CINDERELLA DREAMS

LIFE PASSAGES

Ronald L. Grimes and Robbie Davis-Floyd, Editors

CINDERELLA DREAMS

The Allure of the Lavish Wedding

Cele C. Otnes
Elizabeth H. Pleck

University of California Press   Berkeley   Los Angeles   London

University of California Press
Berkeley and Los Angeles, California

University of California Press, Ltd.
London, England

Library of Congress Cataloging-in-Publication
Data

Otnes, Cele.
   Cinderella dreams : the allure of the lavish
wedding / Cele C. Otnes, Elizabeth H. Pleck.
      p.   cm. — (Life passages)
   Includes bibliographical references and
index.
      ISBN 0–520–23661–0 (alk. paper).
      1. Weddings.   2. Weddings in popular
culture.   3. Consumer behavior.
I. Pleck, Elizabeth Hafkin.   II. Title.
III. Series.
HQ745 .)7   2003
395.2'2—dc21

                              2002151318

Manufactured in the United States of America

13   12   11   10   09   08   07   06   05   04
10   9   8   7   6   5   4   3   2   1

The paper used in this publication is both
acid-free and totally chlorine-free (TCF). It
meets the minimum requirements of
ANSI/NISO Z39.48–1992 (R 1997)
(Permanence of Paper).♾

To Mark and Emily
To Joe and Dan

The pleasure of your company
is requested to share
the dream of a lifetime.
To cherish an event
filled with happiness and love.
To witness the sweet joy of today
and the loving promise of tomorrow.
To admire the perfect dress
for the perfect day.
The pleasure of your company
is requested to share
this romantic moment in time.

Copy taken from the 2001 "Romantic
Wedding" Barbie doll package.
Courtesy of Mattel, Inc.

CONTENTS

ILLUSTRATIONS

ACKNOWLEDGMENTS

Ours was a marriage brought together by mutual academic interest. Both of us had written about weddings, as well as about children's birthday parties and gift giving, when we realized we had offices four floors apart in Gregory Hall at the University of Illinois. We were both looking at the relationship of ritual to consumer culture: Cele from the vantage point of advertising and marketing; Liz from the stance of society, family, and women's history in the United States. There were similarities in our personal backgrounds as well. We both married in white dresses, white veils, and white shoes at ceremonies where we exchanged rings. We both had receptions where we cut white cakes, and we both had honeymoons. Yet we were also looking at the lavish wedding from the stances of two generations of educated American women: Liz married in 1968, one week after Robert F. Kennedy was murdered; Cele, in 1987 in the midst of the revival of interest in traditions and rituals, including the luxurious wedding. Liz remembers family conflict because of the then-impossibility of finding a priest and a rabbi to perform a Jewish-Catholic wedding ceremony where one member of the couple did not convert to the other's religion. Cele remembers family harmony and joy at a Protestant ceremony and large reception for two hundred in Austin, followed by a more intimate and casual reception at a lake house that had been in her husband's family for over forty years. We talked about our own experiences when we began to put together this book, as well as those of others. But telling others about writing a book about weddings is akin to being a doctor at a cocktail party; someone always has a story to tell, and almost everyone is interested in comparing the stories of their weddings to those of others. We hope some of the flavor of affirmation and ambiguity of these conversations has carried over into our book.

Researching and writing this book took longer than the thirteen months it usually takes to plan a lavish Western-style wedding. And as is true when most people plan those kinds of events, we had help and wise counsel along the way. We wish to thank the following undergraduate students for helping us: Jodi Bielenberg, Stepheneta Hoff, Elaina Joyce, Tracey Lee, Catherine McDonald, and Amanda Ronayne. We also found the help of many graduate students invaluable, namely Irina Chubukova, Junyong Kim, Shimantika Kumar, Kyoungmi Lee, Omar Ricks, Lan Xia, and Linda Tuncay. Our research benefited from funding from the McNair Program and the Summer Research Opportunities Program of the Office of Minority Student Affairs, the James Webb Young Fund in the Department of Advertising, the Sheth Foundation awarded through the Department of Business Administration, and the summer research grant program sponsored by the Office of Research in the College of Commerce and Business Administration, all at the University of Illinois. We also thank the faculty and staff in the Department of History and the Department of Business Administration for their support and assistance.

A great deal of our understanding of contemporary weddings in other cultures comes from Eileen Ford, Kyoungmi Lee, Nicole Ranganath, and Nancy Hafkin. Nancy Hafkin was not only a valuable informant but also an excellent source of interview contacts and photographs on her most recent trip to east Africa. Richard Hertel provided a detailed translation of *Mariage,* a review of bridal fashion published in French. A number of research collections proved significant in our work. These include the archives of *Bride's* magazine at Condé Nast; the American Life Histories at the Library of Congress; the Warshaw Collection of Business Americana at the Smithsonian Museum of American History; and the Hartman Center for Sales, Advertising, and Marketing History in the Rare Book, Manuscript, and Special Collections Library at Duke University. We thank Ellen Gartrell, Jacqueline Reed, Elizabeth Dunn, Eleanor Mills, and Stacey Tomkins for their assistance at Duke.

Supportive colleagues have shared their research and insights about advertising, fashion history, and their own study of weddings. They include Jean Allman, Antoinette Burton, Abbie Griffin, Kristin Hoganson, Tina Lowrey, Michelle Nelson, Winifred Poster, Julie Ruth, and Sharon Shavitt. We also thank all of the brides and those who work in the wedding profession who were willing to be interviewed over the years for this project. Cele's parents, Cecil V. Crabb Jr. and Harriet F. Crabb, provided guidance, advice, and support while she was thinking about and writing this book. Mark and Emily Otnes have been a source of strength and a respite for Cele. Joseph Pleck has been as always an extraordinary resource of information and clippings, as well as a good editorial critic. Daniel Pleck has contributed news about Liza Minelli's wedding and has called his mother to the television when there is a wedding on a sitcom he is watching.

We value the comments, writings, and insights of Ronald Grimes and Robbie Davis-Floyd, editors of the Life Passages series. We appreciate the feedback from our friends and colleagues who read and commented on this manuscript, notably Russell Belk of the University of Utah, who provided us with helpful and wise advice. Thanks to all of our colleagues who reviewed the manuscript or the prospectus: Eileen Fischer, Pauline Greenhill, Beth Hirschman, Kristin Hoganson, Ellen Lewin, Ramona Faith Oswald, Michael Solomon, and an anonymous reviewer for the University of California Press. Thanks also to those who supplied the clippings, documents, permissions, and photographs for the book, including Sidney J. Levy, Dan Cook, and Jackie Kacen. We started this project with Doug Abrams of the University of California Press. Reed Malcolm, who took over the project upon Doug's departure, has patiently answered our numerous queries and guided us through the publication process. We thank him, Cindy Fulton, Jennifer L. Morgan, and the members of the editorial, production, and marketing teams responsible for shepherding this book through the University of California Press.

We hope we have offered readers an intriguing look into the contemporary wedding and that they find the trip down the aisle we have provided enlightening and enjoyable.

Chapter 1 | ROMANCE, MAGIC, MEMORY, AND PERFECTION

On June 22, 2001, millions of viewers watched *Good Morning America* as retired firefighter and cancer survivor Lorenzo Abundiz married Peggy Beeuwsaert in the middle of New York City's Times Square. The bride and groom had won a contest, sponsored by the program, in which viewers voted for the couple they felt was most deserving of a "fairy-tale wedding." In the weeks leading up to the event, viewers watched as Peggy and Lorenzo selected their wedding gown, cake, flowers, and bridesmaids' dresses. After taking their vows, they were serenaded by British classical star Russell Watson, given a honeymoon to England and Ireland by ABC, and then driven away in a horse-drawn carriage down Broadway. To help create the dream wedding, ABC enlisted the help of the Web site Weddingchannel.com, wedding gown designer Amsale, specialty baker Sylvia Weinstock, jewelry designer Scott Kay, cosmetics maven Estée Lauder, and designer Ralph Lauren.[1]

It was not the first time a television program had given away a wedding; in fact, that was the whole *raison d'être* of *The Bride and Groom Show,* which aired on NBC in the 1950s. But what has changed since that time is how pervasive weddings have become in our cultural landscape. There are television programs devoted to following wedding planning; films centered on weddings; wedding plots in soap operas, situation comedies, and dramas; an increasing number of magazines devoted to the ritual; coverage of celebrity ceremonies; a plethora of wedding-themed toys and costumes for young girls; and, of course, Web sites. But why are Westerners—and increasingly, people who live in other parts of the globe—fascinated with elaborate weddings? Why are we equally absorbed by those staged either as fairy tales or as absurdities (e.g., the Fox network fiasco *Who Wants to Marry a Millionaire?*).[2] And why—given the availability of alternative forms of luxury such as McMansions and Mercedes—do couples still feel that weddings must provide moments of luxury as well?

Consider these statistics: from 1984 to 1994, the average cost of a typical American wedding quadrupled, from $4,000 to $16,000.[3] In 2002, an estimated $50 billion was spent on wedding-related products and services (including the honeymoon), for an average of more than $22,000 per ceremony.[4] In other countries, especially capitalist countries in Asia, these events can cost substantially more. For example, in South Korea, a lavish wedding cost the couple's families an average of $40,000 in 1990.[5] Likewise, Hollywood has long known that weddings, especially elaborate ones, can draw large audiences. Sociologist Chrys Ingraham identifies more than 350 films produced since 1890 with the word "wedding" or "bride" in the title.[6] And as we will discuss, some recent wedding films such as *Four Weddings and a Funeral, Runaway Bride,* and *The Wedding Singer* have been enormous hits at the box office. Televised weddings—both real and fictional—have also often proved captivating. When Prince Charles and Lady Diana Spencer were married in 1981, more than 750 million people worldwide watched the ceremony.[7] Just months after this real-world event, Luke Spencer and Laura Baldwin, characters in the soap opera *General Hospital,* finally made their long-anticipated trip down the aisle, and a photograph of the couple graced the cover of *Newsweek.*[8] More recently, 30 million viewers watched Chandler and Monica tie the knot at the end of the seventh season of *Friends* in 2001.[9]

Moreover, television has now discovered the lure of offering weddings in *cinema verité* format. In 1997, The Learning Channel began producing *A Wedding Story,* which follows ordinary U.S. couples—consisting of hairstylists, nurses, police officers—from their engagement through the process of buying goods and services for their ceremonies and receptions and ultimately to their weddings. By the beginning of its third season, the program had helped the network earn double- and triple-digit ratings gains among the prized audience of women 18 to 54.[10]

Not surprisingly, Web site developers and "e-tailers" have also jumped on the wedding bandwagon. One of the largest, Weddingchannel.com, has the backing of Federated Department Stores, which owns Bloomingdale's and Macy's. Claiming access to between 300,000 and 400,000 browsers in 1999, Weddingchannel.com was designed to offer couples everything from "the ins and outs of bridal etiquette to providing customized timetables for planning the big event."[11] Yet while Weddingchannel.com boasts of an audience that is male as well as female, most marketers and advertisers of wedding services acknowledge their true target audience is women, who have always been seen as central figures in the lavish wedding.

What is telling about all of these examples is that, except on the lowest rungs of the socioeconomic ladder, the decision to plan and execute elaborate weddings is rarely questioned, and seems now to be considered not only a rite but also a right in North American culture. Furthermore, the "traditional" or lavish wedding denotes a religious setting, a bride dressed in a long, white gown, a multitiered white cake, abundant flowers, attendants in matching finery, a reception, and a honeymoon and is the dominant form in much of global culture today.[12]

Certainly on one level, lavish weddings can be regarded as wasteful affairs, especially when one considers the months (and sometimes even years) devoted to planning a series of events that span a mere weekend, and the alternative ways the same amount of money could be spent. But are these events alone in this regard? Consider the billions of dollars spent on Christmas gifts in America, many for people with whom the givers have little or no social contact outside of the Christmas season.[13] The money spent on holiday gifts is rationalized in the name of preserving social networks, and wedding spending has always been even easier to excuse, because the ritual is seen as something one does once (or a few times) in a lifetime, not every year. In fact, the lavish wedding satisfies the definition of the "binge" offered by anthropologist Richard Wilk: "the consumption of large quantities of goods in a very short period of time."[14]

Given its highly commercial aspects, and the fact that at least half of the couples who take vows in the United States do not remain together, can the wedding truly still be considered a ritual? Or has it merely become a big party, an excuse for once-in-a-lifetime embossed ecru invitations and ice sculptures, that has lost much of its religious and communal meaning? Unfortunately, as ritual scholar Ronald Grimes has recently observed, definitions of ritual are often contradictory and convoluted, ranging from the narrow (ritual is "sacred behavior") to the broad ("culturally defined sets of behavior," which seem to include everything).[15] So how can we distinguish ritual behavior from other types of social expression, such as play?

What separates ritual from other types of behavior is the set of functions it fulfills (or is perceived as fulfilling) for both individuals and society. We agree with sociologist Diana Leonard that rituals are social events that are "largely expressive, symbolic, formalized acts [through which] we can get profound insights into [the] values and institutions" of cultures.[16] Likewise, Tom Driver has eloquently described three "social gifts" of rituals: (1) to impose order in society; (2) to provide connectedness to others, both in one's social circle and beyond (what Victor Turner calls *communitas*);[17] and (3) to effect real and perhaps even lasting transformation in the lives of the ritual participants. Driver de-emphasizes the need for rituals to be somber occasions because he believes, as do we, that rituals can be joyous, carnivalesque, and creative as well.[18] In fact, the resilience of rituals in contemporary Western societies is notable, given the sweeping global and technological changes that constantly bombard these events and their participants, pressuring weddings to metamorphose or disappear altogether. As Leonard observes, "each repetition [of a ritual] allows the accommodation of new developments and new interpretations . . . change therefore not only occurs in rituals, it is endemic."[19]

Certainly, if rituals impose order, enable us to feel connected to others, and transform us in some significant manner, then weddings qualify as rituals. Given the relative absence of initiation rites in Western cultures, and the declining amount of flourish that people put into funerals, weddings in the twentieth century have become *the* major ritual of the entire life span. As Grimes observes, the wedding has become the single ritual performance upon which families "spend the largest amounts of time, energy and money."[20] Both legal and religious institutions encourage marriage, and as a result, weddings effect a multitude of legal changes for individuals and formalize their relations with kin groups. Moreover, for the pregnant bride, the wedding and ensuing marriage offer legal rights to her unborn child.

However, because men and women are marrying later in life all around the world, the wedding has lost its potency as a rite that marks the transition from adolescence to adulthood. Nevertheless, people still perceive it as the most significant ritual in contemporary culture. As fewer marriages in the world are arranged and more countries embrace a capitalist economic mode, elaborate Western weddings are becoming more popular around the globe. In fact, given its importance, the wedding has been surprisingly overlooked by social scientists, historians, and even scholars of contemporary consumer culture.

Consumer advocacy in the 1960s and 1970s spurred several journalistic and critical surveys of weddings, and some scholarly studies in the 1980s and 1990s as well. Taken together, these works offer four useful but insufficient arguments for the popularity of the lavish wedding. First, the complex of events that make up this elaborate event obviously supports and bolsters the institution of marriage, which despite rising rates of voluntary singlehood, cohabitation, and divorce, is still a state highly desired by most people around the world. Almost 90 percent of adults in the United States will marry at least once in their lifetimes, and most who divorce also end up remarrying.[21] Even though the number of single-person and female-headed households is on the rise all around the world, marriage is still regarded as the more acceptable state for adults, and couplehood as the norm. In most Western countries, marriage is rewarded socially, legally, and financially. Marriage grants a number of concrete benefits, including escape from estate and gift taxes when transferring assets to a marital partner, eligibility for a greater range of employment benefits, rights to visit a partner in prison or the hospital, and sick leave benefits to care for a spouse.[22]

Obviously, the link of the wedding ceremony to marriage contributes to its popularity. But lavish weddings are not required for this change in status to occur; it is certainly possible to marry at the city hall. However, the lavish wedding remains one of the most visible means by which individuals can both demonstrate and enhance the quantity and quality of their social connections, since not everyone can afford such an event. Hence the second argument for the popularity of the lavish wedding: it is a prime mechanism for the communication of social prestige. The idea behind conspicuous consumption is that because one's bank balances are typically hidden from view, visible spending becomes the best way to communicate wealth. Thus, the conspicuous consumption that characterizes many wedding ceremonies today provides families with an efficient but extravagant way to illustrate not only that they can afford to give the bride and groom the send-off they deserve but also that they have arrived socially themselves and enjoy comparable status with, or even higher status than, their new in-laws.

Moreover, as consumption has become more democratized through rising incomes and increased access to credit cards and loans, the lavish wedding has become the standard in both middle- and working-class households.[23] Although the wedding-as-status-symbol model is undoubtedly true for some families, the difficulty with this argument is that extravagant weddings now permeate almost all classes of society. Writing about luxury goods in general, philosopher Christopher Berry observes that as such goods "become cemented into daily life . . . they can be thought to be socially necessary."[24] As a result, while weddings remain important markers from the standpoint of social visibility, their ability to make an overarching statement about prestige within their social class has become diluted as previously inaccessible goods and services have trickled down. Where there is great affluence, people then search for individualism and self-expression. Thus, the importance that was attached to the cost of the wedding is now superseded by the emphasis on making these goods and services distinctive (e.g., offered in combinations never before seen by others in attendance). It is not enough to have champagne; one must now have a variety of liquor served by white-gloved waiters. Likewise, black-and-white photographs suitable for a museum exhibit are preferable over the canned list of shots in once exclusive, but now cliché, color. In short, we will argue that distinctiveness is now as important as luxury, because taste becomes as much a marker of class as money.

A third argument for the popularity of the lavish wedding is that because the woman's status (and even her name) changes more than the man's through marriage, she has more need of ritual recognition of the event. Therefore, most of the desire for a lavish wedding has stemmed from women. As this type of event began to take hold, the "grand affair" was understood as a type of recognition for the years of sacrifice the woman was about to endure. Historian Ellen Rothman has argued that the elaborate wedding was critical to a Victorian woman's identity because it was her reward for having remained a virgin and was perceived by the bride as the greatest moment in her life. Women were supposed to willingly sacrifice themselves on behalf of their husbands, children, and relatives, so the elaborate wedding was a reward (perhaps even a bribe) for a future of unpaid labor and thwarted ambition.[25] Although we believe this argument had its merits in the Victorian era, applying it to contemporary culture suggests that as bridal virginity has disappeared, and as women's employment opportunities have approximated those available to men, the lavish wedding should have become superfluous. It also implies that as women widen their spheres of home and family, they will no longer want or need a "special day." Obviously, these assumptions have not been supported in recent history, as nonvirgins with independent incomes, now the bridal majority, not only contribute to the weddings of their dreams but also have redefined the meaning of white as a symbol of tradition rather than of purity. In short, the demand for lavish weddings has increased even in the face of women's increased education, income-earning ability, and political participation. Staging such an event is now understood as the right of the couple, their families, and the ritual audience to immerse themselves in a luxury-laden experience, rather than as a compensatory reward for years of sacrifice and perhaps even drudgery.

The fourth explanation for the increasing popularity of lavish weddings proceeds from the premise that rituals become more elaborate when the public perceives the social institution being celebrated (in this case, marriage) as tenuous and vulnerable. This explanation assumes that people are extremely anxious about the prospect that a marriage will end in divorce. A fancy wedding is therefore sometimes understood as "divorce insurance"; if a couple spends a great deal of time and money on a wedding, it surely must follow that they are committed to the marriage. Conversely, it is assumed a "quickie marriage" will not be long-lasting because the couple has not devoted time and effort to contemplating the seriousness of their marriage.

Most children in the age of divorce (whether their parents remain married or not) can cite statistics about the frequency of marital breakups.

But most brides and grooms, regardless of the marital status of their parents, think their marriage will last because they have "found the right person." Members of Generation X do tend to approve of family values and think of the wedding as a ritual that symbolizes stability. However, the growth of the lavish wedding is also burgeoning in countries where divorce is relatively rare. Rising prosperity is therefore a more likely explanation for its popularity than the attempt to ward off divorce with an opulent occasion.

Is it true that the lavish wedding deters divorce? No statistician has taken up the question. But recently, divorced journalist Pamela Paul interviewed sixty white, college-educated couples who had divorced within five years of marrying. She discerned that "matrimania" kept couples from thinking about their relationships while they were absorbed in booking reception halls and tasting wedding cakes. However, these couples also told her the wedding was the one consistently happy moment of their brief marriages. Moreover, couples who eloped or married at city hall regretted marrying in haste. But couples who had "the 300-pound circus" also regretted their weddings were so impersonal. Thus, both the quickie and the mammoth wedding seem to prompt regrets, but it remains unproven whether either type of wedding reduces the chances of divorce.[26]

Certainly, the arguments presented above have helped to further our understanding of the popularity of the wedding. The desire for marriage and prestige contributes mightily to the popularity of this event, and there is little doubt many women enjoyed, and still enjoy, their time in the limelight during their engagements and wedding ceremonies. However, we believe these motivations do not truly take into account the appeal of consumer culture and the many meanings the wedding can connote for the couple and their families, especially for the bride. Instead, we believe there are four additional reasons why weddings have captured imaginations and incomes within contemporary Western culture. These are that the lavish wedding—more than any other event—has the ability to (1) "marry" the tenets of both consumer culture and romantic love; (2) offer magical transformation; (3) provide memories of a sacred and singular event; and (4) legitimate lavish consumption through the "ethic of perfection"—or the standard that includes the desire for both flawless beauty and a perfect performance—as well as an appreciation and recognition of the occasion by both participants and guests.

It seems almost a truism to observe that consumption is now the dominant ethic in Western and Pacific Rim cultures. Many scholars have observed that what really distinguishes modern from postmodern society is the fact that modern society was producer- rather than consumer-oriented, while in postmodern society the reverse is the case.[27] However, "consumer culture" is more complicated than this reversal. Scholar Celia Lury lists the features she believes distinguish material or consumer culture from previous types of economic and social systems. Many of these features have had a direct impact on the development of the lavish wedding. For example, in an age of plenty, weddings "require" many more artifacts than was the case just twenty years ago. Likewise, an increasing number of stores and service providers assist consumers in fashioning the wedding. The growth in the visibility and consumption of sports, tourism, and shopping has made it socially acceptable for a couple to plan an adventure-packed wedding weekend, rather than a quiet one in a more rustic rural setting.

Likewise, the fact that the shame of borrowing money and going into debt has dissipated means it is perfectly acceptable to finance a wedding on a credit card or to take out a home equity loan or second mortgage in order to create an unforgettable wedding weekend. Finally, an increasing emphasis on having a life filled with aesthetically pleasing images and objects—reinforced through messages found in advertising, product design, and fashion—means the ideal of the beautiful bride and the ceremony, reception, and honeymoon that she and her husband enjoy is now a culturally sanctioned ideal, and not one that is reserved for the elite.[28]

In consumer culture, people believe spending will buy happiness, self-fulfillment, autonomy, and personal transformation. Moreover, the same mechanisms that support and reproduce consumer culture in Western countries—namely advertising, the media, retailing, and merchandising—now assist global marketers and manufacturers in fostering consumer desire and emulation of elite lifestyles. As a result, there is increasing emphasis on satisfying individual versus collective desires, of pursuing a "myself-that-could-be" through consumption.[29]

Many critics of consumer culture believe advertising and marketing manipulate desire and create false needs. But desire for luxury, status, prestige, and romance—along with greed, vanity, and lust—all have very ancient roots that existed prior to modern enticements. Advertising and marketing do play to these qualities within people, even as they have become major mechanisms of communication and creators and reinforcers of individual and group identities. Marketing scholar Jonathan Schroeder recently observed: "Advertising has a tremendous hold on how we conceive of the Utopian good life, including our desires, fantasies, wants and dreams, providing meaning in a myth-like way that helps us make sense of our world."[30] Indeed, it has become impossible to communicate in our culture without the symbolism conveyed by goods and services. Moreover, the days have long since passed when it was possible to distinguish false needs from true ones in societies with rising standards of living and subjective definitions of need. Wants have been turned into needs; this is the core of marketing, and of the subjective nature of the word "luxury." The wedding has become a part of the "standard package" of both working- and middle-class life. The entire wedding industry creates an abstract desire for the lavish, elegant wedding and then provides the consumption rules for different social classes to follow when enacting the event.

Of course, neither weddings nor the businesses they support could flourish—or remain recession-proof, as some have argued—without being accorded special status in the culture. In short, from its relatively humble roots that featured ceremonies in the parlor and receptions in the church basement, the wedding has been elevated to the special status of luxury good in contemporary consumer culture. Berry observes there are four main categories of luxury goods in capitalist societies today: food and drink, shelter, clothing, and leisure.[31] Perhaps one reason the wedding has proved captivating is that it essentially encompasses all four of these, if one interprets "shelter" as a posh location for a reception or a ten-day stay at a swanky hotel in Maui. Moreover, we can think of other types of luxury goods and services—for example, limousines, fresh flowers, and musical performers—that have become mandatory for this event. Berry also observes that conspicuous consumption involves "consumption, the satisfaction of which derives from audience reaction."[32] Certainly, the increasing size of the guest list for weddings is testament to the fact that it is important for more and more people to both witness and revel in this form of luxurious consumption.

Given that consumer culture implies an increasing infatuation with goods and services, it is not surprising some scholars have noted a connection between romantic love, which emerged as a desirable basis for marrying in the nineteenth century, and the love of goods, made possible through simultaneous developments in commerce and transportation. In fact, the connection between romance and consumption has grown even closer in postmodern consumer societies, as incomes have grown and romance has become such an important appeal for advertisers. While "pure" romantic love might seem at odds with the crass desire for material goods, sociologist Eva Illouz notes people seek to escape a world laden with bureaucracy and technology for a "romantic utopia,"[33] and actively employ goods and services that have been accorded a sacred "aura"[34] in order to fill their lives with romantic overtones. We now inhabit a world where "the romanticization of commodities and the commodification of romance" go hand in hand.[35]

Of course, such a union of romance and consumption makes weddings the perfect event at which to valorize both. Moreover, it is no coincidence that advertising, fashion, fiction, and film—the same mechanisms that further the goals of consumer culture and encourage emulation of the fashions of Hollywood celebrities and European princesses—also portray being in love as one of the most highly sought-after states of existence.[36] Perhaps most important, these images contribute to what Illouz calls the "democratization of romantic love," offering images and ideas to working-class couples previously unexposed to the idea of love as consumption-laden leisure.[37]

Love and consumption share another common bond; both are considered primarily to be the domains of women. Girls and women consume the goods that support a "love culture": fairy tales, dolls, soap operas, romantic movies, romance novels, and popular magazines.[38] As sociologist Francesca Cancian observes, "we identify love with emotional expression and talking about feelings, aspects of love that women prefer and in which women tend to be more skilled than men."[39] Yet with the blurring of gender boundaries in contemporary times and the acknowledgment that men can satisfy emotional needs through consumption as well come increasing ambivalence among men glad to not be responsible for the wedding plans, but also not wanting to be left out entirely. Thus the symbiotic relationship between consumer culture and romantic love ensures that advertising, marketing, and the media will constantly remind women (and to a lesser extent, men) that their lives are incomplete unless they (a) experience romantic love, and (b) once having found it, reward themselves for doing so by consummating the accomplishment through the bestowal of a diamond engagement ring, a lavish wedding, and a honeymoon. After all, marriage is still seen as the endpoint of romance, and a lavish wedding as the best portal to marriage.

But the relationship between consumption and romance is insufficient to explain the appeal of these nuptial extravaganzas. Most real-life examples of the potency of the lavish wedding are contained in epiphanies experienced by the bride-to-be. One woman told us that when she received her engagement ring, she was able to "see her future, and that she'll have children someday."[40] After trying on fifteen wedding gowns, another bride-to-be burst into tears and exclaimed, "This is my dress!"[41] What gives these items their power among women? It is not just that brides want to be transported in order to escape from the ordinary or even disenchanting world. Instead, they are pursuing a particular form of fantasy or utopia, that of "living happily ever after" in a time outside of time. This fantasy is usually a story of female passivity and male redemption, but it is now by no means limited to highly traditional gender roles; such romantic fantasies also appeal to gay couples, even if those couples do not subscribe to divisions of labor that mirror those of heterosexual partners.

In short, people want lavish weddings because *they want to experience magic in their lives.* Consumer behavior scholar Russell Belk has observed that we continually seek to reenchant our lives through magic "clothes, jewels, and perfumes. We drive magic cars. We reside in magic places and make pilgrimages to even more magical places. We eat magic foods, own magic pets, and envelope ourselves in the magic of film, television, and books . . . the rational possessor is a myth that . . . fails because it denies the inescapable and essential mysteriousness of our existence."[42] Ritual scholar Ronald Grimes argues that magic is transformation by ritual and mysterious means, and that the magic has to "work" and achieve an end (or at least, the couple has to believe it has worked).[43] In the case of the wedding, the ritual ceremony is laden with artifacts that make people feel truly changed (even if only for a short while), and the empirical end is the creation of a paradise on earth.

Figure 1. Romantic bridal photography, landmark Chicago building, 2002. Courtesy Steven E. Gross, Chicago.

Because lavish weddings also embody our sacred beliefs in marriage and religion and feature luxury goods that make the couple feel like celebrities for a day, these events have more potential than almost any other ritual to help people experience the feeling of being transported out of everyday space and time. When we say weddings offer the potential to experience magic, we mean to distinguish this magic from the "everyday" kind promised by advertisers, who have long appealed to the idea of transformation of self. A recent study of women's magazines from 1955 to 1992 revealed that more than one-third of ads featured claims that promised a product or service would somehow transform the user.[44] Yet ironically, the sheer number of slogans such as Disney's "Remember the magic" increases the risk this promised magic will generate consumer cynicism and parody and be rendered meaningless. What shields wedding magic from cynical interpretation is its association with religious symbolism, its status as a once-in-a-lifetime occasion, and (at least in Western countries) the use of products and services so sacred and cherished that they will be preserved prior to the occasion, used only once, and then packed away.[45]

Perhaps one might assume that because by 2002 the average age of brides and grooms in the United States has increased to 25.1 years old for women and 26.8 for men, couples ought to know better than to waste money on a wedding, and save for other more rational purchases such as a home.[46] This is the familiar "weddings are wasteful" argument we identified earlier in this chapter. If the distinction between needs and wants has become almost entirely subjective, the decision about what is frugal and what is wasteful has become subjective as well. Moreover, it is impossible to deny lavish weddings provide the ability to escape everyday routine and elevate to center stage decisions pertaining to once-in-a-lifetime costumes, two- or three-tiered confectionery delights, rare and wonderful flowers, stretch limousines, shrimp puffs, champagne fountains, and musicians, all typically topped off by the trip of a lifetime as well.

Just how sought-after is the magic attainable through the wedding? Consider the growing phenomenon of couples who actually have *two* events. First is a low-key trip to Las Vegas to marry in a wedding chapel, or a small ceremony with a cake-and-punch reception. Yet these types of ceremonies are often followed by full-blown affairs that feature the ubiquitous white gown, tuxedo, and bouquets, sometimes even after the couple has been married a year or more. And as the number of cross-cultural couples who have to negotiate two sets of customs and kin across borders continues to grow, this two-wedding strategy has become an increasingly popular means for them to reconcile cultural differences surrounding the ritual.[47] The bride and groom legally become husband and wife at the smaller first ceremony, but the magic is missing. The second wedding may reinforce the couple's connection to their social networks, but its greatest appeal is the promise of magic, especially for women.

Through fairy tales and beauty ads, brides are the ones surrounded by the story of Cinderella finding Prince Charming and being transformed through marrying him.

Most of the objects of memory at the opulent wedding do not predate the early nineteenth century. Prior to the 1830s, when daguerreotypes replaced the artists' portraits prevalent among the upper class, most families had few tangible visual souvenirs to commemorate family gatherings, so they relied on their own memories to re-create past events.[48] Historian John Gillis argues that during the nineteenth century, the meaning of family changed from "the people whom one lived with" to "a culture of commemoration" that connected family members to distant ancestors through family trees, Bibles, and heirlooms.[49] And although contemporary attics and basements often overflow with photographs and albums that preserve images of friends and relatives, in truth, all of the moments in our lives are inextricably bound to the present, such that even before the last bit of rice has fallen from a couple's hair, the wedding begins to disappear from consciousness.

The annual calendrical round of birthdays, national holidays, and anniversaries provides us with ample opportunities for special and memorable moments. But at the same time, because they occur once a year, these occasions are less unusual and special. The wedding still retains its place on the "once-in-a-lifetime" pedestal—bar and bat mitzvahs, confirmations, graduation parties, quinceañera celebrations, and coming-out parties notwithstanding. And because most couples marrying for the first time still adhere to the assumption that one wedding day is their lifetime allotment, there is heightened pressure to mark the occasion indelibly and to capture it visually and tangibly.

As a major ritual in the life course, even a simple wedding is no doubt considered what psychologist David Pillemer calls an "originating event," a moment the couple believes will profoundly influence their mutual destinies.[50] When pollsters in 1988 asked American couples to recall their most memorable day, about one-fourth of adults said it was their wedding day.[51] But the lavish wedding is much more than a day to remember. As one of the few recently democratized portals to reenchantment in life, the wedding does not so much hold up a mirror to who we really are, but instead offers a temporary dream world for all in attendance, a celebrity-like world of elegance, elaborateness, emotion, and ease. Other rituals can promise lavishness, but none can convey a memory of having once felt like Cinderella and Prince Charming.

Retaining the memories of special occasions also seems to be especially important to women, who are typically responsible for organizing family gatherings and rituals.[52] As the custodians of family ties, women place more importance on the momentous occasions in their lives than men, are more likely to want these moments recorded, and tend to use their ritual photos and videos to show others so that they can relive special times. Women not only shape and mold their identities in part by retaining and reliving special memories, but also decorate their homes as shrines to weddings and kin relations. Wedding photographs, originally intended to prove status and formality, have become ways for a couple to encapsulate and enshrine their romantic feelings for each other, preserving the magic for all time.

Every "traditional" lavish wedding is therefore part of the great chain of marrying, tied to every one that preceded it and every one that follows. Mothers, and even grandmothers, who enjoyed their own lavish weddings become key factors in transmitting the meaning and method of the ritual to the next generation. The commemorative connections to specific events are often made through intimate familial actions such as the bride wearing her mother's veil, or including a family Bible or prayer book in the ceremony. But the choice of engagement and wedding rings, a designer gown, a particular type of band at the reception, and a honeymoon locale represent not only an affirmation by the bride and groom that they want their ceremony to be remembered as commemorating the union of romantic love but also a consumer culture characterized by abundance, novelty, and the latest fashions.

Of course, as is true of photos in family albums in general,[53] not all incidents at weddings are preserved, even on the happiest day of one's life. Few if any bridal albums contain allusions to hurt feelings, lewd toasts at the rehearsal dinner, or heated arguments among members of the bridal party or drunken relatives in their cars on the way home. As historian David Lowenthal observes, "memory transforms the experienced past into what we later think it should have been, eliminating undesired scenes and making favored ones suitable."[54] Only those items that foster an image of the happy and perfect wedding—a wedding program, a champagne cork from the wedding night, a dress that transforms

Figure 2.   Wedding souvenir mirror, 1939. Courtesy Museum of
the City of New York.

a working woman into a fairy princess—are carefully stowed and preserved. But whitewashed memories, while inaccurate, create an emotional connection between the past and the present and are intended to
provide a ballast to offset hard times.

For all of the fuss surrounding it, the wedding is really a brief respite
from the everyday world, and its participants may live fifty, sixty, or even
seventy years after the event. Given that the memories of the wedding are

supposed to last a lifetime, it is essential there be a broad range of artifacts upon which to rely to resuscitate those memories. As the above discussion demonstrates, the photographs of the event are the most important relics and are usually encased in frames or bound in leather albums. Because weddings often feature mini–family reunions, photographs affirm a belief in family solidarity and may represent one of the few times when certain relatives are visually included in the family circle.[55] As such, they express an anxiety about the family's loss of kin contact by showing an illusory moment when the relatives gather, and perhaps even astonishment that relational ties are as strong as they are in an increasingly mobile society. And of course, photos both provide the bride and groom with tangible evidence that they had their day to shine as the stars of their social network and provide them with a means of reviving their belief in "happily ever after."

One-use-only items, such as cake toppers, champagne glasses, and the gown and veil, serve another important memory function as well. Because they can play recurring roles in future family weddings, they become heirlooms that enable the essence and collective memory of earlier weddings to be transferred to future generations and give a material concreteness to the idea of "tradition." For all of these reasons, the memories that the wedding produces are almost as important as the magic generated by the occasion.

While weddings valorize romantic love, consumption, and magic, one of the most important reasons they can do so is because consumers are encouraged to engage in emotional and financial excess and are completely spared any guilt for doing so. Emphasis on "the perfect wedding" appears to date to the 1920s, when the phrase came into common use. Standards of perfection, which implied no limit on spending and an increasing reliance on paid professionals, were created by advertisers, marketers, and bridal magazines. Couples were urged to buy expensive engraved invitations, proper-vintage champagne, an ornate wedding cake, and of course, the perfect designer gown, which now typically costs the bride over $800.[56] A cursory glance at advertising copy in a recent issue of *Modern Bride* brings home this point: "Whatever happens, the Lenox is always perfect"; "Register for the gifts that make your home perfect together" (Pier One Imports); "The Perfect Match" (J. C. Penney

Bridal Registry); "Make Your Day Picture Perfect" (Gingiss Formal-wear).[57]

Of course, one important implication of the perfect wedding is that people do not search for perfection on a budget. Even guests are unwilling to skimp on a gift because they do not want to look like skinflints. A rule of thumb that now seems to be *de rigueur* is that guests spend as much on a wedding gift as they believe is being spent on them at the reception.[58] In a consumer culture, perfection is synonymous with lavishness, because what perfect really means is spectacle, romance, luxury, fashion, and entertainment—the combination of which is never cheap.

In summary, we believe that while lavish weddings do glorify the institution of marriage, enhance the status of the participants, and have special appeal to women, these explanations are insufficient to explain the popularity of this event. This is because these explanations do not acknowledge the ability of consumer culture to generate meaning. Nor do they recognize the ability of romantic love to embed itself within consumer culture. Thus, the rite of the lavish wedding is increasingly popular because it glorifies both romantic love and the love of "romantic" consumer goods, promises transformation to its participants, provides a repository of memories of this magic and romance, and offers the promise of perfect (e.g., boundless and guilt-free) consumption.

Like most events that glorify conspicuous consumption, the big wedding has long generated controversy and critique. Feminists dislike the patriarchy of many customs, such as the bride's vow of obedience to her husband and the loss of her name at marriage.[59] Gays and lesbians challenge not only the legal and religious barriers that preclude their right to marry, but also the pressure to conform at the celebrations of straight friends and relatives. And as we discuss in the next chapter, of all critiques, the most entrenched has been that the lavish wedding constitutes extravagant and wasteful spending, especially among those who cannot afford it.[60]

The current reasons given as to why wasteful spending on weddings is bad are that it depletes the savings of the poor, pollutes the environment, and belongs in the nebulous category of the tasteless. However, the common argument that people of modest income should not spend beyond their means has been largely replaced by the new belief that the lavish wedding is the best chance ordinary people have to "rise above their station," as incomes have risen and a democratic society holds out the promise that everyone has the right to spend, and even to spend lavishly.

In addition to individual critics, governments have often taken direct measures to express their dislike of marrying in luxury. The Athenians in the fourth century B.C.E. introduced so-called sumptuary laws designed to curtail consumption in a variety of contexts.[61] Two of the main reasons these laws were enacted were to curtail envy and hostility among the have-nots and to control the spread of luxury, which was viewed as an "effeminate" indulgence that might weaken men's desire to participate in military action.[62] Even some of these early laws specifically governed consumption at weddings; in Athens, only thirty guests were allowed to attend weddings in an attempt to limit spending.[63] Sumptuary laws spread throughout Europe, where the consumption of particular types of food and drink were regulated, as were lavish weddings, which were prohibited in Italy in the mid-sixteenth century.[64] As we will discuss in chapter 2, such laws were also common among the Puritans in England and New England, where they were designed to "curb the sins of pride and envy."[65]

More recently, sumptuary laws have had a more blatant political intent in authoritarian and/or Communist countries, where they were intended to curtail consumer desire. In Korea, Pakistan, and the Soviet Union, politicians have sought to place an arbitrary lid on how much families can spend on weddings in order to keep them from going into debt and to ensure that a pool of savings could be tapped for economic development rather than luxury. Invariably, such bans are lifted, and when they are, very fancy and expensive weddings spring up. As Russell Belk observes, "the power of consumer desire to thwart sumptuary laws is seen in the strategies developed to legally circumvent these laws as well as in their outright disregard."[66] Even when governed by the most oppressive of regimes, such as the Taliban in Afghanistan, people have risked severe punishment, imprisonment, and even torture to create and participate in a lavish wedding. After the Taliban government began to crumble, one Afghan family handed a *Time* magazine reporter photographs of the bride in a long peach gown that also featured family members who had gathered stealthily to enjoy special foods and to lavish gifts upon the couple.[67] Leveling down by fiat, it seems, is inherently unworkable. Given the social pressures to spend lavishly and even competitively, it is doubtful luxury spending can be limited by legislation. Nor does imploring people to rein in spending for weddings find many adherents.

Such evidence supports our belief that the freedom to choose— whether the choice is ultimately an elaborate wedding, a more simple ceremony, or to not marry at all—will ultimately be a stronger determinant of the style of the celebration than any legislation. Perhaps in these days of easy access to credit cards and low-interest loans, decision-making ability is as strong a factor as family income. However, not all people truly have the same range of choices, even people with sufficient and steady income. Moreover, affluent couples who do not choose to have a lavish wedding swim against strong familial, social, and cultural currents and may face social sanctions for not choosing the traditional route. On the opposite end of the spectrum, we have talked with, and even consoled, women from both modest and wealthier backgrounds who years later regretted they did not have the wedding of their dreams.

Of course, since luxury consumption is about status and the ability to spend freely, it is inevitably a system of inequality. Some couples who want to marry lavishly cannot afford to, and many of the poor have given up on marriage as a bad bet because underclass men seem to have such poor prospects for becoming providers. Yet the democratization of the "wedding bash" since World War II indicates the mass of (heterosexual) couples have come to enjoy—and perhaps even expect—a style of celebration previously reserved for the elite. Not surprisingly, then, many of the people still denied a lavish wedding—by virtue of their limited resources, their sexuality, or their status as a single parent—covet it. Yet the lavish wedding is quite capable of evolving so that the previously excluded can participate and symbols of patriarchy or fertility can be reinterpreted in more benign ways. In fact, the capacity of this rite to respond to change, and even upon occasion to constitute itself as a form of protest without losing its status in culture, is part of the reason for its appeal and vitality. The lavish wedding has withstood interfaith marriages, previous divorce experienced by the bride and/or the groom (and their parents), non-Western religious traditions, gay liberation, satirization through popular culture, and even images of pregnant brides in white wedding gowns. It can be environmentally friendly, vegetarian, and feminist. And in the days of "everything dotcom," it has assimilated high-speed connectivity as well.

In the 1980s and 1990s, some feminist writers acknowledged and accepted the appeal of beauty and fashion to women. As much a rebuke to this tendency as to anything else, several important critiques, which were part academic, part journalistic, were published between 1999 and 2002. Sociologist Chrys Ingraham elaborated upon the feminist critique of the "white wedding" in arguing these occasions are socially lauded manifestations of heterosexual, patriarchal, and racially biased ideologies. She also declared that weddings further heterosexual interests; that bridal magazines, etiquette guides, and newspaper announcements have ignored racial minorities; and that many of the traditions in wedding ceremonies reflect the legacy of patriarchy. Like many other critics of consumer culture, she perceived the time and spending on the lavish wedding as a distraction from civic responsibility and work toward social equality. Lesbian studies scholar Ramona Oswald has extended this criticism by arguing that traditions such as the bouquet toss and the "singles" table at the wedding reception often marginalize and ostracize lesbians and gays in attendance. To counter this situation, Oswald has created a brochure for those planning weddings that includes guidelines to help minimize the discomfort of homosexual guests.[68]

Jaclyn Geller, an English literature graduate student and self-professed single woman, takes these arguments a step further, claiming that in celebrating heterosexual coupledom, marriage and the rituals that surround it effectively ostracize not just gays and lesbians, but all singles who choose not to marry. She has adopted the strongest stance possible—not only against lavish weddings, but also against the institution of marriage as a whole—arguing, "We must stop repeating the absurd mantra, 'It's OK to be single,' and adopt the more aggressive stance that 'It's not OK to be married.' "[69] Literary and queer studies scholar Elizabeth Freeman favors the gifts, the processional, and the honeymoon. However, she also advocates removing all special tax and legal benefits for married couples or even domestic partners.[70] It is hard to deny that lavish weddings valorize heterosexual coupledom, religion, fertility, and traditional gender roles. At the very least, there should be increased sensitivity to the feelings of those in attendance, as well as to members of society whose interests are not served socially, legally, or economically by the inability to have a wedding, or by extension, to marry. Some will choose the path to conformity as the avenue least likely to upset relatives. Others embrace a bit of reform in how they marry. Some ponder the perplexing question of how to balance majority sentiments with minority sensitivities.

But ultimately, marriage is a civil right, and the wedding ceremony is both the legal and most socially desirable means to attain that right. We do not agree with Geller or Freeman that marriage or weddings should be discouraged or stigmatized; rather, we believe they have crossed the line between advocating greater respect for the nonmarried and imposing their own exclusionist standards that demand adoption and advocacy of the single life or take away benefits for dependents.

Nor do we believe it is wrong to begin a marriage with a lavish wedding. Some argue that such an occasion results in unrealistic expectations for the ensuing marriage; in truth, however, the elaborate wedding is not necessarily guilty of teaching the lesson that money can buy happiness. In fact, its message—that luxury is permissible once in a lifetime—is a much more limited embrace of the consumption ethic than that espoused by credit card companies. Ultimately, it is a question of whether the fantasy of a lavish wedding totally obliterates reality. Probably the best answer is that it does—but only to some extent, and for some people. No doubt, some women have expressed postwedding depression as the realization of a relatively routine married life dawned upon them. And of course, living in a fantasy world all of the time is a sign of mental illness. But in a society replete with images of aspiration and achievement, not being able to inhabit a dream world at least some of the time seems an impoverished way of living. After all, one of the reasons we may choose intermittent escape is so we do not feel compelled to drastically or impulsively transform our lives in their entirety. While "born to shop" may be an extreme consumption-oriented position, we embrace the *right* to shop, as well as the right to marry, and believe those societies that are the least coercive with respect to these issues, and other basic human freedoms, are the most democratic and the most equitable. Our purpose in this book is not to evaluate the rights and wrongs of the lavish wedding, but to understand how this magical moment (or monster, depending on one's point of view) came to occupy so much of the consciousness of contemporary consumer cultures around the world.

Given the critiques levied against the lavish wedding, it may seem the occasion has had to dodge more bricks than bridal bouquets. And in fact, most studies of lavishness and luxury in consumer culture tend to be highly judgmental, missing the point that consumers genuinely attribute meaning to such activity. We do not believe brides are "dupes" of the wedding industry because they page through magazines, attend bridal expositions, or compare samples of wedding cakes. Consumer culture can be wasteful, redundant, and inequitable; likewise, it can also be liberating, magical, democratizing, and the basis for defining oneself. In short, we believe in trying to find neutral ground when discussing the lavish wedding by being fair to all sides and recognizing the tears, joys, and happy memories the wedding brings to most, but also acknowledging the pain, feelings of exclusion, or boredom it evokes in others. At the same time, we will reflect on the implications of the lavish wedding for society and culture as a whole. These approaches mean we strive to understand how and why the elaborate and luxurious wedding has always generated criticisms, reforms, and alternatives that have in turn shaped this event, and to understand the meaning and appeal of alternatives that have emerged.

While we trace the origins of some customs and traditions pertaining to the wedding back to the Hebrews, Greeks, or Romans, our primary focus in this book is on the development of the lavish wedding from World War II to the present. It was during this period that a consumer culture of luxury and abundance became available to ordinary North American couples. It is also the time when the bridal industry developed new magazines, professional organizations, and suburban shops. The postwar era was also an extraordinary couple- and family-oriented time period, when brides and grooms were marrying quite young and were often making "choices" that were in fact dictated by their parents.[71]

In the chapters that follow, we respectively explore the historical and cultural conditions that contributed to the rise and popularity of the lavish wedding, as well as the evolution of the engagement period, shopping for the event, the ceremony, the honeymoon, the portrayal of the wedding in Hollywood films, the development of alternative weddings, and the variants of the lavish wedding across the globe. In our final chapter, we reflect on the paths the lavish wedding may take in the future.

Chapter 2 | THE RISE OF THE LAVISH WEDDING

"Ellen," who was married in 1966, recently described how she and her fiancé spent less than $500 for the knee-length wedding dress she bought at a department store, her flowers, a professional photographer, and the reception. The groom wore a dark suit and tie. Her reception was held at a local restaurant, but there was no music or dancing. Ellen remembered:

> We paid for everything ourselves, because our family wasn't too happy about our marriage. My parents were upset that he wasn't Catholic and his parents were upset that I wasn't of the same ethnic background as they were. . . . One of our friends made the cake. I don't remember the flavor, but she gave us the cake stand as a wedding gift. [My attendants] were just my sister and brother [and] just our immediate family, probably about twenty people [attended].

Twenty-seven years later, in 1993, when Ellen's daughter Clarise married, the wedding was three times as large and thirty-six times as expensive. Clarise and her fiancé took twelve months to plan the festivities, which cost $18,000. Both sets of parents, as well as the bride and groom (who each had four attendants) helped pay for the event. They invited 325 people to the wedding, and 275 came. "We almost couldn't fit our reception into any halls in the area!" exclaimed Clarise. The reception featured both a band and a disc jockey, as well as a "five-layer cake, all frosted in white, with real flowers at the top!"[1]

Although Ellen's wedding may have been slightly more subdued and smaller than average when it was held, Clarise's was a typical middle-class event for its time. In the contemporary wedding, champagne fountains, limousines for the bridal party, a dessert buffet that supplements the cake, a release of doves or monarch butterflies as the couple leaves the reception, and honeymoons with multiple destinations are not uncommon. On the whole, the trend in weddings in the past century is that an event that was once relatively modest in scale has become much larger and grander and takes longer to plan. As we have already observed, the most significant contributor to this change was the development of a romantic consumer culture. But to understand one of the main reasons why this kind of culture could flourish, we must go back farther in time.

"Fairy tales," writes one literary critic, "are bedtime stories of the collective consciousness. . . . They are shared wish fulfillment."[2] Unlike myths, fairy tales are stories about ordinary people, not the gods. Unlike legends, the ordinary people did not necessarily encounter the gods or get involved in extraordinary events.[3] Elders told the first fairy tales to an assembled group as a means of entertaining them and perhaps instructing the young. The earliest recorded version of Cinderella appeared in a Chinese book written around C.E. 850–860.[4] The topics that arose in the story, such as incest, arranged marriage, the tensions of the stepfamily, and sexual longing, had wide appeal because they appeared so often in patriarchal families.

The Western history of the Cinderella tale is more recent, the legacy of the telling of European peasant tales. With the rise of the printing press in the fifteenth century, oral stories were written down in Latin and printed in books. Written versions of peasant stories have been called "wonder tales," because a wonder or some magic was required to effect miraculous change and a reversal of fortunes. Because of the presence of magic in these tales, anything could happen, and anything was possible. These stories also contained predictable patterns. The main character in a wonder tale, whether male or female, invariably was blocked by some prohibition in realizing his or her goal and was compelled to violate the prohibition. The villain gave the hero or heroine an impossible task to accomplish. Helpers were required to assist in the quest. In the case of Cinderella, the heroine accomplished the task of finding a way to the ball, and eventually found marriage, wealth, and happiness.

Written versions of peasant wonder tales, published in the 1600s in western Europe, were called literary fairy tales. These were no longer critical of the aristocracy; in fact, they were often written with an aristocratic audience in mind. Charles Perrault, a French poet and lawyer, did not write the first European literary fairy tale of Cinderella, but his *Cendrillon,* published in 1679, became the best known. Perrault transcribed the stories French peasants told him and dressed them up for an aristocratic reading public. He left out many elements of the wonder tale versions, but added the fairy godmother, the glass slipper, the pumpkin coach, and the drama produced by the arrival of the bewitching hour of midnight.[5] His version was translated into English in 1729.

Jacob and Wilhelm Grimm, two German brothers who collected and compiled wonder tales, had their own version of Cinderella, which never became as popular as Perrault's. But their heroine was more resourceful and did not rely on a fairy godmother. In their version, Cinderella had a more direct role in realizing her dreams, since she planted a hazel tree and watered it with her tears. The Grimm version has to be considered more sadomasochistic as well, since the wicked stepmother succeeds in convincing her marriage-minded daughters to cut off a toe or part of a heel in order to fit into the desired slipper. Publishers of children's books in the middle of the nineteenth century preferred Perrault's story because it was filled with charming animal characters (plump white mice and whiskered rats), and perhaps because they believed a more passive female protagonist would be more popular with readers. Perrault's tale was also one of the major plots of a new literary form, the novel, which became one of the most prized objects for sale in the eighteenth century. Charlotte Brontë's *Jane Eyre,* published in 1846, offered a determined, not-at-all passive "Cinderella" who was willing to make her way into the world and not wait for a man to rescue her.

Subsequently, Cinderella's story has been told in poems, musicals, operas, plays, and novels too numerous to count. Advertisers have long understood that fairy tales are fantasies realized; they are about dreams that come true, and these stories that are ostensibly for children have an equally powerful hold on the adult imagination. In the United States, they are also a statement of national ideology, since Cinderella is the expression of the dominant belief in success (she moves from rags to riches) and fantasy (the American dream). In the consumer culture of the nineteenth and twentieth centuries, many products, from cosmetics to cars to crystal goblets, were sold to the public as a means to fulfill the wish to live happily ever after. The fairy tale, originally an oral tradition unconnected to commerce, became central imagery for a consumer culture and for the romantic version of that culture. The term "storybook romance," such as in a child's book of fairy tales, refers to romantic love leading to marriage. Two central ideas—romantic love as the basis for marrying and magic as the means of reversing fortune and realizing one's dreams—became embedded in products and services in a culture dependent on magazines, stores, visual imagery, advertising, radio, and finally, wedding services.

These ideas became embedded through narrative, the ability of advertising to tell a story that began with "Once upon a time" and ended with "They lived happily ever after." Where once advertising had merely described the merits of products, by the early twentieth century it came to focus on telling a story, and some of the best stories in that commercial genre were fairy tales. The Cinderella story has been employed in bridal advertising since around 1900. In 1904, a Libbey advertisement, which showed a bride admiring a large glass vase, contained the headline, "The American Cinderella."[6] Moviemakers have also fallen in love with the once-wealthy orphan girl, making three silent films and four motion pictures about her realization of luxury, romance, love, and marriage through magic.[7]

Ever the symbol of the good, beautiful, deserving woman, Cinderella has been portrayed and understood as resourceful or passive, but rarely as both. She has usually been a blonde beauty, but illustrators have sometimes drawn a short, brown-haired girl in rags. (Whatever her hair color, she was Caucasian with fair skin until the Disney television movie version starring Brandy as Cinderella and Whitney Houston as the fairy godmother was produced in 1997.) Cinderella was not always the most popular fairy tale, but the Disney feature-length film of 1950 seems to have elevated the tale to that status. Adult women interviewed in the 1970s remember reading the story; their male counterparts claim not to recall any tales from childhood.[8]

Merely considering the Disney version will not suffice to understand the meaning of the Cinderella tale. As is true of all cultural texts, fairy tales can be read in several ways. Exactly what type of tale about womanhood the listener or reader takes from Cinderella seems to vary widely with the times, the age and gender of the reader, and the specific version being told. Modern feminists certainly hear a story about female passivity and beauty being rewarded, with the happy ending in life being marriage and wealth. Cinderella had been an object of scorn for feminists such as Simone de Beauvoir or Anne Sexton, who interpreted the 1950 Disney version as a paradigmatic statement of female passivity and the belief that women are in need of male rescue. Likewise, self-help writer Colette Dowling identifies the female fear of success as "a Cinderella complex." But others have noted that the popular fairy tales are stories for a female audience about girls coming into their own.[9]

However one interprets the meaning of the fairy tale, it was central both to romantic consumer culture and to advertising. The tale of Cinderella came first, then the idea of romantic love, and after that, a consumer revolution in part fueled by the belief in romantic love. Throughout most of human history, marriage has been a property transaction between two families, and love has had little to do with the reason for marrying. Marriage was designed to ensure the legitimacy of heirs and provide a man with sexual service and a good housekeeper. Even the initial stirrings of romantic love had nothing to do with why a couple married. The French like to say they invented romantic love. To be more accurate, they seem to have invented the notion of "courtly love." This variant featured fine manners, chivalry, lovesickness, and the pangs of unrequited love between a knight and a married aristocratic lady. The French queen Eleanor of Aquitaine and her daughter, Marie de France, are given credit for creating a new literary ideal of selfless devotion of a knight to his lady, although Arab storytellers may have had as much influence as French queens. When the idea of courtly love emerged at the end of the twelfth century, it was confined to a small section of women in the aristocracy. Such a vision was actually a love triangle: a husband, a wife, and the knight in shining armor who was in love with the wife. Courtly love declined with the demise of feudalism, but love and chivalry endured, even if they became detached from courting and marrying. There were always a few couples who married for love, but for centuries, such marriages were discouraged and thought to be foolish. Historian Lawrence Stone argues that by the middle of the eighteenth century, in Europe, the North American colonies, and especially Britain, the rise of the novel, the concept of individualism, and the belief that the individual had the right to emotional happiness laid the basis for the idea of romantic love as a rationale for marrying.[10]

Sociologist Colin Campbell makes the claims that romantic love was one of the prime reasons behind the consumer revolution at the end of the eighteenth century and that a revolution in consumer behavior likewise was a major stimulus to the growth of the Industrial Revolution. Factories were producing pottery, thread, and cotton cloth. The public had to come to accept the idea of wanting and needing more things; once acquired, however, goods never seemed to satisfy completely. Campbell notes that consumption and romantic love were both about longing, about fantasies, about dreams coming true. People were seeking to buy the pleasures they dreamed about. With their imaginations and desires never completely satisfied, consumers earnestly embarked upon a never-ending pursuit of novelty through the purchase of goods, services, and experiences.[11] Romantic poets such as Keats and composers such as Beethoven valued expressing passion, love of beauty, and individualism. The romantically inclined saw purchases and gifts as expressions of individuality, the means to cement relationships, and items necessary to make a home a haven. As historian Peter Stearns notes, "Material objects, emotionalism, and a new sense of self [were] intertwined."[12]

Although Campbell identifies the period of the Industrial Revolution as the beginning of a romantic consumer culture, some scholars have pushed back the origins of consumer culture (minus the romance) to prerevolutionary France, seventeenth-century Holland, or Florence during the Medicis.[13] There was a consumer culture at all these times, but it affected relatively few people and lapsed during periods of cultural somnolence. The consumer culture of late-eighteenth- and early-nineteenth-century Britain, Europe, and North America was more developed, more sustained, and increasingly yoked to romance as an inducement to buy.

We date the growth of the lavish wedding to the British Queen Victoria's wedding to Prince Albert in 1840. Their marriage was certainly arranged, and since it was between first cousins, would hardly meet most modern standards of legality, let alone romantic intimacy. Moreover, Victoria's choice of husband was restricted in that she was required by law to marry a Protestant. It was not that Victoria's wedding gave birth to a romantic consumer culture but rather that certain features of the consumer culture already in place publicized this royal wedding and created the desire to emulate several features of it.

Brides had been marrying in white much before Victoria, but royal brides, who had always been of interest to the general public, typically did not follow this tradition. Victoria's immediate predecessors had usually worn velvet capes trimmed with ermine, and perhaps heavy brocaded gowns embroidered with white and silver thread, when they wed their (typically royal) husbands. Since red had once been more popular than white for weddings in western Europe (and certainly in China as well), what made white—pure white without any silver threads—so appealing at this time? Quite simply, white was the color girls were supposed to wear at court. It was also hard to keep clean, and cleanliness was becoming more valued as a sign of privilege (and later became associated with good hygiene and fighting germs).[14] More important, the queen herself, and the era she lived in, valued the ideal of female sexual purity and associated this trait with the color white. In Western culture, there were only two kinds of women, good ones (mothers or virgins) and evil ones (whores). The Victorians had their own twinning of women, the pure versus the "fallen" (their term for a prostitute). At her wedding, the pure woman wore a white veil and gown to signify her virginity. She deserved to wear white because she and her family had protected her sexual virtue.

Since Victoria had white skin, and many believed in the superiority of Anglo-Saxons, the color white also seemed to signify racial superiority. But even in Victoria's day there were some African American women who thought white an appropriate color to indicate their own strongly held beliefs in the ideals of sexual purity and cleanliness.[15] Moreover, Christian missionaries thought the ideals of Christian monogamy were so important to impart to nonwhites and nonbelievers around the world that they incorporated teaching the custom of the white dress and gown into their evangelistic duties. Thus, racial minorities were supposed to (and often did) share in dominant ideals about the purity of white as they became assimilated. Moreover, they did so despite the fact that they were underrepresented in magazines and advertisements.

Women's magazines of the time, which were targeted for a largely white audience, obviously touted the white middle-class woman as the standard for beauty. Such magazines thrived because they recognized their readers' interest in the home and in beautiful clothes. Magazines and newspaper articles described the white Spitalfield satin of Queen Victoria's dress, the handmade Honiton lace, the orange blossoms in her hair—the kind of detail readers began to expect in fashion reporting. But magazines also offered more helpful clues as to the expense of various fabrics and made clear the dividing line between the vulgar and the tasteful. Thus in 1849, *Godey's Lady's Book* told brides: "White silk stockings and satin slippers should always be the accompaniment of a bridal dress. Kid or prunella have a vulgar look."[16]

Popular novels of the nineteenth century may have included weddings, but their main story lines focused on removing the obstacles to finding one's true love. The novel can be seen as a literary form often dependent on the fairy tale, and was a new consumer product itself that was often purchased by women who were not well-to-do. Urban working girls at factories in Lowell, Massachusetts, read popular romantic magazines and novels in the 1840s. Because of the limited routes of economic mobility for poor women, "marrying up" (or hypergamy) was the most promising means of rising in economic and social status. Popular novels were created by publishers and sold for only a dime. As early as the 1880s, working-class girls were purchasing these novels, many of which conveyed and reinforced the desire to find Prince Charming. Dorothy Richards, an educated woman and writer, took a job in a box factory around the turn of the century to learn about the lives of women factory workers. Her co-workers described how they loved romantic stories such as *Little Rosebud's Lovers.* One garment worker excessively prized a writer whose stories were so realistic that they made "you feel as if you were the poor girl yourself going to get married to a rich duke."[17] The women even called themselves by the names of heroines in romantic novels.

Although the term "department store" was not used until the 1880s, these large retail institutions, located in major cities with special separate departments for apparel, toys, and housewares, were established by the 1850s. They would prove to be key centers of the nascent wedding industry. Plenty of mirrors, frequent organ recitals, and display windows at street level helped to create the magic of the big city department store.

Figure 3.   Wedding gowns, 1861, *Godey's Lady's Book.* Courtesy Library of Congress.

The large emporiums such as Marshall Field's in Chicago, Macy's in New York, Filene's in Boston, and the huge Wanamaker's in Philadelphia were founded by the mid-nineteenth century.[18] By the early 1900s, such urban spaces had elevated the store window display of merchandise to an art form and often featured palatial interiors and live music to enhance the shopping experience.[19] Brides had always collected their necessary house-hold goods before they moved out of their parents' home, but with ever-increasing numbers of household goods from which to choose, depart-ment stores quickly devised ways to entice and educate them on the importance of various merchandise. In 1908, Wanamaker's dedicated two whole weeks to an event titled the "Bride's Jubilee":

> The "whole store was surcharged with wedding vibrations." Pink and white colors appeared throughout on nearly every floor. Demonstrators, who worked in the furnishings department in the basement, conducted a cooking school for brides, showing them how to operate new "gadgets" and cooking

equipment. High up on the eighth floor, a "bride's totally furnished house, rich in suggestion," was on display. Situated on nearly every floor . . . were tableaux[,] . . . the "bride at breakfast," two scenes showing the bride in French lingerie-like gowns for receptions, dinner, and balls, the bride "receiving friends in the new home," the "bride's afternoon on the porch," the "bride in the kitchen," and so on. . . . An organist . . . played wedding marches at intervals.[20]

Through displays and color schemes that were decidedly feminine, these commercial establishments made clear dual equations: woman = consumer, man = provider. Men had once selected the family's food at open markets and frequented small shops or country stores, where they spent time chatting with other male customers and the shopkeeper. In rural areas, women remained at home and gave men lists of items to buy at these country stores.[21] But the new urban and suburban middle-class woman, confined by gender definition to the domestic sphere, found the department store safe, bright, and filled with mirrors so she could admire herself. Stores offered comforts for leisurely shopping, such as restrooms and restaurants, as well as delivery of packages. Department stores have always been seen as offering instant gratification in the form of ready-made goods. But in fact, they also sold bolts of satin or taffeta, the raw material for dressmaking, as well as offered in-store seamstresses and fitters.

Retailers often worked with merchandisers to determine appropriate ways to educate consumers and display new products. In their jewelry departments, stores encouraged buyers to select fine cutlery for wedding gifts.[22] Jewelers and department stores understood the bride was not just a one-time customer but was about to become "the family buyer," a potentially very valuable lifelong customer.[23] Jewelry stores also had smaller windows at eye level. The glass-encased wooden display case became an item that in the jewelry store signified things out of reach but that in the home was a valuable piece of furniture. In a wooden credenza with a glass front, a middle-class woman showed off luxuries such as the china and silver she received as wedding gifts.[24] The department store also pioneered another kind of display, the fashion show, which was first tried in New York City in 1857. Live models walked down a runway wearing Parisian-style fashions. The finale of these shows was occasionally a model wearing a bridal gown.

Department stores were only located in major cities, so most of the population had no access to such shopping experiences. After all, the bride, her mother, or a seamstress sewed most gowns for women in the nineteenth century, if indeed a woman wore a new gown for her wedding at all. Nonetheless, entrepreneurs began introducing new products for bridal sewing. The tailor Ebenezer Butterick and his wife introduced the tissue paper sewing pattern with graded sizes in 1863. Their 1892 catalog included a pattern for a wedding gown and veil that required 6½ yards of material 44 inches wide.[25] The mail-order catalog was a marketing innovation that disseminated luxury goods to rural America, where there were no department stores. The Sears catalog of 1902 sold no wedding dresses, but did offer lace, veils, and silks for the discerning dressmaker. In addition, it featured frock coats and tuxedoes for men, wedding bands, diamond engagement rings, a Queen Cathedral Gong Clock advertised as an appropriate wedding present, and a white trousseau lingerie set.[26] Because blacks in the South suffered discrimination in Southern stores, those who could afford to do so often preferred catalog shopping.[27]

Newspapers and magazines began to publish black-and-white photographs of celebrity weddings in the early twentieth century. *Photoplay*, the first movie fan magazine, was founded in 1910. A celebrity-crazed culture was nothing new. Victorians were fascinated with their queen, Edwardians with Sarah Bernhardt, and everyone with racy tabloid tales. But Hollywood created a new class of celebrities and new visual and written means for people to be able to look at the lives of the stars. Originally, the players in silent films were not named and moviegoers received no information about their private lives. By around 1910, Hollywood studios and publicists began to realize that publicity about film actors was one of the best ways to promote films. Because film performing was perceived as more natural than performing on the stage, the viewers thought the actor on the screen was portraying his or her true self. The audience hungered to know about the sexual and personal lives and the glamorous, expensive lifestyles of the stars. These actors, often from humble, ethnic, and/or émigré backgrounds, symbolized a panoply of consumer ideals: the fit body, the rags-to-riches story, the allure of luxury, beauty, youth, and celebrity.

Advertising has always both reflected and shaped the popular imagination. It became the lifeblood of mass circulation magazines. Since advertising provided magazines with a generous and stable revenue source, subscription costs could be lowered, making the publications more accessible to the reading public. Around 1910, advertising in newspapers and magazines began to shift from practical descriptions of products to descriptions of the emotions that products could elicit. The change was accompanied by a new design format, with larger images and a smaller amount of text. Wealthy women or film stars often endorsed the products. The text did not always require an accompanying photo of a film star, but merely pictures, words, and perhaps slogans that evoked romance, beauty, and luxury.

Advertising that sold romance had become a way of selling goods, especially goods associated with women, such as cosmetics, soap, food, fashion, jewelry, and housewares. A pair of silk pajamas brought pleasure, sensuality—and magic. Of course, romance was only one of many ways to sell products, since advertisers also appealed to envy, anxiety, snobbishness, traditionalism, family values, and the desire of ordinary people to live on the same plane as the fashionable set. Much of the credit for the birth of romantic advertising goes to Helen Landsdowne, then a 29-year-old copywriter at the J. Walter Thompson advertising agency. She recognized that selling romance was usually facilitated by creating a catchy slogan. While Woodbury's had touted its soap as a cure for pimples and skin disease, Landsdowne saw the potential to market the soap as a beauty product. In 1915, she devised the famous slogan for Woodbury's, posing male and female models in intimate settings and adding the mildly risqué, "A skin you love to touch."[28]

Advertising, which identified women as "Mrs. Consumer," also raised the level of importance of being a beautiful woman. Of course, valuing women for their loveliness was a centuries-old practice. Prior to the development of the marketing industry, a woman's beauty drew the eye of the viewer to a portrait by Rubeiro or Rubens; advertisers simply copied this convention of European art.[29] The male viewer could project a sexual, voyeuristic fantasy onto the body of the fleshy nude in a painting. In contrast, women viewers hoped to remake themselves in the images of the subjects of these paintings. In art, the lovely woman of unknown marital status was the main visual attraction, but advertisers used beautiful brides to sell products because the bride was a symbol of purity, joy, and happiness. These ads helped to make brides into a symbol of luxury.

Advertisers also made implicit promises that using their products would bring about the desired matrimonial result. In 1939, a famous national advertising campaign for Pond's soap revolved around the headline: "She's Engaged! She's Lovely! She Uses Pond's!" and featured a description of a socialite whose skin obviously helped her make an appropriate match.[30] (Indeed, there is no real difference in the associations fostered by the bride in this 1930s campaign and those conjured up by Elizabeth Hurley when she was the "model bride" for Estée Lauder's "Beautiful" perfume.) Like the Pond's ads, those for Gorham silver assured working- or middle-class women they could become upper class. Gorham sold silver flatware to brides using photographs of "Philadelphia's Most Important Brides" or "The Smartest Brides in Washington." But the image of the bride also made a product for the entire family more attractive and even magical. Thus, an advertising campaign for "Bridal Tomato Soup" included a newspaper ad featuring the image of this icon of beauty on the soup can.[31]

The new visual culture was a spectacle; it had sights, sounds, and motion. And while the spectacle was not only used to sell the idea of the lavish wedding, it conveyed the belief in romantic love through many updated variants. Musical comedies that made their way to the Broadway stage at the turn of the twentieth century, such as *A Stubborn Cinderella* and *The Silver Slipper,* were song-and-dance versions of the fairy tale—poor girl meets and eventually marries rich eligible man while she warbles beautiful love songs.[32] But even when the music was simply accompaniment, as in silent films, the large audience was still interested in seeing how lovers kissed or how a woman moved in glamorous silken clothes. As we discuss in chapter 7, film can offer a prolonged visual display of luxury goods, including wedding gowns, jewelry, and bottles of champagne. On screen, goods and services have more emotional appeal than they do on display in the store window because of the music and motion that accompany them, the size of the viewing audience, and the audience's identification with "the stars."

There was always a very close relationship between new imagery and new forms of personal intimacy. In the 1920s, when a man wanted to show interest in a woman, he no longer simply brought her flowers or chocolates. The idea of the "date," or commercialized leisure in pursuit of romance (even though this romance did not necessarily lead to marriage), developed at this time. The "date" was an unknown concept in the Victorian era. In that period, a suitor might pay a call on a woman in her parlor or sit with her on the front porch swing. She or her mother invited the man to pay the call. On a date, however, the initiative passed to the man. He asked the woman out, rather than waiting to be invited to her home. The trend began with the urban working class, which had no parlor for entertaining. But it spread from there to the middle and upper classes, who longed for the freedom of public entertainment. Dating also became more popular because of the growth of coeducational high schools; the availability of discretionary income; the rise of new leisure industries such as dance halls, amusement parks, and movies; and access to automobiles.[33]

Going to a baseball game, movie, soda fountain, or amusement park, while a typical activity on a date, fell short of the romantic ideal. The truly glamorous evening out involved dining at an elegant restaurant, one with music, waiters, a white tablecloth, candlelight, good food, and fine wine or champagne. Eating in a restaurant became the smart way to court before World War I, even if it was a style popular only with the cosmopolitan elite. Such dining was romantic because it was so different from eating an ordinary meal. The drudgery of cooking was kept from sight, and there were high expectations of the level of service provided by the uniformed waiters. Tables were arranged so each group of diners was set apart from the rest, and couples were able to inspect and compete with each other in their expression of elegance. Because the meal had to be ordered and served, dining out took more time than eating at home. With time to wait for the food, and the serving of one course at a time, the couple could talk to each other and achieve a kind of emotional intimacy.[34]

Pulp romance magazines founded in the 1920s, such as *True Romance* and *Dream World,* conveyed the idea of romantic love to a readership of mainly working-class women.[35] Radio, with no visual images, provided information in the form of on-air advisers and stirred fantasies of romance and dream worlds. The first wedding on the radio was broadcast live from the Central Palace in New York City in 1922 to an estimated audience of four thousand listeners.[36] Many of the department stores had their own shows as well. Macy's bridal secretary had a weekly radio program that discussed what the "up-to-date" bride should buy.[37] At first, broadcasters were at a loss to know what types of programming to air in the daytime. They devised the soap opera, a program sponsored by national brand soap companies like Colgate-Palmolive or Proctor and Gamble. With widespread ownership of radios by the end of the 1930s and the isolation of married women in the home during the daytime, soap operas had a ready-made audience. In 1930, Irna Phillips was the first writer to inject wedding planning and the occasion itself into the plot of a soap opera, *Painted Dreams,* to generate excitement.[38]

The release of best-selling "how-to" books offered not only a new consumer product, but also a way for wedding planning to become ingrained in American culture. Emily Post's etiquette guide, first published in 1922, appeared at the same time as many innovations in consumer culture—and concurrently with so much open flouting of convention by the educated young of the Jazz Age. At the time the first edition of the guide was published, Post, a 49-year-old former novelist and short story writer, was divorced from her blueblood husband. Her first edition was intended for people who owned a Social Register or other Visiting Book from which to select their guest lists for their weddings. In subsequent editions, however, Post broadened her audience to include the female equivalents of Jay Gatsby, the *nouveau riche* who envied the owners of the big houses across the bay. In order to rise in status, they needed to master the manners of the elite. Post not only provided the rules for the proper way to do things but also specified the aesthetics of the occasion. She publicized the tripartite division between formal, semiformal, and informal events, with corresponding rules for male and female dress. People insecure in their new status felt more comfortable conforming to the rules she mandated and less likely to be exposed as imposters in the world they wanted to join.[39]

Women had long understood that because marriage was a competitive endeavor, they had to package themselves attractively. Purchasing Emily Post's guide was a step in learning external conformity; nevertheless, there was much work to be done for women to transform their hair and bodies to make themselves attractive to men. In order to win the heart of a prince, the cinder girl of the 1920s had to make herself beautiful and wear lovely clothes. The beauty industry in that decade offered transformation. It focused new attention on the woman's face and hair and created the ideal of the slim, boyish body. Standardization of dress sizes imposed new ideals about the body. The discovery of the calorie as a measurement of food intake and the increasing availability of scales introduced the idea of dieting to achieve an ideal body size. Just prior to World War I, French couturier Paul Poiret introduced a new straight-line, knee-length sheath dress, which became synonymous with the "flapper" outfit. This new dress further encouraged women to diet in order to achieve the ideal of a slim-hipped silhouette. Moreover, the slim body became the new beauty ideal of the age because it was seen as the sign of good character; it meant that a woman had achieved self-control.[40]

The impact of Hollywood stars and studio publicity photographs changed women's attitudes toward makeup. Once only prostitutes and actresses used rouge and colored their lips. By the 1920s, however, "putting on paint"—lipstick, mascara, rouge, and nail polish—as well as bobbing one's hair and getting a permanent wave became means of expressing oneself, even if they were slightly rebellious acts. In the beauty "makeover"—a project of magical transformation of both the face and the body—a woman could change her self-concept and even her personality. In other words, she could reinvent herself.[41]

Through the concerted efforts of advertisers for cosmetics such as Helena Rubenstein and Max Factor, makeup came to be regarded as bringing out the true self rather than hiding it. But other products offered illusion, a way of concealing blemishes to create an improved self. Advertisements for many products raised anxiety only to demonstrate how these products could alleviate this condition. A woman who failed to use Listerine mouthwash was "often a bridesmaid but never a bride."[42] Many ads in the 1920s included personal testimony of nuptial success: "I Cured My Pimples—and Became a Bride."[43] Men were given identical advice; in one campaign, a man who did not wear garters to hold up his socks failed to win the hand of a beautiful girl.[44]

There were no major beauty innovations in the 1930s, but the decade was highly significant in the history of the long, white gown. Before that time, there were fashionable bridal dresses in brown in the late nineteenth century and high-society second-time brides such as Wallis Simpson, who wore a light blue suit when she married the Duke of Windsor. Moreover, there were still shops that rented gowns. However, in the

1930s, three norms governing the bridal gown coalesced: it should be white, it should be worn only once in a woman's lifetime, and it should be a fashion statement all its own that was not ruled by the hemlines and styles of the moment. The idea of the white, wear-once gown probably originated with the department store bridal salon. Altman's in New York City seems to have been the first to promote this idea in 1927. A distinctive bridal style arose as a reaction to "flapper" fashion. Many bridal gowns of the 1920s were knee-length flapper sheaths. As skirt lengths for this fashion trend rose, many brides began to prefer a full-length gown as more suitable for a church service. Needless to say, dress manufacturers were highly in favor of the development of a separate, wear-once style that required more material. In the 1930s, brand names began to emerge in bridal gowns (Alfred Angelo) and in the rental of men's formal wear (Gingiss), and the infusion of brands into this area encouraged the trends toward formal and "once-in-a-lifetime" apparel.[45]

Bridal promotional literature of the 1930s helped to convey and reinforce this tripartite notion of a white, wear-once, long gown to customers of the department store bridal salon. In truth, the bridal magazine was an outgrowth of the bridal salon more than it was a concept originating with any magazine publisher. Department stores liked to hand out free books, pamphlets, and magazines (termed "promotional collateral" by marketing professionals) to shoppers. Businessman Wells Drorbaugh founded *Bride's* magazine in 1934 under the original title *So You're Going to Be Married.* Department stores bought copies of the magazine in bulk. They handed them out to customers and mailed them to lists of engaged couples. In return for distributing the magazine, *Bride's* carried free advertising for their department store distributors. Department store bridal salons across the country handed out the *Wedding Embassy Year Book,* a free book rather than a magazine. It eventually became a freestanding wedding etiquette guide.[46] Advertising from bridal shops, florists, honeymoon resorts, and companies selling champagne supported both *Bride's* and the *Wedding Embassy Year Book.*

Such print material appeared to offer benevolent and neutral advice to brides as they planned their weddings, but in following that advice, customers naturally had to acquire products in the department store. Bridal shoppers were a prime audience for pamphlets about wedding etiquette, rules about the appearance of the gown, and the procedures to be followed at the wedding and reception. Afraid of making mistakes and insecure in a situation that required expensive purchases, these brides sought refuge in publications offering assurances found only in a firm set of rules. The standard format was a series of loosely connected topics, from the trousseau and bridal attendant wear to menus for wedding receptions, rules of etiquette, and answers to questions posed by bridal consumers. This "Q-and-A" format appears to be an especially effective method of conveying bridal information.

Capitalizing on the public's belief in the ideal of romantic perfection, and with mass media, advertising, and retail stores firmly ensconced in both the culture and the marketplace, the bridal industry was free to create and communicate the idea of a perfect wedding and to represent this event as an expression of the ideal of perfect love. The idea of the perfect wedding was simply the application of rules, regulations, and the right to spend taken to the extreme. "Perfect" was an adjective applied to virtually every product and element of the lavish wedding. Moreover, the perfect wedding had found its own soul mate in its association with perfect love, a concept that had a long history. Throughout most of that history, love had little to do with the reason for marrying. In fact, the Swiss philosopher Denis De Rougemont argued that passion thrived only when lovers were prevented from satisfying their erotic inclinations. Plato also held this view, as did romantic troubadours during the era of courtly love. As we have already observed, romantic love became the basis for selecting a marriage partner in western Europe and in North America between the middle of the eighteenth and the nineteenth centuries, because it seemed to fit with the emergence of individualism. It was at that time, then, that the ideal of perfect love became linked to romantic love, and romantic love became linked to marriage.[47] Thus, the highly popular "O Perfect Love," often sung at Victorian weddings, was an expression of the joining of romance with marriage.

What made the 1930s a distinctive period along the way toward realizing true love was that perfection was thought to be achieved by attention to the kind of rational planning and systematic order created and epitomized by the rules of bridal magazines and promotional materials. Perfection was the watchword, the central belief, and the rationale for the bridal industry. Thus, the word appears in the founding statement of every bridal magazine or bridal association, even predating the late 1940s, when so much of the bridal industry moved into the phase where it was both professionalized and legitimized. The first issue of *Bride's* in 1934 portrayed the future marriage as a combination of roles and adventures that needed a perfect beginning to get off to the right start:

> . . . you have set the date for your great day. Your day. It is the one day you have dreamed about since first romance was born in your heart. . . . It must be perfect in every particular. Everything about it should be just as you desire. . . . It's the culminating of exciting weeks of preparation—hectic shopping, sending out invitations, opening presents; it's the symbol of great adventures to come—your honeymoon, your home, your role as a hostess.[48]

Hollywood first began to use "perfect" in association with weddings in its 1946 promotion campaign for *Abie's Irish Rose*. The promotion included ads for wedding rings, a honeymoon, a caterer for the reception, new furniture, a veil, and Peach Bloom makeup under the headline, "Be Fully Prepared for That Perfect Time—The Wedding Day."[49] The first etiquette book to use "perfect wedding" in its title was Leola Coombs Kelley's *How to Conduct a Perfect Wedding* (1957), which, as expected, focused more on rules than on feelings. Nonetheless, the equation of perfection with magic was far more important than etiquette in the 138 books that contained the words "perfect wedding" in their titles between 1957 and 2000.

The ideal of the perfect wedding was present in the 1920s and 1930s, but the majority of Americans did not have the means to achieve it. It was only a matter of time before this would no longer be the case. The first period of mass prosperity and consumer buying occurred in the 1920s. Although working people were buying Fords, radios, and vacuum cleaners, most couples were still marrying rather simply. Following the boom years of the 1920s, the pinched incomes of most ordinary Americans—when the bottom half of the society was suffering and the Depression spread economic misery upward—put dreams of lavishness and luxury out of reach, or more accurately, confined them to the movie screen. During the 1930s many families were too poor even to be able to afford printed wedding invitations. The bride baked her own cake, and her mother cooked the food for the reception to keep costs down.[50] Nieces gathered wildflowers for bouquets. A single portrait, taken at the bridal studio, often sufficed to remember the occasion.

Wartime scarcity and three-day leaves kept luxury to a minimum during World War II. At the end of the war, some brides were making dresses out of parachute silk and could not secure scarce film and flashbulbs. Yet even during the war, the bridal industry insisted that a long, white bridal gown and a diamond engagement ring were democratic rights. The American Association of Bridal Manufacturers relied on patriotic rhetoric in asking for an exemption from the War Production Board's L-85 guidelines that rationed the silk needed for parachutes. They argued to key representatives in Congress, "American boys are going off to war and what are they fighting for except the privilege of getting married in a traditional way?"[51] The industry won its exemption.

In the United States, an economic crisis lasting almost a decade followed by a four-year war with battlefield deaths numbering more than 400,000 had produced families where women had to make do, respond stoically to tragedy, pack up at a moment's notice, defer childbearing, and bring in extra income. At the end of World War II, all of these adaptations came to be regarded as unfortunate responses to hardship and crisis. The advent of the Cold War so soon after World War II encouraged Americans to turn to the family as a bulwark of stability in a threatening time. Just as American foreign policy promoted the containment of Communism from spreading beyond the Soviet Union, China, and eastern Europe, so, too, the domestic ideology of the Cold War era emphasized containment of erotic impulses within stable marriages.[52]

The 1950s American dream of joining the middle class included owning a single-family home, a car, and a television set—and the lavish wedding soon became a part of that dream. A middle-class woman sought to acquire a diamond engagement ring and have a luxurious wedding, with gifts of silver, china, glass stemware, a toaster, and salad bowls. With incomes on the rise, an opulent wedding was soon construed as a social necessity. Greater acceptance of luxury had caught up with the abundance of goods and the incomes to buy them. Luxury was no longer seen as morally corrupting, but instead as an entitlement for the masses.[53] Savings, earnings, and small loans were used to pay for the wedding in the years before Diner's Club, American Express, and Bank of America began issuing credit cards.

Postwar prosperity also helped create a marriage boom. The average marriage ages for both men and women fell to the lowest in a century. In 1950, the typical first-time bride was 20.3 years old, and the groom was 22.8. By the mid-1950s, these ages had fallen even lower. Singlehood went out of style as the marriage rate rose to an all-time high.[54] Since couples were so young, the bride's parents typically paid for the fifties wedding. As the 1950 film *Father of the Bride* made clear, such nuptials were often the realization of the mother's dreams, because she had been unable to have a lavish ceremony of her own during years marred by economic depression and war.

In addition to the spread of the lavish wedding, the 1950s also saw the democratization of shopping for this event. For the first time, blacks in Southern towns could enter stores through the front door, and they began to be treated with the same respect as white customers. But in other Southern cities, blacks were still not allowed to enter department stores. Black customers had to use the restroom marked "colored women" rather than the one for "white ladies." As a result of a boycott by blacks in Baltimore in 1951, blacks were allowed to shop at the city department stores but were still not allowed to try on clothes. In fact, not being allowed to try on wedding gowns was a frequent indignity for black bridal shoppers. Later boycotts, initiated by the civil rights movement in the South, addressed the entire racial etiquette of shopping and also demanded the hiring of African American sales clerks. By the mid-1960s, the system of racial segregation in shopping had been completely overturned and the lavish wedding was beginning to lose any association with racial indignity and exclusion.[55]

Surveys of bridal magazine readers in the 1960s and 1970s showed that black readers were represented in numbers equal to their share of the population. Readers with Spanish surnames were overrepresented according to some surveys, since by the 1960s, a large quinceañera and a large wedding were the means of gathering together a sizable extended family, and in Hispanic tradition, the events could be paid for by both sets of relatives.[56]

The democratization of bridal shopping signaled one basic fact: the demand for the lavish wedding was growing and beginning to attract consumers who had never considered such extravagance before. The bridal shop was as much a product of suburbanization as the shopping mall located near the exit ramp of an interstate highway. It was a new kind of business that siphoned off customers from department store bridal salons. Previously, salons had been incorporated as sections within downtown department stores. By contrast, these new bridal shops were relatively small, freestanding stores, spreading throughout the country in smaller cities and in the suburbs. Moreover, for the first time, photographers could make a living specializing not only in taking bridal portraits at the studio but also in photographing wedding-day rituals. Most of their customers wanted "candid" shots at the home as well as pictures of the ceremony and reception, not simply posed portraits taken in a studio.

There were important visual additions to bridal fantasy in the 1950s as well that were not necessarily evident in the parade of white and pink dresses on the covers of some bridal magazines. Besides developing the standard for the Cinderella tale and depicting a heroine who conformed to the 1950s ideal of blonde, bosomy, passive beauty, Walt Disney created a highly interconnected set of commercial products spawned by his retelling of the fairy tale. The Disney corporation manufactured toys, books, records, clothes, and items for children. The theme of his *Cinderella,* loosely based on the Perrault version, was "The dreams that you wish will come true." Moreover, the film demonstrated that success would come to those who are decent, good, and bold. Disney turned Perrault's Cinderella, who had suggested magical ideas to the fairy godmother (such as changing rats into coachmen) into a passive "good girl," patiently singing "Some Day My Prince Will Come."[57] Ultimately, Disney's Cinderella is a girl who wants love, not riches, since Cinderella falls in love with the prince before she realizes he is royalty. In the end, she is rewarded for her virtue by eventually marrying the wealthy, handsome, and royal man of her dreams.

One component of girlhood socialization in the 1950s was learning the story of Cinderella from Disney cartoons or Golden Press storybooks. A woman psychology professor asked her thirty-two female students at Kalamazoo College what appealed to them most as children in the tale of Cinderella. She conducted her interviews among women who had grown up in the forties and fifties. They told her they loved the idea that Cinderella got to go to the ball and marry the prince. Many of them recalled that as little girls they also had wanted a fairy godmother who would grant their wishes. One student replied that as a little girl she loved "the way the godmother just touched some rather ugly object and it was transformed into a beautiful object for Cinderella."[58]

We do not know how often little girls played "dress up" as brides before the 1950s, or whether they had magical fantasies about their weddings. However, bridal dolls in Victorian times had been intended entirely for display. Moreover, because public display of grief was so important to Victorian culture, far more dolls were dressed in mourning costume than in bridal outfits.[59] As was true with all other aspects of the wedding business, the big boom in bridal dolls occurred in the 1950s. A host of different companies introduced these dolls, which transformed fantasy into girlhood play. The popular Madame Alexander bride doll of the 1950s had a girl's body but a woman's features, and wore high heels and a white satin dress. Likewise, although the Betsy McCall doll that was sold from 1957 to 1963 resembled a young child complete with Mary Jane shoes, she had more than one hundred outfits made from velvet, taffeta, felt, and other materials. Her bridal outfit was created the first year she was manufactured. By 1958, the "Dress-Up Delights" section of the Sears catalog included a picture of a young girl in full bridal regalia admiring herself in the mirror. In 1965, the advertising copy for the "radiant bride" costume in the catalog featured an "acetate taffeta gown, long nylon net train with a finger loop to hold, and a lavish lace-trimmed nylon net veil. Extras too[,] . . . glitter mitts, wedding band ring, corsage, bridal bouquet, a lacy hanky" for $3.97.[60]

If the 1950s brought bridal fantasy within the reach of the average seven- to ten-year-old American girl, the 1960s brought her counterpart in contact with a more sexualized consumer culture. The bridal Barbie was both a sexier and a more fashion-conscious bride. After watching her daughter act out young-adult-themed play with paper dolls, Mattel cofounder Ruth Handler realized there was a market for a three-dimensional doll promoted as a shapely teenage fashion model. She introduced Barbie in 1959 and the first wedding gown for Barbie, titled "Wedding Day Set," that same year: "This dreamy mass of lace and satin appeared in the first fashion booklet. . . . Of all clothing sets sold, the wedding gown each year is the best seller."[61] By 1962, young girls could

Figure 4.   Reproduction of 1960s Wedding Barbie, Courtesy of Mattel, Inc.
Barbie is a trademark owned by and used with permission of Mattel, Inc.
© 2001 Mattel, Inc. All rights reserved.

buy the life-size Barbie costume set, which featured eight different outfits, including a wedding dress.[62]

Barbie, the best-selling doll in history, was the ultimate consumer, a
fashion-conscious and long-legged beauty with a bevy of outfits to buy,
choose from, and change into. Like Disney's Cinderella, she typically had
creamy white skin and long, beautiful, blonde hair. Barbie taught little

girls the basic lesson of fashion and cosmetics—that by changing their makeup, hairstyles, and costumes, they could acquire a new and more beautiful identity. As they ushered their Barbies through pink and white wedding boutiques, girls played with the accessories brides acquired through shopping. They projected onto Barbie the American cultural ideals of beauty, roles for adult women, and ideals of fashion and femininity, and although Barbie began as a white beauty ideal, black and Hispanic versions were created as well in the 1980s.

With so much reinforcement of the ideal of the lavish wedding, and so many girlhood dreams to fulfill, it is surprising that any young woman rejected marrying in an opulent manner. Yet some members of the educated classes turned decidedly antitraditional from the late sixties to the mid-seventies. These were the years of long-haired rebellion against all societal institutions, including the institution of marriage. College-educated children from white middle-class families were rejecting a key ritual of middle-class life. The slogans of the generation, "Make love, not war," and the Beatles' song lyrics, "All you need is love," demonstrate that the sixties counterculture was decidedly in favor of both sexual expression and romantic love. Some did cohabit as an alternative to marrying. But for the most part, it was the style of the wedding, and not the ceremony itself, that was the object of rebellion. In order to cater to brides who took an antimaterialist stance, Bloomingdale's put in its window a mannequin wearing a white cotton Mexican wedding dress. What constituted a perfect wedding for these brides was no longer found in the pages of bridal magazines. Although a distinct generational minority, the antiestablishment, college-educated segment seems not to have purchased as many magazines. As a result, readership of *Bride's* magazine declined, and it was even threatened with business failure.[63] The recently retired editor of *Bride's* confessed about her experiences in the sixties, "People would laugh at me at parties." Even after campus protest died down, Tricia Nixon's nuptial splendor on the White House lawn in 1971 was considered decidedly square.[64] There was, in fact, a linkage between antitraditional attitudes toward wedding and nuptial behavior. The number of marriages continued to decline in the mid-1970s, in large part because more couples began to choose cohabitation either as an alternative to marriage or as a temporary option prior to it.[65]

Then came the true-life Cinderella tale, broadcast to the world in a way that had never been possible before the age of global media. Cinderella was alive and well and being played by Lady Diana Spencer. Of course, there had been royal brides since the first regal in white, Queen Victoria. In 1956, Grace Kelly's marriage to Prince Rainier of Monaco was also a storybook romance loaded with spectacle and filmed by MGM. But if Hollywood's queen was becoming a princess, it could be said she was suffering a demotion. And since the elegant Kelly had already achieved fame and fortune before her wedding, there was simply more magic in Diana's story. Although titled and from the old English aristocratic Spencer family, Diana had dropped out of school at age sixteen and had never gone to college. Her résumé consisted of work as a kindergarten aide while she shared an apartment in a ritzy London neighborhood with friends. As she donned her taffeta Emmanuel gown and Spencer tiara and rode to her ceremony in a horse-drawn black and gold carriage, her transformation from giggling, gangly teenager to fairy princess was complete.

The royal wedding reinvigorated the Cinderella fantasy, providing permission for celebrities and commoners alike to emulate royalty. Magazines described Diana's ivory silk taffeta gown, studded with 10,000 pearls and sequins and bearing a 25-foot train, as "fit for a fairy princess." She was the true heir to Disney's Cinderella and to Barbie: a long-legged, blonde-haired beauty. Despite his bald spot, Charles was a prince who looked like a military hero in his medal-laden uniform with gold epaulets. Diana's shyness only reinforced the ideal of the demure bride who (at least initially) bowed her head or looked away from the camera. The wedding was "magic in the daylight." "PERFECT" proclaimed the *London Daily Mail* as their caption to the photograph of now–Princess Diana kissing Prince Charles on the balcony of Buckingham Palace.[66]

In America, the effect was immediate. A new professional organization, the Association of Bridal Consultants, was formed to cater to the increased demand for skilled managers to arrange large and lavish weddings. "The big wedding is back," trumpeted the headlines of several magazines. In every town and suburb, brides dressed in ruffles, flounces, and bouffant skirts, their huge puffed sleeves trimmed with lace and their dresses direct copies of Diana's.[67] Perhaps it would be stretching the point to attribute the marriage boom of the 1980s—which featured a record number of marriages in U.S. history[68]—to a single wedding.

Surely the boom was also related to the swing of the pendulum back in favor of traditionalism and to the onset of "luxury fever," thanks to the increasing number of corporations that touted luxury goods for aspiring consumers at all socioeconomic levels.[69] Martha Stewart's *Weddings* magazine, first published in 1987, provided the aesthetic and decorative patina for the Di-Charles wedding boom and conveyed the highly contradictory message of perfection achieved by doing it yourself.

Some U.S. trends, as well as those of British origin, were also vital to the growth of the lavish wedding. In 1980, the United States had a new president, a former Hollywood actor whose wife had been a lesser-known starlet. First Lady Nancy Reagan wore beautiful beaded Adolfo gowns, bought expensive new china for the White House, and invited friends from Hollywood to gala East Room events. What the spectacle of a royal wedding in 1981 did was provide a model of how to spend new wealth once the eighties turned prosperous. "If you've got it, flaunt it" was a popular maxim of the decade. In contrast to the upper-class norms that had frowned upon conspicuous consumption in the past, the wealthy no longer needed to conceal their love of luxury. A former catering consultant explained the growth of the eighties wedding extravaganza, remarking, "It's part of the whole yuppie thing. . . . Going back to tradition. The Reagan Administration. The economy. Princess Diana and Prince Charles."[70] But going back to tradition usually meant adopting a tradition not one's own. Couples by the droves were repudiating Emily Post's advice that people of modern means should not overspend. The wedding now presented a "chance to reach beyond your station."[71]

By the 1980s and 1990s, wedding etiquette guides emphasized how to consume in good taste, with expanded coverage on parties, presents, clothing, invitations, and transportation. Social critic Mark Caldwell argues that etiquette writers in these decades were less preoccupied with where to stand and how to greet guests, and more concerned with how to assemble the necessary goods and services for the occasion.[72] Emily Post's etiquette guide for 1955 devoted ninety pages to weddings; the 1997 version logged in at 161. In her day, Emily Post had worked with Towle, manufacturers of silver flatware, in publishing a special guide to *Bridal Silver and Wedding Customs*. Her heirs at the Emily Post Institute recognized the market potential for "name-brand" advice. They published a special guide to wedding etiquette, a checklist-planning book, a wedding audio book, and a CD-ROM. As always, etiquette guides offered reassurance to offset anxiety, but the fears that had to be allayed shifted to those pertaining to mistakes that could be made in purchasing as opposed to social errors. Although there were many questions as to how to handle hurt feelings caused by divorce, most questions and conversations in wedding chat rooms on the Internet were devoted to how to find a good photographer, baker, string quartet, or other service provider, or how to track down cut-rate copies of expensive items.

Changing demographic patterns were bound to result in couples having increased input about their weddings. The typical bride and groom in the nineties had sex before marriage and were much older than the youngsters who were married in the fifties. The average bride in 2000 was twenty-five and the groom was twenty-seven.[73] Older, more cosmopolitan couples also had more buying power. Both were probably employed and could contribute to their wedding, if not foot the entire bill. Because they were helping to pay for the event, the couple, not the mother of the bride, began to evaluate potential churches, synagogues, reception halls, caterers, and florists, often without consulting either set of parents. Couples were moving away from home and engaging in sex without having to tie the knot. About half of these brides and grooms had already lived together before marriage. If cohabitation became a middle-class norm, why bother with a ceremony at all? Because a marriage, everyone recognized, reflected increased public commitment to the relationship. For some, it was religiously sanctioned. For many others, it represented success, personal fulfillment, and a more secure way to raise children and seemed to provide the sense of privacy so many people found lacking in other areas of their lives.[74]

Among African Americans, the frequent resort to cohabitation proved a less enduring alternative to marriage.[75] Black women experienced higher divorce rates than others in society, as well as a higher chance of never marrying. They therefore were less likely to experience a lavish wedding, and it was more likely that their dream of a stable marriage would not work out as they planned. A small but growing segment of the poor, especially the African American poor, never married at all. The general reasons for nonmarrying among African Americans were the shortage of marriageable black men, limited job prospects for black men who were poorly educated, a lack of income, and the low probability that some could become reliable family breadwinners. There were also more eligible black women because of the higher homicide and imprisonment rates among black men. As more black women were able to support themselves, marriage to a man with dim chances for economic success did not necessarily look like a better choice than raising a child on one's own, with considerable help from family. Choosing a white spouse tended to be an option that was more appealing to black men than women, who often associated a white man with a legacy of inequality. Eventually, for many of the black poor, the nineties were also a time of prosperity.

The nineties started out as a rejection of the eighties, with designer Vera Wang's sleek straight-columned gown that showed plenty of bare back replacing the frou-frou overkill of a Demetrios creation. There was a brief flurry of interest in the simple life in 1991, about the same time the country experienced a mild recession. Then the longest peacetime economic expansion in American history arrived and spawned day traders, McMansions, Internet billionaires, and a boom in spending on luxuries—what one commentator called "luxury fever" and another called "opuluxe."[76] The nineties were a much more prosperous version of the eighties. The conventional wisdom is that, as was true in the 1950s, couples are more prone to marry when times are good. In fact, the marriage rate actually continued to fall in the nineties as more couples postponed marriage or simply cohabited in order to continue their education, start their careers, and delay the date of commitment.

Consumer culture took the longing for love and packaged it as a longing for goods, services, and experiences that express love. There is thus a strong connection between Charlotte Brontë's *Jane Eyre* and arriving in a glass coach and being married near the spires of Cinderella's Castle at Disney World. One gave rise to the other, and both stemmed from the yearning to live in a world where every desire was satisfied, every wish fulfilled. It is thus not a surprise that the Cinderella Wedding is the most requested type of "fantasy wedding" at Walt Disney World. In the fairy tale, characters have their wishes fulfilled through magical intervention. In the world of consumer culture, people acquire their magic through the purchase of goods, services, and unique experiences.

No one needs to be reminded of Princess Diana's bulimia, messy divorce, and tragic death to realize that "happily ever after" is a myth. But the desire for magical fantasy was not simply created by the bridal industry or made appealing to today's couples because of fears of divorce. Female desires, longings, and illusions are as old as the folktale of Cinderella; consumer culture rose up in part to meet these wishes. The idea of the perfect wedding is not age-old but instead was created by the bridal industry and eventually accepted and embraced by the public. This idea was the logical culmination of a romantic consumer culture, premised on the belief that utopia can be achieved in this world, not the next. Perfection was clearly a pragmatic notion as well for the bridal industry, since creating a perfect, magical wedding required so many services.

From Emily to Elizabeth Post, Priscilla of Boston to Vera Wang, Wells Drorbaugh to Martha Stewart, stylemakers contributed to the growth of the opulent wedding by developing new ideals to be achieved through extensive planning, spending, and new and constantly updated versions of etiquette, beauty, and distinctions in taste. The romance that was made tangible in things and that was once attached mainly to novels and fashion became equally affixed to dining, jet and auto travel, and photography in the twentieth century. Women were claiming their right to luxury, fashion, and pleasure. Consumerism was bound up with identity, and however much women's roles in public and economic life have changed, the identity of the bride seemed to offer singularity and beauty.

In the second half of the twentieth century, the belief that every bride could be Cinderella became a girlhood fantasy, a democratic right, and *the* central preoccupation of the wedding. People were able to buy the pursuit of happiness. Having the money to buy the dream brought a form of equality, even in a society of vastly unequal wealth. As we will discuss, the opulent wedding is no longer only for wealthy white people or heterosexuals. Lavish commodities and fashion have become symbols of romantic love for all, and utopian fantasies are widely shared. Consider this testimony from a shopper at a gay and lesbian bridal fair: "I've dreamed of the big party and beautiful white gown all my life. . . . Just because I'm a lesbian is no reason to deny myself my dream. We're paying for this ourselves, so why shouldn't we have it exactly the way we want?"[77]

Chapter 3 | THE ENGAGEMENT COMPLEX

Given the amount of detail involved, the lavish wedding obviously does not happen overnight. Engagements in the United States now last an average of thirteen months, a far cry from Emily Post's admonishment in 1922 that "A long engagement is trying to everyone. . . . It is an unnatural state, like that of waiting at the station for a train."[1] Of course, in case the bride and groom are unsure of how best to use this time, bridal magazines and etiquette books provide detailed checklists of goods and services that must be acquired, altered, maintained, and stored for the wedding, according to a month-by-month timetable.

But just what does it mean to be engaged? In Western countries, where couples choose their own mates without parental influence or supervision, it means two romantic partners who have created a "love match" openly declare their intention to marry in the near future. The event that marks the official beginning of the engagement is the proposal, which in most cases still depends on male initiative. The period is marked by a set of ever-evolving rituals, most of which are designed for women participants, and which revolve around lengthy preparations for the "big event." These rituals have become more elaborate in recent years, as if a fancier wedding somehow requires or deserves a more dramatic and magical warm-up.

Renowned ritual scholar Victor Turner defines a liminal condition as one during which a ritual participant "passes through a realm that has few or none of the attributes of the past or coming state."[2] During their engagement, the prospective bride and groom each have one foot in both the single and married worlds. But because they are not full-fledged citizens of either and are occupying a "celebratory never-never land," they may be unsure of their roles and identities.[3] As a result—and as is true of all states of liminality—engagements are often characterized by emotional ups and downs, and some of these are caused by the sheer enormity of the tasks involved in planning a lavish wedding.[4]

Throughout the centuries, the engagement period has evolved from one designed to reinforce the ceremoniousness of the marital bond and help prepare the couple to adjust to the roles of husband and wife characterized by premarital gifting and shopping sprees, particularly in consumer cultures. Engagements today are largely secular and consumption oriented. Once, they included their own religious betrothal ceremonies, viewed as legally binding, and featured an exchange of rings between the couple. These ceremonies originated in Roman times because some couples apparently seemed "forgetful of their plighted faith [and deferred] the fulfillment of their nuptial contracts."[5]

In fifteenth- and sixteenth-century England, an engagement became official when the couple participated in "handfasting" or "contracting," during which they exchanged solemn vows similar, if not identical, to those repeated in the actual wedding.[6] Although not required, if a couple participated in handfasting, "there was no backing out."[7] However, if an impediment such as an existing spouse or another woman pregnant with the groom's child was discovered, the ceremony could be declared invalid. Bindings were considered vital parts of engagements by the middle and upper classes and were sanctioned by parents, the church, and the community, all of whom had a stake in reinforcing the solemnity of the marriage commitment.

Around the same time, another religiously sanctioned tradition, the reading of the "banns," or intention to marry, began to take hold in England. This custom had been made compulsory in France in 1176.[8] Its purpose was to allow parties potentially harmed by the marriage to come forward and make their cases public. In order to marry in Catholic Europe in the sixteenth and seventeenth centuries, couples had to either have the banns read three times in church, get a license, or have a public notice posted, usually on the church door.[9] Reading or posting the banns had virtually supplanted handfasting ceremonies in England by the late 1600s,[10] and the custom was imported to America by the first settlers. But by the mid-nineteenth century, it had died out among Protestants in the United States, although reading the banns persisted among Catholics as late as the 1930s.[11] The tradition was slowly replaced by a nonbinding form of announcement, the placing of engagement notices in the newspaper, which began as an indication of high society in the large cities in the Northeast. In New York City, only families included in the *Blue Book of Social Registries* were permitted to be included in the paper. A prominent name and marriage at the fashionable Episcopalian church were the usual principles of inclusion in large metropolitan dailies outside New York until around 1900. Occasionally, such papers did carry announcements for Catholics and Jews but none for blacks, Hispanics, or Asians, except perhaps those of daughters of foreign diplomats.[12]

Although banns were no longer required by the end of the nineteenth century, the engagement period still retained its legal status through two mechanisms. The first was the waiting period imposed by the various states, a designated number of days between the time the couple acquired a marriage license and the time their ceremony could take place. Although typically lasting just a few days, most waiting periods were designed to prevent hasty trips to the altar.[13] Of course, some states like Nevada discovered that eliminating the waiting period boosted the state's economy, since all heterosexual marriages that take place in one state are recognized as legal in the others.

The second way the engagement period was legally upheld was through "breach of promise" or "heartbalm" lawsuits.[14] Breach of promise lawsuits were authorized by common law to protect mainly female plaintiffs who claimed injury to their reputations, their future chances at marrying, or their emotional states because of a broken engagement. After posting the banns became optional, there was no longer a clear legal standard as to when an engagement agreement had been reached. Some Victorian judges had accepted a suitor's love letters as indication of a promise to marry. But by the late nineteenth century, while the law still permitted such suits, public attitudes had changed. Women who claimed breach of promise were no longer seen as wronged and virtuous daughters, but as gold-diggers who cheapened the institution of marriage. Moreover, as romantic love became the ethic that governed whether a couple would marry, the courts became more convinced that love should not be regulated by jurisprudence, and that "treating a marriage like a contract made it 'soul-less' by subjecting lovers to contractual compulsion."[15]

The major period of reform for heartbalm laws occurred from the 1930s to the 1950s. By the end of this period, the only lawsuits permitted were those enabling the man to sue for the return of the engagement ring if his fiancée backed out of the wedding. This item, it was argued, deserved special status because it was given on the condition of marriage and would not have been provided otherwise. Since the 1970s, a "no-fault" ethic has dominated these cases, meaning the ring must be returned, regardless of who ends the engagement. Interestingly, while men can sue for the return of the ring, the courts do not permit women to sue for any costs they may have incurred for the wedding itself, even if they are stranded at the altar. Obviously, such statutes illuminate sexist assumptions about engagements and weddings; while these occasions may be more "for" women, they have no legal recourse to recoup their investments in the events.

In the eighteenth and nineteenth centuries in the United States, the engagement period was a time for both the bride and groom to accumulate goods for their new household, and for the man to solidify his financial prospects and acquire a home. The couple often had to wait until the groom could demonstrate he could provide a dependable source of income. In many cases, the bride lived with her family after the marriage until her husband could provide a separate residence for the couple.[16]

Besides getting to know her fiancé and his family more intimately, nineteenth-century brides typically spent their engagement periods acquiring the necessary clothing, linens, and other furnishings for their trousseaux. They usually made these items, both because stores were far away and because most did not have the means to buy embroidered hand towels or a floral quilt. A Rockefeller, Morgan, or Carnegie daughter had to allow time for items to be made for her or for a trip to Paris in order to secure the desired linens, lingerie, and dresses from the House of Worth. In 1878, when young Frances Folsom returned from Europe with her mother prior to her marriage to Grover Cleveland, they reportedly had the "rumored trousseau carefully packed in their trunks."[17] If a girl was from a family of modest means, the bride, her relatives, and other women friends usually made a quilt and woolen blanket for the bed and hemmed a few towels. She might also have been given bowls, pewter dishes, a coffee pot, some tablespoons, and perhaps a mirror from her parents.[18]

Wedding gifts were typically received only from members of the family and a small circle of intimate friends. More widespread gift giving did not begin until the 1880s. As a result, until that time, future brides "shopped, and sewed, and packed, and sewed, and cleaned house, and sewed some more."[19] Setting up the household was especially important before the marriage, not only because women were expected to create well-feathered nests for their hard-working husbands, but because children typically followed within a year or two of the wedding. And while the bride and groom were busy with gender-specific tasks, they devoted little time to planning the ceremony or even inviting guests. Nineteenth-century weddings were often simple affairs, and relatives who lived far away rarely traveled to them.

The Industrial Revolution brought advances in transportation, communications, and manufacturing, as well as a proliferation of sewing machines and machine-made goods. With all of these developments, it would be logical to assume the bride's workload would have shrunk and the engagement period consequently would have shortened by the early twentieth century. But paradoxically, a higher standard of living, the development of advertising as a vehicle for the creation of consumer desire, and improvements in retailing merely shifted the arena for completing engagement-related tasks from home production to shopping.[20] Instead of relying on her own skills or those of her mother, the bride now turned to seamstresses and department stores for her "necessary luxuries." As historian Regina Lee Blaszczyk observed, home furnishings, linens, crystal, china, and glassware became consumers' "major vehicles for expressing class affiliation and individual style."[21] Retailers raised the required standard of goods for a household from a homely frying pan, iron kettles, and pepperboxes to a wide range of aesthetically pleasing items typically used on special occasions.

Moreover, retailers had quite a bit of help from authorities who also shaped brides' ideas of outfitting the household. Solid farm folk rarely described the gathering of a bride's bundle before the marriage as a trousseau. But there was some agreement that she would bring some fancy lingerie and items for the household to the marriage. Emily Post began her list for the trousseau with "trimmed lingerie, tea gowns, bed sacques, pajamas," items of "gossamer and lace . . . for the sole admiration of her husband."[22] Then came the specifications of household items, divided for three classes of brides: the wealthy, the average, and the moderate. In the most extravagant category, her recommendations included the following:

> One to three dozen of the finest quality, embroidered, or otherwise trimmed linen [or silk] single-bed sheets, with a large embroidered monogram. If linen, it is dyed to match the color of the rooms.
> One to three dozen of the finest quality single-bed linen sheets, plain hemstitched, large monogram.
> Twelve to eighteen blanket covers of thin washable silk in white or in colors to match the rooms, and edged with narrow lace and breadths put together with lace insertion.[23]

The socially catastrophic events of the Depression and World War II meant different types of work besides acquiring household luxuries pervaded the engagement period. Moreover, there was an increase in the number of "telescoped" courtships and engagements (those lasting a few short months) during World War II, when couples quickly married before a man was shipped overseas.[24] This compression, along with the increase in women's employment, limited the amount of time available for setting up a household. Yet even during turbulent times, the work of the engagement was shifting from women's unpaid labor into the social and commercial realms. As we have previously discussed, the two most visible causes of this shift were the increase in access to automobiles and the spread of dating, romance, and a culture of couplehood in this country.

Given that engagements were no longer associated with the relatively somber realms of religion, law, labor, or betrothal contracts, why have the "recommended" engagement periods continued to lengthen since the 1950s?[25] Given that many women live with their fiancés before marriage, haven't they already acquired the goods necessary for setting up a household? The answer to this second question is probably "yes."

Because this is so, the engagement has evolved from being a time for "getting to know you" to "getting it all done" to "getting it all done right," and now to "getting better or different things" than the couple currently owns.[26] In short, the paramount function of the engagement is now to allow enough time for the wedding and honeymoon to be meticulously planned so the couple may revel in romance, magic, memories, and perfection.

Changes in the wedding checklists published in *Bride's* clearly illustrate this point. In 1959, the magazine recommended the bride begin planning a mere two months before the wedding and specified twenty-one tasks for her to complete.[27] By 1970, the number of months had increased to six, and the number of items on the "to do" list to forty-seven.[28] Although these numbers stayed relatively stable in the 1970s and 1980s, by the 1990s the magazine was advocating a twelve-month planning calendar with forty-four tasks, including such signs of the times as "Inquire about ATMs near your honeymoon site" and "Check final details with wedding professionals." And while the number of points on the "to do" list seemed to decrease throughout the 1990s, this was only because similar tasks were consolidated (e.g., "Book consultant, caterer, photographer, videographer, florist, and musicians").[29] Even among second weddings, engagement periods are becoming more common, as these types of weddings have come to resemble first marriages in their elaborateness.

Not surprisingly, those rituals of the engagement that have survived are the ones best able to reinforce the increasingly lavish nature of the wedding. One item, the diamond engagement ring, seems "quintessential" in that it is key to fulfilling the promise of romance and magic for the bride.[30] In countries from the United States to China, when a woman becomes engaged, she will probably receive an engagement ring containing a semiprecious or precious stone. Most likely, it will be a diamond; consumers in thirty-four countries spend approximately $74 billion a year on these gemstones.[31] The "average" diamond ring is now over a carat and is often the first (and sometimes only) piece of expensive jewelry a woman owns. Moreover, these rings are now so inextricably intertwined with the engagement ritual and so devoid of meaning in any other sphere that they have little if any resale value.[32] In fact, if a woman divorces, the only acceptable way to dispose of her engagement ring is to pass it on to a daughter or other female relative. Reusing or even resetting diamonds that have lost their meaning as emblems of a romantic relationship is typically not an option because of the stigma of failed romance these diamonds carry.[33]

Like many other customs associated with the lavish wedding, the tradition of the diamond engagement ring began with European royalty. Archduke Maximillian of Austria supposedly gave the first diamond engagement ring to Mary of Burgundy in 1477.[34] However, less valuable betrothal rings were known to exist since the second century C.E. in Rome, with brides-to-be receiving circlets of iron or rush as tokens of their upcoming marriages.[35] While brides who were royals and members of the nobility sported brilliantly cut stones, wealthy Americans in the mid-nineteenth century had bejeweled gold bands with pearls and engraved romantic sentiments. In the late 1880s, Tiffany jewelers in New York City devised an open mount for the stone that elevated the diamond on six prongs and allowed it to catch the light.[36] But what really caused the tradition of diamond engagement rings to take off was, simply put, a marketing campaign as brilliant as the gemstones themselves.

Despite antitrust legislation in the United States, the monopolistic diamond industry has found ways to flourish in this country. It has its roots in a discovery by a 15-year-old boy of a "glittering pebble" on the farm of the De Beers brothers in South Africa in 1867. In 1881, British empire builder Cecil Rhodes bought the mineral rights to the farm. In 1888, the Rhodes mine merged with a nearby Kimberley facility to form De Beers Consolidated Mines and control production in the entire region. As Rockefeller had recognized with regard to oil, Rhodes realized that the main threat to profitability was overproduction. Diamonds are plentiful, not scarce; but the marketing of diamonds was built around making them appear scarce so their price would not plummet when new fields were discovered.

But the story of diamonds is only complete if we acknowledge the Boer men, women, and children and African, often Zulu, men who dug Kimberlite rock out of the ground. They lived amid pneumonia, frequent accidents, and freezing temperatures. Eventually whites secured the skilled and supervisory mining jobs, and the African men who worked underground lived in walled compounds where the sale of liquor was prohibited. The mines resorted to elaborate strip searches and bodily purges to ensure that workers had not swallowed diamonds. Needless to say, diamond miners could not afford to purchase diamond engagement rings. Even today, few miners are married in Western fashion. They usually are wed in traditional ceremonies in the countryside, then leave their families behind and work in the mines, where they live in all-male hostels.

Ernest Oppenheimer, who bought De Beers from Rhodes's successors in 1929, secured a monopoly on the production of diamonds. In 1934, he established the Central Selling Organization to coordinate the marketing of gems around the world under one umbrella. As was true for all luxury trades, the Great Depression played havoc with the diamond business. Higher-quality, larger diamonds were no longer selling in Europe, but with the Nazi regime encroaching, the black market flourished as anxious refugees sewed uncut diamonds into their coats as mobile assets. In England and France, the appeal of diamonds had never trickled down to classes below the aristocracy. Prosperity in the United States had increased the popularity of diamond engagement rings during the 1920s, so it was there Oppenheimer set his sights as the market most likely to absorb excess production. Even during the Depression, Americans bought diamonds, albeit smaller, cheaper stones that featured "illusion settings" to make them look more impressive.[37] In 1938, assuming America would remain neutral during the war in Europe, Oppenheimer sent his son Harry to meet with the N. W. Ayer advertising agency.

Through its initial market research, the agency learned that consumers thought of diamonds as symbols of love.[38] It became apparent that the key to increasing the diamond trade was persuading the average man that buying a diamond engagement ring for his fiancée was both a necessity and a luxury and that the ring represented proof of his love. Of course, it was easy for Ayer to create a corollary to this idea: the larger the diamond, the greater the love expressed.

Ayer quickly began a campaign designed to alter "social attitudes" about diamonds and capitalize upon the links between luxury items and romance touted throughout the burgeoning popular culture industry. In a memo to De Beers in 1938, Ayer defined the target audience for its promotional efforts as "some 70 million people 15 years and over whose opinions we hope to influence."[39] In order to convince retailers that advertising would not cheapen the image of diamonds, Ayer ran ads in jewelry trade magazines explaining the marketing effort and listing the magazines where ads would be placed. In actuality, Ayer ran five campaigns in the 1930s and 1940s, each with a different strategic purpose. The first campaign, targeted to men, appeared in September 1939. The copy argued that giving a woman a diamond was an affirmation of masculinity, in that it reflected the man's financial acumen and achievements.[40] A few years later, Ayer ran a series of ads targeted to women that featured famous churches and cathedrals, thereby associating diamonds with the sacred, elegant church wedding.[41] Using public relations, advertising, product placement in films, and dealer promotions (a tactic known today as "integrated marketing"), Ayer promoted diamonds as indispensable luxury items that all "proper" engaged women should acquire.

One of Ayer's most famous advertising efforts, the "Great Artists" campaign, began appearing in 1939. Featuring highly romanticized paintings by modern artists such as Picasso, Dufy, and Dali, the basic strategy was to "marry" diamond engagement rings with images of high culture, taste, and sophistication. (In 1982, Absolut Vodka used this same strategy to revive its brand.)[42] The message was that the diamond ring was as unique and priceless as a master work hanging in the Metropolitan Museum of Art. Ayer placed full-page, four-color ads in such magazines as *Fortune, Town & Country, Vogue, Harper's, Look, Life, Saturday Evening Post, Time,* and *New Yorker* to reach a middle- and upper-class audience. In addition to original artwork and poetic copy, the ads also highlighted four sizes of stones—half carat, one carat, two carats, and three carats—and the price ranges for each. Thus, Ayer set the agenda for the appropriate size of diamonds men should acquire and provided a way for less affluent brides to still get their diamonds.

The "Great Artists" campaign was a both a strategic and aesthetic success. But more important for De Beers, it helped increase retail sales by 25 percent in the first six months of 1940 and by 55 percent in 1941.[43] Ayer's use of "guilt appeals"[44] to tug at the heartstrings of hapless grooms was clearly successful. A 1940 ad that employed these appeals also managed to attribute magical qualities to the diamond engagement ring while reminding grooms of the consequences of withholding magic:

[T]here are some things that, neglected now, can never be made up in later life. Not in many a month of somedays. Not in the accomplishment of all his plans for time to come. His engagement diamond is such a gesture. No other ring given in later years can ever hold its precious significance for both of them. Given unworthily, foregone in a sweet gesture of self-sacrifice, it can never be replaced—for in its shining light is stored the treasure of their hearts.[45]

After the war broke out, the American public became aware that diamonds were needed for industrial production. However, Ayer created a campaign that educated consumers on the differences between industrial-grade and jewelry-grade diamonds. Thus, women were told it was perfectly acceptable to acquire a diamond, and moreover that the purchase price of diamonds used for jewelry helped offset the cost of mining the industrial diamonds needed for the war.[46]

In addition to creating multiple advertising campaigns, Ayer arranged for movie stars and celebrities to wear the gems in movies and at gala events. Ayer even persuaded Hollywood to feature diamonds in movie titles and plots. The agency convinced Paramount to change the title of *Diamonds Dangerous* to *Adventures in Diamonds,* and even managed to have a long scene inserted in the 1941 Claudette Colbert film *Skylark,* in which her character shopped for diamonds.[47] Ayer also created a series of seminars on diamond engagement rings: "all of these lectures . . . are reaching thousands of girls in their assemblies, classes and informal meetings in our leading educational institutions."[48] Jewelers gave talks (prepared by Ayer) at service clubs, women's luncheons, and the like with titles such as "The Right Ring for the Left Hand."[49] Gladys Babson Hannaford, known as the "Diamond Lady," logged 25,000 miles a year for Ayer while lecturing about diamonds across the country.[50] Such public relations efforts extended beyond U.S. borders as well. In Great Britain, Princess Elizabeth's engagement ring, acquired in 1947, and her 1953 coronation jewels swelled public interest in diamonds.[51] Elizabeth also toured the De Beers mines in South Africa and accepted a diamond from Oppenheimer.[52]

Through the mid-1940s, De Beers ads featured diagrams of four different-size diamonds but no positioning line. One night in 1947, Ayer copywriter Frances Gerety, a high school graduate from Philadelphia who had been working for the company for four years, was finishing an ad that needed a slogan: "I thought: 'Dear God, give me a line.' " She then wrote down "something, not sure if it was right or not, and went to bed."[53] The line she had scribbled was "A diamond is forever." Perfectly encapsulating both the lasting asset value of the stone and the romantic aspirations of couples entering into marriage, this slogan became the mainstay of the De Beers campaign in the United States. It also conveyed the idea that the ring should not be resold because of its sentimental value. Ayer immediately incorporated the slogan into all efforts for De Beers. Except for a brief but disastrous experiment during the "Me Generation" of the 1970s ("A Diamond Is for Now"), it has remained a mainstay of De Beers advertising.[54] In 1999, just a week after Frances Gerety died at the age of 83, *Advertising Age* named "A Diamond Is Forever" the best advertising slogan of the twentieth century.[55] Yet it is important to remember that for all its fame, it was actually the five advertising campaigns Ayer created for De Beers prior to the appearance of this slogan that contributed to the widespread adoption of the diamond engagement ring tradition.

Savvy jewelers, movie producers, and other entrepreneurs also helped spur the sale of diamond engagement rings during the 1950s. In 1951, Mary E. Lewis, president of the Federation of Doll Clubs, created "Little Queens and Big Diamonds." These crepe de chine dolls were replicas of monarchs and celebrities in wedding or other renowned gowns and featured genuine miniature engagement rings. The ring for the Princess Elizabeth doll was an authentic diamond solitaire of one-tenth of a carat in a six-prong setting. The series also featured Queen Victoria at her Diamond Jubilee; Elizabeth I, the Queen Mother; and Her Serene Highness, Princess Grace of Monaco.[56] In 1953, the movie *Gentlemen Prefer Blondes,* starring Marilyn Monroe and Jane Russell and featuring the hit song "Diamonds Are a Girl's Best Friend," was an enormous box-office success. The association of Monroe's blonde-haired, big-bosomed beauty, sexuality, and femininity—showing off her diamond while wearing a strapless pink taffeta gown—helped make the allure of these stones undeniable for women. In short, these messages about diamonds led to the formation of the "diamond mystique," which contains several seemingly contradictory polarities, including hard/soft, giving/receiving, ice/fire, virgin/whore, and temporal/eternal. Diamonds are perceived both as virtuous and as passionate, which makes the meanings of the dia-

Figure 5.   De Beers "Great Artists" ad, 1954. Courtesy of De Beers, Inc., and the John W. Hartman Center for Sales, Advertising, and Marketing History; Rare Book, Manuscript and Special Collections Library; Duke University Libraries.

Figure 6.   De Beers "Great Artists" ad, 1969. Courtesy of De Beers, Inc., and the John W. Hartman Center for Sales, Advertising, and Marketing History; Rare Book, Manuscript, and Special Collections Library; Duke University Libraries.

monds deep, complex, and awe-inspiring. Such contradictions no doubt make diamonds all the more appealing and desirable to their owners.[57]

The message that worked was that the diamond was an expression of love from a man to a woman. Henry Peterson, another entrepreneur who worked in the jewelry industry in the 1950s, was a former engraver who became president of the Feature Ring Company of New York City. In 1956, he created the "Acceptance Ring," designed for a woman to give to a man once she had said "yes" to his marriage proposal. The rings featured brilliant-cut diamonds mounted in white gold and were engraved with the phrase "Omnia Amor Vincit" (Love Conquers All).[58] The Acceptance Ring never caught on because the diamond was seen mainly as a feminine object. Jewelers were trying to double the "target market" for engagement jewelry, but the public refused to accede.

Spurred by its success in the United States, De Beers began to export the diamond engagement ring tradition to other parts of the world in the 1960s. To spearhead its overseas campaign, De Beers chose another advertising agency, J. Walter Thompson, because the agency had already established international offices in many key cities in Europe and Asia. J. Walter Thompson translated "A Diamond Is Forever" into several European languages, beginning in 1962. At first, Europeans were slow to embrace the idea that diamonds could be more than elite jewels or investments. But in 1967, De Beers discovered that the "tri-set," a third wedding band studded with diamonds, was popular among Germans. The popularity of this variant of diamond jewelry helped Germany soar to first place among European markets in adopting diamonds.[59]

It was in Japan that De Beers met with unparalleled success. Prior to World War II, the jewelry collection of a Japanese woman typically consisted of pearls and coral. When the De Beers campaign began in 1968, fewer than 5 percent of women in that country received diamond engagement rings; by 1981, the figure was 60 percent. De Beers's success in Japan can be attributed to J. Walter Thompson's inspiration that the ring should be positioned not as a gift from the groom to the bride, but as part of the *yuinōhin* bundle of gifts offered from the groom's family to the bride's household.[60] By the 1980s, the Japanese were typically spending three or four months' salary on an engagement ring, as opposed to the "two months' salary" norm established by Ayer in its American advertisements.

With the diamond engagement ring tradition now firmly entrenched in its most profitable markets, De Beers could tailor its advertising messages to the most prevalent sizes of diamonds available from its mines. When an excess supply of small diamonds became available in the 1960s, Ayer developed the "Four Cs" of diamond buying—cut, color, clarity, and carat weight—and emphasized these features over the size of the stone. When there was a shortage of clear diamonds, the agency emphasized those with a more yellow hue. Unfortunately for the cartel, by the mid-1970s the suggestion to downsize had worked too well, and the average size of solitaires fell to .28 carat, down from one carat in 1939.[61] In 1983, De Beers ordered Ayer to execute an about-face in its advertising

Figure 7.   Men's Acceptance Ring ad, 1957. Courtesy of the John W. Hartman Center for Sales, Advertising, and Marketing History; Rare Book, Manuscript, and Special Collections Library; Duke University Libraries.

and reemphasize the importance of having a "rock," with headlines such as, "A full carat or more. Halfway isn't your style."[62]

That the tradition of diamond engagement rings has become an undeniable part of American culture, and that it also represents a return to security and comfort, was evident in the wake of the terrorist attacks of September 11, 2001. Many Americans decided to advance the dates of their weddings, even if it meant cutting back on the elaborateness of the ceremonies.[63] However, diamond engagement rings soared in popularity, especially among the small but nevertheless profitable segment of men who had never given their wives an engagement ring. During the ensuing recession of 2001, which worsened after September 11, consumers changed the way they shopped for diamonds, shunning Tiffany, Cartier, and other high-priced jewelers and paying half price for comparable diamonds at the more than four hundred merchants in the "Diamond District," a two-block area in midtown Manhattan, the largest diamond market in the country. Just as was true in World War II, many diamond shoppers were brides or wives sent by their grooms or husbands to preselect their rings. One customer, married for fifteen years, reported she and her husband were going to renew their vows for a fourth time, and after she had picked out her (most recent) diamond, her husband would " 'surprise' her someday with the ring and another marriage proposal."[64]

Etiquette has always dictated that it is perfectly acceptable for a woman to be involved in selecting her engagement ring. But Ayer had discovered what the customer above exemplifies—that women still want an element of romance and surprise when their rings are presented to them. But how could men make this joint purchase a surprise? The answer was by ritualizing the *giving* of the ring, so that even if the bride knew what she was receiving, and might even help pay for it, she would not be privy to the "magic" surrounding its actual receipt. An internal report created for Ayer in the 1980s recognized this fact, noting "the giving should not be made to seem casual. The elaboration and creation of ritual and ceremony would work to sanction more giving and getting of diamonds in keeping with the spirit of the diamond."[65]

The ritualization of the proposal seems to be an invention of the twentieth century. Prior to that time, at least in America, there appeared to be only two phases to proposing: the man asked a woman in person or in a letter and then met with her father to ask his permission. The potential groom was expected to outline his financial assets and prospects, and the woman's father might have asked the couple to delay their plans if the man's status seemed tenuous.[66] In unusual cases, because of a father's absence or death, the groom asked the bride's mother for her hand.[67] Only in groups featuring unusual chaperonage, such as wealthy Southern planters or Hispanic ranchers, did the suitor ask the bride's father before going to the bride. The tradition of the man "on bended knee" seems to be merely a dramatic flourish in stereopticon pictures and silent films. None of the great suitors in nineteenth-century literature—Mr. Darcy in *Pride and Prejudice,* Mr. Rochester in *Jane Eyre,* or Laurie in *Little Women*—actually fell to their knees.

As late as 1969, Emily Post still mandated that the groom should ask the bride's father for her hand. With the impact of feminism, this custom began to die out, both because it suggested that the bride was property to be exchanged between men and because it implied the bride's father deserved more respect than her mother. Like many patriarchal gestures, this one has been reinterpreted as a bow to "tradition" or "respect for parents." Etiquette manuals and magazine articles written in the last twenty years label the ritual as optional, suggesting instead that the bride inform her parents with the groom at her side.[68] Moreover, a recent article in *Newsweek* recommended that even though the couple has probably discussed marriage, it is important for the would-be groom to "put in a call to the parents" and either plan a surprise trip to a romantic location or "propose in a wildly creative fashion or on a meaningful day and place."[69]

As is true of the wedding reception, the proposal has become more theatrical in the past two decades for several reasons. First, the event does not really represent the beginning of the marriage process as much as it does the end of the dating process, and as such, an end to (or decline in) the restaurants, roses, and concert or show tickets dating and courtship imply. Second, there is a crude economic calculus that operates; simply, all expensive wedding-related goods require increasingly theatrical gestures surrounding them. Third, lavishly romantic scenes from movies and advertising have incorporated the engagement process in their dramatizations of wedding luxury, along with the wedding itself. Gestures are supposed to be not merely romantic, but novel, nutty, and zany, injecting potentially staid and even stale occasions with "the illusion of rebelliousness" while discouraging true iconoclasm.[70]

As a result, opulent and high-status props such as flowers, limousine rides, champagne, elaborate dinners, concerts, high-priced sporting events, and even foreign trips to romantic Tahiti or Paris are now standard elements of proposals. Women also often seem to expect these kinds of proposals and are often disappointed if a man "pops the question" in an ordinary or profane manner. One bride even described how her disappointment with her fiancé's failure to utilize "the typical proposal days" of Christmas, New Year's Eve, and Valentine's Day—and his choice to propose on the living room floor on a Thursday evening—caused her to resent him for the first four years of their marriage.[71]

As some venues for proposals (such as romantic restaurants) have become cliché, proposals have become more expensive, and perhaps even outlandish, in order to help the presentation of the engagement ring remain magical and memorable and distinctive from the proposal narratives shared by others. Tales run rampant of prospective grooms dressing as knights in shining armor, proposing via the New York Yankees scoreboard, or burying "ancient" bottles containing proposals on beaches.[72] And for those men who are "romantically challenged" or strapped for time, on-line services are available to orchestrate these events.[73]

While not all brides experience magical and memorable proposals, most will participate in other sanctioned prenuptial rituals designed to affirm the social and commercial nature of the wedding, the female community surrounding the event, and the greater importance women typically attach to rituals. These include the bridesmaid's luncheon, multiple bridal showers, the bachelorette party, and shopping trips for wedding-related goods. In fact, there is really only one "male-only" activity (the bachelor party), and a few optional events for the couple (the engagement party and perhaps a couples shower).

Assurances that the bride and groom would have enough possessions for their new household were typically made in the form of dowries (called "marriage portions") until the early nineteenth century in America, and a little later in Europe.[74] After dowries disappeared, the custom of giving gifts to the couple spread to family members, and then by the 1880s, to family friends. Originally, gift giving provided the couple with necessities such as linens, pots, and bedding. But retailers in jewelry and department stores began to promote the more elaborate goods available, and they successfully touted silver, china, and crystal as symbols of proper middle-class homes. Brides typically displayed these gifts on a white linen tablecloth in the dining room of their parents' home before the wedding, and sometimes on their wedding day as well.

One of the most prevalent mechanisms for giving wedding gifts was, and is, the bridal shower, which began in urban areas in the United States in the 1890s. From their beginnings, showers were designed to reinforce domestic roles. At these parties, neighbors provided brides with money and basic items for the kitchen or bedroom. Likewise, costumes and themes reminded women of their soon-to-be-prevalent household duties. At one kitchen shower in 1905, "the invitees dressed in aprons and cooks' caps and prepared the luncheon. . . . [A]t another . . . guests were requested to come 'dressed as spinsters' and bring their sewing."[75] Showers were named after Japanese parasols, "which, when opened, showered the bride with gifts. . . . [T]he shower was a female ritual, usually held at the home of a female friend or relative, which underscored the responsibility of the women's community in helping the bride acquire the necessary goods for homemaking."[76] However, even early showers did not completely exclude men: sometimes grooms attended and received gifts of "dustpans, aprons, brushes and household tools."[77]

Showers in the United States thus began as mainly female parties among the urban upper middle class and made their way to rural areas by the 1930s. Etiquette books of the time observed that showers should be "purely spontaneous and informal, and should surprise the bride."[78] A 1937 magazine article described six types: kitchen, pantry, linen, electrical, glassware, and bathroom. Showers were intended both to furnish a home and to define a woman as cook, housewife, and sexual partner. For example, by 1948, one book contained thirty-five variants of the bridal shower, ranging from the more traditional kitchen and linen varieties to those focusing on specific types of items, such as books, records, soap, and handkerchiefs.[79] Even in the prim 1950s, the boudoir shower was also suggested as a sexual party theme. This was merely a new twist on the once-prevalent custom of displaying the bride's panties, bras, and nightgowns, often made out of silk or embroidered cotton, for other women to see and touch. One regional custom, not confined to immigrants, was to schedule this display of "the frilly things" about a week before the wedding at a tea hosted by the bride's best female friend.[80] In Canada, a more communal event, the "hall shower," emerged. Popular among Ukrainians and immigrants from Italy, Malta, and Romania, it featured a rented hall, up to three hundred guests (all women), expensive gifts such as refrigerators, money collected at the door for the couple, and an unwrapping ceremony that usually lasted a few hours.[81]

Since their inception, bridal showers have typically followed a fixed format of events, with time set aside to enjoy specially prepared foods, games, and a formal gift-opening ceremony complete with a recording secretary who lists each giver and gift so the bride can write thank-you notes and record her gifts in her wedding memory album. With the decline in male guests at showers, the other rule of the event was to invite the bride's mother and female kin, her soon-to-be-acquired relatives, and her own female friends. Given the increasing number of guests invited to weddings, it became a matter of course that a bride would have not one but many showers. With the emphasis on proper hosting, party guides featured lengthy discussions of etiquette pertaining to invitations, foods, and "cornball" party games. The types of games seemed to correspond to the types of gifts expected. For example, a 1940s shower might feature "Name Your Beauty Aid," where guests matched products cut out of a magazine with their brand names. During "Pick Your Perfume," guests took turns guessing whether certain perfume samples were from dime stores or department stores.[82] At the lingerie showers, the banter was blatantly sexual.

Nowadays it is common for guests (and even some brides-to-be) to confess to boredom with these events. They dislike playing childish games. Guests comment on the "strained politeness or reserved atmosphere" of the event. The shower assembles (largely female) friends and relatives from both sides without the liquor that lubricates interaction at the wedding reception. The most dissatisfied guests seem to be nontraditional women. One invitee in her twenties, who rarely cooked, was stymied by the hostess's request to bring her favorite recipe. Refusing to play along, she submitted instead the telephone number for Domino's pizza.[83] The satisfied guests are recent or future brides who recognize the reciprocal nature of gift giving and understand that when it is their turn, they will also "pick up loot" from all of the brides whose showers they had attended.[84]

These days a minority of bridal showers might be coed events. Like the "stock the bar" showers that emerged in the 1980s, these parties typically feature a gender-neutral theme.[85] Both the bride and the groom are present and the guests are not limited to women. The couple, rather than the bride, are made coequal guests of honor and the community being affirmed is a male and female one. Yet while some feminists praise the coed shower as an affirmation of more egalitarian household roles and intimacy between the couple, women sometimes tease the male guests about their lack of domestic skills, knowledge of the games, and gift-receipt norms, albeit in a good-natured manner.[86]

Given that many women now have multiple bridal showers, it is not surprising the popularity of one mechanism fueling wedding gift giving—the bridal registry—has soared. Combining rationality and efficiency with wish fulfillment and desire, the registry systematically enables guests to find gifts for the couple. The registry is used as a guide to purchase gifts for the shower and the wedding; guests who attend showers are expected to give two sets of gifts, although the shower gift is usually thought of as less expensive than the wedding present. The idea of a bridal registry seems more impersonal and systematic than the earlier practice of brides attaching notes to the wedding invitation indicating the kind of goblets, bonbon dishes, and punch bowls they would like. The founder of *Bride's* is often credited with inventing the registry in the 1930s, since he promoted the idea with managers at Lenox China.[87] In truth, however, stores had begun using informal notations at the beginning of the twentieth century, asking brides to provide them with a list of gifts they wanted.

The first recorded instance of an in-store bridal registry was at China Hall in Rochester, Minnesota, in 1901. Herman Winkle, a clerk, began to list brides' names on index cards, along with the gifts they received and their preferred patterns.[88] Brides liked the idea of the registry, at least in part to increase the sets of glassware or china already selected. Because stores assumed men would not want to enter these "feminine" departments, clerks took orders from their male customers over the phone, selected a gift for them, and then sent them cards describing what the department store had sent on their behalf.[89]

Advertising campaigns such as the one created by N. W. Ayer for Fostoria Glass Company in the 1920s fueled the desire for fine household items such as china and crystal. Fostoria encouraged women to buy large sets of china so they would have enough to always have a clean set for entertaining. As such, the company "redefined dining traditions, presenting forty-two-piece luncheon sets as perfect accessories for the era of the servant shortage."[90] By the mid-1930s, ads in bridal magazines were touting registries.[91] With its initial emphasis on luxury goods, the registry reinforced the message that fine store-bought items such as linens, china, and crystal were *de rigueur* in order for the bride to be outfitted properly. In the 1950s, Amy Vanderbilt warned: "*If you don't get your sterling now, you may never get it.* [A family's] constant needs absorb funds . . . so we 'make-do' over the years with ill-assorted cutlery. . . . [T]here is nothing that can be done about shabby flatware."[92] An ad that ran in *Bride and Home* magazine in the early 1960s also made the connection between romance and wedding-related consumption abundantly clear. It depicted a bride raptly admiring her new china in her wedding gown and featured the headline "Another Romance Is Just Beginning."[93]

The message that wedding gifts should be somehow distinct from ordinary gifts also trickled down to potential wedding guests as well. Studies have shown consumers often compare more brands for wedding gifts than for other-occasion gifts, even when buying for close friends, and will also buy items with more features when buying wedding gifts.[94] Moreover, consumers rated the attributes "practical, high quality, and lasting" as more important when selecting wedding gifts than when selecting the same types of items for themselves and typically spent more on these types of gifts.[95] One study demonstrated that when purchasing a gift for a wedding, consumers seek out "risk-reducing" properties, such as statements about its performance on government-sponsored tests and a warranty. Givers also avoided products of poor quality, those that reflected a lack of thoughtfulness, or those that could be described as "gaudy."[96]

Obviously reflecting the increasing pervasiveness of the consumption ethic, the typical bridal registry has become increasingly elaborate. It is now so popular that almost 90 percent of *Bride's* readers indicated they were planning to register in 1997, up from 60 percent in 1984. Moreover, more than half of brides who were recently surveyed indicated they were registering for crystal stemware, bed and bath linens, fine china, small appliances, cookware, stainless and sterling flatware, and table linens.[97] As the number of wedding gifts has increased (to an average of 171 in 1997), couples may want more control over the types of items they will receive.[98] Guests now spend between $60 and $100 on gifts, and the bride and groom probably do not want to be stuck with unwanted expensive items.[99]

But because some couples regard these luxury items as too cliché for their registries, and some want to make more distinctive statements about their identities to prospective wedding guests, brides and grooms have begun to supplement lists of these standard gifts with other items such as camping gear, tools, and stocks and bonds. Many of these innovations of the bridal registry have the added advantage of appealing primarily to men.[100] Although the "correct" places to register for most of the twentieth century were specialty and department stores, retailers such as Target and Home Depot, which want a share of the $19 billion bridal gift market, now offer this service.[101] These types of retail outlets are also popular among couples in which one member has already been married and has already traveled the traditional wedding registry route.[102] A final twist to registering has been the changes brought about by the Internet. Couples now direct potential wedding guests to special Web sites where they can view wish lists containing everything from traditional items to Blockbuster video vouchers, stocks, mutual funds, frequent flier miles, down payments for a mortgage, and hiking treks to Nepal.

Travel agencies and tour operators have also jumped on the bandwagon and offer potential guests the ability to finance portions of the couple's honeymoon. Some even provide discreetly worded cards for the couple to include with their invitations, providing directions as to how guests can contribute to the honeymoon fund.[103] For their six-week tour around the world, one Australian couple received a limousine tour of Singapore, a guided excursion in Santiago, and a night at a Cuzco monastery as wedding gifts.[104]

Couples also now include desired gift lists or the location of their preferred on-line registries (of the more than five hundred from which to choose) inside their wedding invitations, a move that has etiquette experts reeling.[105] But in truth, brides specified the types of items they desired on their invitations in the early twentieth century, prior to the development of the registry. Moreover, while cash or checks have always been acceptable and welcome wedding gifts, even if the amount was discreetly hidden from view when gifts were displayed, couples now are more blatant about asking for money, and sometimes even suggest the amount they would like to receive.[106] In short, the quest for magic, memories, romance, and perfection has made some couples (especially those who want their honeymoon or home down payment covered by their guests) more vocal in enrolling others to achieve their goals. Some brides, described as "aesthetic compulsives," want only exorbitantly expensive or even one-of-a-kind items as gifts. As a result, some stores now allow guests to pool donations toward items such as limited-edition vases, Mies van der Rohe Barcelona chairs, or even commissioned sculptures.[107]

Besides bridal showers, the engagement period may include two other types of parties. After waning in popularity for a few decades, the engagement party is reemerging as a lavish event among celebrities and East Coast society families. Emily Post observed in 1922 that the proper way for an engagement to be announced was for the family of the bride to host a small party. During the salad or dessert, the father of the bride would rise, announce the happy news, and toast the couple.[108] By the late 1940s, the need to have the "big news" announced by the family patriarch had diminished. Surprise engagement parties, where the bride announced her news to friends and family, came into vogue. Often she would disguise the news in a clever way, for example, by placing a miniature suitcase decorated with stickers from romantic travel destinations at each place setting at the party. When the guests opened their suitcases, they found an engagement announcement.[109]

Compared to weddings, engagement parties are still relatively intimate affairs, with typically only family and a close circle of friends attending. As is true with rehearsal dinners, these parties have resisted the trend to become increasingly elaborate, except among the wealthiest families. We suspect several factors have contributed to the decline of engagement parties as the "proper" way to present the happy couple. First is the increasingly elaborate nature of the wedding reception, with its often-sumptuous meals, live music, and pressure for providing an open bar. Second, increasing geographic mobility in American society, as well as the rising ages at which couples marry, makes it more likely family and friends may not be able to attend an engagement party. If the couple lives far from the bride's parents, her family members may in fact learn about the engagement after it has been announced to nearby friends. Finally, the engagement party is no longer a required mechanism through which the couple becomes legitimized in the eyes of family and friends, and the patriarchal gesture of the father's toast has lost its meaning as the official legitimizing symbol for the engagement.

While engagement parties may remain relatively subdued, the one male-only event, the bachelor party, has taken the opposite direction. Once decidedly optional, it began among the elite as a sedate "bachelor dinner," with the groom and his friends solemnly toasting the bride and then smashing their champagne glasses in the fireplace at a men's club or private hotel dining room. In the 1930s, etiquette experts tried to minimize the potential for decadence by advising that the bachelor dinner should be "a dignified occasion, free of that rowdy spirit so abhorrent to refined men[;] . . . there is no reason for ribaldry and cheap jests."[110] Somewhere after the 1950s, when the bachelor dinner became a common event among almost all social classes, it was transformed into a bachelor and then a "stag" party. The transition in both the language and activities at these parties coincided with the shift of the bachelor persona in American culture. From 1953 to the 1970s, *Playboy* publisher Hugh Hefner successfully reinvented the desired image of the American bachelor as a "successful, urbane, unfettered, and sexually conquering male."[111]

Since the 1970s, the required elements of the bachelor party have included an all-male guest list, copious amounts of alcohol, pranks played on an inebriated groom, and the inevitable stripper. One goal is to thoroughly humiliate the groom and affirm a form of aggressive, joking, and even hostile masculinity. The primary means to do so is as follows. First, the stripper attempts to sexually excite the bachelor. Next, she disrobes him until he is naked in front of the other partygoers. He then becomes the subject of jokes and jeers, which symbolically represents his expulsion from the group and his readiness to enter into marriage in a humbled state.[112] The party extends into the night, but many brides insist it not be held the night before the wedding so hangovers or hijinks (such as kidnapping the groom and transporting him to a faraway city) do not mar their special day.

As is true with other aspects of the engagement and wedding, bachelor parties are becoming more elaborate. Some now involve travel to fancy resorts in or out of the country, where men spend time playing golf, skiing, riding horseback, and bonding, as well as tapping a keg of beer in anticipation of the still-mandatory stripper. Men justify these prolonged events as their last real time "with the boys," and it provides them with a way to use both disposable income and frequent flier miles.[113] In other words, although the engagement period is loaded with "female" activities, men seem to want a little magic of their own as well. With the growing equality of women, as well as female disenchantment with the "boring" shower, many female friends of the bride now provide her with a "bachelorette" evening that mimics the format of the groom's night out. The bacchanalian night for the bride indicates women's increasing sexual assertiveness. The evening includes an all-female guest list, copious amounts of alcohol, pranks played on an inebriated bride, and a male stripper. There is often "a racy scavenger hunt" in which a bride must ask men for condoms or their underwear. A drunken bride and her guests squealing at a man in a G-string appears deceptively similar to the event for men, but women guests seem to betray less hostility toward the bride because they sense that other women find aggressive joking "offensive." Like the bachelor party, the female version occurs two or three nights before the wedding so that the bride "has some fun" before she returns to "getting ready" for the big event.[114] The norm of perfection for the wedding also extends to planning the perfect bachelorette party. An executive at a company selling exotica for such parties indicated that women spent quadruple the amount on "lewd items" as did men.[115]

The current engagement rituals clearly are designed to reinforce the couple's (and more so, the bride's) belief that it is appropriate to expect one's wedding to deliver a renewed romance with consumption, magic, perfection, and memories. The souvenirs of elaborate proposals, gifts, airline ticket stubs, and photographs make these experiences tangible and help contribute to the perception of the engagement as a magic, liminal time. But given the size and complexity of the contemporary wedding, engagements often involve as much work as play, especially for the bride and her mother. In the next chapter, we explore one key aspect of wedding planning, shopping for key artifacts.

Chapter 4 | THE RITUALS OF WEDDING SHOPPING

The engagement ring is on the bride-to-be's finger and the planning for the parties and showers is in full swing. And now the bride, who these days probably already has a full-time job, takes on what will seem at times like another one: selecting the important ritual artifacts for her wedding day. As we will discuss, in about half of couples, the groom will help with certain aspects of shopping. In 1995, a new retail chain called "We Do" was launched. The chain attempted to be a "category killer" and put everything a bride would need under one retail roof. The investment team ran out of capital before the idea could become profitable, and the chain dissolved in 1997. Yet given that in the 1990s customers visited an average of thirty different retail sites when creating their weddings and that most of the sites were small family businesses and cottage industries, it is understandable how these investors perceived an opportunity to consolidate wedding shopping for harried brides, their mothers, and their grooms.[1]

Of course, not all wedding goods and services are created equal with respect to the time, money, and effort spent acquiring them. Sociologist Emile Durkheim argues there is a fundamental difference between sacred and profane objects and events, and sacred ones should be kept separate from the profane so as to not dilute their power.[2] Because wedding planning involves months of information gathering and decision making that sometimes border on the tedious, the process of planning this type of event clearly has profane aspects. Nevertheless, it involves a few sacred objects and sacred moments that are unusual and extraordinary and that transcend normal routine. In the wedding context, some brides even claim that items seem to magically reveal themselves as they shop (a process called "hierophany"), help fulfill the fantasies for their wedding day, are imbued with tradition, have communicative power, and "contaminate" the wedding with positive energy.[3] Such items meet the definition of sacred artifacts as described by scholars in religious studies, consumer behavior, and other disciplines.[4]

It is not surprising the wedding gown is the object brides mention most often as possessing sacred qualities, given its distinctiveness from everyday attire, its ability to make a woman feel like a princess, and the fact it is the object most likely "to provoke an intense emotional response in the congregation" during the ceremony.[5] Brides also describe veils, wedding rings, and photographs in the same manner.[6] As symbols, the white gown and veil have long ceased to represent purity and virginity, two meanings they embodied from the Middle Ages through the Victorian era.[7] Yet even though their meaning stems more from commercial than spiritual sources, the gown and veil are still vessels of sacred power.

But why should the bride's ensemble be elevated to sacred status and the other costumes involved in the ritual not be? One reason is because the bride herself has such a special role to play in the ceremony, and her costume reflects that fact. Since the nineteenth century, the wedding day has been regarded as the bride's day, even more so than the couple's day. And only in cultures where kinship is revered over coupledom (e.g., in those areas where arranged marriages are still the norm) has the wedding ever been considered the family's day. However, the gown did not always stand out from the other costumes used in the wedding. Until the 1880s, female attendants often dressed in gowns identical in color and style to the bride's, supposedly to ward off evil spirits, confuse any potential kidnappers who might wish to disrupt the marriage ceremony, and also to rattle the groom when he came to marry his true love.[8] By the late nineteenth century, apparently in order to make the bride the center of attention, attendant attire was made in colors other than the bride's gown and became less ornate (and sometimes even plain) in order not to overshadow the bride's costume.[9]

Moreover, with the exception of the engagement ring, the gown and accessories are typically the most expensive tangible wedding artifacts purchased. And of course, with the Cinderella myth firmly embedded in so many countries, it is natural that the wedding gown—with its ability to transform a "commoner" into a princess—would be considered the focal point of the ceremony. Ads in bridal magazines, most of which feature the bride alone demurely modeling her gown, reinforce this myth.[10] So do retailers, who are aware that the public regards the wedding gown as a sacred item and have sought to combine profit making with the redesign of the bridal store as a quasi-sacred space. For all of the effort the bride (and her mother or the groom) expends while planning the wedding, one of the distinctive satisfactions of the whole experience is the very special moment when the bride finds "her" gown.

In truth, seeking transformation through dress is probably not a phenomenon limited to the bride on the wedding day; other participants may seek, and feel entitled to, this experience. The writer Stanley Elkin described his feelings upon wearing his tuxedo:

> [There is] something possessive in the feel of the thing, something hospitable and generous, father-of-the-bride, say, founder-of-the feast, chairman-of-the-board, leader-of-the-band, master-of-ceremonies, maitre-d'. Something patrician, the long, deep bloodlines of first families and old money. I didn't want to take it off. I never wanted to take it off.[11]

Another member of the wedding party who feels increasingly entitled to some transformation is the mother of the bride. Until recently, "MOB" dresses were often dowdy, monochromatic, and conservative. One author and MOB recently wrote that when she shopped for something to wear at her daughter's wedding, anything "over size 12 look[ed] like something Mrs. Khruschev would wear. . . . I tried on turquoise crepe. I looked like a wall in the hospital."[12]

These days, more daring MOBs who crave the magic and admiration a fancy dress can offer wear strapless, body-hugging gowns that show off their figures, or even dresses that feature bustles and elaborate trains. Many choose such gowns because they never had elaborate weddings of their own. Personal bridal consultant Phyllis Finkel remarked: "Nine times out of ten they will tell you . . . 'I want nothing on the dress.' But then comes the transformation[,] . . . all those tulle bottoms and bustier tops. All they need is a veil, and you could push them down the aisle."[13] In a similar manner, attendants who once had to resign themselves to matching polyester or taffeta ensembles now find themselves wanting to float down the aisle in designer sheaths that mirror the creations of Vera Wang.[14] Some may even get permission from the bride to pick out their own style of attendant dress, so long as they adhere to the bride's choice of color.[15] This was the case at Liza Minelli's fourth wedding in early 2002. Her sixteen attendants were instructed to wear floor-length gowns of their own choosing, as long as the gowns were black.[16]

The wedding gown, the headpiece, and the veil alone can now cost the bride an average of about $1,000, with the clothes of the groom, attendants, and mother of the bride requiring another $1,400.[17] Given the high visibility and cost of these items, it is not surprising that shopping for wedding apparel is a vastly different experience from shopping for everyday clothing. Many of the observations that anthropologist James Carrier makes about another ritual, Christmas shopping, are relevant here. He notes that as much as people complain about holiday shopping, it is an integral part of the ritual. In fact, it is the hard work of making choices between the offerings in the marketplace that actually transforms an object from a mere commodity into a "special thing" that "demonstrates that we can celebrate and recreate personal relations with the anonymous objects available to us."[18] In the case of the gown, choosing the "special thing" also makes a woman feel like a bride and conditions spectators to look upon her in the expected way—as beautiful, special, and a symbol often associated with hope and joy.

There are, however, major distinctions between shopping for rituals such as Christmas and birthdays and shopping for weddings. With the annual rituals, most shoppers are at least familiar with the major products and brands of toys, housewares, and apparel available in the marketplace. Yet weddings feature truly specialized artifacts, and with the added distinction that weddings supposedly occur once in a lifetime, consumers are less likely to be familiar with the goods involved. With fewer brand names upon which to rely, there is more difficulty in discerning a product's quality. Nor are consumers likely to be well versed as to the rules pertaining to the timing and display of these items, or what consumer scholar Dennis Rook calls the "ritual scripts."[19] So a bride must rely more heavily on retailers and service providers not only for the right goods and services, but also for training in how to use them. In understanding the rituals of wedding shopping, we focus on two of the most visible types of wedding retailers: wedding planners and retail bridal salons.

Wedding planning truly began to emerge as a profession in 1979, the year 4.6 million people got married in the United States, a record at the time.[20] Since then, the surge in employment among young and older women alike has meant they have had less time to devote to activities such as planning the important rituals of their lives. Yet at the same time that most women have devoted more energy and effort to further their education and careers, the lavish wedding has taken hold of consumer consciousness. Taken together, these trends have led to an increase in couples seeking help from wedding planners.

The idea of brides seeking outside help to plan their weddings has its roots in the last third of the nineteenth century, when the elite began to hire "masters of ceremonies."[21] These precursors to modern-day wedding coordinators emerged as department store bridal salons began to hire specialized employees in the 1920s. One of the primary purposes of the "bridal secretary" was to "be a sort of arbitor [sic] on etiquette[,] telling with authority who should stand where and whether the bridegroom wore a pearl gray tie. She was the chief of protocol and the Emily Post and the last court of appeal."[22] In the decades before World War II, the term applied to a wide range of women who offered advice about etiquette and wedding-related merchandise and who sometimes also traveled to upper-crust weddings to provide the kind of on-the-scene assistance now routinely associated with wedding planners.

Initially a position occupied solely by women, a bridal secretary could be the head of a bridal shop, an employee responsible for the bridal registry at a department store, or an independent businesswoman. This last category mushroomed during the postwar wedding boom of the 1950s. Barbara Wilson, who had worked for ten years as head of the Tailored Woman bridal shop in New York City, was a typical secretary of that period. Her clients were white women from relatively well-to-do families who had professional jobs in the city and therefore no time to plan their weddings themselves:

[Wilson] comes to the business girl's apartment in the evening with a longish list. Point by point they talk over the church, the flowers, the reception, the wedding cake, receiving the gifts, etc. . . . Just because she [the bride] is working all day and doesn't have time for the fuss doesn't mean she doesn't like the fuss. . . . Miss Wilson makes an appointment for the bride to go look at dresses over her noon hour . . . [and] will go to the fitting of the bridal gown if desired but sometimes the girl just goes alone.[23]

In an atmosphere of increasing postwar abundance, wedding consultants tried to gain stature by promoting their service as a profession and offering specialized training. The first association for bridal consultants, the National Bridal Service, was formed in 1951 by retired jeweler Jerry Connor. A watchmaker by training, in 1926 Connor devised the first registry system for sterling flatware in the nation at a jewelry store in Champaign, Illinois. Spurred by its success, he began to offer educational programs to other jewelers, touting the high profits that could be reaped from bridal customers. Connor became convinced that "the Wedding Market had become the single most important thing in the retail jeweler's life."[24] Connor began to travel across the United States encouraging jewelers to expand their offerings to include china, crystal, and unique gifts for the bridal party. In this way, he made jewelers competitive with department stores, where "the Wedding Market was being exploited to the fullest."[25]

By 1950, many jewelers across the country had begun to carry china, glassware, and stationery in addition to jewelry and silver place settings in order to attract brides. When Connor formed the National Bridal Service, he created manuals and educational training courses for prospective bridal consultants. By 1954, the NBS had members in forty-one states and had accepted its first international membership in Australia. Its consultants often included women who had not previously worked outside the home. One NBS employee, Doris Nixon, described how she had been a farm wife before receiving her training as a bridal consultant, and subsequently how Connor had "changed her life."[26]

The duties of the NBS bridal consultant included "consultation on wedding problems, coordination of table-top patterns, proper guidance in the selection of [the bride's] wedding invitations and announcements and other items of her paper trousseau."[27] Advertisements for the association that appeared in *Modern Bride* in the 1950s revealed that NBS consultants typically worked in jewelry stores.[28] Other associations, such as the American Association of Professional Bridal Consultants, founded in 1955, soon followed.[29]

Harried brides and mothers who were working outside of the home quickly got over their initial unease about having a stranger plan their intimate family affairs. Early consultants earned commissions from vendors who provided goods and services for their clients. In many ways, then, the role of the bridal consultant is similar to that of a building contractor, who oversees the work of others and coordinates the logistics involved in creating what is typically a weekend's worth of activity. These days, most consultants charge 15 percent of the total cost of the event.[30] At the pinnacle of the profession is Australian-born Colin Cowrie, a modern-day "bridal consultant to the stars" (and, some claim, the model for Franck Eggelhoffer in the 1991 movie version of *Father of the Bride*). Cowrie charges a $12,000 starting fee to his celebrity clients and $150 an hour thereafter.[31]

According to sociologist Angela Thompson, the wedding industry now recognizes three categories of planning professionals: wedding consultants, who give only advice for a fee; wedding coordinators, who work with both the couple and a variety of vendors to stage the wedding; and wedding day directors, hired by the wedding party to assist with setup, delivery, and cleanup on the day of the event.[32] Only about 10 percent of couples use the services of a coordinator, and they tend to be middle- or upper-class brides who spend much more than the average cost of a wedding. One coordinator told Thompson she was sometimes hired when brides and their mothers were fighting over how much should be spent on the event.[33]

Wedding consultant Debi Kephart of Austin, Texas, observes that because of the wealth of information now available on the Internet, brides and grooms who are technologically savvy and who have the time to plan are least likely to use the services of a wedding coordinator.[34] In fact, Web sites such as Theknot.com and WeddingChannel.com have transformed wedding shopping in one significant way: they tend to get men more involved in the decision making than was true in the past. In fact, it is just recently that the number of women who shop on the

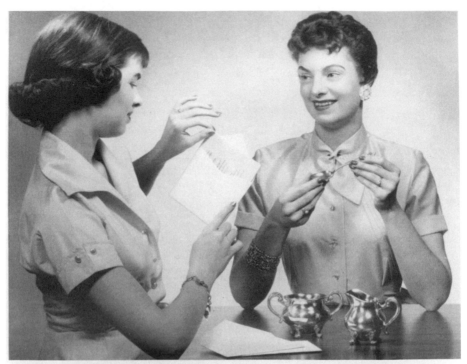

Figure 8. National Bridal Service ad, 1957. Courtesy, National Bridal Service; courtesy the John W. Hartman Center for Sales, Advertising, and Marketing History; Rare Book, Manuscript, and Special Collections Library; Duke University Libraries.

Internet has superseded the number of men.[35] As is true when shopping for other types of goods, men seem more willing to make purchases over the Internet than to visit traditional types of retail stores. This may be because technology has always been understood as more of a "man's domain," and no doubt most men perceive interacting with the computer as much more of a "masculine" activity than standing awkwardly in a bridal salon that contains wall-to-wall satin and lace.[36]

Couples—or more correctly, brides—who bypass the choices available on the Internet and use a traditional wedding coordinator typically seek help with the minute details regarding invitations, flowers, deliveries, and so forth. However, Thompson observes that one of the main duties of the coordinator is to manage what sociologist Arlie Hochschild has called the "emotion work": the highs and lows experienced by the bride and/or groom during the year or more it takes to plan a lavish event. Weddings possess both social visibility and a high degree of personal meaning, and because clients typically have limited experience with such events, they often swing between elation, desperation, and depression in planning the wedding.[37]

Yet it also may be true that one of the most common sources of these mixed emotions for brides is the gap between their expectations and the reality they encounter when working with wedding retailers. Many brides report how their excitement over shopping for their weddings was dampened by the apathy with which they were met in the marketplace. Some also felt outclassed by the planner, who knew more about party favors and little boxes of chocolates for the guests than they did, a situation that may have contributed to the brides' emotional distress. Just as shopping in a salon may be an affront to a man's sense of masculinity, not appearing to be in the know about wedding shopping and planning may threaten a woman's sense of femininity.

Sociologists Robert K. Merton and Elinor Barber observe that often when individuals must seek the advice of experts in a profession, they experience mixed emotions because the expert always has the upper hand in terms of knowledge of the problem being solved. As a result, customers may simultaneously experience relief at having a professional in charge and anger because their choices are more limited than they may have perceived them to be.[38] In fact, a recent study on wedding planning found "sociological ambivalence"—or the mixed emotions that occur when role conflict emerges between two people—highly visible in that particular context. As the acclaimed scholar Zygmunt Baumann observes, "[T]he expert bridges the gap between guarantees of being in the right (which can only be social) and making the choices that one wants (which can only be personal). In the ambivalence of his skills, he is, so to speak, resonant with the ambivalent condition of his client."[39] One bride reported on her encounters with the owner of a bridal shop:

> I'd heard many, many horror stories about this lady, that she had the entire wedding party in tears. . . . [She'd say,] "This looks horrible together, you can't do that." [But] she has what the girls want. She has the big-name dresses, she has all the fancy beads. . . . So that's why people go there, and she had what I wanted. . . . [I]f you can get past her, it's the best store in town.[40]

Although brides can sometimes manage their own mixed emotions by switching stores or "toughing it out"[41] with planners, wedding coordinators can find themselves acting in the capacity of therapists, calming their clients' fears "much like a flight attendant would allay the anxiety and fear of an airline passenger"[42] and providing socially sanctioned reactions for the feelings expressed by the bride and groom. Thompson argues that counseling and consoling are "similar to the guidance and transforming wand of Cinderella's fairy godmother" as she prepared the princess for the royal ball. Some coordinators even include images and phrases pertaining to the fairy godmother analogy in their promotional materials.[43]

However, all of the magical powers wedding coordinators might seem to possess must also coexist with the disenchanting qualities of planning an event on a budget that might not be adequate to make the bride's dream a reality. Weddings are also times when family tensions that have been bubbling close to the surface may erupt. Sometimes the way the bride imagines her wedding clashes with the vision held by another family member—usually her mother.[44] Moreover, the bride might experience mixed emotions as she tries to reconcile her values or expectations with those of the groom's family or her guests.[45] For example, brides who do not drink alcohol and who do not want it served at the reception must decide whether to stand their ground against relatives and guests who expect a cash bar, wine, and champagne. One bride described her feelings about alcohol at her celebration:

> We might have free beer . . . and then champagne punch. . . . The alcohol, I don't want any, hardly, I don't drink. . . . But I mean there would be like, "What, no alcohol at the reception?" So I mean it's just tradition, I guess. But I'm not going to have an open bar or anything. I'd just feel responsible if someone got too drunk and got into a wreck.[46]

As orchestrators of the wedding, coordinators must find a way to resolve these tensions while still focusing on the floral displays and monogrammed matchbooks that are absolutely imperative for the bride, the couple, and/or the family to realize their vision for the ceremony and reception. Moreover, even though they work in an industry responsible for creating the ideal of the perfect wedding, consultants often criticize bridal magazines, discourage clients from thinking their wedding is the most important day of their lives, and remind the couple that no event is *ever* perfect. Because the actions of the florists, caterers, and photographers whom they hire are essentially beyond their control, planners must warn that weddings are not always perfect so their own reputations are not blemished by others' mistakes. Instead, planners fall back on another appeal—that the bride will have an entire lifetime of great memories, recognizing that, as is supposedly the case when a woman endures labor, her memories will inevitably blot out any imperfections that occur on the wedding day.[47] In fact, it is the vendors who glean their profits from sales of gowns, slips, or headpieces who must continue to foster the belief that the wedding is the most important day of a woman's life.

Outside of any possible involvement with bridal Web sites, just how involved are grooms in the wedding planning process? Beginning with an emphasis on the "togetherness" of the couple in the 1950s, articles in bridal magazines often encouraged the bride to seek the groom's opinion. Many of these attempts, however, seemed to spring from the fear that the man's ego would be damaged if the bride received all of the attention. At the same time, attempts to involve men had to make wedding planning appear manly—no small task for an industry built around creating the quintessential image of femininity.

In the early 1950s, Jerry Connor created the "Bridegroom's Guide" for the National Bridal Service, a "man-to-man letter" designed to increase the involvement of the groom in the wedding process.[48] During the same decade, bridal secretary Barbara Wilson assisted grooms with planning the honeymoon, finding an apartment, ordering flowers, selecting their wedding attire, and purchasing the engagement ring.[49] More recently, etiquette advisers and the publishing industry have tried to acknowledge the impact of feminism on wedding planning, urging grooms to be involved in order to share the burden that months of arrangements entail. The first official male-oriented wedding guide, a British one published in 1974, was directed toward the best man, who not only was supposed to organize many details, but who, in England, was also expected to give a witty toast at the reception. In the 1990s, there were five American etiquette guides published for grooms; one was a mother's guide for her son. Still, most assumed men were reluctantly dragged to the church and they had to be reassured that choosing calligraphy for invitations was not unmanly. Much of the writing is characterized by a cynical, sardonic, I'm-a-cool-guy tone. *Esquire's Things a Man Should Know about Marriage: A Groom's Guide to the Wedding and Beyond* even seems distinctly antifeminist, instructing the groom as to how to persuade his bride not to adopt a hyphenated name.

To the degree men help shoulder the responsibilities of planning the wedding, or in the atypical cases, work with a hired professional, the meaning of the wedding seems to be shifting from the bride's special day to the couple's. As we have suggested, some grooms may also feel transformed by their wedding attire. But while there are more than a few grooms who pick out the china pattern themselves (because the bride is too preoccupied with her job), their participation has not been enough to eradicate the Victorian belief that the wedding day belongs to the bride. The coordinators in Thompson's study reported most of their clients were women. One planner noted about half of grooms say "I don't care" to wedding plans, and only approximately "one in ten [of the grooms] is actively involved."[50] At the four bridal fairs Thompson attended, she never saw a groom without a bride by his side.[51] Charles Lewis, who studied the wedding planning process of fifteen Minnesota couples in the 1990s, found only three grooms participating to any great degree in the planning.[52]

However, in focus groups conducted with undergraduate and graduate students in an Illinois college town in 1991, half of the brides participating said their fiancés were helping them.[53] Kephart reports that about 60 percent of the time, her clients are the bride and groom together, along with whoever else is interested in helping plan the wedding (or pay for it).[54] Yet she reported grooms often participate in selecting more gender-neutral items such as the reception hall, food, and music. They steer clear of bridal expos and often evaluate decisions or vote among choices already winnowed down by the bride, rather than take part in the necessary initial legwork themselves. Even in times that profess more gender equity, the bride and her mother still appear to be the major decision makers, with certain tasks delegated to the groom.

There seem to be many reasons grooms do not embrace the idea of wedding planning, and they all stem from the fact that shopping, decorating, beautifying, and contacting kin are still largely women's domain. First, men recognize the tremendous amount of work involved in this event. It is much easier to shirk tasks traditionally defined as a woman's responsibility in the first place—and especially those pertaining to the wedding—that supposedly made a woman a "true" woman.

Men also feel unskilled at comparing china and silver patterns or deciding on themes or colors. As Diana Leonard notes, "Men are culturally defined as less interested and less knowledgeable about wedding rituals."[55] Moreover, not only might they consider it unmanly to go to bridal fairs, but other men might ridicule them when they take on "feminine" tasks in planning the wedding. One bride mentioned her fiancé's friends teased him about attending a bridal show, and afterward he stopped participating in the wedding planning.[56] Until recently, whenever Hollywood has portrayed men who enjoyed making decisions about wedding details, they have been depicted as effeminate and probably gay.

Likewise, the wedding industry itself restates and magnifies assumptions about gender and supports the assumption that women are by nature the best consumers. Wedding magazines are for brides, not grooms, and they imply women are more skilled at decorating and therefore should arrange these events. Most wedding vendors consider the bride, not the groom, to be their ultimate customer. In fact, department stores used to classify a listing in their wedding registries according to the bride's last name, and did not even record the groom's last name.[57] Even the context of buying the engagement ring, typically identified as the man's bailiwick, often involves the bride. Moreover, when a groom selects his tux, his fiancée typically accompanies him to make sure whatever he chooses is in keeping with her vision of the wedding.[58] Although men clearly possess the skills to help create an event of this magnitude—after all, some have managed invasions and run corporations—bridal magazines nevertheless still portray men as "incapable of organizing a wedding."[59]

Moreover, even if men show interest in wedding planning, some brides may be afraid their fiancés would merely be in the way. Simply put, women's identities may be more vested in the wedding than men's. After all, the wedding is still connected to marriage, and women are more likely than men to say a happy marriage is important to them. So it is logical to assume women are supposed to be more interested than men in planning weddings. Several of the brides we have interviewed said they were planning their weddings themselves because they knew exactly what they wanted and because they, more than their fiancés, possessed the skills to get the job done.[60] Moreover, perfectionist brides—or "Bridezillas"—want the flower petals in their bouquets to be a specific number of centimeters across, the officiant to be attractive for the sake of the photographs, and even overweight or tattooed friends to be banned from the wedding party.[61]

The profile of grooms who are more involved in planning their weddings is sketchy. Research indicates they tend to be older and previously married, which suggests they may be trying to find ways to involve their children in the festivities.[62] Moreover, these fiancés and their brides often help to pay for the event themselves; if the bride's parents pay, grooms tend to regard the event as the in-laws' show.[63]

Just as gender role assumptions may limit the participation of grooms, they seem to have put a damper on the number of male consultants as well. Jeff Stockard, president of the Association of Wedding Professionals, estimates only about 2 percent of his members are men.[64] It is telling, however, that there seems to be a glass ceiling even within this "feminine" profession; the few male wedding coordinators tend to be at the top of the hierarchy, with men heading all three major professional associations.[65] Moreover, Thompson observes that when she interviewed these executives, they tended to feel the need to assert their masculinity by describing their military service records and backgrounds in business. These men also seemed to perpetuate gender stereotypes by describing how their female counterparts enjoyed picking out pew bows, while they themselves liked to create spreadsheets enumerating the costs of the reception.

Regardless of whether grooms accompany brides to the wedding coordinator, there is one business establishment—the bridal salon—where men are rarely seen. Until recently, the bridal salon has traditionally only offered attire for the women in the wedding party. Although many salons now rent tuxes, these items are typically available only in one corner of the store. If a bride plans to wear a long gown for her ceremony, she will most likely purchase (not rent) this item from a bridal salon, which tends to be a single shop managed by the owner. More and more, salons in department stores are disappearing. In 1980, J. C. Penney was the largest bridal retailer in the country, but after shifting its bridal business entirely to a specialty catalog in 1989, it closed the last bridal salon in its stores in 1999.[66]

At the turn of the century, brides in immigrant neighborhoods in the United States often rented their gowns. Likewise, in countries such as Japan and Israel, where space is at a premium, renting is often the preferred option.[67] As we have shown, since the 1930s, magazines and bridal salons encouraged women to own and not rent their wedding gowns and to wear the gown only once, although renting does become more popular during recessions. When women want to find their perfect wedding dress, they often turn first to the bridal salon. And of course, almost all women care deeply that their wedding gown will be perfect. Sheryl Nissinen, author of *The Conscious Bride,* observes:

The wedding dress is both a mythological and spiritual symbol of perfection. . . . A woman wants to be a princess on her wedding day, adorned in the most beautiful gown she can find as she prepares to meet her prince. . . . When a woman understands that on her wedding day she is elevated to a spiritual state where her transformation can occur, the wedding dress ceases to be merely an object that will make her "look perfect" but rather can be utilized as an amulet to assist her during her rite of passage.[68]

France is associated with luxury and fashion, and luxury and fashion are associated with prestige. The French word "salon" distinguishes the retail establishments that carry wedding gowns and accessories from mere stores, denotes them as high-status establishments, and contributes to their mystique as havens of pampering, exclusivity, and even magic. A bride choosing her gown from a salon typically makes her first visit six months before the wedding, tries on samples of gowns in her size, selects a style, and waits for a copy to be made for her. She then returns to the salon probably several times for alterations and then stores the gown at the salon until her big day.[69] With the exception of celebrities and the fabulously wealthy, most women buy their everyday clothes off the rack. Buying a wedding gown will be the one time a woman will own a custom-fitted (but nevertheless machine-made) dress,[70] as well as receive the attention that accompanies the assistance with fittings and alterations. Philosopher Christopher Berry explains the appeal of custom-tailored (even if no longer hand-sewn) clothes as "distinguished by expert workmanship and quality material. . . . [O]wnership of such goods conveys the meaning of exclusivity and its associated qualities of power, wealth and taste."[71]

Yet bridal salons can be sources of disenchantment and even discomfort. The expense and perceived risk of making a wrong choice is one reason, but the bride must also contend with the sheer weight of the gowns, which makes trying them on akin to engaging in physical labor. The bride is often exasperated by the six-month waiting period for her finished gown, the lack of samples in her size, bloated charges for alterations and storage, the fact that retailers remove tags so brides cannot compare prices at different salons,[72] and even the not uncommon practice of sewing designer labels into nondesigner gowns.[73] But the greatest fear is that a salon can go out of business before the customer has her gown in hand. Newspapers are replete with stories of angry women describing how they placed deposits of hundreds and even thousands of dollars on gowns months in advance, only to return to the stores to watch the inventory and fixtures being removed. These skittish brides must then frantically call manufacturers directly or visit other stores to find last-minute alternatives.[74]

Retailers try to minimize these concerns and meet their customers' needs to elevate shopping for the wedding gown to a sacred experience because they know many women want the shopping experience itself to make them feel magical. When Vera Wang opened her salon in Manhattan in 1990, it featured "a curved staircase of French limestone, white oak paneling, beige draperies, plump sofas, crystal chandeliers and copious arrangements of fresh flowers," with "each selling area . . . like a living room."[75] Many more modest salons offer their clients gourmet coffee and, of course, French croissants (which is ironic, considering the strict diets and adherence to exercise regimes many brides follow) and decorate the bathrooms with ornate gold fixtures.[76] At Kleinfeld in Brooklyn, which bills itself as "America's largest evening and bridal specialty store," clients are provided limousine service to and from the salon. Kleinfeld also offers "special religious consultants . . . to advise on dressing for a certain occasion."[77] Reinforcing the link between celebrity and the uniqueness of a woman's wedding day, Kleinfeld heralded the fact that one of the investors who purchased the store in 2000 was Wayne Rogers, famous for playing "Trapper John" on the television series *M*A*S*H.* Among the innovations Rogers has supervised is a new lounge for the men of the bridal party, where they can relax and watch television while the bride tries on gowns.[78]

Employees of bridal salons also use specific rituals to distinguish shopping for the gown and veil from more mundane activities. Most salons follow the Kleinfeld model and require brides to make appointments. Moreover, salons in Canada, and even the bridal sections of department stores in that country, request that potential clients and their entourages remove their shoes and leave them at the door before entering the salon. This action serves to reinforce the perception of these areas as "pure" ritual spaces and emphasizes their cleanliness and need to be separated from the mundane world. It also reinforces the fact that like Cinderella, women have to leave behind their mundane and sometimes even messy workaday worlds before they can entertain the possibility of transformation.[79]

In some cases, brides are rejected if they do not have enough time for a gown to be selected and altered or if they are unwilling to spend a minimum dollar amount on a gown. Retailers often screen brides over the telephone to determine if they will meet these criteria. When author Jaclyn Geller "went undercover" and tried to secure an appointment at Kleinfeld, she was told over the telephone that she could have one the next day, but she would have to be willing to spend at least $1,800 in the store, the cost of the least expensive gown.[80]

In the 1970s, communications scholar Irving Rein noted that once a bride came in for her initial appointment, in some salons an attractive male clerk, or "charmer," often recorded the vital information about her wedding. He would then escort her flirtatiously to a special room containing both the bridal gowns and a female salesperson waiting to assist her. On her way out of the store, the charmer would ask for the bride's telephone number so she would still feel attractive to other men, even though she was "spoken for." The point of this activity, Rein noted, was to make the bride associate feeling special and desirable with that particular salon.[81]

Although charmers are not as common today because brides are older, more sophisticated, and more cynical, brides still cross a threshold into a special area of the store, and the bride's passage through one or two inner rooms reinforces the out-of-the-ordinary nature of gown shopping. (Many jewelers created "ring rooms" in the 1940s and 1950s for the same purpose.)[82] Consumer psychologist Susanne Friese observes that salons serve a particular ritual function as well:

> The physical crossing of the doorstep to enter a bridal store can be viewed as the tangible equivalent of the emotional crossing of the intangible boundary a bride experiences when she leaves her social group. . . . A bridal store is not an ordinary store in which people look around and browse through other items[;] . . . it has the feel of a special, sacred place.[83]

Once inside the "gown room," salespeople enact another series of performance rituals: they bring the bride special undergarments, typically show her one gown at a time, assist her with the heavy dresses and petticoats, poof out sleeves, fluff skirts, billow out trains, adjust bodices, and provide patter that instructs the bride on the many accessories she will need.[84] At the same time, one or more women—the bride's mother, grandmother(s), maid of honor, or other attendants—accompany her, admire her, and offer advice, reinforcing the communal aspect of the event and that this is no ordinary purchase.

We have already argued that perfection was a standard created by the bridal industry. But while bridal consultants downplay this ideal, retailers in salons take on the responsibility of educating brides in, and enforcing, norms pertaining to perfection. Salespeople instruct brides in the proper care of gowns, the headpiece (possibly a tiara), bridesmaids' attire, and issues of etiquette. Moreover, in order to guarantee that the gown will be as perfect as possible, salon employees inform the bride of two primary rules of the wedding world: plan far ahead, and avoid losing or gaining weight once a dress has been selected. Sociologist Marisa Corrado observes that brides who ignore these rules at the outset are likely to be rejected as potential customers, because their actions could lead to the selection of an imperfect gown, which would in turn reflect badly on the retailer.[85] Salon employees cannot run the risk of outfitting the bride in an unbecoming way, because if that happens, the bride will likely blame them. Because the wedding business is based almost solely on referrals, the retailer's emphasis on making sure the gown is perfect is a way to protect future business. In short, salon salespeople enforce their rules about planning ahead and weight control because "temporal deviance robs them of essential time to produce a quality product (a bride), while physical deviance undoes all of their efforts and generates more work for them."[86]

The salon insists the bride adhere to its schedule for ordering and alterations, but at the same time, it attempts to engineer a magical experience for the bride. Given the strict policies enforced at these salons, it is worth asking: are brides truly able to spontaneously experience magic while trying on gowns? The answer seems to be "yes." Many brides whom we interviewed have described how their gown almost magically appeared to them while they were shopping:

> When I found that dress, I mean I put it on . . . I started crying, 'cause it was like, "This is my dress, . . ." and the whole thing seemed so much more real; that we were really getting married, and that this was going to happen. . . . [I]t just was a really overwhelming type of feeling.[87]

As is true in the above example, many brides described how the most tangible cue that their search was over occurred when they, or someone else in their entourage, cried at the sight of the future bride in her wedding gown. Rachel Leonard, the current fashion editor of *Bride's,* reports that the moment "has something to do with being plucked from ordinary life and suddenly becoming a symbol—set apart but also connected in a long chain with one's mother, grandmothers and brides everywhere."[88] Time after time, brides pinpoint the act of crying as their moment of discovery and epiphany. This feeling is not diminished even in the face of subsequent disasters pertaining to the gown.[89] The absence of tears seems to be what keeps brides searching for the perfect gown. But some never feel they find it and cannot disguise their disappointment over this fact:

> I tried on a good 18 dresses, I'm sure. . . . I feel like I never actually found the dress: "That's the dress and I can't live without it." I bought a dress that I'm happy with and I'll be glad to be married in it . . . like I said, I was too tired. I was about ready to cry or hurt somebody. . . . I guess the hardest part was you keep trying dresses on and you would expect to have that "perfect dress" feeling. And I never did that.[90]

Some brides take the less traditional path and select luxurious material that will be made into a gown by friends and relatives. Even without an actual garment to try on, the shopping trip might feel magical to them. Whereas most brides must rely on the mirror to tell them a gown is magical, those who can afford expensive fabrics rely on their sense of touch. Author Kate Cohen describes her experience buying silk and lace, the fabrics she wishes to use for her gown, at Casa dei Tessuti in Florence, Italy:

> Signor Romano and I picked silk crepe de chine. Rather, he picked it and I agreed, reluctantly; I wasn't certain that something so luxurious belonged on my body, but this store, this man, made one feel that luxury was the way it was supposed to be. Not a sin, not a sign of weakness or greed, but a hymn to God. Manmade fibers, stiff fabric, anything poorly wrought was an error, an insult, a waste of our precious time on earth. Yes, that snowy white crepe de chine would be just right.[91]

While it might appear that the discovery of the perfect gown is accidental, a closer look at bridal shopping behavior reveals bridal salons often actually serve as "clearinghouses" of merchandise. In truth, many brides have already chosen the gowns they want, or at least the styles they prefer. Often they enter the salon with a file folder full of photographs clipped from bridal magazines and ask whether particular gowns (by particular designers whose merchandise is featured in glossy, art-directed ads) are in stock. In other words, the magic they experience may result not from the gown being a total surprise but from their ability to fulfill their quest for a previously selected item.[92] However, even though the bride has engaged in extensive research prior to entering the salon, the transformation engendered by the gown is no less meaningful.

At other times, the talismanic power of the wedding gown can take a woman completely by surprise. Even Jaclyn Geller, who detested the white candles and strewn rose petals at the average bridal salon, was not immune to the power of the perfect dress. Her case was even more unusual, since she had only the saleswoman's opinion to rely upon rather than the bevy of female relatives and friends whom most brides consult as they step out of the dressing room for the first time. This author of an antiwedding, antimarriage treatise describes her feelings of transformation as she studied herself in an Oleg Cassini gown:

> I pull at the skirt and catch my own reflection in the mirror. For a moment I don't recognize myself . . . in this A-line gown, with the long, smooth skirt, I look like a different person, the heiress to the throne of a small country, a duchess. . . . I actually think to myself, "I look amazing. I look like a queen. It would be worth getting married just to be seen in this dress for a few hours. I will never take this dress off."[93]

While salon owners seem convinced their customers need the ritualistic aspects of pampering and expensive gowns to feel like Cinderella, two retail practices—one fairly old and the other more recent—fly in the face of this thinking. Since 1947, discount retailer Filene's Basement has held a daylong sale on bridal gowns; it now occurs four times a year in Boston and twice a year in Chicago. During the sale, the store is stuffed with gowns that normally sell from $1,000 to $8,000 but are marked down to $249. It takes only 45 seconds from the time the doors open at 8 A.M. for the entire inventory of 800 gowns to disappear. Yet the shopping experience is more similar to the bridal salon than might first seem to be the case. Brides usually still have their entourage of women in tow. In fact, the bride usually relies on one woman to act as a scout for desired gowns in the bride's size and another to stand guard over her cache of merchandise while she swaps gowns with other brides at the sale and tries them on in the open area of the sales floor amid a huge crowd of women. Two marketing scholars observed that, at first, what appears to be "a competitive, warlike environment [in fact has] a lot of cooperation going on."[94] But still, how is it possible to explain the attraction to a gown-purchasing scenario so different from the traditional salon experience?

Letters from Filene's customers reveal that the lunacy of the event does not overshadow feelings of joy in finding the perfect dress. In fact, women exulted over the fact that their gowns made them feel like Cinderella. Even though a gown was marked down and sold in a basement outfitted with linoleum floors, and no fawning saleswomen with tape measures, its transformational power was undiluted. One woman reported finding a "French lace over satin gown, full train, bustle and all, rolled in a ball under the . . . stairs. . . . [T]he original price was $100, a fair price for a gown back in 1952, that I purchased for $2.99."[95] What the bridal industry thought—that no bride could be price-conscious—turned out to be a myth, as this woman combined her thrill in getting a bargain with finding the perfect dress. Perhaps the lesson of the sale is that in a badly lit room packed with haggling women in bodysuits or underwear, finding the perfect dress becomes even more serendipitous, more incredulous, more magical than ever.

A second, more recent event that has had more nationwide repercussions was the opening of David's Bridal in 1990, a chain that offers discounted wedding gowns, accessories, and costumes for all members of the bridal party, including the groom. This chain did not originate simply in response to a new trend of the-bride-as-bargain-hunter, since the Filene's bride demonstrates she had existed for decades. Instead, the David's customer has neither the time nor the patience to shop at multiple stores and is almost as price-conscious as the Filene's shopper. David Yontie, a Florida retailer who had leased bridal boutiques in department stores, founded the store. He had originally named his new enterprise David's Bridal Warehouse but soon realized even brides proud of their bargain-hunting skills might not want to admit they had purchased their gown in a warehouse. In an effort to offer some of the pam-

Figure 9. Trying on gowns at Filene's Basement, 1995. Courtesy George R. Cross; Filene's Basement.

pering bridal customers expected, in the late 1990s, David's added consultants, spacious dressing rooms, large mirrors, stylish fixtures, and displays to its stores.[96]

David's Bridal can undercut its competition because of its size and contracts with multiple dress manufacturers in Hong Kong and mainland China. The retailer offers only foreign-made gowns because foreign labor is cheaper, and making a gown often involves about one hundred hours of work. Moreover, David's has revolutionized the way bridal gowns are purchased by stocking the same bridal and attendant gowns in different sizes rather than just carrying samples. Although some thought brides would turn up their noses at the idea of an off-the-rack bridal gown, David's has single-handedly invented the concept of the "bridal superstore," six times the size of the average salon. David's now has more than one hundred stores in thirty-five states. Each carries about 2,600 gowns, and all are available off the rack for less than $1,000. David's understands, as traditional bridal salons do not, that a wide selection and the convenience of a cash-and-carry operation do not seem to preclude a bride from delighting in the magical moment when she finds "her" gown.

Clearly, reveling in the sacredness of items featured in the lavish wedding does not begin once brides bring home shopping or garment bags but rather as they thumb through magazines, scrutinize numerous gowns, taste wedding cakes, and ingest the reams of information provided to them by bridal coordinators and salespeople. The transformations experienced at the wedding take place on the pedestal of a bridal salon, or even at a discount retailer. More often than not, women who are purchasing gowns "made for them" are, in actuality, buying gowns that are machine-made by low-paid workers in factories in Asia, Mexico, or Central America. Yet it is the bride's illusion of having "her dress" created for her from scratch that gives the retailers who offer these garments (as well as the fancy salons where they are housed) their power.

Certainly, sociologist James Carrier is correct when he argues that it is the ritual of shopping, not just the items themselves, that invests goods with meaning. And equally correct is a statement by consumer culture scholar James Twitchell, who observes that shopping is an "adventure in self-creation."[97] Given the powerful emotions and memories evoked as women shop for their weddings, we can understand now why women (and some men) want to experience for themselves the same magic spilling over from the tales of brides who have found their perfect dresses or who feel transformed into Cinderellas as they don formalwear. Such feelings explain why women devote so much time, energy, and money to selecting the items they will use in their weddings. Yet to achieve their full potency, all of these artifacts obviously need to be used in their intended ways in the next phase of the wedding, which is the subject of our next chapter: the ceremony itself.

Chapter 5 | THE WEDDING WEEKEND

A groom married in St. Louis, Missouri, in March 1992 recalled his wedding three months later: "The wedding was a hit," he gleefully confided. "The white orchids gracefully arched over the center of each table. The cake—chocolate French cream with raspberry filling and braided icing—seduced all die-hard dieters. The dancing didn't stop until midnight and the videotape caught it all." Late in the evening he held his bride in his arms and danced with her to the strains of "You Send Me." He had only one question. Would the picture of this dance grace the walls of the photographer's studio for all to see?[1]

Putting on a big—and these days unique and distinctive—show has always helped secure a family's social standing and make visible their wealth and prestige. Indeed, the bride's parents paid $16,000 for the white orchids, chocolate cream, and other obvious trappings of this St. Louis wedding. But prestige was only part of the wedding mystique for the groom. Like so many others, the groom thought of his wedding not as a religious ceremony but as a well-reviewed theatrical event. Beauty and luxury were supposed to seduce guests concerned about calories and cholesterol. The groom's greatest hope was that a bridal photographer would make his celebrity public as a shining exemplar of the perfect wedding. For him, as for many others, the lavish wedding was his coronation as much as it was the bride's. Surely the contemporary wedding is an exercise in narcissism, with the circle of pleasure and self-admiration spreading from the bride outward to include the groom, the mothers of the bride and groom, and sometimes the guests.

Having the special day seems now to be equated with the culture of celebrity. The values of entertainment—being the star of one's show; providing guests with a properly paced spectacle; often borrowing the concept of themes from parties, restaurants, or Disney World—appear more and more in the reception as well as in the ceremony itself. A culture of celebrity prizes fame and employs photography and special experiences to make individuals feel like film stars or royalty. It offers couples artifacts and photography as memorabilia to prove they were royally treated. As shopping, television, and movies have saturated the public with images from and the values of the entertainment industry, both the happy couple and their guests have come to expect more "spectacle." Primarily, this means increased dramatic sights and sounds, including the release of doves or butterflies from white boxes, the shooting off of fireworks, or a dramatic exit from the reception by the bride and groom.[2]

To outsiders and many critics, the mini-rituals of the special day may prove to be profoundly disenchanting, because so much of the day is routinized and highly scripted. The standard American wedding follows a format: it has a sequence and timing of each of the many events. Most weddings include the obligatory walk down the aisle, the cutting of the cake, the bouquet toss, the special exit, and so forth. Often couples and their families seem to be seeking some kind of balance between conformity and slight innovation so that the event appears personal, memorable, and not like other, "cookie-cutter" nuptials. But the kind of equilibrium to be achieved now must also take into account the profound changes sweeping U.S. society. Interfaith and intercultural marriage, the resurgence of ethnic identification since the 1970s, the frequency of divorce, the impact of popular culture, increasing social informality, the women's and gay rights movements, rising marriage ages, and the virtual disappearance of the virgin bride all have had an impact on the special day.

The greatest impact on the wedding is found in the highly subjective but ever-changing project of defining luxury. Luxury provides the feeling of being treated like royalty. Moreover, luxury is seen not just as requiring expensive and even unique items but also as calling for elaborate, indeed chivalric, gestures. The greater the luxury, the more dramatic flourishes required. Indeed, the wedding and reception can be thought of as a highly stylized performance before an eager audience. Therefore, there is a profound linkage between luxury and the theatricality of the wedding and reception. The most appropriate kind of analogy for the theatrical performance one finds at a wedding and reception is the musical, because this genre is based on song-and-dance numbers and usually ends happily.

The analogies with a musical are numerous, if we assume all weddings can be viewed as the same long-running show the audience has attended several times before. Various paid directors, such as photographers and videographers, are hired to help make the performance more romantic and magical. There is the cast and an audience, and the audience responds with applause and whistles at dramatic moments along the way. The cast has two major stars, with dozens of extras. The cast members wear color-coordinated costumes that help to identify the supporting characters and facilitate their roles. The actions of the major actors are choreographed; they must walk at a certain pace, often in time to music, and stand in certain places. The major action occurs up and down an aisle and at the front of the interior space. The actors use small props to help them perform their parts and provide a sense of visual display.[3] Many of these props—the bouquet, the rings, the Unity Candle, the bride's gown—become transformed into sacred objects by their association with the wedding and the fact that they are used for one purpose, and often one time only, before being saved in a memory box.[4] As at many other performances, theater critics abound. The reception is highly susceptible to these kinds of instantaneous reviews: the limousine driver got lost; the filet mignon is too well done; the dinner is served too late; the band is too loud; the photographer is too pushy.

Exactly where the rehearsal ends and the actual performance begins is not always clear these days, because as the wedding has become more expensive, it has become lengthier. The wedding day has turned into a wedding weekend, and in the upper middle class, it is common for out-of-town friends and relatives to travel by plane to attend a wedding where they will arrive on Friday night and leave late Sunday or early Monday morning. With a widespread geographic dispersion of relatives, the guests look for more opportunities to meet kin they rarely see and for "cheerful camaraderie" among friends. Within the wedding weekend, the rehearsal dinner has been transformed from a picnic or a potluck in the church basement into a fancy warm-up dinner that includes not only the bridal party but also out-of-town guests. More often than not, it is now held at a fancy hotel or restaurant, rather than a relative's home. There are now toasts at this event as well as the reception, but prior to the marriage, toast makers sense they have permission to disclose sexually revealing secrets about the bride or the groom.

The wedding day itself—a consumer event and a musical—has a spiritual dimension. To be sure, it is a day to exchange sacred vows of commitment for a lifetime. Religious officials marry most couples in sacred or religious settings. Moreover, as we have shown, the bride and groom endow purchased objects with a sacred character. Nonetheless, the values of the bridal and entertainment industries, and of consumer culture, prevail. As such, they inject magic, romance, perfection, and memory into countless elements of the ceremony and the reception in ever-increasing doses.

This way of describing the lavish wedding is considerably different than that favored by anthropologists, who have long considered the wedding a major rite of passage, a symbolic way to mark the movement from dependency to full adulthood and from being single to being married. As a result of undergoing such a rite, the individual is transformed and perceived differently as well. Supposedly the rite is a one-way passage—once an adult, always an adult. But given the increasing age at which couples marry and the likelihood that the average couple may be living together at the time of marriage, the meaning of the day as an official marker of becoming an adult has been diminished. Contemporary Americans tell psychologists they think an adult is an independent decision maker who is also financially independent. They have decided being an adult has little to do with being married.[5]

However, the anthropologists were correct in thinking the wedding provides a profound sense of transformation. And for the couple, this transformation results from their belief that they have produced a hit show and were treated royally. To put on a good musical, the major actors, but mainly the bride, pay attention to posture, skin, makeup, diet, and working out at a gym.[6] Although the bride and groom are both performers, the bride, not the groom, takes to heart the bridal industry ideal of perfection for a number of reasons. First, consumer culture has adopted perfectionism as its watchword, because consumers who buy "perfect" items are promised emotional and perhaps even financial rewards for doing so (e.g., owning the "right" car could result in a promotion). Advertisers often employ an appeal to perfection as they tout homes, cars, clothing—indeed, almost all goods and services in capitalist cultures.[7] Moreover, the bride is aware that on this day, everyone will be looking at her. Whereas slimness has been an ideal for women since the 1920s, the workout ethic, which touted the benefits of slim thighs and defined upper arms, came into its own in the 1970s. After that time, the bride had to exert more effort in achieving the ideal body. At the time of her wedding, author and feminist Kate Cohen was cohabiting in a farmhouse with the groom-to-be. She nonetheless felt compelled to join the local Gold's Gym two months before her wedding. She writes, "Since I was going to be a bride, I wanted to be a perfect bride, and the perfect bride had to have a perfect body."[8] The bride's body, face, and teeth have become part of the wedding planning project. It is now not uncommon for U.S. brides-to-be not only to go on a crash diet but also to have their teeth whitened—and, for some, to have plastic or Lasik surgery.

A late afternoon wedding, followed by a dinner and reception in the evening, enables the couple to feel most special, because this scheduling assumes a higher standard for the kind of food and entertaining guests will receive. Many couples before the 1950s married in the morning and served their guests lunch, followed by a reception at the bride's home. Or they married in the morning and had a reception at a public hall in the evening. Catholic weddings, which often used to occur in the early morning, followed by a morning nuptial mass, have largely shifted over to the afternoon/evening pattern as well.[9] Since love is often associated with candlelight and twinkling stars, the changing time for the wedding reception seems to make the whole event not only more expensive but more romantic as well.

Production values often govern both the timing of the ceremony and where it will occur. The value of the religious setting has long been viewed through the lens of romance. A lovely chapel in the woods, a cathedral with stained-glass windows, a temple overlooking a duck pond—any of these is supposedly the perfect place to marry. The interior can then be decked out in altar vases and pew bouquets. A few couples have a deep attachment to a particular house of worship, but many more drive around leafy suburbs looking for a church with the right look on the outside and the appropriate lecterns, pews, pipe organs, Bible stands, stained-glass windows, and wood trim on the inside.

In fact, a church or synagogue wedding is a bit less common now than at the end of World War II because of the rise of interfaith marriages and the decline in religious affiliation among first-time brides and grooms. In 1948, 81 percent of first-time brides married in a religious ceremony, according to government compilations of marriage statistics from reporting states. The figure had fallen to 74 percent in 1987. But there was also a countervailing trend. As attitudes toward what is acceptable for non–first timers have become more liberal, the percentage of religious ceremonies among remarrying brides has risen somewhat from 51 percent in 1948 to 57 percent in 1987, the last year that the government collected these statistics.[10]

The religious setting of the ceremony and/or the selection of a religious officiant to perform it constrain both theatricality and lavishness. Therefore, luxury is much more subdued in the ceremony than in the reception. To be sure, many brides are given some latitude to decorate the church with vases of flowers rather than pew bows, but few religious institutions are eager to have their space transformed into a wonderland. Many individual officiants and specific churches restrict the freedom of movement of the photographer and the videographer. Some denominations offer opportunities for personalized vows and readings while others have a standard script that cannot be altered. Moreover, the ceremony is performed before an audience restricted to their seats. For those who insist upon regarding the ceremony as a consumer option, there is the destination wedding, say, in Las Vegas or at Walt Disney World. Thus, the mother of a bride whose daughter was married by a minister at Disney World touted the ceremony precisely because "Disney is very, very accommodating. They'll do just about anything you want."[11]

Most couples and their parents prefer some version of a standard script, some recognizable words and gestures to suggest the couple is calling upon tradition and religion to bless their union. Vows, pledges, blessings, the joining of hands, archaic language, and a kiss express a cherished hope for monogamy, fidelity, and everlasting love. In the Catholic and Protestant wedding, the officiant either walks down the aisle to the front or enters the front from a side door. The rabbi and cantor lead the walk down the aisle in the Jewish ceremony. A hush falls over the audience just before the show is about to begin. The audience sit in their chairs or in flower-bedecked pews. The ceremony usually starts soon after ushers show the mothers and grandmothers to their seats. These women are admired, either as matriarchs in corsages or as women who have managed to preserve their beauty and their figures, including a few who want to garner appreciation for their shape and their dresses. Once everyone is seated, the groom and his attendants wait at the altar in anticipation. Slowly, and often using a special theatrical processional gait, timed to music, the bride's attendants proceed down the aisle, one by one.[12]

One index of luxury at the wedding is the number of aides to the bride and groom; thus, the larger the number of attendants, the fancier the event. There have always been extremely large bridal parties among the social elite. But it is the style of the average couple's marrying that has become grander. The growth in the average number of attendants at a wedding affords proof of the increasing scale and theatricality of the ceremony. According to wedding announcements published in metropolitan U.S. newspapers in the 1950s, which tended to describe weddings of the Social Register set, the typical number of bridesmaids was about three. The average had crept up to four by the 1980s; by the 1990s, bridal magazine readers planned to have five bridesmaids and a wedding party of ten.[13] With a corresponding rise in the number of ushers, and required gifts for all attendants, the number of key participants, as well as the spending by and for them, has also escalated.

The lavish wedding is based on expressing exaggerated forms of masculinity and femininity, along with religious views of marriage as a monogamous and lifelong institution that encourages men and women to bear children. Roles pertaining to gender and sexuality are expressed through the presence of child attendants who symbolize fertility, as well as through the bride's white gown, veil, and shoes, which once symbolized sexual purity. There is no necessary reason why a theatrical and lavish event must fall back on highly traditional gender roles. However, the opulent wedding evolved out of multiple wedding traditions based on the idea of the wedding as a property exchange between the father of the bride and the groom. In addition, many of the theatrical gestures of the wedding are also rooted in the ideal of chivalry—of exaggerated gestures and manners between the knight and his lady.

Moreover, some of the gestures and statements in the ceremony have their origins in religious liturgies intended to restate views of marriage for the purposes of fidelity and procreation and portray the wife as an obedient servant of her husband. There is also the highly differentiated way the groom and bride appear at the ceremony. The groom enters before the bride, but without attendants or musical accompaniment. The bride waits and walks up the aisle with her father. At both typical weddings in the 1950s and those held today, it is usually the bride's father who escorts her down the aisle. In sociologist Erving Goffman's phrase, the bride participates in a "ritual of subordination" by putting her hand on her father's arm, "in effect marking the boundary of his social property."[14] Goffman noted that such rituals are particularly pronounced at the beginnings and endings of ceremonies. There is more ritual of subordination at the front of the sanctuary as well, because typically the bride's father or maid of honor lifts her veil. For that reason, the father's gestures—as well as his affirmation that it is he who gives his daughter away to be married—are often highly criticized by feminists.[15] Today there are some Protestant and Catholic brides escorted by both parents. Catholic liturgy has favored that variation since 1965, but few Catholics seem to have paid notice to these reforms. Once again, most contemporary brides redefine paternal escort as "tradition" rather than a ritual of subordination. In 2001, a Web site reported that 82 percent of prospective brides expected to be escorted down the aisle by a father, stepfather, uncle, or brother. Only 12 percent planned to walk down the aisle alone or with their mothers.[16]

Although we have argued that the contemporary wedding is a form of entertainment with two major stars, the bride clearly has top billing. While both the bride and groom may want to feel "special," the bride is much more than a first among equals. At the same time, many couples have chosen to eliminate some overt sexism in the event, although subtle layers of it remain. The readings and garter tosses express retrograde views of gender roles at the same time that personalized vows and new-style cake toppers represent the idea that the couple seeks to convey their individuality, shared interests, or postmodern sensibility rather than their shared roles. Even the guests revert to gender stereotypes: it is mainly women who cry at weddings. Instead of thinking of the luxurious wedding as merely an expression of patriarchy, it is preferable to recognize the highly contradictory messages of the contemporary wedding day—an odd mix of patriarchy and gender conformity with egalitarianism and individuality.

The exchange of rings makes the service lavish, dramatic, and egalitarian, for example. The exchange between the bride and groom of jewelry that is intended to be permanent and worn continuously is a visual statement of commitment, marital identity, and/or sexual exclusivity. Originally only a wife had a wedding ring. She was publicly bound by her marital status in a way her husband was not. But in the exchange of rings a ritual of subordination has become symmetrical. The best man now hands the ring for the bride to the groom. A blessing of the ring is optional.[17] The groom slips the ring on the fourth finger of the left hand of the bride. Among the Greeks it was believed that there is an artery connecting the fourth finger of the left hand directly to the heart. The idea of a double ring ceremony was common in many parts of Europe. The fact that two rings cost more than one emboldened jewelers in the United States in the 1920s, who marketed the idea but without much success. A ring for the groom seems to have caught on during World War II, when soldiers wanted to place a ring in their duffle bags as a memento of their marriage. Since that time, the double ring ceremony has become the standard form of ring exchange.[18]

There is an additional example among Christians of "an invented tradition," a new symmetrical ritual that has become very popular and is now regarded as traditional. In the 1980s, Catholic and fundamentalist Protestant couples adopted the innovation of lighting a Unity Candle. Exactly how and why lighting this candle has become so popular is hard to explain, but we suspect that candle manufacturers were supportive of the idea. The lighted white candle has a double meaning. Lit candles were often part of Catholic and Eastern Orthodox religious devotions. Moreover, such items are *de rigueur* at an elegant romantic dinner, since lit white candles are a symbol of romance. Because it is a new ritual, however, lighting the Unity Candle has no standard location in the order of the ceremony. It often occurs after the exchange of vows and rings. The bride and groom each light a candle, and together they light a single Unity Candle. In some ceremonies, after the couple blows out the flames on their individual candles, they are pronounced husband and wife.

There are many theatrical set pieces within the wedding ceremony itself, and the new tradition of lighting of the Unity Candle suggests there is time in a relatively short ceremony to add some new ones. But the single most romantic moment of the wedding occurs after the couple has been declared legally married. The officiant then grants the groom permission to kiss the bride, symbolic of religious permission to engage in sexual intercourse. (The kiss was originally understood as a gesture to seal a bargain.) The nuptial kiss can be short, sweeping, embarrassed, or something in between. Guests sometimes clap or whistle. The photographer tries to be in exactly the right place to capture the moment on film, but it can go by quickly. The kiss is male-initiated romance, much like the traditional date and the marriage proposal. The recessional reprises the walk to the altar and provides the kind of symmetrical repetition that makes the ritual complete and satisfying.

The experience of the wedding itself has increasingly receded in importance compared to the recording of the event. This is not simply because photography and videography preserve memories, but because they make the couple feel like celebrities. Perhaps a bride and groom have always remembered their wedding day, but for a long time they had to do so without visual representation. Photography helps to capture and preserve the magic and transform the event into a visible artifact to prompt memory. The photographs saved, displayed, and shown to others are supposed to provide a record of perfection, a "portable utopia."[19] As with every other aspect of the luxurious wedding, the memory bank has received an ever-increasing number of deposits as the average size of the wedding album has grown. The ritual of taking bridal photos has also changed considerably. The first daguerreotype of a bride dates to the 1850s and was taken at a studio. Even so, pre-wedding photos were uncommon, perhaps because it was considered unlucky to photograph the bride before her wedding. However, the middle class soon began to see the daguerreotype as a less expensive version of the artist's oil portrait.

Nineteenth- and early-twentieth-century photographers did lug their equipment to the homes of the wealthy, but most people could only afford to pay for a portrait in their finery at the studio. In some cases, they went there as much as a year after the wedding. Bridal photography became part of the wedding day in the 1920s because customers wanted their photographs to represent how they actually looked on the big day. Nonetheless, for the majority of couples, photography remained studio based. In 1939, a New Haven, Connecticut, couple got into a car and rushed from the ceremony to the photographer's studio. The photographer snapped a minimal number of standard shots to reduce costs. These were photos of the bride, the couple, members of the wedding party, and, if requested, of the parents of the bride and groom.[20]

By the 1930s, the society crowd was inviting photographers with big-view cameras and electric floodlights into the sanctuary. Two decades later, about eight or ten photographers would show up at a church with their roll-film cameras and flashbulbs to compete for the couple's business.[21] Photographers began to go on location to both the wedding and the reception in the 1960s. At that time, strobe lighting replaced flashbulbs, making it less cumbersome to take many shots. Likewise, color photos replaced black-and-white, adding warmth and emotion to the photographs.

Just as artists developed certain standard techniques, so, too, bridal photographers developed any number of visual clichés in the postwar era. In keeping with the belief that it was the bride's, not the groom's, special day, the first shots showed the bride looking in the mirror and preparing herself for the ceremony. Even in Disney's movie *Snow White,* the mirror was an artifact of magic, even of divination. The "mirror shot" reveals a part of the room in the mirror hidden from view, imitating the classic Van Eyck bridal portrait from the 1400s. It became a standard photograph in the late 1940s when the business of wedding photography took off. The bride was actually already prepared for the ceremony by the time the photographer took the photograph. According to a guide for wedding photographers, the shot is supposed to be "dreamy or contemplative, and should tell the story of her [the bride] preparing for her new life."[22]

Because wedding photography is central to the day, it is understood that photographers must be given a great deal of power to adjust or bring to a halt the schedule of events for picture taking. One way is by interrupting the reception so as to pose the couple, the bridesmaids, the groom's family, the bride's family, and so forth. In "altar returns," a sec-

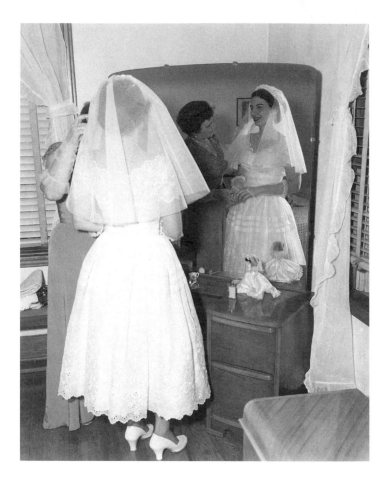

Figure 10.   Bride in mirror, 1956. Courtesy Florida State Archives.

ond option, the couple, their attendants, and the wedding official reenact the ceremony for the photographer.[23] The photos taken in this manner are simulations of the ceremony rather than the actual event. Or the
couple has photographs taken at the religious site two or three hours
before the ceremony commences. This last method poses the difficulty of
challenging the superstition that it is bad luck for the groom to see his
bride before the wedding.

    In posing photographs (as well as in making seating arrangements and
deciding who stands where in the reception line), the impact of divorce
on the wedding is most keenly felt, because physical proximity is taken as

a sign of emotional connection. Therefore, the best way to indicate emotional distance is to sit separately or pose in separate family portraits. Will there be a photograph of the bride with both her mother and her father if they are divorced? Will ex-spouses even allow themselves to be in the same picture?[24] The wedding photographer acts as a diplomat, negotiating in advance who should stand or sit next to whom.

While divorce forces certain practical accommodations in posing shots for the average working photographer, the actual style of photography is set by royalty and celebrities. Just as Paris or Hollywood designers establish the desired style in bridal dress, so, too, bridal photographers for the Kennedys and other celebrities have set trends in this field. The fashionable style swung back and forth from a documentary photojournalistic style to the highly posed, very romantic statements so popular from the 1960s to the 1980s created with soft-focus and starburst filters. Photographs of Grace Kelly in the palace at Monaco on her wedding day created a demand for a portrait of the "pensive bride," deeply immersed in her own thoughts, who also represented the ideal woman, too demure to look directly at the camera.[25]

In the romantic, post-Diana mode of the 1980s, shots of the couple superimposed over the church, like angels looking down at the altar, were common. Photographers in the 1980s also took standard shots of groups of relatives, but the taking of these couple-as-angels photos reflected a far greater emphasis on the purity and sacredness of the couple's romantic love. Then there were eighties photographers, trying to stimulate spontaneity and joy, who encouraged the wedding party to jump in the air, as in the famous Toyota ad campaign of the same time.

In the 1990s, the photojournalistic style of Denis Reggie, famous for photographing the wedding of John F. Kennedy Jr. and Carolyn Bessette in 1996, cost a great deal more, because Reggie took only a few posed shots and snapped as many as 1,600 unposed pictures. Many of these photos were taken at fairly close range while the event was unfolding in order to capture a magic moment; for example, he trained his lens on a grandmother's face when she saw the bride and groom cutting the cake. Even though Reggie's technique was different from that of his peers, he was able to supply as many shots of relatives and friends as photographers who posed their subjects. Reggie's shot of JFK Jr. bending down a bit to kiss his bride's hand as they left the church also confirmed the pub-

Figure 11.   Bridal photography style, 1983. Courtesy Charles Lewis, Mankato, Minn.

lic's view that the dead president's only son was a Prince Charming who upheld the ideals of chivalry.

Videotaping made the bride and groom into stars in their own television documentary. Videotaping weddings began in the late 1970s but was technically difficult at that time (the camera still came with an electric cord rather than a battery pack, and the images were of poor quality). Clergy had the same initial distaste for videographers as they had for photographers, ordering them to remain in the rear of the church or synagogue. Moreover, there were guests who resented the disruption of being interviewed when they wanted to enjoy their meal or talk with relatives at the table. Couples had been experimenting with Super-8 sound cameras in the 1970s, but the attractiveness of video over these other methods was the ease in viewing it. With the rapid spread of the VCR, this new service became a booming business. By the middle of the 1990s, the majority of weddings were being videotaped.

This interest in photojournalistic shots also trickled down to the middle class, but of course, most could not hire a Denis Reggie. The trade association of wedding photographers, Wedding and Portrait Photographers International, reported a fivefold increase in photojournalistic black-and-white shots between 1995 and 2000. A favorite was a shot of the usher's shiny black-and-white shoes against the pavement or of the bride's arm holding a bouquet of flowers, without her face or body visible.[26] Involving the guests reached new heights when they were encouraged to take photographs as a form of memorabilia and self-entertainment in addition to, not instead of, professional picture taking. Guests had always been allowed to be amateur photographers, but traditionally they had brought their own cameras. As both a souvenir and a means of entertaining guests, the disposable camera began to appear on tables at the reception. In 1994, Kodak introduced a flash wedding edition of its Fun Saver camera and successfully capitalized on the idea that couples should offer guests disposable cameras to use at the reception.[27]

Videographers turn off their cameras so as not to record embarrassing moments, edit the tape to include reaction shots, add sound to action, and record the event as it occurs.[28] Videography no more duplicates photography than a dessert table duplicates the wedding cake. It increases the magic by enhancing the illusion that ordinary couples are celebrities for a day. It does so not simply by following ordinary people around before, during, and after the festivities, but through the playback process at a later time, giving the sense of watching history live and seeing what appears similar to a televised event, like the royal wedding, on a television monitor.[29] Neither the video nor the photograph is an accurate reflection of what happens on the wedding day, but instead they are different types of idealized representations of the event. A wedding video usually features sentimental background music, the bride and groom dancing, and shots edited to reveal a couple in a state of heavenly bliss. A videographer explains how memory and celebrity combine: "You can take an ordinary wedding, where nothing really out of the usual happens, combine it with some powerful music, some cool effects and freeze frames, and all of a sudden the wedding looks incredible."[30]

CHAMPAGNE AND CELEBRATION:
THE RECEPTION

The reception, where half of the wedding budget is spent on food, flowers, entertainment, liquor, and rental of a hall, is the key event in the day that symbolizes distinctiveness. It is also the part of the wedding the couple or their parents have devoted the most time to planning. The reception is supposed to occur in the evening, a good time for romantic candlelight and spectacles such as fireworks. People also feel more permitted to drink—and dance—in the evening. Then there is the standardization that renting a facility or hiring professionals imposes. Many of these events last for precisely five hours because the reception hall, photographer, and disc jockey charge by the hour and impose time limits on availability. To thwart these restrictions, some couples have an after-the-reception party for a smaller group of friends.[31]

The 1950s are a convenient starting point for the growth of the celebrity reception simply because they were the beginning of mass participation in the luxury wedding. Then, as now, there were many types of receptions, although most of them seem to fall into four categories: high society, upward-striving, modest, or communal. Who you were in the 1950s determined the elaborateness of the "wedding breakfast," as the reception was then called. There were—and still are—strong class differences as to the location for the reception. Only high-society couples hosted luxurious events; many others were, or had to be, content with the modest or communal variant. The fanciest events took place on the lawn of the family or vacation home, provided the lawn was sufficiently grand and well manicured and there was money in the budget to rent and set up tents and a dance floor.

Perhaps the Kennedys did not become America's royal family until John F. Kennedy was elected in 1960, but the Bouvier-Kennedy wedding in September 1953 had all the markings of a royal wedding. When 24-

year-old Jacqueline Bouvier, wearing a dress of fifty yards of ivory silk taffeta, married the junior senator from Massachusetts, she had ten bridesmaids, fourteen ushers, and six hundred invited guests at the ceremony. Crowds lined the steps of St. Mary's Catholic church in Newport, Rhode Island, to catch a glimpse of the couple, and cameramen filmed the event. The main drama of the day was that "Black Jack" Bouvier got too drunk to walk his daughter down the aisle, and Jackie's stepfather had to step in. At the insistence of the Kennedy family, fourteen hundred guests were invited to the reception on the grounds of Jackie's stepfather's estate, Hammersmith Farm. The bride and groom danced their first dance to the music of Meyer Davis's orchestra.[32]

Then there were the modest, upward-striving, and communal events. In the 1950s, and in earlier decades, too, the reception at home was the modest and common choice for both the middle and working classes. In the upscale version, there was a luncheon—but only for immediate family—either at a restaurant or at the home of the bride's family. Guests might arrive at the family's home for cake and punch, perhaps with sandwiches and ice cream added. The punch was often made from fruit juice mixed with champagne and ladled out by the corsage-wearing mother of the bride. Many families set up the wedding cake on a white tablecloth on the dining room table. The standard of elegance was fairly low not simply because of limited budgets but also because of the generally held belief that one should not display wealth beyond one's means.[33] In the typical house, there was no room for an orchestra or musicians. The parents placed long-playing records on the turntable. Working-class couples often hosted their version of the communal reception (a dinner for guests in the finished basement of the family home), and guests might spill over into the upstairs room. They dined on a home-cooked meal and there was often dancing and drinking.[34]

The communal reception was held in an unglamorous setting, and for the most part, female church or family members were responsible for preparing the food and cleaning up the reception site. In the 1950s, it was equally common to hold receptions in the church basement or, on a sunny day in the summer, on the church lawn. In many cases, however, caterers, rather than the bride's family, made the meal, reflecting the combination of some commercial services with the rather unattractive environment in which the reception was held. Or a local baker or caterer would prepare the meal, and the female church members served it.[35] There was a logic and convenience to this arrangement: the ceremony took place in the church, and immediately afterward guests walked downstairs to the church basement, where aesthetic standards were low. The guests did not look up at the exposed heating pipes or glance down at the linoleum floor. Folding tables were covered with white tablecloths, and the guests sat on metal folding chairs.

Even when there was a rented reception hall in the 1950s, guests were typically welcomed in an undecorated public space without floral displays. In large cities, working-class couples who had the money for a reception not held at home invited their guests to a large public hall. The guest list was long; virtually every friend, relative, and neighbor was invited since the wedding was an inclusive rather than an exclusive event. Food was homemade rather than prepared by caterers. Women loaded a buffet table with provolone, roast beef sandwiches, crackers, homemade cookies, and pitchers of beer. By the 1950s, many parents who had moved up from the working class wanted their daughters' weddings to signal prestige; thus, it was often "their wedding" more than it was their daughters'. The sit-down multicourse dinner, live orchestra, and white-gloved waiters in white jackets were designed to show that the parents of the bride had moved up the social scale.[36] For many Orthodox and Conservative Jews, both the wedding and the reception were held at a hotel or a catering hall because it was still considered a defilement of the sanctuary to marry in the synagogue.

So, too, the way an ethnic group signaled prestige was to ask the caterer to serve the standard American fare: roast beef, potatoes, and green beans with almonds. At some of these fancier hall events of the 1950s, the reception took place in the evening. But the atmosphere was more like a prom, an appropriate image since most brides in the 1950s were so young. As a means of making a grand entrance into the reception hall, there was a Grand March for the bridal party. To the accompaniment of music and applause from the seated guests, the bridal party walked around the entire room and the bride was able to show off her gown and long cathedral train.

The kind of food selected and the way it was served was initially intended to communicate prestige. How the dinner meal was served was a language filled with class, generational, and regional distinctions. In the

1950s, a buffet with hors d'oeuvres and cake was still quite common; so, too, were luncheons at a downtown Regency.[37] Receptions held in the evening in the 1950s or 1960s seemed to require that the groom and his ushers rent tuxedoes. Children of couples who had a reception at the American Legion hall wanted to chose "the perfect wedding menu" along with a catered sit-down dinner or a buffet with serving stations (popular in the 1990s). In the South, the buffet was more common than the sit-down meal. Southern fertility rates had always been higher than those in the North, and as a result, Southern families were larger in size. Southern families regarded the buffet as a way to invite all the relatives but keep costs down, and a more casual lifestyle was reflected in a greater number of outdoor receptions than in the North.[38]

These days, the sit-down dinner at a public reception hall has become the preferred (and often expected) mode of feeding guests, and also often the cause of anxiety among brides who cannot deliver this type of meal.[39] The sit-down dinner is the most expensive and elegant form of reception dining. Moreover, it now often comes served on rented china place settings, with place cards bearing the guests' names in calligraphy. The sandwiches and ice cream of the 1950s, and even the chicken of the 1970s and 1980s, are often replaced by prime cuts of beef, or for the cholesterol-conscious, by even more expensive seafood entrees such as grilled salmon. Sit-down dinners resemble the types of meals served at five-star restaurants or on fancy dates, with wine for each course, a fruit course, salad, entree, and desserts. Yet while the sit-down dinner reinforces the message of opulence, it often cannot be a reflection of the couple's own tastes or their desire for customization because of the logistics of serving so many guests at once from ill-equipped kitchen facilities. One bride, disappointed with the choices offered by caterers, remarked, "The wedding meal's spiritual kin in the culinary world is probably the airline meal."[40] Because flowers are perishable and expensive, flower arrangements at each table serve as symbols both of romance and of luxury.

Such food also deserves a glorious setting. Couples often request linen tablecloths, floral centerpieces, and festive displays of balloons. Some brides veto balloons because they associate them with birthday parties and baby showers, and not as part of the wedding tradition. But balloon manufacturers have tried to change the meaning of the object from a decoration for a children's party to one that more broadly symbolizes joy and celebration, as well as distinctiveness. They have tapped the language of romance by renaming their arrangements: "Ring of Love," "Enchanted Bubble and Fantasy Cloud," and "Magical Dove."[41]

The brands of liquor served at the reception can provide an index to the level of luxury and expense of the event. For example, the prestige of the wedding is tied to the name brand of the champagne served, whether guests are charged for liquor, and the brands of liquor available. Frugality, as we have seen, was a hallmark of the modest reception of the 1950s—but no longer. Wedding feasts are now associated not just with waiters pouring champagne but with serving liquor at a cocktail hour and then during the reception as well. At an open bar, a guest can request any kind of drink, served free of charge. At a cash bar, a guest must pay for liquor and sometimes even for soft drinks. Thus, the kind of bar influences not only the cost of the event but its prestige as well. Once guests have begun to drink, prestige takes a backseat to play, rowdiness, and sexual innuendo. Drunken men get up to sing, guests look a bit disheveled, and libidos overflow into ribald gestures. One wedding photographer cringed when "the father, after a few too many toasts, forgot the name of one his kids and his wife hit the roof."[42] However, the free flow of liquor at weddings varies from one social group to another, with new norms arising about excessive drinking. Of course, some social groups like the Mormons have always had a tradition of nonalcoholic receptions because of their religious beliefs.

The gestures of subordination embedded in the wedding ceremony reappear in certain fixed segments of the reception, such as the toast. The toast is a speech, usually given by a male with a glass of liquor in his hand. Public speaking, especially of the ribald and potentially hostile kind, is still a male preserve. Senior-ranking males at the event, such as the best man or male relatives, still largely, if not invariably, make the toasts.[43] Men speak and interject humor, whereas women listen and laugh at the appropriate moments. These norms of public speaking have proven more impervious to feminism than public statements in the religious service, perhaps because changing these norms would require mothers and bridesmaids to be unusually assertive in a situation where they are supposed to be largely decorative and admired for their dignity or beauty. A woman who gives a toast is thought of as aggressive, even unfeminine.[44] During the meal, the toast maker either stands or gives another signal (e.g., clinking his knife against his glass) to get the attention of the guests and begins his toast to commemorate the couple. Toasts can range from the heartfelt to the very short to the slightly ribald to those that blatantly make some kind of social gaffe. The best man often expresses fear that he is losing his buddy the groom, but also affirms that the bride is someone who will welcome him into the couple's life. Many toasts celebrate the ethnic heritage of the bride and/or groom, such as "Mazel Tov!" or the famous Irish blessing that begins "May the road rise up to meet you." Others are intended to signal intercultural acceptance by demonstrating knowledge from the heritage of both the bride and the groom.

Cutting the cake appears to be a ritual similar to the ring exchange: it was once a gesture of subordination and is now more often one of symmetry. It always takes place after the meal, and although a standard ritual practice, only a few guests who are eating and talking near the cake table usually witness it. Through the 1930s, the bride usually cut the first slice, and at fancier receptions, a caterer cut the rest. Since she was soon to become a housewife, it made sense for the bride to take on these serving activities as preparation for a lifetime role. By the 1940s, bridal photographers began to prefer a more interesting shot of the bride and groom cutting the cake together. One cake expert claims the tradition originated because the icing on early wedding cakes had to be extremely stiff to support all of the layers, so the groom needed to apply brute force in order to work the knife through the icing.[45] Sometimes the groom steadied the bride's hand by putting his underneath (a 1950s style, demonstrating the male provider role). At other times, she provided the foundation. After looking at dozens of such photos from the 1950s, we could find only one photograph of a groom feeding his bride a piece of cake, and none of mutual feeding. With the dominant ethic these days one of egalitarian sharing, each partner is supposed to offer the other sweet sustenance.

The 1950s married couple symbolized marital stability; indeed, the stability of the nation in its fight against Communism depended on the two of them standing together. At the top of the cake in the 1950s stood a little plastic likeness of the couple called a cake topper. It consisted of a replica of a groom in a tuxedo and a bride in a long, white dress. Many brides still choose cake toppers, but now often prefer ones that represent the hobbies of the couple (a surfer bride and groom, a bride and groom with fishing reels) or their favorites from popular culture (the Simpsons) rather than ones representing formality and conjugality. Accompanying this personalization of the couple's joint identity is a tendency toward featuring likenesses of the couple on the cake toppers, or toppers of guardian angels or of floral arches. To many, however, the couple cake topper symbolizes 1950s "togetherness" that is no longer fashionable, as in this inquiry on a bridal Web site. "Ikbwitched: Do I have to have dorky bride and groom dolls on top of my cake? Modern Bride Expert: No, you can have dogs, cats, parrots, but you don't need the typical bride and groom."[46]

The wedding cake is a sugary sculpture and is often regarded as an object of beauty now intended to impress and awe the guests more than it is a symbol of romantic love. When Elvis Presley got married in Las Vegas in 1967, he had a six-tiered wedding cake. There will always be some brides and grooms who associate height with status and power. But that equation seems largely to have been replaced by a new ideal of the cake as frosted fantasy. In the upscale version, it is an expression of something unique about the couple or their personalities. The luxury is in the novelty of reinventing a standard item, rather than its height. Cakes can take different shapes: there can be an octagonal bottom, with rounded layers on top; some prefer Cinderella's castle. Cakes can be almond, hazelnut, yellow, chocolate, carrot, or even cheesecake flavor; likewise, fillings can range from chocolate mousse to lemon cream. There are more colors, more choices as to fillings, more variety and amount of floral decoration, and more sauce on the side. Cakes can be an expression of luxury or of popular culture–centered kitsch. One cake at a recent reception cost $5,000 (five times more than the bride's gown) and was laden with 14-carat-gold decorations.[47] Other couples, however, choose "cakes" made of tiers of Krispy Kreme doughnuts. Originally just stacks of doughnuts created by the bride and groom, the manufacturer of this brand, which has achieved almost a cult following, now offers templates for local decorators to follow when creating these "cakes."[48]

Of course, since the cake is now a requirement for almost all weddings, the most fashionable not only find ways to make theirs more unique, but also enhance the overall lavishness of the event with other sweets at the end of the meal. The trend is to supplement with a dessert table—gourmet cookies, petits fours, mousse, flaming desserts like Cherries Jubilee, liqueurs, and coffee—all to make important distinctions in taste and add to the level of magic at the reception.[49] In addition, gifts for the guests such as personalized mugs, small picture frames, wedding chocolates, mints, or ethnic signifiers such as sugared almonds are offered as souvenirs of the occasion, ensuring that the event will live on in the guests' minds long after the last dove, balloon, or butterfly has been released.

There may have been elements of rowdiness in weddings for centuries, but usually it was guests who had poked fun at, tricked, or made lewd gestures toward the bride or groom. Beginning in the 1980s, couples started to think of themselves as entertainers who engaged in hijinks toward each other. The bride and groom were no longer merely stars in a television documentary but slapstick comedians, "kooky protagonists starring in a nuptial farce."[50] Elements of slapstick comedy incorporated a new ideal of "adorable nuttiness" into the wedding ritual.[51] The bride and groom began to smash a piece of the cake in each other's faces, rather than mutually feeding each other, with guests often egging them on. One wedding photographer was peeved at the drunken sorority sisters at one wedding when they began to chant, "In his face. In his face."[52] Miss Manners complains that smashing the cake at the wedding is related to a growing show-business trend evident in the bride's "stage makeup," applause for the couple as they enter the reception, and comedy routines from guests offering the toasts.[53] She also suggests that couples want to inject more informality into a ritual that prescribes so many routines.

Another sign of the growing expectation of lavishness and distinction through entertainment is the increasing inclusion of dancing at the reception. Before the 1980s, dancing was optional. The communal reception often had a band—polka or klezmer or banjo and string. In the modest home celebrations, those couples who wanted some music at the reception sometimes resorted to the phonograph or a tape player, which had fairly poor sound quality. Usually a guest would be responsible for changing the records or tapes. A live band or orchestra was always an expensive alternative. By the 1980s, a reception was supposed to feature paid entertainment in the form of a live band or disc jockey. The DJ played recorded music, with a large variety of selections chosen with the couple's wishes and their desire to blend the musical tastes of different generations of guests in mind. The DJ began to take on the role of the

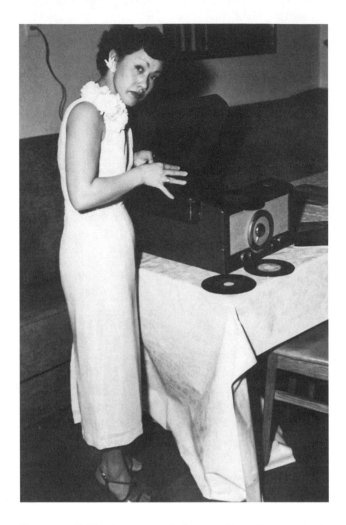

Figure 12.   Bride's sister at record player, 1956 (wedding reception).
Courtesy Shades of L.A. Archives/Los Angeles Public Library.

announcer, providing a schedule for the ritualized moments of the reception, such as the formal presentation of the couple to the guests, the first dance, and the bouquet and garter tosses.

The musical entertainment was intended to create a mood of romance. The bride and groom made sure the guests understood that the first song to be played at the reception was personal and unique; it was "their" song. In each decade, this first song has usually been a contemporary one, from "Because," popular in the 1950s, to the always popular "The Way You Look Tonight" to Elvis's rendition of "Can't Help Falling in Love," which represented 1990s nostalgia for the fifties.[54] The music at the reception, however, makes clear the event is not simply a celebration of the romance of the couple, because the reception must also be a theatrical hit. Therefore, while the first dance is a celebration of the couple, the group dance is a way for guests from both sides of the family to enjoy themselves. Changes in popular dance reflected the dissemination of Brazilian, then African American, then Hispanic culture on popular taste: from the Chicken Dance (1960) to the conga line (1970) to the Electric Slide (1980) to the Macarena (1990).[55] Eastern European socialists who moved to what was then Palestine established the first kibbutzim between 1905 and 1914 and introduced folk dancing, including the circle dance, the hora. After the founding of the state of Israel in 1948, it became very common at Jewish receptions for guests to dance the hora to the music of "Hava Nagila" and to rediscover the ritual of the guests joining hands, encircling the bride and groom, and lifting them up on chairs.[56]

There are two final acts to the script of the standard wedding reception: the bouquet toss and the garter removal. The bouquet toss is a statement about the importance of being married for women; the garter toss is a symbolic feigning of the sexual act. The bouquet toss is a woman-to-woman ritual that symbolizes the importance of a single woman finding a mate. The woman who catches the bouquet is supposed to be the next to marry. The toss makes many single women these days feel uncomfortable because it so clearly suggests that singlehood for women is a second-class status. In the 1950s, when the rate of singlehood was so low, the bride was seen to be passing along a magical talisman to a valued friend or relative. But by the 1990s, the toss was fraught with tension. The film *Picture Perfect* (1997), starring Jennifer Aniston, acts as both a paean to romantic love and a scathing commentary on the bouquet toss. Aniston plays a single Madison Avenue copywriter in her early thirties, in love with both her career and her philandering supervisor. She attends her best friend's wedding and participates reluctantly in providing a videotaped greeting to the bride and groom. But she cringes when she is the only youngish and eligible unmarried woman available for the bouquet toss. In reluctantly accepting the bouquet, she says, "Oh, give me the f——g thing."[57]

The toss has been made more dramatic as it has become more difficult to execute. Photographs from the 1950s show the bride making a simple forward pass to a group of single women standing in their places. The group of women is usually small, never more than five; the bride faces the women. By the 1960s, brides were turning their backs and tossing their bouquets over their shoulders. The purported rationale for the backward turn is so the bride cannot show favoritism in awarding the bouquet. More likely, a bridal photographer found the backward toss a more interesting picture.[58] This action forced the single women to become more active participants in catching the flowers. Florists in the 1990s recognized that most brides, like their wealthy Victorian counterparts, wanted to keep their expensive bouquet rather than give it away. Thus, they made up a complimentary "toss bouquet" to throw, smaller and lighter than the one the bride carries.[59]

Traditional, egalitarian, individualist, romantic, nutty—after assuming so many varied poses in a single day, the groom's toss of the bride's garter is finally the sexiest act of entertainment performed by the couple, occurring almost at the end of the reception. It is another tradition that did not exist at fancy weddings in the 1920s or 1930s and whose origins are less ancient than most commentators claim.[60] If garters were worn at all during medieval times, they were silk sashes tied below the bride's knee. The male guests would pull on the sash until it came off. There were also older traditions of removing the bride's (and groom's) stockings when the couple was put to bed.

There were tosses in the 1950s and 1960s, but the modest bride in those decades removed the garter herself inconspicuously and handed it to the groom, who threw it to his ushers.[61] The garter removal has become a much sexier bit of drama in the wedding. During the sexual revolution of the 1960s, grooms began to act on their own initiative, perhaps encouraged by photographers. The bride sat in a chair, smiled with embarrassment, and let the groom feel up her leg to about mid-thigh, which is the sexier, post-1960s way of wearing the garter. The groom removed the garter with his hand, stood up, and tossed the garter to a male guest, perhaps one of the ushers. Sometimes the man who caught the garter then placed it on the leg of the single woman who caught the bouquet, thus providing symmetry and closure to what were, after all, rituals of subordination and adding another element, like the bouquet toss, that was supposed to result in the marriage of a single woman.

Photographers of the reception often showed the groomsmen appraising the beauty of the bride's legs as the groom removed the garter.[62] Some grooms approximated the more masculine pose of an archer, putting the garter around one finger and drawing an arrow before propelling it outward with a snap of the finger. *Betsy's Wedding* (1990) was the first movie to show the groom removing the garter with his teeth to the accompaniment of "The Stripper." This action, occurring in real weddings as well as in a film, probably arose not only because sex was more visible in the media but because oral sex had become a common part of couples' sexual repertoires. The objectification of the bride's body, as she looked on and smiled, seemed to fit with the rebellion against the prudery of the fifties wedding and the rejection of the feminism of the sixties and seventies. Moreover, if she had spent months making her body fit, the bride was eager to show her perfect thighs. The new ritual offered a way to incorporate ribald gesture into wedding ritual at a point in the wedding at which many of the guests had had several drinks. Throwing the garter, sexually explicit dancing, the smashing of the glass at the Jewish wedding, enforced kissing, and the joint cutting of the cake are as close as the contemporary wedding comes to symbolic mimicry of the sexual act.

Spectacle requires a very singular finale. At expensive weddings it is no longer enough for the couple to simply walk out of the reception hall in a hurry of birdseed or bubbles, although a cheering audience has always been a part of the departure. The truly lavish exit has to be dramatic and magical. The bride and groom, sometimes wearing new and stylish outfits, now ride off in a vintage automobile as fireworks are shot off into the air, trot off on horseback, climb into a golf cart, board a double-decker bus, or even fly off in a plane to experience the next magical phase: the honeymoon.

With such a sumptuous banquet of choices, as well as the high expectations of the couple, family, and guests, today's bride is not content with the modest reception in the family living room so common in the 1950s. Genteel respectability, which after all was only one of several competing styles, has lost its sway. So, too, the communal reception—the prom, the picnic, the church supper—all seem as dated as a rerun of *The Lawrence Welk Show.* For many a couple, the idea of a reception without dancing or alcohol is incomprehensible. All aspects of the day are supposed to be aesthetically pleasing and provide magic. Luxury and distinctiveness have been democratized and personalized as celebrity culture permeates more of the choices and styles for many features of the wedding and the reception. Champagne and fresh flowers, once found only at the fanciest of weddings, are now standard for people from humble backgrounds and limited parental incomes. One Bethlehem, Pennsylvania, bride, married in July 2000, defined her goals this way: "I wanted the whole day to have a sophisticated, elegant feel."[63]

Celebrity culture reaches down and affects virtually every wedding, even those where the bride does not explicitly buy a dress like Jennifer Aniston's or Catherine Zeta-Jones's. The editor of *Bride's* writes, "The bride and her bridegroom are stars at their own show . . . with the footage, if not the ratings, to prove it."[64] A photographer follows the couple's every move so they can remember the beautiful romantic moments they shared. Prestige is a signal, whereas distinctive and romantic consumption is a fantasy of utopia. The fantasy of the wedding day is what couples (and in most cases, especially the bride) hope they can purchase from the caterer, the florist, the jeweler, and so forth. Perhaps we should think of the couple, and especially the brides, as producers of their own movies. They arrange the financing, select the location for filming, and cast themselves in the two major roles. More and more, they hire directors to make sure the action goes smoothly and the film will be entertaining and stylish. Wedding professionals, from florists to photographers, help to create the fantasy, some by supplying the flowers and the cake, others by directing the events of the day. But the professionals whom the couples hire tend to impose a script and a schedule on the proceedings. The photographer hands the bride and groom a checklist of shots that serves as a routine for the wedding day. As one 1997 Minnesota bride observed, "Those checklists aren't just proof that all weddings are alike; they *make* all weddings alike."[65] There is thus a huge discrepancy between the reality of standardization and the ideology of the wedding industry that each wedding is unique and different.

The creation of magic requires a form of standardization not all that different from the registry or an assembly line. A somewhat disillusioned wedding photographer writes, "Wedding-party members may be stars in their own movie, but it is the photographer and ultimately the wedding industry that largely determines much of the mood and impact. The production process and its resulting images are largely formulaic, and it follows that the understandings they promote are also quite formulaic."[66] Where the photographer emphasizes the formulaic side, we give equal weight to the meanings of romance, perfection, magic, and memory that emerge. That romantic consumption generates a standardized experience, as well as the exhausted and happy feeling of having had one's special day, is at the heart of the contradictory nature of the contemporary wedding.

Chapter 6 | FROM THE CABIN TO CANCÚN

As the 98 percent of newlyweds who take a honeymoon know,[1] the wedding festivities may be over, but after months of planning and hours of meeting, greeting, and standing, another ritual lasting approximately eight to nine days usually begins immediately thereafter. It was not always so. As the wedding and reception lost their moorings as home-based rituals expressing ties to family or kin, the same became true of postwedding trips. Instead, the first trip of a married couple has become a perfect chance to collect lifelong memories and pay homage to the ideals of romance on magic Maui, at the Magic Kingdom, or on Disney's *Magic* cruise ship. In the space of fifty years, the honeymoon has quite literally moved out of the woods and into the world of airline travel and packaged tours.

The word "honeymoon" first appeared in English in the 1500s. It referred to a period lasting approximately one month after the wedding, to be filled with honeyed affection. After this period, the emotional climate of the couple supposedly underwent a change, just as the full moon appears briefly and then begins to wane. Thus the word "honeymoon," a sardonic and cynical term, made no reference to travel or a holiday.[2] Indeed, the assumption was that the couple would simply remain in one place and perhaps drink honeyed nectar for a month to ease their inhibitions prior to having sex.

The nuptial journey, or "bridal tour," as the honeymoon combined with travel came to be called, developed in the first half of the nineteenth century. The honeymoon was a ritual that corresponded with the Victorian wedding, since both were English and elite in origin. It consisted of rail or coach travel to a secluded destination and became the proper way to begin a marriage after the ceremony and the wedding feast. Such journeys began in the 1830s at about the same time upper-class urbanites were undertaking tours to view scenic vistas in the countryside. Initially, relatives often accompanied the couple on their travels as they stayed with family members whom the bride or groom had not met before. Just as the wedding had enveloped the couple in their network of kin, so, too, the bridal tour was designed to include additional relatives in the couple's social circle. By the middle of the nineteenth century, however, relatives accompanied the couple only part of the way or bid them good-bye at the train station. The couple's interest in privacy, the shift in the meaning of the wedding to a romantic rather than a kinship-forming event, and the bride's desire to escape "vulgar comments" of friends and relatives about her sexual relationship with her husband all seem to have contributed to the idea of the honeymoon as a trip exclusively for the couple.[3]

The honeymoon the Victorians created served several purposes. First, it reaffirmed the emphasis society placed on the ideal of privacy for a newly married couple. They were deserving of a brief but special time when they would tell each other their innermost secrets and deepen the candor and rapport already developed during courtship. The journey to a secluded spot was a ritual with a distinct beginning and end. Supposedly, the pair departed from their separate residences before the wedding ceremony and then returned to their new home, where the groom carried the bride over the threshold. Then the groom was expected to initiate his bride sexually on the wedding night, and with increasing assurance during subsequent days and nights. The couple, it was widely thought, needed to become familiar with each other as sexual, economic, and spiritual partners. The wedding night, where the virgin bride prepared herself to be deflowered by her groom, was a ritual within a ritual. She was supposed to take down and brush her hair and don a beautiful white nightgown, an especially valued part of her trousseau, as she made herself ready for the groom. Reticence with respect to the activities of the wedding night prevailed in the second half of the nineteenth century, except for the hushed and unhappy testimonies shared by bitter wives to free lovers and women anarchists. They told of "spoiled honeymoons" and husbands who locked the bedroom door and forced intercourse against the bride's will. As brides became more sexually experienced, or could at least claim rights to sexual pleasure, accounts of such terrible first nights became less frequent.[4]

A third but more latent goal of the honeymoon was to initiate the husband and wife into their proper sexual and gender roles. As they assumed the identity of husband and wife, men and women needed to become familiar with the duties and obligations that went along with those identities. With the advent of popular interest in Freudianism and behavioral psychology in the 1920s, people were thought to have sexual identities either normal or deviant. It was also around this time that heterosexuality acquired the meaning of being psychologically normal. The couple, but especially the bride, who was a virgin, was proving their sexual normality at the same time they were beginning to adjust to their future roles.[5] Moreover, in the twentieth century, the groom was no longer portrayed as an insensitive brute. Patient but masterful, the gentle groom was supposed to instruct the bride "not only how to behave in coitus, but, above all, how and what to feel in this unique act."[6]

There were also gender roles to be affirmed on the honeymoon. Before the wedding, most men and women understood what was expected of them as husbands and wives, but the honeymoon included rituals to point the couple in the proper direction. Signing the register as "Mr. and Mrs." was thus not just a ritual of the honeymoon, but a statement of altered consciousness. Marital advice literature in the 1950s made such assumptions explicit. A wife had to recognize that "his job will likely come first, if it is a choice between his and hers. And she has become a part of his family in name. At first the very sound of 'Mrs. Anthony' seems quite unreal. It will take some time to get used to it, but it is the goal for which life up to now has been prologue."[7] Meanwhile, marital advisers described the wife as swelling with pride in introducing her husband because she had acquired a protector and provider. These authors decreed that joint activity fostered adjustment to proper gender roles. It did not matter if the honeymooners played doubles tennis or bingo so long as "the adjustment process . . . took place in the context of the activity."[8]

One obligation that was distinctly within the husband's domain was that he was to pay for the honeymoon and select the locale, since he was supposed to be the provider and make such decisions for his family. But although the groom was still paying for the trip, by the 1950s, choosing the honeymoon destination had become the woman's domain. In cases where she did not make the choice herself, she usually had veto power over the groom's selection. Just as the wedding has come to be thought of as the bride's special day, so, too, the honeymoon had increasingly becoming the special vacation to fulfill the bride's dreams.[9] Like Kay in the 1950 version of *Father of the Bride*, young women began to veto their fiancés' preferences for a fishing cabin in Nova Scotia. In the remake of the film in 1991, there was no discussion or conflict at all, and the couple chose Hawaii. The degree to which this pattern has changed is probably roughly similar to the increasing involvement of grooms in wedding planning. These days, many couples probably engage in mutual decision making, although it seems likely that many still define the honeymoon as the bride's special vacation. Although wedding advice books still cite the rule that the groom is expected to pay for the honeymoon,[10] virtually all inquiries to chat rooms about good destinations come from prospective brides. Moreover, most hotels and resorts recognize the bride as the special guest who is choosing among destinations.

A final goal of the honeymoon was to express the language of romance through spending on souvenirs, tickets, and meals. Like the wedding itself, a honeymoon was also purchased, and as such it incorporated elements of consumption such as novelty (a place never before visited), luxury, and choice of destinations, accommodations, and activities. All of these choices provided consumers with the opportunity to signal the prestige of their honeymoon. The honeymoon was also the kind of consumption we have been examining in this book, affording perfect memories "to last a lifetime," as well as romance. It, too, offered perfection: the perfect place, perfect sex, perfect understanding of one another. Souvenirs and photographs provided the artifacts to prompt memory. With the increasing luxury in the accommodations and spectacular entertainment at vacation spots since the 1960s, more and more honeymoons offered "magic" moments and were overflowing with symbols of romance: sunset cruises, flowers, candlelight dining at expensive restaurants, heart-shaped tubs, champagne toasts.[11]

It is easy to see that the honeymoon has lost several of its original reasons for existing. First of all, a honeymoon in Las Vegas, at Disney World, or on a cruise ship is not a private and secluded experience, and it is not particularly relaxing either. Couples choose these places because they are exciting, even if public and crowded. Second, the honeymoon is no longer supposed to initiate a couple into their roles as "Mr. and Mrs." but instead provide a satisfying and memorable experience for two unique individuals. The bride seems to be deciding the destination, but certainly some couples engage in mutual decision making. Most basically, the honeymoon is no longer a rite of sexual initiation. It is not easy to choose an exact date when this was no longer so. During the sexual revolution of the 1920s, most college-educated brides were not virgins when they married, according to sex surveys. But then again, the average Jazz Age bride had only a ninth-grade education. She probably was more traditional and less sexually daring than the "flaming youth" in colleges. But we also know that as late as the 1950s, women who "went all the way" did so only when they were engaged. As a result of the sexual revolution of the 1960s, however, the odds were fifty-fifty that the bride lost her virginity to a man she ended up not marrying.[12] With the steep rise in cohabitation beginning in the 1970s, the honeymoon no longer served the purpose of acquainting the couple with each other's personal habits, since at least half of them had been sharing the same bedroom and bathroom for quite a while. According to sexologist Edward Laumann, in 1999 only 20 percent of brides and 15 percent of grooms were virgins on their wedding nights.[13] Still, the honeymoon was never intended to be travel solely to accomplish the goal of sexual initiation. It was, and still remains, a trip designed for the purpose of achieving happiness, with spending on a travel holiday helping to fulfill fantasies and dreams about amorous eroticism and perfect love.

In these respects, the magic of the wedding continued into the honeymoon. But in fact, the honeymoon was higher on purchased experience and lower on purchased material goods. There was, after all, no expensive clothing to be selected, no ring to be bought. Even souvenir shopping is not simply about purchasing a material good but about being able to take home "a piece of the experience."[14] The couple was purchasing entry into a dream world, a paradise, a special place reached through a journey, a distinctive and special experience, and a return home.[15] The tourist industries invoked the ideas of magic, memory, romance, and perfection and applied them to places that were specially decorated and staged to elicit a romantic aura. Just as the idea of perfect love could be translated into the perfect wedding, so, too, the tourist industry turned the religious image of the Garden of Eden into a honeymoon paradise. Utopian desire, so necessary to consumer culture, was thus joined with journey to a magic place.

What really put the honeymoon show on the road were the increasing forms of convenient travel available to couples. In the nineteenth century, train travel was cheaper, faster, easier, and more comfortable than travel by steamship or coach.[16] Beginning around the 1920s, mass ownership of autos, the availability of inexpensive gasoline, paid holidays, and the building and paving of roads encouraged couples to take "a short motor trip" for their honeymoon. They were usually headed for an affordable place within about a hundred miles of their point of origin.[17] There were propeller flights from the West Coast to Hawaii in the 1930s, but they took about twenty-two hours and were costly. As late as the 1950s, travel outside the continental United States usually meant going on a cruise. Since it took ten days to sail to and from Hawaii from the West Coast, only those who had flexible schedules and sufficient resources could take such trips.[18] However, as jet travel became affordable beginning in the 1960s, the average couple could board an airplane for their honeymoon destination.

The shift in the locales chosen—from nearby mountain cabins and lodges to faraway theme parks, cruises, and tropical islands—reflected not only an increase in the expense of travel but also a change in the kind of romantic fantasies honeymoon couples were seeking. American nationalism contributed to travel to the wilderness. European nations had monuments and medieval universities; the Americas had mountains and streams.[19] A cottage in the woods was less rustic than camping in a tent, but it was still "roughing it." The wilderness seemed to offer town dwellers "the strength, health, and vigor" they felt deprived of.[20] In Frank Capra's *It Happened One Night* (1934) the runaway bride, having fled one annulled marriage, weds her true love and the film ends with her honeymoon. The happy couple is off-screen in their rustic cabin, while the married owners of the establishment decide their customers are definitely newlyweds because the couple has shown them their wedding certificate. Lights out at a honeymoon cabin in Glen Falls, Michigan, was perceived to be a deeply romantic ending to a film filled with deep sighs and sustained longing. Capra movies celebrated the common folk, not the bankers and their spoiled daughters. The rustic cabin with the car parked outside made perfect sense, since it was an ordinary place for a couple where the wealthy bride deliberately chose to join the people rather than to remain special.

Making use of the honeymoon as a means to express a consumer/romantic identity is relatively new, since before the 1950s, honeymoon travel was a form of class and race privilege. The majority of couples in the nineteenth century did not go on a honeymoon; in fact, they had no holiday time of any kind. Low income and an inflexible and demanding work schedule did not allow for a vacation. Men in industrial or outdoor labor worked six days a week, when they had a job; recreational travel was out of the question for the unemployed. On the farm, cows had to be milked and chickens had to be fed. Only wealthier farmers could hire laborers to do chores in their absence. Sharecroppers and migrant farm laborers, ditch diggers and teamsters, washerwomen and domestic servants never imagined being able to afford a honeymoon. They usually spent the wedding evening at the home of one set of parents and returned to their duties the next day. One Polish immigrant who married right after the end of World War I explained she and her husband "never knew what honeymoon meant."[21] In the 1920s, many middle-class, salaried employees were entitled to vacations with pay, but the rest of the labor force was not. Only in the 1930s and early 1940s did working-class couples begin to go on a honeymoon. They often offered the backseat of their own or a borrowed car to kin to reduce the cost of gas.[22]

In the postwar world, both the lavish wedding and the honeymoon became understood as democratic rights, part of the American way of life. Both were promoted by bridal magazines, which, beginning with *Bride's* in 1934, had begun to carry ads for honeymoon resorts. What was once a luxury had become an entitlement. General survey figures about the extent of postmarital travel bear out this chronology. Between 1920 and 1960, about 75 percent of Washington State couples went on a honeymoon, but such a long stretch of time includes the experiences of about three generations of couples. Two other, more time-specific studies reveal the growth of the right to leisure after the war. Between 1925 and 1944, 47 percent of Detroit, Michigan, white and black couples in a survey took a honeymoon as compared to 90 percent of nine hundred white couples married in New Haven, Connecticut, between 1949 and 1950.[23]

But the New Haven survey of only whites inflated the extent of honeymooning. Since the rate of black poverty was higher, more black couples were unable to afford such a vacation. In addition, there were barriers other than income to honeymoon travel among African Americans. The democratic right to a honeymoon was compromised by racial discrimination, just as the wedding itself was compromised. In the late 1940s, a Niagara Falls restaurant on the Canadian side was charged with denial of service on grounds of race. In 1950, a black couple from Kansas won the annual honeymoon contest sponsored by a Niagara Falls hotel. They received a tour of the city and a greeting from the mayor but not the free meal and night at the hotel other contest winners were given.[24] Motels in the 1950s had relatively small rooms but often had small bridal suites. At such motels, especially in the South, black couples suffered from racial discrimination before the Civil Rights Act of 1964 was passed and widely enforced. After being married on the lawn of her parents' home in Marion, Alabama, in 1953, Coretta Scott King and her husband Martin could not find a bridal suite in a motel or hotel that would rent to blacks. A local funeral home owner provided them with a place in his establishment. In later years, Martin Luther King Jr. would tell friends, "Do you know, we spent our honeymoon at a funeral parlor."[25] Most middle-class black honeymooners, anticipating racial discrimination, seem to have selected black-only resort communities such as Oak Bluffs on Martha's Vineyard, Massachusetts; Highland Beach on the Chesapeake Bay in Maryland; Sag Harbor on Long Island, New York; or Idlewild in northern Michigan.[26] Similarly, Jews faced discrimination at many resort hotels. In fact, before World War II, the resort hotels on Waikiki and Miami Beach did not admit Jews or racial minorities.[27] With the large Jewish population in New York City, a honeymoon closer to home was the likelier option. Jewish couples from New York City as early as the 1890s were choosing Jewish-run resorts in the Catskill Mountains. The resorts, which could be reached by train from New York City, offered kosher dining.[28]

Many other working-class and middle-class couples also faced the barrier of limited incomes, having to choose between traveling and buying new furniture. During the war, Niagara Falls became known as a spot for brief and affordable honeymoons for servicemen and their brides. With its cheap souvenir shops and garish signage, the Falls acquired a reputation for sleaziness. But after the war, Niagara Falls boomed as a tourist destination for working-class couples who lived within easy driving distance and found this hallowed spot within their budgets. Most honeymooners who came there were satisfied tourists for whom the Falls represented their first hotel stay, their first restaurant meal, their first glass of wine.[29]

While some hotels catered only to honeymooners at Niagara Falls, the first postwar *resort* specifically for honeymooners was "the Farm on the Hill" in the Poconos, near Swiftwater, Pennsylvania. In 1945, retired New York executive Rudolf van Hoevenberg and his wife, Eleanore, started "the Farm."[30] Similar resorts for honeymooners were developed in Florida about the same time. Since the 1820s, vacationers from the East Coast had been attracted by the fresh, clean air and water, lakes, and hiking paths of these Pennsylvania mountains. Because of the proximity to New York City, soldiers during World War II who had to marry quickly before going overseas often took their brides camping or to a cabin in the Poconos. Some veterans wanted to return to the same area for a "real honeymoon" after the war.[31]

A resort offered tennis courts and a swimming pool, daytime activities, evening entertainment, and a large number of other couples staying close by in a single compound. Socializing among peers, not retreat from society, was the goal of many a 1950s honeymoon. A Poconos honeymoon was a vacation among other newlyweds.[32] There are a number of reasons why postwar couples wanted not a cabin in the woods but instead one at a resort. First of all, such facilities had evening entertainment and more amenities. However, a Poconos owner also speculated that a bride liked the idea of not having any single women who might compete for her husband's attention on the scene. A more compelling additional reason is that the conformity of the postwar years heightened the long-held American desire to inhabit a "peer group" society. The honeymoon resort seemed to carry this national desire to its extreme. Couples ate at long tables, like summer campers. The van Hoevenbergs went to great lengths to choose couples who would get along with each other. They selected their customers on the basis of a submitted statement, which included a description of the couple's future plans. Honeymooning in the Poconos thus prepared a couple for their future life in the suburbs; it was time spent with married couples of one's own age, education, and social status.[33] The Poconos in the 1950s also had a mainly white, Christian clientele, since resorts in the Poconos discriminated against both blacks and Jews.[34] Then, too, couples seemed to require that other honeymooners be in proximity as the bride underwent sexual initiation. They wanted to be kept busy and stick to a schedule as a form of distraction.

Who were the patrons of these Poconos resorts? They tended to be the sons and daughters of Catholic, working-class parents. The grooms were firemen, postal clerks, and repairmen; the brides were nurses, secretaries, sales girls, and waitresses. In the 1960s, the average Poconos bride was nineteen—younger than the national median age for brides—but at twenty-two, the groom was about average age. The resorts in the Poconos attracted guests from all over the country but drew mainly from small cities or medium-sized towns in the East or Midwest. Most chose the area because friends had recommended it. The typical couple had a big-splurge wedding and drove to the resort right after the reception. Social science surveys as well as offhand remarks by resort owners suggest that while Victorian mores had disappeared, sexual virginity was still common.[35] The bride who was a virgin was seen as both more deserving of a honeymoon and more in need of special instruction. (The owner of Cove Haven recalled the bride who left her cabin in the middle of the night and hitchhiked to her parents' home.)[36] Being less sexually accomplished than their peers, couples who registered at resorts in the Poconos often found the prompts, cues, and winks of resort managers and stand-up comics an aid in lessening inhibitions. As the location of the first honeymoon resort, the Poconos pioneered the development of a key component of the post-1950 honeymoon experience: live entertainment.

The sexual revolution of the sixties arrived at the Poconos as more of their clientele came to include the sexually initiated, if not the truly experienced. As honeymoon options increased, the resort was losing its appeal. In part to remain attractive to its base of clients, a Poconos resort owner, Morris Wilkins, who had once been a plumbing contractor, built a special large tub and filled it with bubble bath, thus creating an enduring honeymoon symbol. The appearance of the bubble-filled large tub coincided with the availability of the birth control pill and the onset of the swinging sixties.

Compared to previous marketing efforts for honeymoon locations, advertising the bubble bath seemed akin to mass-marketed pornography for honeymooners. To be sure, sexual fantasy had been implicit in Niagara Falls advertising of the 1870s, which depicted a waterfall on a travel brochure, with the idea that water plunging rapidly into a pool below was a metaphor for sexual intercourse. But there was considerable distance between perceiving the sexual imagery in nature and a photograph of a naked couple in a bubble bath. In 1963, *Life* magazine published a two-page color spread featuring a honeymoon couple at Caesar's Cove in the Poconos immersed in a heart-shaped bathtub. Ads in bridal magazines were more modest, depicting the bride alone in the tub.[37] Because of subsequent publicity, the Poconos acquired its reputation as the "Honeymoon Capital of the World" or "the Land of Love." The heart-shaped tub was intended to send a more erotic signal: presumably a couple sipped champagne in a suds-filled pool and then had sex in the tub or on the pile rug in the bathroom.

Wilkins started with the rectangular, sunken tubs other Poconos owners had installed but quickly switched to heart-shaped ones. He explained, "I think the popularity is because sexual relations are related in some way to cleanliness."[38] Wilkins acknowledged he was borrowing his idea of romantic fantasy from Hollywood films in which the female star soaked in a bubble bath. Since Hollywood was also fueling the desire for the luxurious wedding, it is not surprising to find that it helped shape other romantic fantasies as well. Scenes in Hollywood movies, combined with the symbolic meaning of the heart-as-love, created the romantic association between a plumbing fixture and romantic passion. The advantage of the sunken bath to Wilkins was that "it's glamorous, like Hollywood 1930s movies. . . . Couples call us for reservations and don't even care what kind of accommodations they get as long as they get the big bath."[39] He also borrowed from the décor of a brothel in adding plush red carpeting, floor-to-ceiling mirrors, round mirrors on the ceiling, and a room-sized, heart-shaped bed in cabins painted red. The decoration of the cabins and the ambience of the resort seemed to reflect Americans' dualistic thinking about sex itself: a whorehouse interior combined with the wholesome activities and facilities of a summer camp. Did the combination appeal to the patrons of the Poconos? Cathy, a twenty-one-year-old secretary from Indiana, Pennsylvania, explained, "We came here because of the bathtubs and the beds and the horseback riding."[40]

The Poconos was still the resort of choice as late as 1969, when, according to travel agent surveys, 14.5 percent of honeymooners chose this mountain destination in Pennsylvania, making the area the single most popular honeymoon locale of the time.[41] Wilkins and his fellow resort owners continued to develop the idea of the erotic bath in the 1980s by creating a Jacuzzi 7 feet above the ground in the shape of a champagne glass.[42] But the Poconos were already facing considerable competition from rival destinations. Even in their heyday, the Poconos resorts were a regional and not a national choice; they were too far from the Midwest, the South, and the West to be selected frequently, with many preferring a national park or wilderness site much closer to home.[43]

In the 1960s, luxury travel came to be defined as jet travel to an offshore location.[44] Commercial jet travel began in 1958 with Pan Am's regular flight between New York and Paris and was soon followed by the development of an international route system as well as the growth of charter flights. Long-haul jets, which could accommodate more than a hundred passengers, opened new destinations for mass tourism in the 1960s. As these planes were introduced, the cost of travel to tropical islands fell. Airplane travelers also vastly increased the number of tourists who visited Caribbean spots on cruise ships.[45] In addition, jet travel opened the Hawaiian islands for time-pressed honeymooners and made the airplane trip more comfortable.[46] As a result, the number of visitors to the Hawaiian islands from the U.S. mainland increased a hundredfold from 1952 to 1965.[47]

Along with the jet age, rising incomes and rising ages at marriage led more couples to select offshore locations as their preferred honeymoon destinations. Bridal magazine readers who were planning a honeymoon outside the continental United States rose from 37 percent in 1966 to 66 percent in 1992.[48] The actual destinations chosen during this time period followed a predictable cycle of interest and then decline. All of these

Figure 13. Champagne tub, Caesar's Pocono Resorts. Courtesy Caesar's
Pocono Resorts.

places had ubiquitous palm trees and the necessary "four S's": sun, sand,
sea, and sex. All were hot in the summer, balmy in the winter, and the
water was warm. But there was often the fifth "S": seedy.[49] With the
increase in hotel building and in travel advertising, older hotels became
less desirable and the new was in vogue. The beach was too crowded and

there was too much traffic. Destinations competed for the designation as the new honeymoon capital. Before the revolution, Cuba's political elites, along with American businessmen, built country clubs, hotels, racetracks, casinos, and nightclubs where the entertainer was Nat King Cole and the beat was bongo drums. Nassau, Bahamas, benefited from the demise of the honeymoon in Havana after Castro came to power. Bermuda, Acapulco, Miami Beach, and Waikiki—other favorites of the 1950s and 1960s—fell out of favor. Meanwhile, resorts with new hotels took their place. In the 1960s, developers turned former sugarcane plantations and grazing land into a planned tourist boulevard of hotels and golf courses adjacent to a white sand strip in west Maui; in the 1970s, government planners in Cancún, Mexico, joined a small fishing island to the mainland and laid out a gigantic hotel zone, which they landscaped with fully grown palm trees.[50] Both of these destinations offered white sand beaches and a great many hotel rooms, and they came equipped with elaborate hotel pools that often had water slides or swim-up bars.[51] Travel marketers from these tropical locales identified honeymooners as a key market, in part because these vacationers spent three times as much as other tourists.[52]

In the 1990s, the entertainment honeymoon, to be experienced in Las Vegas, at Disney World, or on a cruise, became a highly popular rival to the offshore, tropical variations.[53] A cruise ship offered plenty of nonstop entertainment, from gambling to floor shows, and served meals. Fourteen percent of couples in the 1990s went on cruises, with those to the Caribbean rivaling the Florida honeymoon in popularity. The cruise combined the Las Vegas and the tropical honeymoon, since the ship made stops on tropical islands while offering gambling and floor shows at sea. The Royal Caribbean's *Voyager of the Seas,* built in 1998, claimed to have the world's biggest roulette wheel. The romantic television program *The Love Boat,* which aired between 1977 and 1986, popularized the idea of the lovemaking potential of evenings spent on the deck of a cruise ship looking at the stars and listening to the waves. The program, a one-hour romantic comedy that placed and then removed obstacles in the paths of couples realizing true love, was filmed on board a Princess Cruises ship. The 1980s cruise ship was a modest ocean liner compared to the behemoths of the 1990s that came equipped with an ice skating rink, a basketball court, and an outdoor golf course.

There was a second, equally predictable cycle of interest and decline related not to the destination but to the unending process of making class distinctions. As soon as a locale became defined as a mass destination, celebrities and people of wealth sought a new and more distinctive one to maintain the social distance between themselves and everyone else. Because consumers loved novelty and the wealthy continually sought to make these distinctions, Maui, Cancún, and Jamaica came to be seen as too crowded, commercialized, and clichéd. Fiji, Tahiti, and Bali (when there was no local unrest or terrorism), as well as Australia and the Seychelles, became the new "in spots" because they were perceived as less spoiled and they cost more to reach. In the late 1980s and 1990s, the upper class took this desire for a private and inaccessible honeymoon one step further by honeymooning on privately owned islands or on yachts (such as the *Royal Brittania,* as in the case of Prince Charles and Princess Diana). Enter also the adventure honeymoon, or a safari in Tanzania. Some of the demand for travel to off-the-beaten-path locales came from older couples who had already visited the standard destinations. Moreover, some highly educated couples, valuing egalitarian relationships, made mutual decisions about the honeymoon destination and often chose a trip that, while still expensive, also managed to express their rejection of either consumer society (camping in Alaska) or of the tropical (a trip to Greenland).[54] These couples may have relied on a travel agent to book their airplane tickets and rental cars, but they had dispensed with restaurant meals, fancy lodgings, and nightclub entertainers.

Since the origins of the honeymoon lay in heterosexual coupling, it might seem that the standard choices and appeals of the tourist industry had no meaning in gay life. For gay couples, there was no need to pay allegiance to the ideal of sexual normalcy. Nor was there any ritual about signing the register as "Mr. and Mrs." Moreover, there is a form of gay tourism—featuring cross-dressers and sex tours—that bears no resemblance to the monogamy and coupledom of honeymoon travel. That gay couples also desired a honeymoon suggests that performing appropriate gender roles on the honeymoon was not a necessary part of the ritual. But in fact, following commitment ceremonies, gay couples tend to prefer the same cruises, trips to the mountains, gambling resorts, theme parks, and tropical beaches as their heterosexual counterparts. To be sure, some gay travelers have been and continue to be attracted to Niagara

Falls as a honeymoon spot precisely because of the opportunity for parody of straight life, long after Niagara Falls has become déclassé.[55] Often, drag shows feature supposedly male and female couples dancing to "Shuffle off to Buffalo." Moreover, beginning in the 1960s, working-class lesbians from Toronto, Canada, have identified the Falls as a "honeymoon" spot, even those couples who presumably did not have a civil ceremony and were defining their trip more as a special vacation. For them, the Falls was cheap, nearby, and had several gay bars.[56] But gays also select destinations, hotels, lodges, and inns where they hope they will not be discriminated against. The surest way to escape discrimination and enjoy the gay lifestyle is by social segregation; thus, many same-sex couples prefer gay-only cruise ships on the Mexican Riviera and the Caribbean. Maui welcomes gay vacationers with explicit advertising. There are also wedding packages for gays in Vermont that offer civil ceremonies overlooking a pond, along with a honeymoon stay at a lodge or bed-and-breakfast inn.[57]

The overriding theme in all honeymoon planning, regardless of sexual preference, is that luxury travel is an opulent way to express romantic love. Just as the lavish wedding offers guilt-free consumption, so, too, expensive postwedding travel is seen as the trip of a lifetime, or at least a very special and very expensive vacation. The average family vacation for a family of four in 1999 cost $956. The typical honeymoon cost almost four times that amount and was a trip for two rather than for four.[58] With greater prosperity, the honeymoon took on new meaning as the first of several expensive vacations a couple might enjoy. In the 1960s and 1970s, the honeymoon might be defined as "the last chance to collect Romance and Glitter, and a few Precious Moments before being besieged for years with bills, children and worries."[59] During the wealth bubble of the 1990s, the expectation was that other luxuries were still to come. Thus, a 1990s wedding guide explained, "This is your chance to take the biggest trip of your life (to date) and splurge to your heart's content—with everyone's deep approval and warm good wishes."[60]

In many ways, preparing for the honeymoon was simply part of the larger wedding planning process. Selecting a destination was just one consumer choice, akin to deciding whether to serve grilled sea bass or tournedos at the reception. The lengthy preparation for the lavish wedding was matched by the hours spent collecting and reading dozens of travel brochures and, more recently, surfing the Web. Until the 1990s, bridal magazines and fairs subsumed the honeymoon under one of the many purchases for the wedding. By the mid-1990s, there were specialized guides to "planning your most romantic trip ever," as well as an entire magazine devoted to the subject. Travel to the tropics had always been perceived as recuperative; what was new was to make explicit that the couple needed to recuperate from wedding planning. Tourist bureaus and advertisers began to describe the honeymoon as a well-deserved rest after planning the wedding and booking the honeymoon travel. An advertisement that appeared in 2000 for the Sheraton hotels in Hawaii featured the headline, "Ten months of wedding planning, instantly forgotten."[61]

Each tourist destination has its own mystique, its own local color, but on the whole, different kinds of resonances emerge from the tropical island than from the theme park. All major tourist destinations are highly manufactured places. But the tropical paradise offers a distinct form of experience—that of being descendants of Adam and Eve. In such lush locales, in the Western imagination, rules need not be followed, food and drink are plentiful, and there are few hardships.[62] The tropical island was thought to decrease sexual inhibitions and prompt romantic passion as the newlyweds smelled luscious flowers and watched the sun set together. In the tropics, explorers, missionaries, travel writers, and later tourists came into contact with native peoples who wore fewer clothes because of the heat. Yet all of these visitors were temporary. Alienated painters like Paul Gauguin, on a quest for the exotic, or writer Robert Louis Stevenson, sought a retreat from civilization, freedom from responsibilities (Gauguin deserted his wife and five children), inspiration, and renewal. The tourist business took the largely male quest for renewal and tamed it into tourism, which was repackaged as an activity for a couple, or occasionally a larger group.

Ever since European explorers landed in the Sandwich Islands or Hispaniola, there have been two competing images of the tropical island. The first was that it was characterized by hurricanes, cannibalism, smallpox, mosquitoes, and bubonic plague and was lacking the necessary constraints of civilization. The second was that it was a paradise, a timeless world offering temporary respite from civilization. Public health measures could rid these islands of infectious diseases, and missionaries helped to eliminate cannibalism. What the tourist industry succeeded in doing was emphasizing the image of paradise and concealing from the traveling public the reality of possible hurricanes.

The international tourist industry emerged at the high point of imperialism in the late nineteenth century. It encouraged seeing the sights, the grand tour along with recuperative travel.[63] While privileged gentlemen led a leisurely life at their country estates and had no need for recuperation, the middle class, living in cities or suburbs, did.[64] Their days were more hurried and more scheduled. They raised children who controlled their emotions and suppressed many of their inner longings. Such people traveled in search of a more authentic and highly intense experience. Some may have found it in their own nation, but many could find authenticity only in another, less civilized culture. In venturing to foreign shores, they sought to see an authentic primitive culture largely unaffected by modern changes, where they would be able to release their libidinal desires. There they encountered "primitive" native peoples. Westerners have invariably regarded dark-skinned native people as savages, closer to nature, and thus less sexually inhibited. They have also tended to see the primitive as feminine, and thus, sensuous, warm, and welcoming. Primitives, although living in the present, were said to represent a timeless past. In sum, the viewing of nature as well as natives through a sexual lens was supposed to decrease sexual inhibitions and prompt romantic passion.[65]

Tourism in Hawaii tapped into such inchoate longings in the late nineteenth century and thus developed the imagery of the tropical paradise upon which the post-1960 honeymoon relies. The first guidebook to the islands was published in 1875. The Hawaiian tourist business began in the 1880s, when a Hawaiian photographer on the islands began to publish a tabloid titled *The Paradise of the Pacific*. He succeeded in enticing mainland travel agents to tour the islands and witness the eruptions of the Kilauea volcano on the Big Island.[66] Perhaps initially the scenery and the weather were sufficient to symbolize a tropical paradise. Soon, however, it was clear scenery was not exciting enough. Large hotels built on Waikiki and steamship companies developed the tourist industry on Oahu in the 1920s. These developers added the beautiful native girl, the native hula dance at the tourist hotels, the native feast (a luau), the costume for the tourist gone native (alohawear), a floral greeting for visitors (handing out leis as the ship docked), and the spectacular on-the-beach arrival via outrigger canoe.[67] Kodak, in combination with the Matson steamship company, inaugurated a free hula show in a Honolulu park in 1937. Unlike the evening nightclub shows, Kodak's version was conducted during the day, providing the tourists with plenty of opportunities to take photos of the hula dancers. Companies in Hawaii marketed tourism through these rituals as well as through guidebooks, advertisements, brochures, songs, recordings, and a 1930s syndicated radio program heard on 750 stations across the world, *Hawaii Calls*. Movie producers and directors who vacationed on Waikiki decided it made an ideal filmmaking backdrop. Between 1920 and 1939, more than fifty Hollywood films, including an occasional one with a Waikiki wedding, were set in Hawaii.[68] Some of the original Waikiki films were made in Hollywood studios, although by the 1930s, Kauai was already becoming a favorite tropical backdrop for prominent directors such as Cecil B. DeMille.

The tropical beach hotel was a Hawaiian invention. The honeymoon couple did not need to leave the grounds of the hotel, since there they could enjoy fine dining, daytime and evening activities, bars, and special events at the pool or on the beach. The tropical beach resort, a separate village set apart from the city or the general population, was an innovation of Club Med. It seemed to fit more with the idea of the honeymoon as a time of seclusion. In 1950, the development of Club Med and French beach resorts in Majorca, Polynesia, and elsewhere served as the first models, even though Club Med was never intended to be a honeymoon resort. In fact, most of its patrons were heterosexual singles, and its villages had a reputation for brief, intimate sexual encounters. But Club Med created the concept of an isolated beach resort with all services included for a single price; tourists used beads, rather than francs, for purchases. Designed as an antidote to civilization, Club Med was actually an outpost of civilization, offering a smattering of elements of consumer culture: a beauty salon, stores, sports equipment, a bar, piped music, and tourist excursions to the local market. Still, there was no native dancing and no entertainment in the evening. It was a much quieter holiday than one on Waikiki. If the Poconos retreats were like summer camp for honeymooners, Club Med was a beach playground for uninhibited children who had nothing to worry about except getting too much sun. At the Poconos, couples were usually clad in Bermuda shorts and tops for fishing and volleyball. The difference was one of playful teenagers at camp versus playful children at the beach. At Club Med, the uniform was a swimsuit—more specifically, a bikini for women—perhaps covered by a sarong. While having limited contact with the natives of the island, the vacationers were nonetheless allowed to indulge in the fantasy that they had "gone native." Club Med also worshiped the sun and a beautiful body, as well as the relentless physical exercise and sports required to achieve this kind of physique.[69]

In the 1980s, a Jamaican businessman created an all-inclusive resort at a small Montego Bay hotel. He went on to develop Sandals, a string of all-inclusives throughout the Caribbean, with the slogan "Where love comes to stay." By 1994, Sandals was the world's largest independent resort group. It offered much more civilization, and indeed, luxury, than Club Med, although it simply borrowed the Club Med idea of the beach village as a retreat from civilization. But since there was always live entertainment in the evening, the all-inclusive combined distinctive regional music with the idea of the beach village. At an all-inclusive, the couple purchased lodging, transportation, meals, and as many rum punches and piña coladas as they might like, as well as use of all the facilities and access to entertainment on the premises. Like Club Med, one of the appeals of the all-inclusives is that the couple did not have to tip, carry around cash, or pay for extras. Being able to eat and have free drinks at all-inclusives led to the moniker "the beach and booze honeymoon." Such places had brand new restaurants; large fitness centers; a swim-up pool bar; king-size, mahogany, four-poster beds; and splashy evening floor shows.[70] The fitness craze in the United States led hotels around the world to install exercise equipment. Most Caribbean islands distilled rum, and the islands generally tolerated drinking hard liquor during the day as well as in the evening. Thus, what distinguished the Caribbean from other destinations was the greater freedom to drink heavily.

Sexual exhibitionism was more overt in the Caribbean than at the Poconos because of the sexual revolution on the American mainland and the freer sexual attitudes of the islands. Most of the guests at Sandals were honeymooners, and at an average age of twenty-four to twenty-eight, they were somewhat older than the average newlyweds in the Poconos. The master of ceremonies at the evening show in the

Poconos went in merely for double entendre. In Jamaica, the nude cruises and pajama parties, where guests came dressed in their nightclothes (no matter how skimpy) and danced to pulsating bass rhythms, conveyed a honeymoon atmosphere more akin to a "swinging singles resort." Just as the reception was supposed to incorporate moments of play, so, too, the entertainment at honeymoon resorts was expected to provide some time for laughter. At these resorts, the new sexual ideal of the honeymoon was no longer privacy and seclusion but public exhibitionism, followed by sexual adventures in the couple's well-appointed room. The couple was also encouraged to relieve the stress of the wedding through yoga or therapeutic massage, and once relaxed, to try out new sexual positions or lovemaking as preliminaries to longer-lasting and sweatier sexual play.[71]

The all-inclusive resorts in Mexico and the Caribbean were also American outposts in the midst of tropical isles, with a local population consisting of black- or brown-skinned hotel workers who lived in shantytowns several miles from the hotels. The honeymoon couple was crossing national borders and entering a different country with a colonial history. Whereas advertising for Hawaii had always featured one native, the hula dancer, independent nations for decades did not include native inhabitants when marketing their destinations. The beach, rather than the inhabitants of the country, was featured instead. In the late 1960s, the advertising executive David Ogilvy eliminated all but one couple on the beach as well as any waiters. He single-handedly created what became an advertising cliché, the happy barefoot couple strolling hand in hand, alone on a sandy beach. National tourist industries gave explicit instructions for these changes. Jamaican tourist advertising in the 1960s had pictured whites being served by black waiters. Under the nationalist leadership of Gerald Manley, advertisers stopped using servile imagery. By 2000, with the colonialist legacy fading, ads portrayed not only tourists engaged in sporting activities but also service personnel. The reason for this change was both to underscore the value of privacy and to acknowledge that couples could expect to be waited on.[72]

Many couples preferred the excitement, the shopping, and the restaurants of Disney World, a cruise, or Las Vegas to tropical beaches. They wanted a supercharged version of the Internet-, media-, and image-driven world they inhabited, but one that was safe, clean, festive, and friendly and offered restaurant dining. Perhaps they were voting against the older definition of the honeymoon as a time of privacy and seclusion. Perhaps they thought the tropical honeymoon was simply too much baking in the sun and too boring and they enjoyed watching the people in the crowds. At any rate, retreat has now also come to mean going unnoticed among a crowd of strangers all wearing T-shirts, shorts, and sandals. Many couples were making their choices because the entertainment locales were cheaper than going offshore. Moreover, ever since the Poconos resorts of the 1950s, evening entertainment has always been a key element of the honeymoon resort. Choosing the Poconos was a vote in favor of entertainment and being with others as against seclusion; choosing these three destinations was a similar affirmation.

Disney World in Orlando, Florida, which opened in 1971, is one of the most popular honeymoon destinations, although it is located in the middle of what was once swampland in central Florida. In 1991, about one in six of all honeymooners who responded to a survey by *Modern Bride* magazine chose Florida, and most of them were headed for Orlando, the theme park capital of the United States. This area offers tourists not only the several Disney parks but also other theme parks in the same city: Universal Studios, Islands of Adventure, and Sea World. Since Disney World was also one of America's most popular vacation destinations, honeymooners were simply choosing more expensive hotel and spending options from a tourist locale that many affluent Americans, Europeans, and Latin Americans selected.

Disney World is an elaborate, heavily marketed fantasyland—a marvel of technology, urban planning, and crowd management. It offers a dense consumer and entertainment experience, with restaurants and gift shops interspersed among rides and exhibits. A tourist entity the size of San Francisco, Disney World is organized around specialty zones (Frontierland, Fantasyland, and others) with theme-appropriate rides, food, and shopping. In the evening there is a nightly New Year's Eve celebration, complete with a fireworks display at an entertainment zone on Pleasure Island, an ersatz tropical isle. Epcot Center, added to Disney World in 1982, offers rides, films, and technological exhibits as well as a staged display of artifacts, performances, and souvenirs from eleven countries, including Morocco, Norway, France, and China. A few hours spent at Epcot provides tourists with the experience of a trip abroad without lost luggage, rude cab drivers, or strange food. Disney developed a zoo with stage shows and rides called Animal Kingdom in 1998.[73] Because Disney World was losing visitors to water slides in Orlando, it also created its own water parks.

There may have been nothing intrinsically romantic about monorail rides, Florida summertime humidity, the threat of hurricanes, animal smells, and long lines for Splash Mountain. But Disney's advertising transformed the mundane and crowded into sun-filled days and moonlit nights. The slogan for Walt Disney World through much of the 1990s was "Remember the magic," with the implication that there was a paradise for every price range and every imaginative rendering. The company also created theme environments representing diverse honeymoon locales in its resort lodges. The tropics were evoked at the Caribbean Beach Resort and the Polynesian Resort and its buffet, the Polynesian luau. Disney even simulated the mountain resort by building a hotel with large logs called the Wilderness Lodge. To be sure, honeymoon couples knew the difference between a Polynesian resort and the Disney version. But Disney was offering the full range of consumer options and romantic associations at a lower price and with the entertainment that a theme park provided. Disney was no more manufactured than Waikiki, originally marshland for growing rice, although it was usually perceived as less "authentic."[74]

The need for heightened sensation in the early nineteenth century led to travel to Niagara Falls, where the honeymoon couple could view "wild, but not too wild, nature." This same need motivated honeymooners to seek out theme park "experiences," events with a beginning and an end that felt "uplifting and out of the ordinary."[75] These three destinations—Las Vegas, Disney World, and cruises—also provided more sanitized versions of the early-twentieth-century amusement parks and carnivals and offered entertainment through spectacles such as fireworks, laser and light shows, costumed cartoon characters, and dancing girls.[76] Las Vegas, a cruise, and Disney World were theme parks, two on the land, one on the sea. Disney and Las Vegas contained resorts within their geographical space; the cruise ship was a floating resort and theme park. Within the theme park, the number of staged performances was very great. All three can be classified as "magical, fantastic, and enchanted settings in which to consume."[77] All three managed to remain competitive in the cycle of resort rise and fall by developing more elaborate spectacles through technology and by creating fabrications (arcades or volcanoes or golf courses).[78]

In short, the simulated environments of these vacations repeat the continuous stream of fragmented television, film, advertising, and Internet images that form postmodern reality.[79] But while Disney may be selling simulation combined with nostalgia for small-town America, Las Vegas seems to hold out the promise of "playful fantasies" presented as spoof or parody.[80] Perhaps at one time the cruise ship was a means of transportation to a destination, but that is no longer the case. Many passengers never leave the ship. Moreover, cruise lines have engaged in fabrication similar to that used at Disney World or Las Vegas. Finding the "real" ports of call seedy and unsafe and the beaches less than pristine, cruise lines have bought private islands and added fine ground sand to serve as ports of call where guests can lie on the beach, snorkel, and glimpse a replica of a ship the companies sank to look like an "authentic" pirate ship. The passengers then can see the Caribbean of "long ago," or at least the Caribbean they imagine.

Given the appeal of these mainly engineered spectacles, how can we account for the fact that a survey in 1999 by *Bride's* magazine found Gatlinburg, Tennessee, in the Great Smoky Mountains to be the tenth most popular honeymoon destination? On the outskirts of the most visited national park in the United States, a couple can stay in a log cabin, fish for trout, hike in the mountains, and visit nearby Dollywood, the country music theme park. At first glance, this kind of honeymoon seems to combine nostalgia for the 1940s honeymoon with an unstated protest against the gambling and drinking in Jamaica, in Las Vegas, or on a cruise ship; the sexual titillation of the Caribbean resort; or even the amorous enticement of the heart-shaped tub. With Dollywood nearby, however, it is clear these couples were not rejecting the excitement of the theme park. More often than not, they chose Gatlinburg for its affordability. The cabins are usually freestanding, not part of a mountain resort like the Poconos. While they come equipped with a digital satellite TV and VCR, there is no maid service and no heart-shaped tub. Nearby major attractions include the Skylift, which carries couples up the side of a mountain in the spring and summer and serves as a ski lift in the winter. Couples can also get married at wedding chapels downtown. If they want to enjoy higher-end accommodations, they can check into one of the newer, moderately priced hotels and stay in a room with a garden-variety hot tub.

One suspects the Smokies have become the resort of choice for born-again Christians who might combine religious sight-seeing (passion plays and gardens illustrating the life of Christ) with the lower-key spectacle that can be found at the Ripley's Believe It or Not Museum, along with Dollywood, and the appeal of mountain scenery. *Christian Bride,* a magazine established in 1999, heavily promotes these resorts precisely because they combine the excitement of the theme park with nostalgia for the cabin in the woods. In so doing, these honeymooners use purchases and travel to affirm a religious identity, as well as their identity as a couple.[81]

The honeymoon was originally intended as a journey from the place where the ceremony occurred to a secluded spot. But the separation of wedding and honeymoon locale began to disappear with the rise of the destination wedding. Favored honeymoon destinations offered either romantic scenery or spectacular entertainment. If such vacation spots appealed to the couple, then they were an equally good place to be married. In fact, because they had so many tourist services already in place, there was an ample supply of the caterers, photographers, and other service personnel needed to create a luxurious wedding. In 1991, Disney World began to offer the destination wedding, a ritual that combined the actual ceremony with a honeymoon on Disney premises.[82] They capitalized on the appeal of their Florida location, but Disney admitted it was responding to inquiries from couples wanting to be married in sight of Cinderella's castle. Whisked away in a glass coach after the ceremony, a little girl's Cinderella fantasy could be complete. Likewise, the all-inclusives offered unusual opportunities for nuptials: an enterprise called "Wedding the Island Way" in St. Thomas flew the bride, groom, officiant, and up to two guests to a private island where they could toast each other with Dom Perignon after saying their vows.[83] So successful had such combination events become that in 2000, 11 percent of *Modern Bride* readers were marrying in this fashion.[84]

In truth, in the 1940s, mountain resorts offered weddings officiated by on-site justices of the peace, with organ music and flowers for the ceremony. Moreover, many couples marrying in Las Vegas stayed on for a few nights in the city for their honeymoon. But such stays were often dressed-up elopements rather than true destination weddings. The dividing line between the two seemed to be whether there were guests at the wedding. Resorts encouraged destination weddings because such events brought added guests to the premises and increased the purchase of services as well. Disney, for example, offers discounted rooms at any one of its fifteen resort hotels for wedding parties. But there were other reasons couples sought out such destinations as a place to marry and honeymoon. Geographically mobile couples found the chosen destination provided a convenient gathering spot for friends and relatives arriving from many points of origin. Being married in the house of worship at home no longer was meaningful to a large part of the population. Children involved in a remarriage were offered a family vacation along with a ceremony and reception. Couples avoided months of planning through the purchase of a package of wedding services coordinated by on-site wedding planners. The smaller the guest list, the more likely it was the total cost of the destination wedding would be cheaper than a wedding back home. Moreover, brides and grooms could legitimately ask guests to pay their own way, because "after all, it [was] a vacation for them, too."[85] If guests were geographically dispersed, then travel to a tourist destination for many might not have been more expensive than travel to the bride's hometown. Moreover, destination weddings offered neutral territories and nondenominational chapels, an attractive and entertaining compromise for feuding families or couples seeking to bridge varied religious backgrounds.

Destination weddings seemed to have appeal for couples in Europe and Asia (especially Japan and Korea), as well as North America. Japanese couples took their search for the cheaper alternative to other parts of Asia, Hawaii, Australia, San Francisco, and Disney World. The destination wedding at Disney World, for example, appealed to Japanese couples who had learned about Mickey and Minnie from visiting the Tokyo Disney theme park and who could marry at Disney World for a fraction of the cost of a Japanese wedding. Japanese companies sold packages that combined airfare, hotel rooms, the wedding, and the honeymoon. Indeed, Japanese and European tourists formed a large propor-

Figure 14. After the wedding, Kona coast, Hawaii, 2000. Courtesy Charla Thompson; courtesy Jacqueline Kacen and James Hess.

tion of the couples seeking destination weddings at U.S. entertainment parks and in Hawaii. In fact, the majority of honeymooners in Honolulu were no longer Americans but instead couples from Japan.[86]

The contemporary honeymoon, like the wedding itself, is an exercise in the fulfillment of fantasy. While the new elements added onto romantic travel included the appeal of the tropical paradise, older ideas about the romance in nature and the sublime were still present. Honeymooners were always seeking some combination of intimacy, entertainment, activity, and perhaps even childlike play. The desire for magic, perfection, and a paradise on earth was an old one. Then it became a long airplane trip to a resort, and from there, a highly scripted experience (Tuesday, 6 P.M., Mai Tais at the pool). However, the same observation we

Figure 15.   Luggage cart, destination wedding, Hawaii, 2001. Courtesy Michelle R. Nelson, Ph.D.

made about weddings also applies to honeymoons: scripted travel can still be remembered as special and magical.

What distinguished the prewar honeymoon at the cabin in the woods from the postwar one were the amenities and evening entertainment. More and more couples wanted the concept of the resort, a self-contained locale that met all their needs for activity, entertainment, and tourism. This idea began with the elite on Waikiki, was applied to mass tourism in the Poconos, and then spread to sandy beach villages. The resort seemed to be able to manage the contradiction between the couple participating in activities and being permitted inactivity. At these magical places, all of their needs were to be met, and the couple could become playful children or perhaps even youthful stars. On such a special vacation being pampered and indulged meant prolonging the wedding feeling of being a star, living the celebrity life for a few more days after the ceremony.

Having lost its function as travel for sexual initiation, the honeymoon takes its meanings from the languages of consumption and from tourism, the largest industry in the world. The honeymoon as part of the consumer rite of the wedding is an extension of magical moments into planned journeys and is now defined as recuperation from the stress of wedding planning. There is a qualitative difference between the magic moments of the wedding and those of the honeymoon. Besides the sexual element, the magic moments of the honeymoon tend to involve paid-for experience, which can only be realized by going to a special place. Instead of the wedding industry promoting the ideal of perfection to be realized through the purchase of goods and services, tourist industries hold out the prospect of paradise: the sex, the photographs, the souvenirs, the memories to last a lifetime. From Paradise Road in Las Vegas to the tropical paradise of Maui, hotels and resorts emphasize indulgence. However, they rely upon quite different imagery—one of the postmodern neon city that does not sleep at night, the other of the primitive, where the sky and the stars enhance the couple's sexual yearnings and the sound of the waves crashing on the beach lull the newlyweds into slumber.

Because the desire to be entertained at home or on vacation has become such a central part of contemporary life (and an increasingly important part of the wedding reception as well), many couples have begun to prefer the crowds. It is probably this element of consumer choice, as well as the rejection of the private, secluded ideal, that makes the entertainment honeymoon such a perfect fit with the celebrity of the wedding. As Kris Bulcroft, Linda Smeins, and Richard Bulcroft argue, "the real key in the mass marketing of the packaged honeymoon lies primarily in the promotion of choice for the couple."[87] At these newer entertainment destinations the couple is offered their choice of romantic fantasies (wilderness, tropical paradise) in resort accommodations and in entertainment. What is being affirmed in such honeymoons is no longer the ideal of seclusion, or even the couple's separate identity, but instead the significance of being entertained in an exciting environment along with being able to choose one's experiences.

Chapter 7 | HOLLYWOOD HOSTS A WEDDING

Why buy a bridal magazine, asks the Wedding Guide 2001 Web site, when you can rent the 2000 blockbuster movie *The Wedding Planner,* which demonstrates the wisdom of signing up for a few dance lessons before the big day? The site observes sagely, "Nobody does nuptials better than Hollywood." The guide also suggests paying special attention to the kiss at the end of the wedding ceremony in the 1950 version of *Father of the Bride:* "It's the perfect at-the-altar smooch, a passionate embrace that says 'I do, I do!' without messing the bride's lipstick."[1]

In all likelihood, a bride-to-be can probably persuade her groom to watch a wedding film even when he might not be willing to glance at an etiquette book. Almost by definition, movies are regarded as forays into magical worlds. The film industry is often referred to as a "dream factory," able to mass-produce and market illusion and fantasy. Undergraduate students who watched 1990s wedding films reported these films portrayed much more elaborate and expensive events than the ones they had attended. Even a bride-to-be felt she was observing a dream world, not finding ideas to incorporate in her own plans.[2] Thus, the wedding movie functions more as a mood prompt and a fodder for fantasy than as a display case for attainable goods and services.

Although studios in France and Germany made the first inroads in the commercial film industry, by the mid-1920s, "U.S. films constituted about 90 percent of all screenings in the world," and Hollywood's dominance of world cinema still holds today, to a slightly lesser extent.[3] Hollywood has been dropping a wedding ceremony or reception scene into films since *The Irish Honeymoon* (1910) and Thomas Alva Edison's *The Wedding Bell*, released the following year. The industry quickly realized the pageantry of elaborate weddings could be a huge draw: publicity for *The Love Parade* in 1929 heralded the royal wedding between Queen Louise (Jeannette McDonald) and Count Alfred (Maurice Chevalier) as "perhaps the most dazzlingly spectacular scene yet witnessed and heard in a talking motion picture."[4] In a smaller number of films, the plot and crucial aspects of the characters revolve around planning a wedding or the actual ceremony itself. But not even the increasing popularity of the lavish wedding in American culture could have predicted the extent of Hollywood's romance with the wedding movie during the 1990s.

Regardless of the era in which they were produced, most wedding films typically include four elements: romance (usually romantic comedy, sometimes romantic drama); fashion; star power (usually actors portraying the happy couple but occasionally just the bride, the groom, or even the parents of the bride); and the filmmaker's attitude toward the lavish wedding (often the dominant view in Hollywood at the time). Usually wedding movies are a subset of romantic comedies, although there is the occasional *Bride of Frankenstein*. Hollywood has long known that, in general, women attend more movies than men.[5] Romantic wedding movies, made to appeal to a largely female audience, shape women's expectations and help them devise the "standard package" of artifacts and activities that should make up a wedding. Moreover, especially in the early stages of a relationship, a man willingly accompanies a woman to these kinds of "chick flicks" to please her and encourage their romance. Women are not only the major consumers of romantic films but also the loyal fans of certain male stars who embody romance and sex appeal, from Clark Gable to Richard Gere to Hugh Grant. Of course, women also idolize female stars, copying their hairstyles and mannerisms, admiring their clothing, and soaking in the consumption-laden contexts in which they are portrayed.[6]

On the whole, the formula of early wedding movies was the girl, the guy, and the gown, and this is usually still the case. In the early days of the film industry, stars of silent films often provided their own costumes, but beginning in the 1920s, Hollywood moguls developed well-funded costume departments so audiences could view good-looking women in beautiful clothes. In the 1930s (if not before), Hollywood, not Paris, set the trends in bridal gowns. While women might have thumbed through bridal magazines to gather ideas for their own wedding costumes, movies have always served as larger-than-life "display windows," and their stars as models for beautiful gowns as well as aesthetically pleasing lifestyles.[7]

From the 1930s to the 1950s, women in darkened theaters wanted to gaze at gowns made by one of the famous studio designers: Adrian, Edith Head, Helen Rose, or Jean-Louis. Of course, the influence of Hollywood on wedding fashions often reflected the importance of lavish weddings in the culture as a whole. In the 1960s, when *haute couture* was somewhat supplanted by mod fashions, Hollywood studios began to cut back on their design budgets, and many were buying bridal gowns off the rack. Moreover, actresses in the 1960s and 1970s often consciously adopted an antifashion image. With fitness becoming more ingrained in Hollywood's consciousness, actresses became more concerned about having perfectly toned bodies than about modeling the perfect gown. While stars today do wear Vera Wang or Donna Karan at awards ceremonies and at their own weddings, the idea of a star inextricably associated with a specific *haute couture* designer (as was the case with, say, Audrey Hepburn and Givenchy) has disappeared.[8]

The appeal of most wedding movies is that they are usually star vehicles the audience enjoys because they like to experience the sparks, romantic sighs, and stolen glances between Clark Gable and Claudette Colbert, Cary Grant and Audrey Hepburn, or Richard Gere and Julia Roberts. Obviously, the reason some of these on-screen duos appeared again and again is because fans wanted to see their favorite couples multiple times. Studio publicity and fan magazines have tended to encourage the blurring of lines between an actor's film persona and his or her real life. The audience likes to fall into idyllic slumber, thinking the attraction they see in the movie is real. However, states of rapture should not be confused with passivity; the audience actively participates in the creation of the fantasy on-screen by buying its premise and the impression of reality it offers. In short, according to film scholar Richard Allen, "this 'projective illusion' is not one that is imposed upon a passive spectator but an experience into which an active spectator voluntarily enters."[9]

The audience also wants to believe an actor plays himself or herself on the screen; in fact, that is the definition of a star. Virtually every article about Grace Kelly's wedding to Prince Rainier in 1956 had one of two story lines. One was that she had played a girl destined to marry a prince in *The Swan* and now she was about to become a princess in real life. The other was that she was the Main Line beautiful bride in *High Society* traveling to Monaco to walk down the aisle in her studio-designed gown.

Most important, films are social barometers of attitudes toward the lavish wedding. Hollywood films are more than merely a reflection of the personal views of the screenwriter or the director. Films are produced and become popular and successful because a major company believes there is an audience for the views the film expresses. Attitudes toward the grand wedding in films may be one step ahead of the culture at large (satirizing such views when they are in fact valued by the audience), but most reflect popular attitudes. In short, most screen movies are mass-marketed fantasy, borrowing from situations familiar to the public either through personal experience or aspiration.

Thus, most wedding movies take place in the United States, and occasionally in England or Australia, between white, childless heterosexuals marrying for the first or second time. Most ceremonies are Protestant; a few are Jewish or Catholic. Outside of independent or foreign films, there are no Muslim, Hindu, or Buddhist ceremonies, and even interfaith ones are rare. The bride usually wears a long, white gown and a veil and carries a bouquet of flowers. Weddings usually occur in churches or hotels, although some take place in the family living room or in the home of a justice of the peace.

As to what Hollywood chooses to say about lavish weddings, the overall verdict depends on the decade one examines and oscillates between two poles: wholehearted acceptance at one end and considerable ambivalence, even contempt, at the other. Some films even manage to offer both points of view. Nor are wedding movies merely about arriving at a judgment about the merits of the lavish wedding. Quite a few tackle larger subjects such as American democracy, gender and class relations, ethnic and regional identity, generational conflict, materialism, and, in the 1990s, homophobia. We focus on some key films, most of which are included as "essential" on entertainment reviewers' lists, although such lists do vary. While we begin with a pivotal film of the 1930s and explore those produced in the decades since, we devote most of our attention to films in the 1990s—*the* decade of the wedding movie. If one of the functions of the wedding film was to venture an opinion as to the acceptability of the lavish wedding, then the many films of the 1990s both endorsed that norm and eventually entered into a debate about the merits of these ceremonies. Mostly, we analyze the messages found close to the surface because these are the ones most likely to be taken in by domestic and global mass audiences. And for the most part, these messages resonate with those presented in etiquette books and/or with the increasing sophistication of public attitudes toward these occasions. Only the rare *auteur* reflects opinions on the lavish wedding totally different from those of the decade in which the film was made.

It Happened One Night (1934) is an appropriate place to begin focused study of the wedding in Hollywood, because it showcased two perfectly paired stars in Claudette Colbert and Clark Gable, a great bias-cut satin wedding gown with a plunging neckline embellished with flowers, and an ambivalent attitude toward the lavish wedding. This type of ceremony was portrayed as nice to look at but not something a girl with character really needed or wanted in order to be happy. Even more important, the film created a whole genre of romantic comedy called "screwball." The term referred to films in which the main characters confronted the problems of life with "cheerful impudence and occasionally a wide streak of lunacy."[10] Screwball comedy shares the basic plotline of the broader genre of romantic comedy: a man and woman are attracted to each other, kept apart by a series of calamities, and finally brought together at the end of the film. The witty repartee between the characters reveals the sexual tension between them. The two are engaged in a classic battle of the sexes, and even in physical battles, since the screwball comedy shares some aspects of slapstick comedy. The sexes are battling for equality, however, since in screwball comedy, a woman needs to earn the man's respect before she can fall for him. And the mutual respect between a man and woman evident in screwball comedy was an entirely new attitude for Hollywood.[11]

In the thirties and early forties, one of the main characters in the focal couple of the screwball comedy was usually extremely wealthy. The main story then was the evolution of the heroine (say, from spoiled brat to true companion) and the tension and subsequent resolution of the tension

Figure 16. *It Happened One Night,* 1934. Courtesy JSP; Shooting Star.

across gender and class lines. In *It Happened One Night,* a rich girl falls for an unemployed journalist, thus reaffirming the Depression-era ideal of a classless society in which sexual chemistry between true equals and decency toward the down-and-out were the marks of true character. The drama of the film takes place on a Miami-to-New York trip by bus, car, and then foot, because only on the road are the heiress and the out-of-work newspaperman removed from their class settings so they can find themselves and learn to appreciate each other. Film critic Elizabeth Kendall writes that director Frank Capra made "a cross-class love affair between two consenting adults, begun on a bus, stand for a renewal of democracy."[12]

Screwball comedy arose because studio heads gave male directors such as Frank Capra, who had already proven they could make successful box-office films, almost free rein to realize their visions. These directors collaborated with female stars, who, instead of portraying heroines who suffered in silence and wept into their hankies, played women who were independent and witty. As Capra's runaway bride in *It Happened One Night,* Colbert represents freedom from marriage to a handsome and debonair but nonetheless stifling playboy. Having decided Gable's character is only interested in a newspaper story and does not love her, Ellie Andrews decides to go through with her society marriage to King Westley. But the audience knows the groom is more interested in show than substance when he arrives on the lawn of her mansion for the wedding in a heliotrope (an early form of helicopter). When the priest asks Ellie if she consents to marry Westley, she bites her lip, shakes her head, hikes up her long train, and sprints across the lawn, her veil streaming in the wind. As Kendall observes, "The runaway bride is one of the most joyous, kinetic and rebellious images produced by mass culture in the Depression."[13] Yet while Ellie Andrews rejects the restrictive life of the upper class and its chief pretense, the wedding of grandeur, Capra allows the audience to see the whole thing. The bride who bolts at the last minute became a cliché but one the audience loved to see in *The Graduate, Private Benjamin, That Old Feeling,* and countless other movies. And of course, the runaway bride would reemerge as one of the most successful box-office images of the late 1990s.

As the Nazis goose-stepped across the heart of Europe, Hollywood in 1939 featured a rash of films that showed life was much simpler in a bygone era. One could not help but notice the films portrayed many decent men marrying in their military uniforms. In the days gone by depicted in *The Old Maid, Wuthering Heights,* and *Gone with the Wind,* all made that year, weddings were opulent and brides wore white silk gowns made by the studio's best designers. In truth, the wedding in *Gone with the Wind* was a minor scene at the beginning of the film and was designed to demonstrate just how far Scarlett would go to make Ashley Wilkes, the man she loved but who had spurned her affections, jealous. Yet Warner Brothers promoted the gown almost as heavily as it did the film. In the South, *Gone With the Wind* sent every bride who had the money looking for a Southern plantation where she could hold her reception. While the symbol of the Lost Cause had existed for white Southerners since the late nineteenth century, bridal salons in Southern department stores seized on Scarlett's gown as a symbol of a distinctively Southern bridal costume: ivory silk, elaborate puffy sleeves, off the shoulder, lots of crinoline, and long, white gloves. Scarlett's wedding gown stood for the Southern belle, a symbol of a lost way of life and the presumed gentility of Southern planters and their ladies.[14] It was ironic, then, that the costumers for the movie had to work to make Scarlett's mother's gown look too big because Scarlett's decision in the film to marry the day before the ceremony was not supposed to leave any time for alterations.[15]

George Cukor's 1940 film *The Philadelphia Story* picked up the screwball wedding movie theme from *It Happened One Night,* but this time the gay director, known for his respect for smart and fast-talking actresses, allowed the grand society wedding to proceed. The lower-class groom in this film is a social climber whom the audience knows is inappropriate for the bride, Tracy Lord, played by Katharine Hepburn, because all he really wants is for the wedding to be publicized in *Spy* magazine, a pulp-celebrity tabloid. With the worst of the Depression over, the audience could enjoy rather than envy a luxurious prewedding ball, the display of silver wedding gifts complete with butler to guard them, and a "ceremony for 93 and a reception for 506" at the Main Line mansion of the socialite bride. The film shared many elements with *It Happened One Night,* most notably a bride who comes to her senses on the morning of the wedding day and (re)marries her true love.

Like Gable in the earlier picture, Tracy's ex-husband, C. K. Dexter Haven (played by the debonair Cary Grant), previously had a fondness for alcohol but has sobered up and proves his noble character when he saves the bride's family from blackmail. In this case, an upper-class rake proves to be the best match. The film demonstrated its ability to perform cultural work by legitimizing the wearing of a designer lavish wedding gown (by Adrian) by a second-time bride, as well as providing a glimpse into the setting for a lavish outdoor luncheon. The film provides a rationale for this decision by having Tracy apologize for eloping with Dexter the first time around and depriving the guests of the type of lavish ceremony to which they believed they were entitled. Apparently, however, it mattered little what the groom wears at a second wedding, because Dexter marries her in a casual jacket, no tie, and pants that do not match his jacket.[16]

Several postwar films such as *The Best Years of Our Lives* (1946) and *June Bride* (1948) showed modest and small ceremonies in the bride's home, and as such were reasonable approximations of the way many couples were marrying. The plot of *June Bride* revolves around a New York City fashion editor trying to bring cosmopolitan style to a small-town Indiana family. The bride whose wedding the magazine had hoped to cover elopes, so the editor then succeeds in transforming the bride's younger sister, a bobby-soxer who had just turned eighteen, into a lovely swan. The fashion editor, another fast-talking Manhattan career woman, also realizes she has always been in love with the (yet another!) journalist sent along to write the story of true love and magical transformation of a dowdy Indiana living room into a lovely floral backdrop for a home ceremony.

In contrast to movies that merely included wedding ceremonies as part of their plot, the box-office smash *Father of the Bride* (1950) focuses on wedding planning from the beginning to the end—and this time it is the family themselves who recognize they have to raise their sights for the wedding, if only to compete with their much wealthier in-laws. Vincente Minnelli directed *Father of the Bride,* and Spencer Tracy, Joan Bennett, and Elizabeth Taylor were the stars. The main character and narrator is a lawyer whose life is turned upside down when his daughter, age twenty, announces at the dinner table that she is engaged. Tracy's character, Stanley Banks, does not want to pay for an expensive wedding and is afraid of losing his little girl. He begins by encouraging his daughter to elope. But his daughter, horrified at the suggestion, replies, "But to get married by the justice of the peace in some dirty little office, with you and Moms not there? I don't know, Pops, but I don't think I'd feel I were really getting married." If that exchange were not enough, Stanley eventually changes his mind because his wife, Ellie, makes him feel terribly guilty about the big wedding she did not have because he did not want a lavish ceremony.

Father of the Bride was one of the most successful films of 1950 and earned Academy Award nominations for Best Picture and Best Actor. In a true case of art imitating life, MGM delayed the release of the film to coincide with Elizabeth Taylor's actual wedding to hotel scion Conrad ("Nicky") Hilton Jr. The Hollywood studio system was at the height of its power. Taylor, like the other stars in the film, was under contract to act exclusively in MGM pictures. The studio controlled the publicity for its stars and liked nothing better than erasing the line between film and reality.[17] In this case, MGM wanted the viewing public to think the on-screen bride was the same as the eighteen-year-old blossoming girl about to marry. The six hundred guests at Taylor's wedding included the heads of all the studios, her co-stars in the film, and managers of the Hilton

Figure 17.   *Father of the Bride,* 1950. Courtesy Shooting Star.

hotels. Taylor's costume designer, Helen Rose, turned out a white satin and lace tight-fitting bodice and pinched-waist gown with tiny seed pearls, close to a duplicate of the one Taylor wore in the film. Rose also designed the yellow organdy dresses and big picture hats for the brides-maids and the beige chiffon outfit for the mother of the bride. Another studio designer, Edith Head, made Taylor's blue silk going-away suit. MGM took care of all of the details of the wedding and the reception as well. An MGM actress sang "Ave Maria" at the Catholic service. The studio's set directors even festooned the church with white carnations and lilies.[18]

While Taylor was on her honeymoon (her first of eight in real life), *Father of the Bride* was playing in theaters across the country. Art Carved diamond rings developed an advertising campaign to sell its product, featuring a photo of Taylor in her gown. A free wedding etiquette pamphlet distributed at movie theaters included the same photo. The week after the film appeared in theaters, a copy of Taylor's gown from the film was on sale in department stores. Again demonstrating the ability of the film to shape popular culture, the tag on the gown said, "As worn by Elizabeth Taylor in *Father of the Bride*."[19] This film was not only important with respect to wedding planning, but probably the most significant film ever made in terms of bridal fashion. Taylor's gown was part of the "sweetheart" style so prevalent in the fifties, one that was an essential statement about the fifties woman. Like all fashion, the sweetheart style fetishized certain parts of the female body. In particular, this style was about breasts (with tight bodices and boning to make them protrude and point), a thin waist, and a hidden but ample pelvis, necessary for childbearing. Edith Head later claimed that despite her 21-inch waist, Elizabeth Taylor was so tightly bound in her cinched-up gown she could hardly breathe. That such gowns were decorative, charming, feminine, and uncomfortable seemed a perfect summary of the prescribed role of women in that decade.[20]

As we noted in chapter 2, Emily Post's etiquette guide had argued that while it was acceptable for upper-middle-class families to set their sights on lavish weddings, members of the lower middle class were best off with a small ceremony in a flower-bedecked living room like the ones in *June Bride* and *The Best Years of Our Lives,* and the working class should not waste money on fancy weddings for their daughters. In *The Catered Affair* (1956), Bette Davis portrays the work-weary mother of the bride who holds the same aspirations for an elaborate wedding for her daughter as Ellie Banks has for hers. Davis's character, a working-class Irish Catholic who lives in the Bronx, is also portrayed as being in an unhappy marriage that had been arranged by her father. Her daughter, played by Debbie Reynolds, is exceedingly practical, not starry-eyed or guilt-inducing. Rather than focus on the foibles of the bride's father, *The Catered Affair* explores the relentless pursuit (and ultimate relinquishment) by Davis's character of the idea that her daughter should have a fancy wedding, even if it means her husband would have to forgo his dream of owning his own taxicab. The film also makes it clear that what motivates Davis's character is her desire to live vicariously through her daughter's ceremony and have the wedding she had always wanted.

True to Emily Post's mandate, and reflecting Hollywood's ambivalence about portraying lavish weddings as proper for working-class families, the daughter in the wedding is quite content to have a simple church ceremony with half a dozen relatives in attendance. Even so, MGM tried to promote the film as a wedding film, but the public, expecting glamour and abundance, recognized the movie's true lesson was the importance of putting practical considerations ahead of romantic ones. Nevertheless, MGM featured the wedding dress the bride tries on, but does not buy, in *Modern Bride*. Another magazine, *Seventeen,* selected *The Catered Affair* as picture of the month in its June 1956 issue. MGM also planned for drive-ins to set aside spaces for real weddings to occur before the picture was shown.[21]

The decline of the studio system in the late 1950s spelled the end of using weddings in films as marketing events. Publicists for stars and films still planted articles about how their clients' off-screen lives imitated the roles they played. But there were no more staged weddings at drive-ins, no more product placements, no sales contests, and no more promotional tie-ins. Nor was the bride's gown especially publicized, except when it was made by a Paris couturier. (In recent years, some veteran stars like Elizabeth Taylor still have attached their names to products such as perfume, but the big stars with box-office appeal, like Julia Roberts, shy away from endorsing products, even those with cultural clout such as bridal dresses or diamond engagement rings.)

Hollywood's fascination with weddings was bolstered by the themes running through popular Broadway musicals of the forties and fifties, such as *Oklahoma, Carousel,* and *Showboat,* and some significant musicals including weddings were also made in the 1960s. Almost every blockbuster show featured a wedding (albeit a low-key one, reflecting the region the show supposedly represented), as well as marvelous songs about love and romance. The 1965 film version of *The Sound of Music,* a great romantic story set amid a family's struggle to escape Austria ahead of Nazi persecution, was almost the end of an era. The wedding scene in the movie encapsulates the transition of Maria from governess to wife and mother, and from country girl to aristocrat. Moreover, the dramatic processional, complete with flowing veil and elegant bridesmaids, contributed to the popularity of floor-length white gowns, which had been a bit shorter in the fifties. The film also underscored the importance of a gorgeous Gothic cathedral as the setting for a dream wedding. Even stars accustomed to being dressed by famous designers were not immune to the magic and the religious epiphanies provided by sumptuous wedding costumes. Julie Andrews commented about her gown, which was designed by Dorothy Jeakins, "I've never felt as beautiful as when I wore that wedding gown. I've never felt prettier before or since. That dress was a miracle."[22]

The second half of the 1960s, however, saw film directors not only portraying ambivalence about marriage but also expressing downright hostility toward institutions such as the family, organized religion, and the military—all of which had been mythologized by the studios since the end of World War II. The film that most clearly expressed the protestor's view of big lavish weddings—that such ceremonies were traditional and that tradition was stifling—was *The Graduate* (1967), starring Katharine Ross, Anne Bancroft, and Dustin Hoffman. While the film borrowed elements of the standard runaway bride movie, it did so with more drama and cynicism and less comedy. Essentially, by depicting the corruption and decadence of the parents' generation, the film echoed Mario Savio's warning, "Don't trust anyone over thirty." The musical sound track, with songs by Simon and Garfunkel, was also a generational call to arms.

At the end of the film, the protagonist, played by Dustin Hoffman, attacks the church while a traditional wedding is in progress. This action represented an explicit rejection of the lavish wedding and the emptiness of the loveless marriage that would merely make a woman financially secure. The heroine, dressed in a long white gown and veil, sees her rejected lover appear at the second-floor window of the church where she has just said "I do." To free her, Hoffman's character picks up a wooden crucifix and uses it both as a battering ram and to bar the door to the church to ensure their escape. The mother of the bride tells her daughter it is too late to run away. The daughter speaks for her generation in telling her mother, "Not for me." The couple's low-cost getaway on a public bus combines the critique of consumer spending with the critique of marriage, religion, and the lavish wedding. On the bus, Hoffman and Ross sit quietly, unsmilingly, and even somberly. So while the film ends with the lovers united, it also reflects the turbulence in American society in that the couple is joined in uncertainty, alienation, and puzzlement about their future.[23]

Robert Altman's 1978 film *A Wedding* belongs in the category of broad satire and comedy akin to *The Graduate,* even though it appeared much later and was not intended as a generational call to war. Although it was the first film in which all of the action takes place at the wedding and reception, it expresses the view that the lavish wedding is vulgar, that family life is filled with secrets people carefully cover up, and that repressed sexual yearnings are bound to break out at such events.[24] The movie unites the cross-class screwball comedy with the chaos of a wedding-planning movie. The daughter of a prosperous trucker is marrying an Italian boy whose father is apparently connected to the Mafia. The action of this film opens with a lavish wedding ceremony, complete with brass band, choir, uniformed ushers, and six bridesmaids in floppy hats and matching peach gowns. The Episcopalian priest is a doddering fool who cannot remember the liturgy, and the bride, with her mouth full of braces, seems to have one foot in the world of bubblegum rock. The wedding planner, played by Geraldine Chaplin, keeps the reception moving despite an electricity outage and the chaos around her. But from her passionate kiss of the bride at the reception, we learn that she is a closet lesbian. Then there is the bride's sister, a nymphomaniac, who announces she is pregnant and carrying the child of the groom. Clearly, Altman meant the lavish wedding to be revealed as a shallow ritual, one that should pale in comparison to the simultaneous death of the family matriarch in the upstairs bedroom.

The upsurge of interest in ethnic identity in the 1970s, prompted in part by growing racial consciousness among African Americans, led both to simultaneous condemnation of the lavish wedding and to loving nostalgia for it as a symbol of an ethnic community and a vanishing way of life. In that sense, the nostalgic impulse resembled that of Southerners attracted to the Lost Cause myth in *Gone With the Wind*. Jewish writers and filmmakers, sometimes accused of group self-hate, were embarrassed by the big splurge of some Jewish weddings. By emphasizing extreme close-ups, eccentric characters, noise, and excessive floral decoration, *Goodbye, Columbus; The Heartbreak Kid;* and *Private Benjamin* all managed to satirize the status-striving and materialism of upper-middle-class Jews. *Goodbye, Columbus* (1969) depicts an upper-class Jewish wedding, which proves to be an epiphany for the boyfriend (played by Richard Benjamin) of the groom's sister (played by Ali McGraw). As a library worker in the Bronx who has been fairly aimless since completing his army service, Benjamin's character realizes he will never fit into her world. In addition, the wedding is mocked as an orgy of excess, with Ali

McGraw's character becoming drunk and whiny at the reception.[25] *The Heartbreak Kid* (1972) begins with a Jewish middle-class wedding and ends with a WASP middle-class one, with Charles Grodin as the hapless groom in both ceremonies. The idle chatter at the receptions, which centers on what people do for a living, makes it evident the groom is bored stiff and that, as a working-class New Yorker who sells athletic equipment, he will be out of place in both groups. Moreover, both the first and second bride seem oblivious to the fact that the groom is a terrible match for them. Grodin's character leaves the first bride after three days, and the audience is left to believe that his marriage to the second will not last much longer.

In contrast, *Private Benjamin* combines a depiction of a typical Jewish upper-middle-class wedding with the reemergence of the runaway bride. The ceremony that opens the film is followed by a scene of the groom insisting the bride perform oral sex in a car in the parking lot at the reception. After her husband dies on her wedding night, Judy Benjamin joins the army and discovers her inner strength by participating in war games and serving as a supply purchaser for NATO. At the end of the film, her wealthy new French fiancé has railroaded her into signing a prenuptial agreement and has revealed he is cheating on her. During her wedding, Judy Benjamin realizes she does not want to give up her new-found individuality, slugs the groom, and runs away in her wedding gown before she takes her vows.

Unlike the wedding movies about Jewish families, Italian American filmmakers tend to see materialism in the service of the wedding as an expression of a family ideal. The weddings of Italians or Ukranians are also often portrayed as symbols of "life before the fall," the happy times loving families share before tragedy strikes. Thus, the blowout for Connie, the only daughter of a Mafia don in the 1972 film *The Godfather,* represents the values of honor, the benevolent rule of a strong father, and family solidarity. Director Francis Ford Coppola shot the scenes of Godfather Don Corleone in his shuttered study granting requests, because a Sicilian father must do so on his daughter's wedding day. By contrast, the outdoor wedding reception is bathed in sunlight.

The Godfather also included another wedding halfway through the film. Michael Corleone, the son of the godfather, marries in Sicily while hiding from his father's enemies. He and his beautiful Sicilian bride,

Appolonia, dance together outdoors in a scene that evokes the simplicity of village life and the groom's romantic and sexual longing for his beautiful bride. Soon after the wedding night, the groom's enemies blow up his car, killing the new bride. Michael returns to America and remarries, but his second wedding ceremony to a woman not of Italian descent, which recognizes the inevitable rather than representing joy and ethnic affirmation, is not even shown.[26] Likewise, the Ukrainian Orthodox wedding scene in a small Pennsylvania town in *The Deer Hunter* (1978) was also intended to symbolize a world that would disintegrate when its young men went off to fight in the Vietnam War.

Most of the 1980s were notable for the marked absence of weddings on the silver screen, even as the wedding of Princess Diana in 1981 and the yuppie consumption ethic worked its way into wedding imaginations and aspirations.[27] In fact, all of the top box-office films in that decade were action or adventure movies with male stars, such as *Taxi Driver* or *Raging Bull.* Eighties story lines typically focused on the travails of action-adventure heroes such as Bruce Willis, Harrison Ford, and Arnold Schwarzenegger; there was little room for white gowns and bouquets in such hypermasculine worlds.

The portrayal of weddings on television was another story, however. Most of the viewers of popular television programs, especially of daytime soap operas, were women. Television producers understood that inserting a wedding into a soap opera or comedy meant increased ratings during crucial sweeps periods. Of course, one of the best examples of this success occurred with the long-awaited wedding of Laura Baldwin and Luke Spencer on *General Hospital,* even though Luke had actually raped Laura in the serial years before. Fourteen million viewers watched the wedding in 1981, setting a new audience record for daytime television at the time.[28] Other programs soon began to realize the benefits of building weddings into their plotlines, and just as had been true on radio programs of the 1930s and 1940s, they proved to be compelling plot devices.[29]

After ignoring its female audience members with heavy action-oriented fare during most of the 1980s, the success of two comedies helped Hollywood realize it was profitable to lure them back. The box-office receipts and critical acclaim of both the Italian ethnic romance *Moonstruck* in 1987 and *When Harry Met Sally* in 1989 made it clear screwball comedies with smart women protagonists still had wide appeal. *Moonstruck* begins with a marriage proposal by one brother, who looks ridiculous as he groans to propose on bended knee in a restaurant. The film ends with his maimed but more passionate (and therefore, the movie implies, more desirable) brother proposing to the same woman in her family's kitchen. It also is one of the last films to depict ethnic wedding traditions; for more than a decade since the release of *When Harry Met Sally*, WASP ceremonies have dominated the big screen. One of the key elements to the structure of *When Harry Met Sally* is the fact that not one but two yuppie couples get married—and both couples feature men and women over thirty who have cohabited, been divorced, and/or had affairs—but who all have lavish weddings anyway. And at the end of the film, Harry and Sally describe their own beautiful wedding, and their enormous coconut cake, in loving detail. The success of these two films, among others, marked the return of the "new romance," in contrast to the more sexually oriented comedies and Woody Allen "nervous romances" of the 1960s and 1970s.[30]

If Hollywood was going to engage in a turnaround and embrace romantic screwball comedies, it was at least going to hedge its bets by casting well-known comedic actors in these films. Capitalizing on his successful portrayal of a stressed-out father in the 1989 film *Parenthood*, Touchstone Pictures cast Steve Martin in the 1991 remake of *Father of the Bride* and made $89 million for its efforts. While the original film was a situation comedy about the chaos that breaks out while planning a wedding, the 1991 remake contains even more slapstick while updating 1950s attitudes toward the wedding and marriage. Because the film focuses on the title character rather than the romantic leads, it does not quite qualify as a screwball comedy; however, it contains elements of slapstick consistent with Martin's roots as a stand-up comedian. The modifications of this film from its 1950 version neatly capture the social changes in race and gender relations, the shift from the proper ceremony to the perfect one, and the growth of the lavish wedding as a middle-class entitlement rather than a luxury.

True to its title, the main focus of the 1950 version centered around Stanley Banks, the father of Kay, who announces her engagement to a "wonderful boy" whom the family has never met. In the 1950 version, the two sources of angst for Stanley Banks—in this order—are the fact that his daughter is leaving home and the realization that he must pay for an extravagant wedding. Because the film places more emphasis on the father-daughter relationship than the wedding planning itself, the original film has been characterized as having Freudian overtones.[31] The most dramatic departure of the new version from the old is that the source of misery for George Banks, Martin's character, is not losing his daughter but his inability to cope with the escalating cost of the wedding.

What is striking is how differently the films portray attitudes toward the lavish wedding in 1950 versus 1991, despite the fact that the basic plot structure in both versions of the film remains the same. Act I in each begins with a soliloquy by the father after the reception is over, in which he laments about the money and effort expended for the wedding. The film is then told in a flashback. In the remainder of Act I, the bride announces her engagement and the prospective in-laws meet. Act II begins when the family sits down to discuss the actual wedding plans. The action shifts to prewedding rituals and the selection of goods and services for the wedding, with the father grousing about each item. The act ends with a fight between the bride and groom, which results in the wedding almost being called off. In the 1950 version, Stanley Banks does not intervene in the fight; however, in 1991, Martin's character pleads the groom's case to his daughter, paradoxically saving the wedding day he has complained about for so long. Act III begins on the actual wedding day with a reverential depiction of the wedding ceremony and glamorous reception. The tension in this act stems from the father's inability to kiss the bride before she leaves. But when she calls before leaving for her honeymoon and tells her father she loves him, he is finally happy, and in both versions, the father of the bride collapses with his wife amid the leftover clutter from the reception.

By the 1991 version, certain racial and gender relationships have disappeared from the Banks household. Delilah, the uniformed black maid waiting on the Banks family at their table in 1950, is long gone; the newer Bankses have no live-in servant. However, the Salvadoran immigrant who works for their wealthy future in-laws—as well as the mansion with a foyer that Banks claims is large enough to hold his entire house—are the two key indicators to the audience of the in-laws' enormous wealth. Moreover, rather than feature a stay-at-home bride who at twenty years old does not attend college or hold a job (as in the original version), the remake presents Banks's daughter as a graduate student in architecture who returns from her studies in Rome and considers the groom's gift of a blender a sexist insult.

The mother's role is updated as well; in the 1991 version, Nina Banks has her own successful consulting business. Although her husband complains about the lavish wedding, Nina does not need to engage in any special pleading to justify the occasion. This lack of manipulation suggests two things: Nina has a more egalitarian relationship with her husband than was true of the Bankses in the original version, and the father of the bride in the 1991 version knows that attempting to argue for a simple wedding is pointless. In fact, the 1991 father does not have enough power in the family to suggest, as did Spencer Tracy, that his daughter elope. Nina merely repeatedly reminds her husband that they can afford a big wedding and that "a wedding is a big deal . . . everybody seems to understand that but you." The modern mother of the bride never discusses her own wedding and seems not to need to live vicariously through her daughter's "big day."

Not surprisingly, the real differences in these movies are found in Act II, where most of the actual wedding planning takes place. George Banks's antics to the contrary, the 1991 version reflects a father much less resistant to spending money than Tracy's character. For all of his protests, Martin's character quickly succumbs to pressure to pay for goods and services he believes are ridiculously expensive, even agreeing to spend $1,200 on a wedding cake after his wife tells him, "This is what weddings cost." But in the 1951 version, even the mother wants to hold down the expense of the reception, asking the caterer for a menu that features sandwiches and ice cream, and concurring with her husband that a cake (then $400) can be eliminated. Nina Banks has much more power in this marriage than her fifties counterpart, and although men still worry more about the expenses of the wedding than women, women rarely, if ever, have to cut back on their plans to please men.

Perhaps the most dramatic shift in the two movies is the movement away from the concerns expressed about having a "proper" wedding in the 1950 version to one that emphasizes creating the magic or perfect event. In the 1991 version, even nature cooperates: it snows for the first time in decades in Southern California the night before the wedding, prompting George Banks to tell his daughter he will remember that evening forever. The 1950s emphasis on "proper" is encapsulated in a long scene that depicts the wedding rehearsal, with Stanley Banks losing his temper over the fact that members of the wedding party are absent, late, or apathetic. That night, his daughter confides she is intimidated about appearing in the church in front of "all those people." In the next scene, which seems borrowed from a Hitchcock film, Stanley has a nightmare and sees himself trapped on a church aisle that apparently has turned to rubber during the processional.

The scenes that pertain to the propriety of the wedding were excised from the 1991 version and replaced by a montage showing the Banks family buying items for the wedding. While a few wedding-related goods, such as the cake and trousseau, are mentioned in the 1950 version, the 1991 home reception features a newly planted tulip border in January, three live swans, ice sculptures, a sit-down seafood dinner, and rose petals to throw at the couple. Moreover, the cost of each guest at the reception escalates from $3.75 a head in the original version (for a total of $1,875) to $250 per guest in the remake (for a whopping $125,000). The updated Banks family also interacts with a slew of wedding experts—interior decorators, electricians, gardeners, salesmen, and chefs. And of course, there is the effeminate consultant with a central European accent, Franck Eggelhoffer, who together with his ponytailed ethnic-hybrid sidekick, an Asian American assistant named Howard Weinstein, almost tears apart the Banks home in his fervor to create the perfect wedding.

Yet even though the wedding features a staggering price tag, the 1991 version never satirizes the event. Instead, the father of the bride is a Dagwood Bumstead, a buffoon, who is clueless as to the importance of this occasion both in his own family and in American culture as a whole. Fool that he is, he actually suggests the wedding be held at the Pit Barbeque restaurant, and fails to realize that his "genuine black Armani tux" is actually a navy blue polyester knockoff, something even a waiter at the reception recognizes. The mother and daughter want to spend extravagantly because the family has the money, because they are trying to demonstrate their status to the wife's business clients, because they are competing with their very wealthy in-laws, and because everyone, including the father of the bride, comes to accept the idea that this is the type of wedding to which every woman in America is entitled.

If the success of the 1991 version of *Father of the Bride* was predictable because it had two bankable American stars, that of the British film *Four Weddings and a Funeral* (1994) seemed to take even the filmmakers by surprise. Made for $4 million, it grossed over $240 million worldwide. As a study in English upper-class weddings, the film skewers these events almost as much as Robert Altman did American weddings but still presents them as inevitable and ultimately desired by most of the participants. Sacred cows are slain as rapidly as rice falls on the departing bride and groom: gold wedding rings are forgotten and replaced with multicolored plastic hearts; a bridesmaid's underwear is exposed as she walks down the aisle; a novice priest blesses the couple "in the name of the Father, Son, and Holy Spigot"; a bride and groom consummate their marriage in a hotel room while Hugh Grant's character crouches in the closet. But these antics aside, the characters describe their boredom with the expected, even clichéd aspects of these weddings. Before one ceremony, Grant's character asks, "Right. Who is it today?" By the end of the film the audience can sympathize, because except for one wedding at a Scottish castle where the groom wears a kilt, the churches, receptions, guests, and attendants depicted are literally interchangeable. In fact, the characters are portrayed as having almost no life outside of either preparing for weddings or attending them.

From our perspective, the most interesting aspect of *Four Weddings* is not that two charming and beautiful people end up together, but the fact that within this upper-class subculture the elaborate wedding has become an accepted part of the weekend routine. By repetitively depicting the same elaborate ritual elements (e.g., the church ceremony, sit-down dinner, live music, and vintage cars) and by associating them with university-educated types with the right British accents, the film endorses these products and services as requirements for upper-echelon weddings even as it lampoons items such as the obscenely priced African pygmy statue on one bride's gift registry.

True, the film ends with a photomontage depicting the elaborate weddings of the ensemble characters, including a gay man and his new lover who may or may not be having a commitment ceremony. Still, the hero and heroine take their own antivows on a rain-drenched London street *not* to marry but to remain together for the rest of their lives. The trailer of the movie, which included the slogan "A film with a message—don't get married," reinforced a pledge in favor of committed cohabitation.[32]

Figure 18. *Four Weddings and a Funeral,* 1994. Courtesy Manifesto Films/Shooting Star.

Instead of a wedding scene, the couple is shown smiling with their young child in the final shot of the photomontage, and no wedding rings are visible. Ritual is for others, while true commitment is expressed through self-marrying. This film is also notable for the appearance of Hugh Grant as the sensitive new man. While not the marrying kind himself, he is the first of an increasing group of men in films who assist the bride with wedding planning to some extent.

Almost every year since the success of *Four Weddings,* a Hollywood blockbuster has debuted in which a wedding or weddings have been an integral part of the story. Moreover, in 1997, 1999, and 2000, a "wedding movie" finished in the top ten U.S. box-office successes of the year, and *My Best Friend's Wedding* (1997) and *Runaway Bride* (1999) rank among the top one hundred best-grossing films of all time. While most of these movies are screwball comedies, each offers its own unique commentary on the ritual. Unlike the films of the 1970s, most wedding films of the 1990s contain little blatant critique of the event. Moreover, most legitimize the need for an ever-expanding support staff—coordinators, wedding singers, bakers, salon owners, caterers, and waitresses—to create the wedding. And no film in the 1990s questioned the right to have lavish events, or the money required to create them, regardless of whether the bride was a waitress, a clerk in a hardware store, a thief, or the daughter of a Chicago multimillionaire. In short, the class distinctions with regard to who is entitled to a lavish wedding, which were so much a part of films in the 1950s, disappeared entirely in 1990s films. The wedding movies that grossed over $50 million worldwide between 1994 and 2001 are included in the table below.[33]

The Australian film *Muriel's Wedding* (1994) is a Cinderella story of sorts. It portrays the lavish wedding as having a much more complicated and psychotherapeutic function in the life of the title character, as if to prove that the indie film can take the same material as Hollywood and make it subversive. The film features an overweight ugly duckling–high school dropout who has a desperate desire for a big, lavish wedding in order to prove to her so-called friends and family that she is a "new person." Muriel papers her bedroom walls with photographs from bridal magazines as an escape route from the real world, where her father belittles her. Muriel's supposed friends from her hometown are so cruel that when she catches a wedding bouquet, they order her to give it to someone who at least "has a chance of getting married." In employing wedding fantasy as therapy for the emotional abuse she has suffered, Muriel races around to bridal shops in Sydney, has her picture taken in wedding gowns, and keeps these photos in a wedding album hidden under her bed. While at her job at a Sydney video store, she repeatedly watches tapes of the royal nuptials of Prince Charles and Princess Diana. Eventually, Muriel surpasses even her own fantasies as the bride in the ultimate event—the "celebrity wedding"—in which she marries a South African swimmer so he can compete for Australia in the Olympics. Yet taken as a whole, the message of the film is that genuine love between women friends is better than an arranged marriage, even if the marriage did begin with a fabulous wedding. Muriel leaves her celebrity husband to care for a female friend disabled by cancer, an ending that has left some critics to wonder whether the two become lovers.[34]

Although Muriel's marriage to the swimmer falls apart and the film portrays the Australian middle class as filled with hypocrisy, adultery, and deeply disturbed women, writer-director P. J. Hogan is no Robert Altman. Although he does make Muriel seem pathetic for caring so deeply about having a lavish wedding, in the end he never ridicules the actual

TABLE 1 Revenues for Recent Films Depicting Lavish Weddings

Film Title	Year of Release	Domestic Box Office (Millions)	International Box Office (Millions)	Total Worldwide Grosses (Millions)	Studio	Stars
Four Weddings and a Funeral	1994	$52.7	$191.4	$244.1	Gramercy	Hugh Grant, Andie MacDowell
Muriel's Wedding	1994	$15.1	$42.4	$57.5	Miramax	Toni Collette, Rachel Griffiths
While You Were Sleeping	1995	$81.0	$100.9	$181.9	Hollywood Pictures	Sandra Bullock, Bill Pullman, Peter Gallagher
My Best Friend's Wedding	1997	$126.8	$172.1	$298.9	Sony	Julia Roberts, Cameron Diaz, Rupert Everett
In & Out	1997	$63.8	$21.0	$84.8	Paramount	Kevin Kline, Joan Cusack
The Wedding Singer	1998	$80.2	$41.4	$121.6	New Line	Adam Sandler, Drew Barrymore
Runaway Bride	1999	$152.2	$129.5	$281.7	Paramount	Julia Roberts, Richard Gere, Joan Cusack
Meet the Parents	2000	$166.2	$129.3	$295.5	Dreamworks	Robert De Niro, Ben Stiller
The Wedding Planner	2001	$94.7	$34.3	$129.0	Columbia	Jennifer Lopez, Matthew McConaughey

ceremony. Even his choice to play a popular song by Abba as Muriel walks down the aisle seems more of a reflection of Muriel's exuberance than of sacrilege. Muriel may not be a beautiful bride in the film, but she is portrayed sympathetically. As a single woman with no prospects, she breaks the rules and tries on dresses she is not really entitled to wear, but the audience roots for her just the same. Muriel, the film says, just wants what every girl wants—and even a sham of a wedding is better than no wedding at all. Moreover, fulfilling her dream provides such a boost to Muriel's self-esteem that she is able to be liberated from her old sense of self, embrace her individuality, and recognize that in the end, she does not need a wedding, or for that matter, even a man.

While You Were Sleeping (1995) was the first Hollywood film produced during this period and one of the least innovative in this enormously successful collection. Nevertheless, it possesses three elements that pervaded Hollywood wedding films from 1994 to 2001: romance, two bankable stars, and a runaway bride. The film depicts an American Cinderella story of an orphaned girl whose fantasy life helps her escape from her bleak job as a subway token collector for the Chicago Transit Authority. Like Cinderella, Lucy dreams of being rescued by a rich handsome man, one who never sees her as he drops his token in her booth on the CTA platform where he waits for his train. Because this is a Hollywood vehicle, the star, Sandra Bullock, gets her man, although as was true in *Moonstruck,* she ends up realizing it is the brother of the man she originally wanted who is the true prince. He also gives her a nice diamond engagement ring and the honeymoon of her dreams (the actual wedding is not shown). But first the heroine almost undergoes a ceremony no bride would want: a wedding to a groom she realizes she does not love in a hospital chapel while he is still hooked up to an IV. At this point in the film, Lucy has no engagement ring, there is no father to walk her down the aisle, and she has had no rehearsal or dinner the day before. She even forgets to take off her coat as the wedding march plays. Both she and the audience know that even though the man she thought she loved has apparently fallen for her, this cannot be her "real" wedding. In yet another twist to the saga of the runaway bride, she objects to her own ceremony and runs from the hospital. At the end of the film, after she marries her true love, they ride off on a Chicago Transit Authority train featuring a "Just Married" sign, while in a voiceover, Lucy dreamily describes her honeymoon in Florence.

After the success of *Muriel's Wedding,* Hogan moved to Hollywood to direct *My Best Friend's Wedding* in 1997, a romantic comedy with none of the deep psychological undertones of his previous film. This time he had a big budget and a big star, Julia Roberts, who began her run as a bride in films with *Steel Magnolias* in 1989. By the end of the 1990s, Roberts had earned the title "queen of the wedding movies," even though, ironically, her only real-life wedding at the time (to musician Lyle Lovett in 1993) took place in a small church in Marion, Indiana, while Lovett was on tour. In fact, one of the most bankable female stars in Hollywood had only a few close friends in attendance, went barefoot, and wore no makeup at her wedding. But in *My Best Friend's Wedding,* Roberts plays a Brown University graduate and New York City food critic who flies to Chicago to sabotage the wedding of her best male friend, whom she realizes she loves after he tells her he is marrying someone else. The four-day wedding weekend in this film is even more splendid than the Banks's grand affair of 1991—but then, this father of the bride is part-owner of the Chicago White Sox. Despite the fact that the bride-to-be is too good to be true, her lavish affair is not belittled because she and the groom are shown as perfectly suited for each other. The film does differ significantly from those that preceded it in the 1990s, because "for once, the female hero does not solve her problems by becoming a bride."[35] Still, the star ends up with a friend but not a lover, as her gay male editor flies in from New York to rescue her from loneliness at the wedding reception.

While *My Best Friend's Wedding* was the first hit to discuss the intersection of homosexual and heterosexual worlds at the wedding, the plot of *In & Out* (1997) made this topic, more than the wedding itself, the central theme. As the film opens, high school English teacher Howard Brackett, played by Kevin Kline, is preparing to marry Emily Montgomery, played by Joan Cusack. At the same time, a former student "outs" Brackett during his Academy Award acceptance speech, throwing the small Indiana town where Brackett lives into turmoil. While Howard insists he is not gay and that there will be a wedding, two crucial scenes help the audience discover his true sexuality even before Howard does. First, Howard admires Emily in her wedding gown. While this was coded as acceptable straight male behavior by a nongroom in *Four Weddings and a Funeral*, in this film, Howard's visit to the bridal salon seems not only effeminate but also to foreshadow doom, because he has seen Emily in her gown before the wedding day. Second, instead of watching pornography and drinking heavily at his bachelor party, Brackett gets into a barroom brawl over whether Barbra Streisand was too old to play the title character in *Yentl.*

As was true of many films with gay characters in the 1990s, the movie was actually more about tolerance for gays and less about the importance of weddings. But at the same time, *In & Out* reinforced two important wedding-related norms to the moviegoing public. The first pertained to the steps the contemporary bride must take to achieve the ideal body image for her wedding day. One main point of discussion throughout the film is how much weight Emily has lost before her wedding day. At one point, she comments, "I didn't want to waddle down the aisle." But after being deserted at the altar, Emily enters a bar in her wedding dress and announces she wants "to eat, to gorge." A second norm is that it is never too late in life for a woman to have her lavish wedding, even if she is already married. At the beginning of the film, Howard's mother reacts to the news about his possible homosexuality by telling him she needs "some beauty and some music and some place cards before I die." In the end, Howard's mother has the full-bore lavish wedding and reception she always wanted—in the form of Hollywood's first vow-renewal ceremony.

Of course, the most inclusive message would have been that everyone, regardless of sexuality, is entitled to a lavish wedding. So what about a ceremony for Howard and his male lover? Hollywood stops short of portraying a gay wedding in a movie intended for a mainly heterosexual audience. One reviewer observed that "as a gay-themed comedy with mass-market aspirations, *In & Out* feels it has to be cautious."[36] Only independent filmmakers, such as the team responsible for *Chicks in White Satin,*[37] the 1993 Academy Award–winning documentary about a lesbian wedding, felt free to explore the topic. Once again, however, television proved more progressive than film in this regard—because less money is at stake—with several successful situation comedies such as *Friends* and *Will & Grace* depicting same-sex ceremonies in the middle and late 1990s.

While the *In & Out* audience realized Kline's character was gay because he was too involved in the wedding planning, the heterosexual male hero of 1998's *The Wedding Singer* could engage in these activities without the audience questioning his manhood. This shift in portrayal was not because attitudes toward male participation in wedding planning had changed but because Robbie, the title character, is perceived as being in the wedding business, and thus knows how to get the best deals. Even so, the shopping activities in which Robbie participates are all of the more masculine variety; he bargains with retailers, investigates his "competition" (other wedding singers), and makes the limo driver demonstrate his skill on an obstacle course.

Although released in 1998, the film was set in 1985 and was an ode to New Wave music and an affirmation of the decade known for big hair and a "greed is good" ethic. Once Robbie is jilted on his wedding day, he becomes depressed and angry and begins to destroy other people's weddings and his own livelihood as well. But he emerges from his funk by helping Julia, played by Drew Barrymore, a waitress he meets while singing at weddings, plan her own nuptials. Her fiancé, Glen, is a junk bond salesman on Wall Street who cheats on her regularly, dresses in pastel sportswear in homage to Don Johnson in *Miami Vice,* and even wants Julia to settle for a quickie Vegas wedding. Like the true heroine in romantic films, in the end Julia does not settle for the safest financial bet but chooses the most decent and romantic man.

After a decade of embracing the lavish wedding, films began to reflect a different attitude that was gaining popularity among the public, that personalization of one's wedding was more important than size and lavishness. *Runaway Bride* (1999) marked a turning point in the depiction of weddings because it was the first to express ambivalence about the necessity for a big wedding, even as it shows the title character almost participating in five ceremonies occurring over a decade. *Runaway Bride* also re-creates one of the central romantic characters from *It Happened One Night,* the cynical and unemployed journalist. Publicity for the film was predictable: it played off the similarity between Julia Roberts's real-life marital woes and those of her character. (In a very real sense, Roberts had been a runaway bride herself, since she had jilted actor Kiefer Sutherland just three days before their planned $500,000 wedding in 1991.) The film generated much advance press, most of it positive, because it reunited Roberts with Richard Gere, her romantic partner in the widely successful 1991 film *Pretty Woman.* Although that earlier film did not depict a wedding, it distinctly contained a Cinderella theme. At the end of *Pretty Woman,* Roberts's character refuses to move in with Gere as a sexual partner, telling him she "wants the fairy tale," which means marriage. And of course, in both that film and in *Runaway Bride* she gets it.

Never in Hollywood history has one single film proved to be such a window display of wedding style and gowns as *Runaway Bride.* The videos of the previous nuptials of Roberts's character, Maggie, play like a primer on the cultural variations of the wedding. The first is a "Grateful Dead" ceremony that features a tattooed Maggie jumping on a trampoline. It is followed by a "high church" ceremony complete with flower girls, bridesmaids, and a processional to "Ave Maria." The third attempt is an outdoor ceremony, where Maggie rides down the aisle on horseback. In the end, she realizes these were not her wedding visions but were in keeping with the grooms' identities. In finding herself, she defines her own wedding style and discovers she "would like to get married on a weekday, when everybody's at work." She and Ike, Gere's character, are married on a hilltop with just themselves and a minister, but guests suddenly and joyfully appear on the horizon. Roberts wears a new and different, off-the-shoulder, long lavish wedding gown, her sixth in the film, for the event. And after the ceremony she and Ike gallop off, side by side, on horseback.

Of course, the decision to have so many weddings is an expensive one. But by the end of the go-go '90s, the days of *The Catered Affair,* in which brides agonized over spending money for one gown, were long gone. One bridal store owner discourages Maggie from choosing a thousand-dollar gown, remarking it is a lot for her to spend on "one of her weddings" since she is unlikely to end up actually being married in it. By insisting it is her right to purchase the gown of her choice, the cynical Ike proves he is not only chivalrous, but the right man for Maggie. Then in a scene almost directly stolen from *Four Weddings and a Funeral,* he falls in love with her as she "swishes like a bell" while modeling the gown for him. (Of course, when she does eventually marry Ike, she wears a different gown, bolstering the social norm that it is bad luck for the groom to see the bride in her wedding gown prior to the ceremony.)

Runaway Bride also illustrates for the audience the importance of dramatic and unique marriage proposals. In one scene, Maggie shows Ike all of the engagement rings she has received and describes the romantic and magical ways her (supposedly) future grooms proposed to her. For instance, one ring was placed in a cocoon at a butterfly farm in St. Thomas, and another fiancé proposed on a baseball scoreboard. In the end, though, after running away from Ike standing at the altar, it is Maggie who proposes to Ike by turning in to him her running shoes.

The surprise proposal is repeated in the opening scenes of *Meet the Parents* (2000), in which Ben Stiller plays Greg Focker. In the middle of Greg's proposal to his girlfriend, she is distracted by a phone call from her sister. The sister announces her own plans to marry and describes how her fiancé has done the right thing by first asking permission from their old-fashioned father. While staying with his girlfriend's parents, Focker rains chaos and disaster on the older daughter's wedding. He breaks the bride's nose two days before the ceremony, floods the site of the reception with sewage, brings home a cat that tears the wedding gown to shreds, and burns down a handcrafted altar where the bride and groom were to exchange vows. Yet the bride and groom marry under the charred altar, even with her broken nose and pink suit bought off the rack. In a departure for a genre that had always treated weddings reverentially, this scene conveys the message that trappings were not all that necessary after all and that a couple can marry even when their "dream day" is ruined.

In the end, Greg decides to leave his girlfriend because he has made such a fool of himself, so in this film it is the prospective groom who is the runaway. To be sure, there is a huge cultural gap between a neurotic, urban, middle-class Jew who is a male nurse and his suburban, WASP, ex–CIA agent future father-in-law. But the film ends up being closer to *In & Out* than to other wedding movies of the nineties, because the classic screwball couple in *Meet the Parents* actually comprises the prospective groom and his father-in-law, mismatched by class and religion, and because the father maintains the view that a male nurse would not be a good provider for his "Pam-cake." But once the father-in-law discovers Greg's potential lifetime earning capacity (in the form of his high MCAT scores), he holds out the two-carat diamond ring that Greg has bought for his daughter and asks, "Will you be my son-in-law?"

The 2001 film *The Wedding Planner,* starring Jennifer Lopez and

Matthew McConaughey, also makes a strong statement about the acceptability of smaller, personalized ceremonies. The fact that two back-to-back hits gave the lavish wedding a gentle nudge seemed to indicate Hollywood screenwriters were advocating something celebrity weddings were also demonstrating—that privacy and intimacy were just as chic as opulence. The opening scene combines the standard chaos of the screwball comedy with the military efficiency of a wedding planner who coordinates expensive weddings for very rich families. The film revolves around planning a wedding for a female business owner and a male pediatrician. The boozy, self-centered mother of the bride cares only about performing a musical number at the reception, and her narcissism and alcoholism explain why her daughter needs a wedding planner in the first place. Likewise, the bride's *nouveau riche* father merely wants his daughter's wedding to be more extravagant than those his business associates have hosted.

But as the Wedding Guide 2001 Web site notes, the movie actually makes a strong case for hiring a wedding planner and presents these professionals as lifesavers for affluent and busy clients. Lopez's character, Mary, is portrayed as a savior, not an incompetent, a cynic, or a gouger. Wearing a discreet headset and reaching into a Batman-like toolkit, Mary sobers up one father of the bride so swiftly and efficiently that the audience is meant to marvel at her ingenuity. Contributing to the portrayal of wedding planners as highly trained, rational professionals, the employees of the wedding planning corporation speak to each other in the language of a law firm: Mary wants to snag big-name "accounts" and "make partner."

As was true of most of the wedding movies in the 1990s, the film is flush with high-end product placements, even though the wedding gown itself is not one of them. The bride, the groom, and Mary whisk along the coastal highway in a Land Rover to Napa Valley vineyards, San Francisco churches are made over to look like enchanted forests, and life-sized sculptures represent the perfect symbol of a couple's union. But while *Runaway Bride*'s Maggie wants a hilltop ceremony for two, Lopez's character confesses to yearning for a simple ceremony on the beach. She fears divorce and claims she can pin down how long a couple will stay together based on the song they choose for their first dance at the reception. Convinced she will never find her Prince Charming, Mary seems ready to marry at city hall, a last-resort wedding option for those entering into loveless unions. In the end, she reunites with the pediatrician, a good dancer and former client who has captured her heart. Yet the director leaves the simple beach ceremony to the viewers' imaginations, and in the true spirit of the romantic comedy, the screen fades to black with a kiss, not a wedding.

In short, the wedding films of the nineties can be reduced to some rather simple lessons about weddings, romance, and consumer culture, summarized as follows:

> *Four Weddings and a Funeral:* Lavish weddings are inescapable, but true love is a highly personal commitment that may not require marriage after all.
>
> *Muriel's Wedding:* Even a loveless wedding can transform one's self-image, as long as it is elaborate.
>
> *While You Were Sleeping:* Unrehearsed, low-budget ceremonies are never right.
>
> *My Best Friend's Wedding:* Elaborate weddings symbolize true love.
>
> *In & Out:* It's never too late for the wedding of one's dreams, but young brides must be thin.
>
> *The Wedding Singer:* Real men *can* plan weddings, but only if they are involved in the wedding industry.
>
> *Runaway Bride:* Women are always entitled to the trappings of a wedding, no matter how many times it takes them to "get it right," but simple weddings are acceptable as well.
>
> *Meet the Parents:* Weddings don't have to be perfect.
>
> *The Wedding Planner:* Get married barefoot on the beach or have a big wedding, but a city hall wedding is a last resort for loveless unions.

The trend toward simplicity in these last three films begs the question: is Hollywood's affair with the lavish wedding over? Even with the newer messages of ambivalence, it seems doubtful. Hollywood still has "dozens of movies in development with 'wedding' or 'bride' in the title." Director

Garry Marshall, who describes himself as "the Wedding Master," reportedly discussed one thousand ways to marry in a documentary for Showtime.[38] Yet these last films of the twentieth century seem to say that the largely female audience feels chastened not only about the prospects for enduring marriage but also about the value of the lavish wedding. While viewers do not mind weddings being the butt of some gentle jokes, they also want some sort of affirming ritual. But what kind? Marrying barefoot on the beach, the model of the destination wedding and the way fashion model Cindy Crawford married, may be the new ideal. It offers something considerably more beautiful than the dirty offices of the justice of the peace but considerably less lavish than the weddings depicted in either *Father of the Bride* or *My Best Friend's Wedding*—and it still offers distinctiveness, if not luxury.

One emerging trend in wedding movies—as demonstrated by releases such as the critically acclaimed *Monsoon Wedding* and the surprise blockbuster *My Big Fat Greek Wedding*[39]—is toward the depiction of weddings from different cultures or of weddings that have a distinct subcultural appeal. Given the increasing popularity of cross-cultural ceremonies and the globalization of the lavish wedding, this trend is not surprising. In all likelihood, the lavish wedding will continue to appeal to moviegoers and to surface in Hollywood films. Simply put, many female moviegoers still love big bashes, and Hollywood loves spectacles, so weddings and big-budget films seem a natural match. What audiences see is what they want, and vice versa. As such, the influence of the film industry on viewers' attitudes toward, and aspirations for, the lavish wedding is undeniable in both the United States and abroad.

Chapter 8 | THE LAVISH WEDDING GOES GLOBAL

Many middle-aged women in the People's Republic of China who have been married for years now appear at bridal studios to pose for portraits in rented long white wedding dresses. Aunts sometimes try on their nieces' gowns and ask to be photographed in them. These daughters of the Cultural Revolution were probably married in gray or blue Mao suits, consisting of tunics and trousers. Their eagerness to own a photograph of themselves looking like a coiffed, made-up Western bride testifies to the pervasiveness of bridal fantasy and to the visual and sensual pleasure photography, fashion, hairstyling, and makeup provide.[1] These women are not alone; every evening a smiling bride appears at a lavish Hilton hotel reception somewhere around the world.

Because goods, images, money, and people move rapidly across the globe, it is difficult to claim that the luxurious wedding is simply Western.[2] Most long white gowns that North American brides wear are manufactured in Hong Kong, China, Mexico, or Central America. Cuisine and music are international. The sushi and samoas served at U.S. wedding receptions are imported tastes, as is the reggae the band plays. More and more people from Latin America, Africa, and Asia migrate to North America and Europe, bringing their wedding customs with them. Many people from North America are traveling to other countries for an "exotic" destination wedding, and honeymoon tourism often requires a passport. Nonetheless, for all of the cultural mixing going on in North America or Europe, the West exports bridal magazine imagery and wedding films much more than it imports the wedding customs, artifacts, or wedding films of other cultures.

This export/import imbalance is causing considerable consternation in other countries. Government agencies, religious leaders, and anthropologists often worry about the burden of debt families acquire in paying for Westernized weddings. They fear competition for prestige between families leads the poor to go into debt and liquidate savings that otherwise might have been devoted to economic development. Many Asian and Middle Eastern countries have tried to impose laws limiting the amount to be spent on weddings. Laws in favor of frugality or even mere appeals for it have rarely succeeded, in part because the desire of families to compete with each other for status is so powerful. Indeed, cultural critics have been worried about luxury spending on weddings, even when these events did not include imported elements.[3] A more pointed criticism of the West is that the spread of the luxurious wedding is part of the larger advance of cultural imperialism, the Coca-colonization of the rest of the world. Such critics worry long-standing costumes and customs are being lost. Cultures around the world are indeed changing, as has been the case for centuries. True, some indigenous marriage customs are lost, but others are being revived. The most important point of cultural change is that as the lavish wedding spreads around the world, it combines old and new, rather than simply eliminating the old.

In the West, the luxurious wedding means not only magic and memory, romance and perfection, but also tradition, even if the tradition is borrowed. Since the luxurious wedding has arrived recently in many countries, it is not regarded as "tradition." The indigenous way—or ways, depending on region, social class, and religion—qualifies for that designation. Therefore, the fact that the luxurious wedding is cropping up worldwide suggests the modern, the new, and the Western are more appealing than tradition. This is so because in many parts of the world, couples, but especially brides and their female relatives, want the fantasy of romantic love borrowed from Western popular culture and from Hollywood films. The long white dress is the realization of the Cinderella dream, the walk down the aisle is the moment of anticipation, and the kiss after the religious ceremony symbolizes true love. In an ever-increasing number of places across the world, the lavish wedding also conveys sophistication, luxury, and status. Indigenous traditions convey some romance as well, but they are perceived as too long and do not have the imprimatur of advertising, celebrity, and Hollywood.

To some extent, people around the world want luxury because they have not had much of it; to some extent, they have wanted novelty, fashion, and sophistication for a long time. Luxury is also one of the best ways for families at a wedding to communicate respectability and status. It seems likely that the greater the scale of the advertising industry in a country, the more magic is part of the wedding's appeal. Even in the absence of national advertising, however, luxury imported goods convey both prestige and magic. A brief continent-by-continent tour will suffice to date the origins of the lavish wedding, the extent to which it has been adopted, and the major countries of influence.

There is wholehearted acceptance of the luxury wedding in the Pacific Rim but rejection of it on the Indian subcontinent and in Indonesia. The Japanese, who have a high rate of savings and a small number of children upon whom to lavish display, especially love the opulent version. The average cost of a wedding in Japan is the highest in the world. To be sure, the Japanese way of reckoning includes furniture and appliances for the couple's new house. Taking these purchases into account, the total cost of a Japanese wedding averaged a whopping $66,000 in 1996.[4] The drubbing that the Japanese economy has experienced starting in the 1990s, as well as price slashing at Tokyo hotels, has kept the cost of the luxurious wedding from rising much higher in recent years and has led some Japanese couples to seek cheaper versions by traveling to Disney World, Australia, Hawaii, or Amsterdam.[5] But on the whole, diminished incomes have not diminished desires.

The luxurious wedding reached British colonial possessions in Asia and in the Pacific in the nineteenth century. The British influence on Australia and New Zealand established the luxurious wedding as the prevailing one, a set of rituals to be taught to native peoples. Because the Philippines were formerly Spanish and then American colonies, the lavish wedding became a religious and consumer element of that culture with Spanish, American, and indigenous influences. In other parts of the Pacific Rim, the arrival of the luxurious wedding is more recent. Japanese wedding businesses began offering white gowns for rent after the end of

World War II, and a boom in building specialized catering halls for weddings started in the 1960s. The luxurious wedding appeared in other Asian countries as part of the more recent emergence of an urban, consumer society. Thus, it became more prevalent in Taiwan, Singapore, Thailand, and Hong Kong in the 1980s and reached the Chinese mainland in the middle of the 1990s.

The lavish wedding is not antithetical to the Middle East, even though it was to the Taliban and is still taboo in much of Pakistan and Iran, and is rarely found in North Africa and Muslim areas of Nigeria.[6] Perhaps anti-Western religious fundamentalism, poverty, and the hold of tradition explain the antipathy in these locations to the lavish wedding. In such places, brides usually are veiled from head to toe and undergo henna dying of their feet and hands as part of the preparations for marrying. Moreover, many Arab intellectuals correctly trace the introduction of the luxurious wedding to Western colonizers and therefore scorn it. Unlike most of the world, where a white dress explicitly means the West, in the Middle East the West is less acknowledged, and white is coded as prestigious and modern.[7] We suspect the reason for this camouflage is because acknowledging the West raises the touchy subject of European and North American influence in that region.

Actually, the lavish wedding is quite common in the Middle East. More and more Jewish weddings in Israel moved out of synagogues into commercial wedding halls beginning in the 1960s. Israeli society underwent a consumer revolution, with a luxurious wedding replacing the older ideal of a modest event on the kibbutz. More Israeli couples than ever before are planning their own weddings rather than relying on parental decision making.[8] Similarly, there are Palestinian wedding halls with luxurious draperies and center stages. Marrying in a long, white gown for the bride and a tuxedo for the groom has been Palestinian, Turkish, and Egyptian "tradition" for decades, although these fashions only reached the Gulf States in the 1990s.[9] Since the overthrow of the Taliban, Afghani brides in tiaras, holding floral bouquets and wearing white dresses and white veils, crowd beauty salons on Fridays, the traditional day for weddings. As to Islam itself, the religion does not proscribe marriage details. Islamic rules about female modesty do not seem to govern bridal attire. Men and women have their receptions in separate rooms in Iraq, but the bride, even a woman who usually wears cover during her daily life, is usually dressed in a long, white gown and the groom in a tuxedo. A young Egyptian woman can wear a headscarf every day to work but show up at her wedding reception in a low-cut white bridal gown. Saudi women, dressed head to toe in the black chador, shop for white wedding dresses in Riyadh.[10]

In sub-Saharan Africa the diamond ring, the large guest list, and the church wedding are mainly found in the megacities and moderately sized towns. In South Africa, such customs are popular among wealthy whites in Johannesburg and Cape Town and equally loved in black townships and Soweto.[11] Enthusiasm for the luxury wedding cuts across religious affiliations on the African continent, even though Christian missionaries were the first to introduce all of the Western customs, from orange blossoms in the bride's hair to the white gown and white frosted cake. Today Muslims, Ethiopian Orthodox, and other Christians are all known to marry in clothes that look like they were purchased in an American bridal salon. As is true in Asia, the luxurious wedding is found more often in urban than in rural areas. Moreover, among urban educated professionals there is some recent interest in the revival of ethnic wedding customs that were beginning to disappear. Because sub-Saharan Africa is the poorest part of the world and the region where the consumer economy is least well developed, there is usually not enough money for both the lavish wedding and the honeymoon. Thus, honeymoon travel is a less frequent part of the wedding ritual in this region than in many other parts of the globe.[12]

There are also more luxurious weddings in Central and Latin American cities than in the countryside, although the lavish wedding occurs in small villages as well as in megacities. Because this area of the world is wealthier, on average, than sub-Saharan Africa, there are more bridal shops, more catering businesses, more jewelry shops, more TV soap operas, and more society pages filled with photos of brides. Mexican bridal magazines extol the merits of honeymoons to Singapore; Thailand; Malaysia; Bal Harbour, Florida; and Las Vegas, Nevada.[13] Latin American countries are not simply wealthier but are also more influenced by U.S. and European fashion. In mainly Catholic Latin America, double ceremonies (a civil one and a second one blessed by a priest) are common. But the style of the church ceremony and the reception that follows is decidedly luxurious among all groups, except for the very poor in the countryside who often have traditions of common-law marriage or adhere to indigenous customs.[14]

In Europe, the luxurious wedding of royalty and then the elite became the middle-class custom after World War II, when it spread from the city to the countryside and from the upper and middle classes to the working class. In the European countryside, brides often wear native embroidered costumes and engage in capping ceremonies, during which the transition from bride to wife is symbolically marked by the substitution of a matron's kerchief for the maiden's wreath or crown. A Croatian bride receives a kerchief signifying her new status as a matron, and a Finnish bride receives a *tzepy* (thin cap) after a ceremonial haircut. These ceremonies, as well as processionals to the church, have not entirely died out, and there is an interest in reviving tradition among the young in Europe as in North America. But the overall trend in Europe is very similar to that in the United States. More modest and even hippie celebrations of the sixties and seventies gave way to elaborate shows of wealth in the eighties. Every major European nation now has its own bridal magazines; fashion designers in Milan, Rome, and Paris rival Vera Wang for their influence on bridal fashion. As we have discussed, in 1994, the British film industry received a huge boost when *Four Weddings and a Funeral* set a trend that Hollywood had to follow. It has been very much of a two-way street between Europe and the United States: we gave them Grace Kelly; they gave us Princess Di.

The typical explanation for the spread of the white wedding is "globalization," a buzzword for bigger, faster cultural exchange. Globalization involves the compression of time and space caused by new technology and airplane travel, freer movement of capital, internal migration within a country and between nations, tourism, and the rapid diffusion of American popular and consumer culture.[15] Globalization seems to best describe the years since 1990—the age of e-mail, cell phones, the fax machine, the VCR, the video rental store, and the World Wide Web. Television clips of celebrity weddings, Hollywood movies, soap operas, and migration to the West from other countries have helped to create a global romantic fantasy. In reality, though, globalization has been occurring since the days of European exploration in the 1500s, and certainly since Christian missionaries and fashion magazines spread the idea of the luxurious wedding in the nineteenth century. Nonetheless, because of migration, tourism, and the impact of new technology, the pace of cultural exchange has accelerated. More people than ever before can view luxury and can import some prestigious goods.

The lavish wedding is part of the global wealth divide, but that division has a spatial dimension. In many countries, the location of the luxurious wedding—Cairo, Tokyo, Mexico City, Taipei, Beijing, Kampala—is usually the largest city in the nation. In fact, it is a truism that the larger the city, the more common the luxurious wedding. Except in the rapidly developing Asian countries, where bridal businesses are found throughout the country, in most parts of the world such businesses are mainly located in big cities. Most photography studios, catering halls, stationery stores, and beauty shops are found there as well, along with the multinational hotel chains such as the Sheraton, Hilton, Marriott, and Radisson.

Luxurious weddings occur most often in cities because urban centers are more modern and more connected with other countries of the globe through modern mass communication, whether television, film, or the Internet. Thus, the clearest indicator of the number of luxurious weddings in a nation is the percentage of the population living in the countryside, where the standard of living is low. Modest income—no electricity, telephone, television, or VCR, let alone a bridal magazine—and a slower process of change best explain the persistence of indigenous wedding customs in such places.

Still, it is the large city where the lavish wedding is introduced and adopted, first by the wealthy who have traveled to the West and later by the middle class. The exception to this rule that the elite lead the way is found in countries that still contain royal families. Royalty often marry in traditional costumes to demonstrate their adherence to the customs of the court and to encourage patriotic sentiments among their subjects. Nonetheless, even more than the ceremonies of royal couples, Hollywood weddings typically set the trend. There is another unique element to urban weddings in some countries. In Jordan, the United Arab Emirates, Taiwan, and South Korea, for example, the urban poor also marry in the Western manner because charitable societies sponsor "group" lavish weddings and make available white gowns, business suits, flowers, and a modicum of gifts for poor couples. In these cultures, the idea of every person being married—and not choosing the single life—is positively valued. Since marrying in luxury has become the preferred form, the charitable societies want to make the ceremony available to all couples eligible to marry, not just to those who can afford it.[16] In so doing, the luxurious wedding becomes a reward for social conformity to the value of legal marriage.

The city is also important to the worldwide diffusion of the lavish wedding because it is the heart of the country's consumer culture. Advertising agencies, department stores, major newspapers, and television stations are located there. Newspapers and advertisements, created and disseminated in the large cities, are the main media for transmitting the ideas and images of this type of event. There are few places in the world where it is not possible to see *Runaway Bride* or *Father of the Bride* with subtitles. Still, it is not always easy to find a bridal magazine. There are none in Ethiopia or Saudi Arabia, although women's magazines in Saudi Arabia often include a section about weddings. Nor are there bridal magazines for sale at Nairobi newsstands.[17] Where bridal magazines are ubiquitous, their format varies from American-influenced ones, such as those in Mexico, to the European-influenced ones found in Latin America. Peruvian bridal magazines, for example, contain translations from the bridal magazines from Spain and Italy.[18] Many countries in Asia and Europe (and even South Africa) are among the small group of nations that have developed their own bridal magazines.[19]

Communist regimes varied as to how spartan an approach they took when regulating the lavish wedding. The Soviet Union, for example, never went to the extreme of encouraging couples to wear the Russian equivalent of matching Mao suits. Nonetheless, all of these regimes had weak consumer economies and could not offer luxuries to compete with those available in the West. Communist regimes, with their bloated bureaucracies, undeveloped legal and banking systems, and overplanned centralized economies, discouraged wedding businesses. They especially discouraged advertising, one of the prime contributors to making the words (and desire for) magic and memory ubiquitous in the United States. The Soviet Union began to offer ceremonies in official wedding palaces after World War II as the state alternative to religious ceremonies, and also as a somewhat lavish compensation for a war generation that had endured so much suffering. But the size of the guest list was rarely larger than the number of people who could squeeze into a cramped apartment. The desire for luxury and consumption helped topple the Soviet Union, whose economic system could not respond sufficiently to consumer demand.[20] Even before its demise, however, the nation was trying to adapt, for example, by offering catering services for weddings around 1975.[21]

With the fall of the Soviet Union in 1991, many Russian couples felt entitled to a luxury wedding for having endured so many years of state-induced deprivation. More lavish events with photographers and videographers soon followed, and many couples wanted to marry in a Russian Orthodox church. Bridal shops, selling gowns and tuxedos imported from the United States and Switzerland, opened to find customers eager to buy or rent.[22] In Cuba, one of the world's last Communist regimes, weddings still conform to the more modest Soviet model. But with profits from the thriving black market, some couples are hiring private caterers and renting Mercedes-Benz sedans to chauffeur them to the state's Palace of Matrimony.[23]

Communist China, from its inception to the Cultural Revolution, was much more eager to eliminate rather than accommodate the luxurious wedding. After Mao took over the government in 1949, catering businesses that depended on the wedding trade had to turn to preparing food for factories or other forms of business in order to survive. During Mao's rule, the typical wedding was very simple. Couples took an afternoon off from work, arrived at the government's registry office dressed in their work clothes (matching Mao suits), and after the ceremony feasted at a big meal hosted by their families. The open-door policy of Deng Xiaoping, begun in 1978, led to the development of more wedding businesses, including bridal gown manufacturers, caterers, limousine rental businesses, and photography studios.[24] Chinese women who manufacture Demetrios bridal gowns sometimes buy them. What united women in Russia, China, or Ethiopia—all countries that began to permit more lavish weddings in the 1990s—was that government-imposed frugality hampered the desire to make the wedding day special and different from the ordinary. With the fall of Communism, the urge to spend freely reemerged, since it had always been present, if suppressed. Because of the spread of Western imagery and consumer goods, the Western wedding became defined as the most luxurious way to spend lavishly.

Globalization of the Western luxurious wedding is different than globalization of the Internet or the cell phone, because acceptance of this way of marrying varies by region. Of all the regions in the world, parts of Asia are the most resistant, especially Indonesia, Pakistan, India, and Nepal. The few Christian brides in large Indian cities do marry in white gowns or in white saris. But among Hindus as well as Muslims and Sikhs, the bride usually does not wear white but instead wears a pink or red silk sari and a gold, probably jeweled, nose ring. Before the wedding, the bride has henna-colored abstract designs applied to her hands and feet as a symbol of wealth and happiness. The rest of the ceremonies of the wedding are intricate, several days long, and do not correspond to the familiar processional walk down an aisle.[25]

South Asians point with pride to the beauty of their ceremonies as the explanation as to why the luxurious wedding has not taken hold. But virtually all the indigenous ceremonies of the world can make that claim, and in most cases, such customs are losing out to a Westernized variant of the luxurious wedding. Explaining exactly why South Asia is so resistant requires we rule out a number of commonsense explanations. These include the following.

Hostility to the West. British rulers tried to eradicate many customs, such as *sati* (widow immolation) and child marriages in India. Those who resisted British changes often defined their resistance as a form of struggle against Western imperialism. However, the mainland Chinese harbor bitter resentments against the Western dismemberment of their country, and government propaganda is able to stir such feelings.[26] Similar points can be made about Iraq or Egypt. However, the Westernized version of the lavish wedding is highly popular in all of these countries. It is thus quite possible to combine nationalism and anti-Americanism with love of Western ideas of beauty, fashion, and romantic love and the Western manner of dress for weddings.

Arranged marriages. Thai, Iraqi, and Saudi couples, who have their prospective spouses chosen for them by their parents, nonetheless still marry in long, white dresses. This is true for many South Korean couples as well. In such situations, the Western luxurious wedding has come to symbolize beauty, luxury, or affluence rather than the couple's love for each other.

White as the color of mourning. In countries such as Taiwan and mainland China, as well as in large parts of Africa, people grieving the loss of relatives wear white clothing. In such circumstances, a cultural exception is made for the lavish wedding. At the same time that white symbolizes mourning, it has also been redefined as an acceptable color for marrying. Still, in the 2001 movie *Monsoon Wedding,* an independent film directed by Mira Nair that is also a classic Hollywood wedding chaos movie, the Indian event planner attempts to convince the father of the bride that a white tent, rather than one draped in bright colors, is an acceptable and modern trend. Signifying the resistance of the older generation to the recoding of white, the father of the bride asks, "Are we having a funeral or a wedding?"[27]

Poverty and lack of urbanization. This same film affirms that the huge middle class living in Indian cities still chooses not to marry in the Western manner, as do the elite in Indonesia. In fact, many Indians see their own wedding customs—such as having four days of ceremonies and inviting fifteen hundred to two thousand guests—as extravagant, and actually regard the smaller and shorter typical American wedding as modest.[28]

The consumer culture infrastructure. There is no shortage of bridal shops, bridal fairs, or wedding planners in India. There are plenty of rental wedding halls where receptions can be held. Brides in India spend freely on cosmetics, linen, emeralds, handbags, silverware, very high heels, red saris, gold chains, rings, and bracelets.[29] The Indian bridal magazine *Bride and Home,* which appeals to an upper-middle-class English-speaking readership, has its own Web site—and there are many other South Asian bridal Web sites as well. Moreover, Surja Diamonds, which is backed by De Beers, has begun marketing diamond engagement rings to the huge Indian market.[30] Indian brides these days are often picking out diamond rings as well as gold bracelets.[31]

A bride-centered culture. People in South Asia also believe the wedding is the bride's special day, but have not accepted Western standards of beauty. Indeed, they have borrowed many Western concepts, such as the ideal of the perfect wedding. An Indian immigrant living in Massachusetts has even written a wedding guide—presumably for Indian immigrants—titled *The Perfect Hindu Wedding*.[32] Perfection, it seems, can be redefined as marrying in Indian-style luxury, not in the Western manner.

Given that the above reasons cannot account for the resistance in South Asia, what can explain the limited acceptance of the Western lavish wedding in this region? One part of the explanation, which we have already mentioned, is that in South Asia, the lavish wedding is defined as a ceremony for Christians only.[33] This is a region where religion defines one's identity and distinguishes and divides Hindu from Muslim from Sikh. The religious definition of the luxurious wedding is unusual and quite different from the definitions in other parts of the world. Neither Jews nor Muslims consider the Western wedding to be necessarily Christian. The Japanese are especially willing to cross religious boundaries. They tend to be church shoppers, who choose a place to marry because it has a long aisle and stained-glass windows. Although only about 1 percent of the Japanese population is Christian, about 30 percent of couples get married in a Christian church or churchlike setting.[34] The Japanese attitude toward adopting customs from other religions can be characterized as highly flexible: they pick and choose one or several, and do so without having to become religious believers in the faith sponsoring the ceremony. Meanwhile, Hindus, Sikhs, and Muslims in South Asia believe it is wrong to transgress religious boundaries. In fact, they appear to have a very strong sense of barriers separating religions and invoke powerful negative sanctions against crossing them.

A second explanation for South Asia's antipathy toward the lavish wedding is the attitude of the region toward gender and modernity. The luxurious wedding often evokes images of fantasy, woman's beauty, romantic love, and the West. Those are powerful, attractive images in Singapore and Seoul but are alien and unappealing in much of South Asia. Luxury is not a problem, but modernity for women is. For many South Asians, modernity conjures up especially frightening ideas about the place of women, such as freely chosen marriage, divorce, sexual freedom, and feminism. These ideas are probably more frightening in South Asia because of the great taboo against marriage for love. The woman is the symbol of tradition, and tradition is associated with nationalism and stability in the family. Therefore, a white gown is perceived as threatening, while a man's tuxedo or business suit is not.[35] And as we noted before, transgressions are punished severely. The woman who dresses in a white bridal gown would be seen not as a fashion plate but as a traitor to her tradition. If a woman does not stay in her place, it is believed, the family will lose its anchor, arranged marriage will disappear, and divorce rates will rise. Of course, these arguments are somewhat circular, because they raise the question of why South Asians need more cultural reassurance about woman's place in the face of global change than other cultures. Perhaps part of the answer is the adherence to arranged marriage. While other cultures are willing to trade cultural reassurance for status, South Asians have loaded their own rituals with enough status to fend off the addition of Western customs.

A third explanation, closely related to the issue of spurning modernity, is the respect retained by many younger-generation Southeast Asians for their indigenous ritual traditions. In *Monsoon Wedding,* Nair skewers the marriage of modernity and tradition in Delhi's upper middle class. The bride's and groom's families live in a world of television, adultery, pedophilia, and porn films. The film even features an Indian wedding planner madly trying to decorate with the traditional flower, marigolds. Meanwhile, the bride and groom in the film are acceding to an arranged marriage in the Hindu fashion. Although the groom has lived in Houston, Texas, for four years, and the couple will return to America after the ceremony, it is the willingness of the young to follow the traditions of their parents that keeps the South Asian wedding alive.

Ideas that undoubtedly seem old-fashioned and even shocking to Westerners, such as the custom of a hopeful groom kidnapping a bride before she is to marry another man in Indonesia and Bali, have steadfastly remained a part of South Asian wedding traditions. A tribal elder in the village of Bonder, Indonesia, estimates that 99 percent of couples still participate in a prenuptial kidnapping, which involves abducting a woman at night, negotiating a dowry for her return, and keeping her secluded until the wedding day. This tradition is about as far from the orchestrated, planned, and public lavish wedding as one can get. One young Indonesian villager explains its popularity simply by saying, "Our parents did the same thing, so we should do it too."[36]

The lack of appeal of Hollywood's wedding films is both a cause and a consequence of the South Asian attitude toward the luxurious wedding. India has Bollywood, the Bombay-based film industry, and it produces its own visual images, including wedding films. Hollywood wedding films enjoy some popularity among English-speaking middle- and upper-class moviegoers in India, but action movies are far more popular. But the smaller audience for *Runaway Bride,* compared to that for an Indian wedding film, *Hum Aapke Hain Koun (What Am I to You?),* results from the continuing allure of South Asian wedding customs. The success of a homegrown film industry, creating its own visual culture, also helps to keep the South Asian wedding fresh and vital.[37]

Since there are many pieces of the luxurious wedding that have been adopted in South Asia, the question is whether the Western form, sans the dress, has in fact been adopted after all. Families in South Asia are clearly not resisting luxury consumption or luxury imported Western goods. As we noted, it is perfectly acceptable for the groom to wear a business suit with a boutonniere. Families hire wedding photographers, videographers, marriage bands, florists, car decorators, dance teachers, and special astrologers to calculate auspicious days to marry. They buy printed invitations and rent hotel rooms for out-of-town guests. Ceremonies take place in rented wedding halls or palaces, and space is rented for catered receptions at hotels. Many hotels also have bridal suites. Indian couples like the Western idea of going on a honeymoon—perhaps to Kashmir—after their wedding.[38] Indian bridal magazines even contain articles urging the couple to choose an exotic location for the honeymoon. Indians living in the United States, who usually import some Indian bridal traditions, nonetheless have adopted the customs of flower girls, ring bearers, and the white cake; Hindu brides in Trinidad wear a sari for the ceremony but change into a white dress for a photo-taking session after the ceremony.[39]

In sum, weddings in South Asia feature their own interpretations of lavishness and some elements of Western luxury, but there is a taboo against bridesmaids, the white dress, and the walk down an aisle. The taboo seems to be directed toward what are perceived as the Christian elements of the luxurious wedding and those that threaten the image of woman as a symbol of tradition. South Asians living in North or Central America change their weddings more, but there is still no rush to adopt two ceremonies.

Other parts of the world are much more eager to embrace the delights of consumption, but exactly how they adopt the lavish wedding varies greatly from one nation to another. There are thus huge differences in the luxury weddings of different countries. Comparing the growth of the luxurious wedding in South Korea, with its dynamic economy, and in Ethiopia, with the lowest per capita income of any country in the world in 1999, will illuminate these differences.[40] These two countries are separated not only by geography but also by their ranks in terms of national wealth. South Korea contains a huge urban middle class, while war-torn, drought-stricken Ethiopia has a small one. In Ethiopia, the white wedding is the preferred form of marrying for the *nouveaux riches* and has spread to the urban masses and provincial towns, but still occurs most frequently in the capital city. The rapidity of South Korean economic development has erased the huge cultural gap between the city and the countryside. The luxurious wedding is now the norm throughout South Korea. In both countries, couples, but especially the bride, want the modernity, luxury, and romance the white wedding evokes, even though it is probably not the tradition the bride grew up with. But at the same time, we see no wholesale effort to repudiate tradition in these nations. In both of these cultures, the lavish wedding is a hybrid, a mixture of traditional elements and imaginative renderings of the West. Except for the bride's white dress, the cake, and the flowers, one would be hard-pressed to consider the South Korean version of the white wedding the same as the Ethiopian one.

SOUTH KOREA

South Koreans have absorbed and mixed many more wedding traditions than Ethiopians because of their greater wealth and more developed consumer economy. At the same time, South Koreans have also commodified their own customs in a packaged format sold to them by caterers, photographers, and bridal shop owners. The lavish wedding took hold earlier in Korea than in Ethiopia. Christian missionaries to Korea introduced the idea of a bride marrying in a white dress in front of a minister in the early twentieth century. But the form of the Korean wedding ceremony owes much more to the Japanese than to missionaries, since the missionary wedding was an entirely modest affair.[41] The Japanese imposed a brutal colonialism on Korea between 1910 and 1945. Most Koreans hated and feared the Japanese; nevertheless, Japanese culture has had a powerful impact on Korean modernization. In many parts of the world, the lavish wedding is imported from the United States. But in Korea, the luxurious wedding arrived via Japanese adaptation, even though most Koreans, because of their attitudes toward Japanese imperialism, are more likely to cite American than Japanese influence.[42]

A professional photo session for the bride and groom in South Korea is virtually a separate consumer rite, so valued is it by Korean couples, and almost an entire day is devoted to picture taking prior to the wedding itself. The photographs produced for the wedding album are entirely of the bride and groom, or the bride only, in romantic poses. Usually the groom pays for the photos. Bridal photographers take couples to settings considered romantic, such as a beach or a park. The photos taken at these settings seem to stand apart from the wedding just as youth culture stands apart from parental control of prewedding and wedding rituals.

Bridal photographs in South Korea represent Western notions of a woman's beauty and of the ideal of romantic love. At the same time, brides are also seeking a photographic record of the magic moment. Some North American couples have wedding photographs taken in advance of the wedding, often in romantic locations. Similarly, in South Korea, bridal photography is supposed to make the couple feel like stars, celebrities, and very special people. The differences are that the South Korean bride undergoes far more expensive makeup and costume changes for picture taking. Also, couples place a wedding portrait, almost three feet tall, of themselves in their bedroom above the bed. One anthropologist suggests the portrait is placed there as a reminder of the bride's beauty before she enters into a life of hard work and self-sacrifice.[43] In addition, the portrait is a kind of romantic totem and object of worship. The beautiful couple blesses the couple's sexual relations even as in real life their beauty begins to fade.

Most South Korean wedding ceremonies take place at special business establishments called wedding halls. These buildings today resemble huge theaters, the size of the Kennedy Center. South Koreans borrowed from the Japanese the idea of one-stop shopping, purchasing an entire range of services and options at a wedding hall and then staging most of the preparation for the wedding as well as the ceremonies themselves—and perhaps the reception—at the hall. Because there is so much on-site coaching on the day of the event, the Japanese and the South Koreans are able to dispense with a rehearsal in advance of ceremony. At the wedding hall, the couple prepares for the event, gets married in two separate ceremonies, and has a sit-down dinner reception. With prices for land so exorbitant in urban South Korea, there is a scarcity of wedding halls. The establishments are fully booked, with a new Christian-style ceremony scheduled about every half hour. In the back of the room, where the Western wedding occurs, a clock hangs in full view of the officiant. Because of the time squeeze, the wedding hall offers a highly structured and standardized experience, but one that is not as off-putting in a culture that places a lower value on personalization and individualism than the United States. But more South Korean couples are beginning to reject the rushed ceremony of the wedding halls in favor of marrying at a hotel or a church.[44]

The wedding is quite expensive, despite the fact that gowns are often rented rather than purchased and flowers are often silk rather than fresh. South Koreans, like the Japanese, have adopted a subtler variation on the wear-once dress. At more expensive wedding halls, the bride gets first use of the gown, as well as another gown for photo sessions days before the marriage. At less expensive wedding halls, the bride accepts wearing a used gown as a means of reducing the overall price of the wedding. However, a bride expects the gown will be thoroughly cleaned before she puts it on.[45]

Wedding halls in both South Korea and Japan offer a package with a very lengthy list of options, each available at a single location and for a price. More important, the package consists of professionals attending to every detail—no amateurishness allowed—with the couple and their families expecting flawless service. The Japanese have shown an ability to incorporate items of foreign origin and reduce their size, whether it is a Sony Walkman or a luxurious wedding. They think smaller is not only better, but also more beautiful.[46] The package, which simplifies arranging the wedding and offers convenience as well as options, is as important as what is being sold.[47] The procedure is that a representative of the wedding hall shows the families of the bride and groom a list of articles and services with a price for each. They then choose the items they want. The couple need not search for a band, a caterer, or a florist. The

Figure 19.   Couple bowing to groom's parents, Seoul, South Korea, 2000. Courtesy Kyoungmi Lee and Woo Jae Lee.

Figure 20.   Korean *p'yeback* ceremony, 2000. Courtesy Kyoungmi Lee and Woo Jae Lee.

Japanese (and therefore the South Korean) method is not only a simpli-
fication of the process—akin to a Disney World or Las Vegas wedding—but a more scripted and scheduled version as well.[48]

Most South Koreans marry at the wedding hall, with other settings for
people of particular religious persuasions. A minority of Christians in
South Korea prefer to marry in a church and have a reception at a restaurant. Non-Christians are not permitted to marry in a Christian church,
although this same rule does not apply in Japan. A few Buddhists marry
in the temple.[49] South Korea has a history of state-imposed limits on the
expense of weddings. Only recently has the government lifted its sumptuary laws so weddings and receptions can occur in hotels as well as in
wedding halls. Before that time, the wedding hall owners enjoyed a
monopoly over the wedding business.

The wedding hall usually contains different ceremonial rooms and
hallways, with dressing rooms in between, where the different ceremonies can occur. The décor of the interior is functional rather than
stately. Thus, the ceiling lights are usually fluorescent and there are no
chandeliers. The Japanese pioneered the idea of a two-wedding, and
sometimes even a three-wedding, ceremony. One Japanese ceremony is
held in a room designed to look like a Shinto temple, where the couple
dresses in kimonos. The second resembles the interior of a Christian
church, where the couple marries in white. The third room, if used, mirrors a Buddhist temple.[50]

Similarly, South Korean patrons of the wedding hall marry in a room
that has a long aisle with a white runner, in the style of a Christian
church, but at the front there is a very large and wide lectern decorated
with large banks of flowers. Wedding hall operators also know that their
clients prefer that the bride and her father walk down the aisle to the
music of Wagner's "Wedding March." The bride does not hold onto her
father's arm but instead holds his hand. The bridal procession is a South
Korean form of the Western one, which, because of the continuing hold
of patriarchy, places greater emphasis on the groom than in the Western
version. Thus, the bridegroom also walks down the aisle and the guests
applaud him. The fathers and mothers of the bride and groom are seated
in large upholstered chairs at the front of the room rather than in a front
pew. There is a bridal bouquet toss after the ceremony, but with less to-
do than the Western version, and there is no garter toss. Exactly why

these rituals have been minimized in the South Korean wedding is not clear, but the important point to note is that South Koreans have selected only certain elements of the lavish wedding as known in the West. However, they have also added elements rarely seen in North American weddings. As the couple faces their assembled guests, they are often surrounded by a fog produced by dry ice. As is true of other elements in the South Korean wedding, it seems likely this one can be traced back to "Japanization," because weddings in Japan often feature this special effect.

The two-ceremony South Korean wedding is another invented tradition, new but appearing to have continuity with the old. The middle class in South Korea grew up after the end of the Korean War; they wanted to show off their newfound wealth but also prove that they were patriots, faithful to an emerging South Korean identity. It felt too Western, and not sufficiently Korean, to simply marry in the Western manner. If an updated version of Shinto provides the basis for one of the Japanese ceremonies, then a modernized version of Confucianism provides the basis for the ceremonial style in South Korea. Instead of a Christian minister, the couple in the churchlike room of the wedding hall is married by a *chur-ye*. He is a "respected elder," a friend of the groom's family, who makes some announcements and gives a speech praising the achievements of both the groom and the bride and giving advice as to how to have a long and happy marriage. Sometimes the couple turns to their guests and remains serious-looking while they listen to a short musical interlude. Then the *chur-ye* tells the bride and groom to bow to each other. After doing so, the bride and groom proceed down the aisle hand in hand. Traditionally, there is no kiss at the end of the ceremony, although friends sometimes insist on seeing the couple kiss after the ceremony is over.

While the Japanese hold their two ceremonies back to back, in South Korea, there is a wedding reception in between the Western and South Korean ceremonies. The cake-cutting ritual occurs at this reception and is a relatively recent South Korean addition. But the cake is wax or Styrofoam and inedible and the cake is cut with a sword rather than a knife. The ritual is performed solely for the purpose of taking a photograph. Japanese caterers originally developed the idea of the wax cake cut with a sword, since many of their patrons did not like Western sweets but liked the ritual and the photograph that accompanied it.[51] During the reception, the couple goes from table to table greeting guests before they adjourn to a separate room and eat with a small group of relatives. Guests at the reception drink champagne and toast the bride and groom, but there is no music or dancing. After the reception, the couple changes into Korean costumes for the *p'yeback* (pronounced *pay-beck*) ceremony. It occurs in a small room of the wedding hall, where the groom's parents are seated on silk mats on the floor. Parental presence is required, but the presence of other relatives is optional. One feature of this second ceremony is the groom carrying the bride briefly on his back, a symbol of his willingness to provide for her.[52]

As in Japan, the caterers and wedding hall operators borrowed from royal or upper-class style in creating their own version of an upper-class Confucian ceremony that might have occurred in the courtyard of the bride's home. The ceremony is intended to convey the image of a home wedding in a rural community. Prior to the Korean War, the rural poor in the country had virtually no wedding ceremony and thus no distinctive wedding clothes. At the *p'yeback,* the bride and groom dress in costumes, exchange bows, eat special foods that symbolize fertility, and sip from cups of wine. The bride's costume—for example, a red skirt and yellow jacket, with a crown on her head and thick makeup—is that of a princess at the palace. Her makeup consists of red circles on her forehead and on each cheek to ward off evil spirits. The groom's costume is supposed to replicate that of a high court official, complete with a hat made out of horsehair. The groom, unlike the bride, is allowed to combine East and West in his clothing because men are permitted to be more modern. Underneath his costume he can wear a Western white shirt and tie. As is true in India, in South Korea women are symbols of the family and of social stability. The couple bows to the parents of the groom and their relatives during the ceremony. They understand the event in the wedding hall is more the ceremony to please their parents than the one they really want. Thus, after finishing at the wedding hall, young couples often join their friends at a bar for a party among their peers.[53]

Bridal fashion seems to be the first element to be adapted to Western custom; patterns of gift giving are much slower to give way. This may be because Western concepts of beauty and fashion have much more appeal than those pertaining to gift giving, which can alter kinship patterns and the way social obligations are recognized and repaid. In South Korea, as in most Pacific Rim cultures, guests at the wedding do not give wrapped presents but instead offer "congratulation money," usually bills wrapped in red paper or a white envelope. Guests check in at the wedding hall, perhaps greet the parents of the bride and groom, and deliver their envelopes. A graceful exit, without attending the ceremony, is permitted. Some close friends do bring gifts for the household. Because giving congratulation money is an expected part of the event, the average expense of the wedding has to be reckoned as a net cost after all the envelopes containing money are opened.[54] While many South Koreans complain about the expenses of gift money, it seems other elements of gift giving cause the most tension. There are many gift exchanges leading up to the nuptials that occur between the bride and groom and between her family and his. Originally, the bride was supposed to furnish the women in the groom's family with silk to make their dresses for the wedding. Now, she may be engaged in purchasing dresses or gift bags as *yedan,* gifts for the mother-in-law. Brides' mothers are said to ask others, "How much money did your daughter-in-law send for the *yedan?*" Dissatisfied mothers-in-law are said to be a major cause of conflict in marriage. Thus, the best mother-in-law for the contemporary bride is the one who suggests no gift giving is required.[55]

The honeymoon is a Western idea that South Koreans have adopted along with the lavish wedding. The South Korean government imposed limits on foreign travel for many years. As a result, Cheju, a tropical island with white sand beaches, palm trees, thatched huts, and waterfalls about an hour's flight from the main peninsula, became the favored destination for South Korean honeymoon couples. The idea of the honeymoon as a separate trip for the couple away from their kin group applies to South Korea as much as it does to the West, even though the South Korean wedding ceremony itself seems much more centered on pleasing parents and kin than its Western counterpart. Moreover, Cheju fits the model of the tropical exotic location so well, it is often called the South Korean "honeymoon haven," "tropical paradise," or the South Korean Hawaii. But honeymooning at Cheju also shares some features found in the Poconos. Some of the wedding resorts on the island host wedding night parties aimed at removing the inhibitions of virginal brides or couples in arranged marriages, which seem akin to the kind of entertainment offered at the resorts in the Poconos. Although there are no overall figures on South Korean honeymoon spending, it is probably a bit more modest than a Western honeymoon, since the number of days spent on this event in South Korea is usually five or fewer rather than the nine-day average of the typical U.S. couple. However, with the lifting of foreign travel restrictions in the 1990s, about half of all South Korean honeymooners in 1997 were traveling to foreign islands in the Pacific, including Guam and Hawaii.[56]

ETHIOPIA

In addition to being the poorest country in the world in 1999, Ethiopia has a largely illiterate rural population; in fact, only about one-third of Ethiopians can read or write.[57] It was one of the last countries outside of South Asia to see the arrival and acceptance of the lavish wedding. Because it was a Communist country for so long and has a scarcity of consumer goods, it shares commonalities with mainland China. There are no wedding hall establishments there. Nor is there any attempt to combine an Ethiopian-style ceremony with a Western one. Unlike in other countries in Africa, Christian missionaries in Ethiopia made no effort to introduce the luxurious wedding. Colonized by the Italians only briefly, Ethiopia was not as thoroughly influenced by European rulers and missionaries as other African countries that underwent a much longer period of colonization. Still, in the Ethiopian countryside as well as in the city, brides are abandoning the white hand-woven cotton wedding dress for the polyester or taffeta long white gown.

If McDonald's is the symbol of the Americanization of the globe, then it could be said that Americanization has bypassed Ethiopia, because even though there are fast-food chains in the country, no golden arches can be found. Nor has American popular culture blanketed Ethiopia as it has the rest of the world. Consumer culture is extremely limited in Ethiopia because the country was under a Communist regime with state stores until 1991 and because of the relatively small size of the middle and upper classes. There are no department stores and no bridal registries. There is no billboard advertising that shows photographs of brides in white dresses, although there are hand-painted signs touting gowns. There is no De Beers advertising of diamond engagement rings. There are no bridal fairs. In most countries, the most ubiquitous image of the lavish wedding emanates from television programs. But Ethiopian television has never shown a live broadcast of a celebrity wedding. There is rarely more than one American television series on Ethiopian TV, and it tends to be an action program, not one displaying white gowns. Bridal shops have been open since around 1998, but none of them have their own Web sites. There are only two limousine rental services in the country, and both can be found in the capital city.

Thus, the bridal industry in Ethiopia is more limited, consisting of photographers, videographers, florists, and neighborhood rental halls that rent tents, chairs, and pots and pans. As in the Soviet Union, bridal shops opened only recently: they provide car and hall decorating and bridal gown and tuxedo rental. The catering industry is also underdeveloped, because families prefer to provide home-cooked meals for wedding receptions. Thus, even if a wedding reception is held in a luxury hotel, the families of the bride and groom will prepare and bring hot cooked food for the event. Moreover, there is not much honeymoon travel; consequently, there are no honeymoon travel packages. In part, this is because the couple cannot afford the extra expense, having gone into debt for the wedding. Also important, however, is that fact that the concept of the couple as a unique and separate entity is not meaningful in the culture. If there is any travel, it is usually a two-day trip to a lake in Ethiopia for the couple with their bridal party.

The luxurious wedding has arrived in Ethiopia quite recently. A generation of young people fled Ethiopia between 1985 and 1990; most of them entered the United States, while a smaller group went to Canada. Some were political refugees from the repressive Communist regime of Haile Mariam Mengistu, who ruled from 1977 to 1991 and who tortured and terrorized his political enemies. Others were economic migrants, hoping to find a better life in the West. As a result of poverty and repression, Ethiopia has had more migrants leave the country than any other nation in sub-Saharan Africa. Certainly enough Ethiopians came to the United States to form an immigrant community, associating with each other but also partaking of American consumer culture. The migrants phoned home and sent remittances as well. When the repression died down, even while Mengistu remained in power, some returned to Ethiopia to marry. When they did so, they married in the Western style.

Figure 21.   Billboard for bridal/beauty salon, Ethiopia, 2001. Courtesy Nancy Hafkin.

For their relatives who remained at home, the migrants brought home objects of prestige, imported luxury items hand-carried by a son or daughter living in the United States or Canada.[58]

Ethiopians who were not refugees or migrants also had an influence on the introduction of the lavish wedding to the country, importing the commodities and styles of many countries, such as American and Italian fashions and printed invitations from India. These groups share an interest in foreign name brands as symbols of prestige so often found among the newly rich. They created a prestige system of ranking, with their weddings defined as the top of the luxury ladder. The goods were new, prestigious, even magical, while the idea of the wedding as a display of wealth was a time-honored one. The cultural innovators were typically wealthy merchants who lived in the capital city of Addis Ababa or pilots employed by the state-owned Ethiopian Airlines. The pilots supplemented their relatively modest salaries by trading in imported goods brought back from their travels. Merchants became wealthy by arranging to import manufactured items ranging from computers to toilets not otherwise available in Ethiopia.[59] Starting with these two groups, the lavish wedding trickled down to the masses, who now rent a specific space reserved for weddings in a public park, and from there it spread to provincial towns. But since most of the Ethiopian population is rural and very poor, the number of couples marrying in the Western manner is still a distinct minority.

There are generally multiple activities for the day of the wedding, interconnected by driving from one location to another in a white Mercedes or other expensive automobile decorated with flowers and toys. Even in the countryside, a car is borrowed if no one in the bridal party owns one. In Addis Ababa, a Mercedes used to be borrowed from a patron, rich relative, or family friend. It is now possible to rent one from one of the two limousine rental agencies in the city. The hood of car is decorated with fresh flowers and many ribbons. This imported Italian custom conveys the idea that the bride and groom will have happy travels together throughout their lives.

The day begins with a procession to the bride's house, followed by a civil ceremony at the city hall. Only the very religious are married in an Ethiopian Orthodox church. After the civil ceremony there is a morning wedding breakfast, then a photography session, and then an outdoor picnic or luncheon at which Ethiopian food is served, usually paid for by the bride's parents. Some guests not previously invited to other events will attend a huge cocktail-hour reception. The groom's parents are expected to pay for this event. Then there is a wedding dinner for a select and smaller group of guests. The food is not catered but instead is cooked by the women of the family, who consider it an honor to be able to provide the food for the wedding feast. The events of the day often do not proceed according to a timetable, because the culture is not as attuned to the importance of keeping to a schedule in business affairs or in daily life as are Western cultures. Because there is no concept of the honeymoon and because the wedding is embedded in a situation of cultural exchange, the festivities continue into the next day, when some of the wedding guests host a party for the newly married couple. In fact, this is just the first of a series of guest-initiated parties that will continue until the couple has their first child.[60]

In Ethiopia, the larger group, not the couple, is the center of attention, because kin ties, not romance, are the vital relationships to be affirmed. Throughout the events of the day, the group make dramatic entrances

Figure 22.   Decorated Mercedes, Addis Ababa, Ethiopia, 2001. Courtesy Nancy Hafkin.

and pose in photographs. They form a distinct unit. The best man has a much larger role, more akin to that of the Western wedding planner, which is an extension of the tradition that the groom's family arranges the wedding feast. The major tension of the wedding also reveals the persistence of tradition. There is fear the potential bride will be discovered not to be a virgin. If she is not, her family can be shamed, even in the contemporary world where sexual mores are changing rapidly.

There are many customs of the lavish wedding that Ethiopians have not adopted. Because the ceremony is a civil one, there is no bridal procession to the altar. Instead, the Ethiopian couple will often enter the wedding reception underneath crossed torches. There is no exchange of rings in a religious ceremony—indeed, there is no religious ceremony. Instead, the groom will deliver traditional embroidered cotton dresses and gold jewelry to the bride in an engagement party that occurs weeks before the wedding. This gift exchange from the groom to the bride's family existed prior to the borrowing of Western customs and fashion. At the reception there is music and dancing to Ethiopian music, including the *iskista,* a dance that involves moving the shoulders up and down. Exactly why there is no garter toss at the reception is not easy to explain. This is one of the few places where South Korean and Ethiopian weddings are similar. Ethiopians have preserved the tradition of women guests ululating at the reception rather than clapping or whistling approval.[61]

As is true in South Korea, Ethiopia has continued its own pattern of gift giving, from the groom to the bride's family. Guests at these weddings are not expected to give presents or money. They are instead obligated to repay through the hosting of a feast or party for the couple, or at a minimum to invite the family to their weddings. The explanation for the feast rather than the purchased gift or a gift of money seems to lie in the importance of the communal feast in a rural society that has no welfare state and no pensions for the disabled or the elderly. It is the constant round of repaying debts through entertaining that creates social bonds. Self-interest and communal feasting go hand in hand, because the repayment through feasting incurs a sense of loyalty and obligation.

The Western-based lavish wedding in many parts of the world is costly, luxurious, wasteful, and a competitive spending splurge, but so is an Indian or Indonesian wedding. It is not the expense that makes the difference. It is the appeal of romantic love, luxury, fashion, and modernity. These ideas are Western, although not entirely from the United States. The global romantic culture emanates from Paris, Milan, and London as well as Hollywood. It also emanates from the dominant culture of the region. Thus, developed countries such as Japan and South Africa create their own bridal magazines and styles of wedding photography that are readily disseminated within their zone of influence. These intermediary countries not only spread Western culture but also create their own innovations. The Japanese contribution to the rest of Asia was much greater than other countries, since the Japanese reduced the scale and the hassle of wedding planning by creating the concept of the wedding package, which has been widely adopted throughout much of the Pacific Rim. The concept has ricocheted back to the West, where it has been adopted as the model for the destination wedding. So which culture has been more influential—Hollywood, with its celebrity weddings, or the Japanese caterers who created Styrofoam wedding cakes? In South Korea, it would be hard to choose; in Ethiopia, the answer is England, Italy, the United States, and Germany, with its luxury vehicles.

Globalization of the luxurious wedding is usually, although not always, an endorsement of Western ideals of romantic love and consumer culture. There is a strong correlation between the spread of the lavish wedding and the decline of arranged marriage. It is the desire of women to marry in a modern manner that is fueling the globalization of the white wedding. To be sure, several members of the family, not just the bride, want the ritual. But on the whole, women in these countries have embraced Western ideas of beauty and fashion. Everywhere, we find that couples and their families want the day to be special, different from the ordinary. Photography and videography have been accepted and understood in the same manner worldwide as preserving a highly constructed portrait of luxury and beauty for future times. Nonetheless, both the South Korean and Ethiopian examples indicate that the celebration of the ideal of romantic love and the couple as a separate unit is not at the heart of these weddings. Underlying the luxurious wedding in these two countries are quite different ideas of family and kinship.

Just as there is a mingling of props, some from the indigenous culture, some from the West, so, too, there is a mingling of meanings. Many customs from the West have not been adopted, because they are unappealing, are too expensive, or challenge fundamental cultural rules of how social obligation should be discharged. Western values accompany the luxurious wedding, but the event is also understood in terms of the local values about everything from symbolic gestures to kinship to sexuality. The flowers, the food, and the limousine are understood in the context of familial, kinship, and prestige systems indigenous in origin. As consumer behavior scholar Russell Belk observes, "What appears to be emulation and senseless pastiche when looking from the outside is seen as sense-making synthesis, and meaningful and coherent symbiosis when looking from the inside."[62]

There is clearly no standard package of luxury in marrying. In most countries, rental rather than purchase of gowns is accepted practice. Wealthier countries substitute caterers and paid labor for home labor. That has not been the case in Ethiopia, perhaps because of the poverty of the country, but also because of the social significance of female relatives preparing food. The absence of gift giving in Ethiopia is a sign both of an underdeveloped consumer economy and of the persistence of customs that embed people in social networks. In sum, consumer culture is reshaping the whole world but not at the same rate or to the same degree everywhere. The greater the economic development of a non-Western country, the more it imports from the West, because Western imports, especially luxury brand names, convey the important symbolic meanings of prestige, status, and high quality and provide some magic.

Far from eliminating national identity, the luxurious wedding has often encouraged it. In Japan and South Korea, globalization does not create homogenization but rather creates and indeed commodifies symbols of national identity. Of all the regions of the world, Asia has kept the traditions of West and East most distinct in terms of cuisine, decoration, and color coordination. The indigenous exists as a choice, a style one can purchase. The culture of the country has been simplified into a service to be sold, an option that reflects the element of individualism so important to consumer culture. Ethiopian nationalism is surely as potent as Japanese or South Korean nationalism, as is evident in Ethiopia's long wars with neighboring Eritrea. But as we have pointed out in our comparison of South Korea and Ethiopia, the purchase of a style is the result of the development of a catering industry and the desire to substitute catered food and packaged services for family cooking. Nationalism, as well as a developed consumer economy, has led to the invention of the two- or three-ceremony wedding. Nonetheless, the two-ceremony solution is no longer limited to Asia; it is now appearing among urban black professionals in South Africa.[63]

Even in North America or Europe, the luxurious wedding is not a coherent whole, since it has so many changing forms. As this variant of the ceremony and reception comes to be adopted around the world, pieces are broken up and rearranged. In fact, what makes the luxurious wedding acceptable in so many places is that it contains many pieces that can be added or subtracted. We have not tried to untangle every possible combination. However, it does appear that the adoption of Western traditions begins in the area of wedding costumes and photography, with brides wearing rented white dresses. The luxurious wedding then evolves into a ceremony(ies) and a reception with changes of costume, including native dress, and then perhaps to a ceremony consisting of the walk down an aisle, the bride in a long, white gown, the groom in a tuxedo. Even so, this kind of progression is becoming evident only in some countries such as Japan, and is certainly not descriptive of the majority of locales around the world.

Beyond this observation, however, the differences around the world are staggering. The safest generalization to make is that people pick and choose elements of the Western wedding, rarely ingesting it whole. As Arjun Appadurai writes, "At least as rapidly as forces from various metropolises are brought into new societies they tend to become indigenized in one or another."[64] The lavish wedding in many countries involves combining local and imported elements. Even if you have seen one of these occasions, you definitely have not seen them all. We have not tried to classify the many different types of luxurious weddings around the world. The most that can be said is that the global lavish wedding is an amalgam of ever-changing elements of various origins. Since the ritual is a product of consumer culture, it is always being remade and updated.

Chapter 9 | VARIATIONS ON A THEME

Although millions of couples all around the world participate in lavish weddings, others have chosen not to marry in an extravagant manner or have been unable to do so. For the most part, however, the absence of a lavish wedding has had less to do with a lack of desire and more with the fact that until recently, strict social constraints dictated the types of couples allowed to indulge in these types of events. Others find that family conflict, especially that stemming from interracial marriage and parental divorce, makes planning a lavish wedding more trouble than it is worth. Then there are the brides and grooms who cringe at the sight of tulle and chiffon, either because they want to protest the underlying ideologies embedded in the symbols and practices of such a consumption-laden event or because they seek personal over social meaning, which they believe can only come from creating their own kind of ritual.[1]

Quite a few types of couples previously regarded as outside the circle of the lavish wedding have actively sought access to it in the last two decades. These include gay and lesbian partners, visibly pregnant brides, couples who hope to preserve distinctive ethnic or religious customs, the previously married, and even long-married husbands and wives who want to renew their vows. Practically invisible to etiquette writers, florists, photographers, bridal consultants, and writers of the society pages, this very diverse lot seems to want the luxuries and distinction the lavish wedding provides. A second category of couples, who both embrace and reject luxury and lavishness, includes those who seek or need a different rite, such as couples marrying in Las Vegas. The Las Vegas wedding is one of the great consumer buffets, offering tradition to those who want it and the ability to reject tradition to those who do not. Finally, a much smaller group of couples, who cannot see themselves tossing garters and bouquets, create their own unique rituals to affirm their cultural and political principles as well as their commitment to each other. On the whole, the "alternative" wedding is smaller in scale, less expensive, and less time-consuming to plan than a lavish one. Most important, alternative ceremonies are less likely to be rehearsed, although none of these features is a necessary and defining difference between two types of ceremonies.

In truth, most of the "alternative" weddings we consider in this chapter have some elements of the lavish in them. After a relatively mundane ceremony, some couples hold separate lavish events; how else to classify a bride and groom who marry at the county courthouse but invite hundreds to a fancy reception two months later? Nor should one generalize about "typical" weddings that might be found in a social group or particular subculture. Some gay couples order engraved invitations and engagement rings and seek the services of liberal clergy; others simply marry each other on the beach, stating their vows to their partners. Some pregnant brides go to Las Vegas because they are embarrassed about their condition; others make no attempt to hide their pregnancies and smile broadly as they cut their cakes. Furthermore, many people typically viewed as falling outside the bounds of the lavish wedding inhabit overlapping categories, such as brides who are lesbian, interfaith, and encore. In sum, traditional and alternative variants are extremes along a continuum, with a great deal of blending going on.

Before examining the range of alternatives to lavish weddings, it is important to remember that for most of human history, *not* marrying in a lavish ceremony has been the norm. In fact, until very recently, millions of couples throughout the world lived together without the benefit of any sort of ceremony at all. Since the sixteenth century, religious authorities and governments in Europe have sought to formulate and harden the rules about who could marry and under what circumstances. In 1563, the Council of Trent declared a Catholic marriage could not occur without an officiating priest and had to take place in a Catholic church. English Protestants in the seventeenth and eighteenth centuries also tried to enforce stricter rules for marrying. Weddings supposedly required enactment by an ordained Anglican priest after the banns had been read. In the American colonies, however, this legislation was never implemented. Meanwhile, in western Europe and the newly formed United States, couples often could not afford a legal ceremony, did not think it necessary, and/or had no clergy nearby to perform one. Most people accepted it was the consent of the parties, rather than the ceremony itself, that signified a marriage. Self-marriage, common-law marriage, cohabitation, and even bigamy were quite common in the early United States, despite religious and legal rules against these arrangements (and in fact, bigamy and polygamy still exist, albeit illegally, in a few states in the American West).[2]

Legal rather than religious barriers prohibited marriage among some racial groups. By law, most slaves in the Americas were not allowed to marry. Nevertheless, slave rituals ranged from lavish weddings arranged by some masters to simple ceremonies outside of log cabins. Slaves were married by white ministers, slave preachers, or even by elderly slave women, with or without the approval of the master. But when the couple did jump over brooms and take vows before witnesses, they were keenly aware, in the words of one ex-slave from Virginia, that "them words wasn't bindin'."[3]

Likewise, U.S. immigration officials were given a great deal of latitude in deciding whether to accept Asian wedding customs. Japanese and Korean immigrants in the late nineteenth and early twentieth century had their own version of self-marrying. The man might select an unknown girl back home from a photograph; at the same time, her parents would scrutinize his picture. The bride was married in a ceremony in Japan or Korea with a proxy for the groom. She would then travel to the United States to join her husband. Once these "picture brides" arrived on American shores, immigration officials acted inconsistently. Sometimes they accepted such marriages as valid, but other times they forced the couple to remarry on American soil.[4] (Picture brides are still common today in many regions of the world, such as in the countries that made up the former Soviet Union.)[5] Finally, many states had laws banning intermarriage between white and nonwhite groups. The

Supreme Court did not overturn the last of these antimiscegenation laws until 1967.

Only after the wealthy had adopted the lavish wedding in the nineteenth century did a new standard for nuptials emerge. In its wake, the shotgun marriage, the elopement, and common-law marriage all became second-class ways of marrying. Couples who flouted the law requiring a marriage license and a ceremony were sent to jail. By the late nineteenth century, American juries stood firmly against self-marrying couples. Lillian Harman, the sixteen-year-old daughter of a radical freethinker, wed journalist and equally freethinking author E. C. Walker in Kansas in 1887. They exchanged their own vows without a minister present and Harman kept her maiden name. The day after their ceremony, they were arrested for failing to have a marriage license or for not being married by a legitimate official. A jury convicted them of violating the state's marriage law, and both received short jail sentences.[6]

Most alternative forms these days do not entail self-marrying, however, and do involve an officiant or celebrant who presides over the couple and pronounces them married. Yet there the similarity between the different variants often ends. The term "alternative" can apply either to the couple (e.g., one previously considered ineligible or undeserving of a lavish wedding), to the type of ceremony the couple chooses to stage, or to both. We begin with a form of alternative wedding that is gaining visibility but that typically does not actually result in a marriage at all because of current legal restrictions in most of the world.

GAY AND LESBIAN CEREMONIES

In April 2001, the Netherlands became the first country to grant gay marriage the same legal status as that between heterosexual couples. In the six months following the enactment of this law, nearly two thousand same-sex couples were married in that country.[7] The first lesbian couple in India to marry were wed by a Hindu priest at a ceremony in their home in May 2001.[8] Yet more typically throughout the world, gay men and lesbians are excluded from the lavish wedding primarily because they are denied the right to marry legally in any form. Most religions also deny same-sex couples the right to a ceremony presided over by a member of the clergy. In truth, same-sex marriage ceremonies have been known to exist throughout history. The Romans and early Catholics conducted such ceremonies, but the Catholic church outlawed them in C.E. 342.[9]

Into the twentieth century, some gay and lesbian couples were wed in churches or city registry offices. Among lesbians in the United States, as far back as the 1860s one partner dressed in men's clothing and pretended to be a man in order to have a wedding ceremony performed.[10] But demands for equality in the 1960s turned both the denial of legal marriage and of religious sanction into a civil rights issue. In 1968, Reverend Troy Perry, an openly gay minister, founded the Metropolitan Community Church in Los Angeles. That year, Perry performed his first same-sex union: a double ring ceremony and an exchange of vows between lesbian partners. He also issued a church marriage certificate, which was subsequently ruled invalid. By 1970, Perry had married two hundred fifty couples. The same year, Unitarians became the first religious denomination to approve same-sex ceremonies. In subsequent decades, Reform and Reconstructionist rabbis and Episcopalian and United Methodist clergy began to follow their lead.[11] None of these ceremonies are legally binding, however, and when the couple's marriage certificate has been challenged in the courts, it has invariably been ruled invalid.

Despite the early ceremonies conducted by Perry and others, the idea of gay and lesbian weddings did not really become popular until the late 1970s and early 1980s, and in fact, a relatively small percentage of gay and lesbian couples hold commitment ceremonies. One lesbian studies scholar reports that only about 11 percent of gay and lesbian couples have participated in such a ceremony in Illinois;[12] another puts the figure at 19 percent for lesbians and 11 percent for gay men in 1998.[13] Undoubtedly, one of the reasons these ceremonies are still relatively few in number is that they are not legal, even if liberal clergy (who do not have the approval of their denomination) officiate.

Another reason is that most gay and lesbian couples do not see the value in these ceremonies. Feminist scholar Susan Krieger observes that with respect to her own long-term lesbian relationship, she and her partner had never exchanged rings: "That would be too heterosexual, too married, too coupled."[14] Others argue mimicking the patriarchal, heterosexual institution of marriage should not be encouraged. Still other gays and lesbians are confused by the roles they should play in these rituals. The author Jane Eaton Hamilton wonders about her own lesbian union: "What kind of rings? Should there be one or two? . . . In a heterosexual marriage, traditions are a given, and they add a significance that's understood by a wider community. Nothing is that simple with queer marriage."[15]

Lesbian studies scholar Ellen Lewin acknowledges that commitment ceremonies demonstrate conformity to what the couple perceives as tradition but that most couples do not see themselves "copying" straight society when they have a ceremony. Rather, they see themselves as demonstrating their commitment to love, and choosing a cermony as spiritual.[16] Many same-sex couples do want to include aspects of the lavish wedding in their own ceremonies and agonize over the choice of DJs and dinner menus in the same way as heterosexual couples. Some even adopt heterosexual traditions that occur before the actual wedding, such as bridal showers. Yet such engagement rituals typically have completely different meanings for gays and lesbians than those experienced by heterosexual couples. One scholar found a lesbian bridal shower did not prepare the bride for marriage but did help the couple feel welcomed by a community of accepting lesbian and gay partners.[17] Considering that gay and lesbian couples often receive less support than they desire from their own families, this change in function is both acceptable and necessary. Moreover, overall spending on a commitment ceremony is often less because there are fewer guests and most couples do not have engagement rings.[18]

AIDS, social conservatism, and the "lesbian baby boom" spurred interest among the gay community in same-sex marriages. The devastation wrought by the AIDS epidemic, which first became visible in the United States in the early 1980s, led an increasing number of gays to view a long-term monogamous relationship as a safer sexual alternative and a more reassuring commitment than having multiple sexual partners with less clear bonds to other people. As with mainstream society, gay culture was also swept up in the general return of tradition. The lavish wedding could provide cultural legitimization at a time when gays became more conscious of the desire to create new families consisting of lovers, friends, and those biological family members who genuinely accepted them. When asked why they chose to marry, couples often said that they were brought together by God and their mutual love.[19]

Figure 23.   Gay wedding in Arizona, 1997. Courtesy Victoria Stagg Elliott.

Moreover, at one time, lesbian mothers only had children from prior heterosexual relationships; these women were usually divorced. With the lesbian baby boom in the 1980s, more women became mothers through artificial insemination and produced children in long-term lesbian relationships. Centuries ago, marriage had been designed as an institution to recognize fidelity, commitment to child rearing, and guardianship of children in the event of a parent's death. Lesbian mothers turned to commitment unions to validate their relationships for precisely these reasons. Still, gays who came out during the height of the liberation movements in the 1960s and 1970s opposed marriage ceremonies because they thought these events mimicked the failed institutions of straight society and relied on symbols of patriarchy.[20] But by the 1980s, many younger gay couples wanted precisely to show they were just like everybody else. So gay assimilationists refer to their relationships as "marriages" and their ceremonies as "weddings," rather than as commitment ceremonies.

In April 2000, Vermont became the first state to pass a law allowing "civil unions" between same-sex couples. This status granted rights to gay and lesbian partners in such domains as inheritance, family leave, and insurance, rights previously reserved for heterosexual spouses. While Vermont's legislation permitted civil unions and seemed to fly in the face of the Defense of Marriage Act that President Bill Clinton signed into law in 1996, it is important to remember the state did not legalize religious ceremonies for gays and lesbians, but only civil unions. Nevertheless, the Vermont decision did open up a potential $40 million market in gay tourism and provided a boon to resorts and bed and breakfasts seeking revenues outside of the ski season. One Web site, Gayweddingguide. com, connects gays coming to Vermont with caterers, clergy, tent rentals, bakers, florists, and photographers. Since gay weddings have no legal status, the business acumen of those involved in this industry in Vermont is notable, because what they are selling is really a facsimile of a desired and renowned ritual.[21]

Gay wedding guides and firsthand accounts all support the belief that gay weddings have the right to commandeer the trappings of heterosexual ceremonies. In fact, in 1994, *The Essential Guide to Lesbian and Gay Weddings* provided a list of "must-haves" that could have been plucked out of any traditional wedding planning book.[22] Moreover, some newspapers in small and medium-size towns began printing announcements of gay unions in the mid-1990s. While standard fare for heterosexual couples, announcements for gay couples received a new level of cultural acceptance when in August 2002 the *New York Times* announced a new policy of inclusion by featuring one couple's ceremony in its Sunday *Style* section and *Vows* column. In making the change, the *Times* adopted the heading "Weddings/Celebrations" to replace the old one, "Weddings."[23]

One unique aspect of wedding planning books directed at same-sex couples is the amount of space devoted to helping the couple cope with resistance from friends and family, some of whom, it is anticipated, will regard the ceremony (and the union) as unnatural, immoral, or suspect. There is very little practical advice on what the "bride" and "groom" or members of the wedding party should wear (and in fact, on whether terms such as bride, groom, and maid of honor should even be used); on who should propose; or on how an engagement should be formalized. Perhaps as these ceremonies become more prevalent, wedding planners and consultants will construct a new set of norms that will provide a guide to this relatively uncharted territory.

Classifying gays as the excluded who want to be included is too simple, because gay ceremonies range from events held in churches and synagogues to Wiccan or Pagan events lasting several days and held outdoors. Most ceremonies combine traditional and alternative elements— a mix of "camp" and convention—although the scale tips toward the highly personalized end. While some couples poke fun at straight society in their ceremonies, for most, the tone is sincere and serious. Since gay life is more integrated by race, culture, and religion than straight life, many more couples use the ceremony and/or reception as a means to bridge two ethnic cultures or religions. In adopting the ritual of straight culture, the symbols are often redefined. Thus, a Jewish gay couple under the chuppah defines smashing the glass not only as a symbol of the destruction of the second Jewish Temple, but also of the destruction of homophobia.[24]

There are other distinguishing features of same-sex marriages. It is very rare that parents of gay children spend as much money on their gay child's wedding as they would for that of a straight sibling. In most cases, the couple foots the bill entirely. Unlike the case with straight daughters, maternal involvement in planning gay weddings seems virtually nonexistent. There is little in the straight world to compare with the pain inflicted by parents or siblings who send their regrets at not being able to attend.[25] One of the most revealing statements of parental indifference is the advice of a wedding photographer that he should be told "which family members will attend, which won't, and how the formal groupings should be handled."[26] In most cases, it is considered a great victory if the couple's relatives stay for both the wedding and the reception. Moreover, because these weddings are smaller and fewer relatives are invited, the gifts the couple can expect to receive are fewer.[27]

The 2000 book *The Wedding: A Family's Coming Out Story* reveals that even for professional, cosmopolitan gay couples who want a religious ceremony and lavish reception, the issues ultimately come down to family acceptance. The book demonstrates the complexities of planning a lavish wedding—complete with reception hall, chuppah, lesbian rabbi, and matching tuxedoes[28]—and illustrates the negotiation of how much a gay man's parents will accept the couple. In registering at Bloomingdale's,

Andrew Merling, a television writer and owner of his own production company, showed he wanted to participate in all of the consumer rituals of the lavish wedding. Moreover, he assumed his parents would willingly pay for the same amount of pomp his sister had enjoyed: "Lavish, hundreds of guests, great foods, photographers[,] . . . all the trappings meant that what they were doing mattered, that it was important enough to warrant all this *stuff.*"[29] Ultimately, it was the squeamishness of Andrew's mother over the decision of her son and his partner, Douglas Wythe, to kiss at the end of the ceremony—rather than any objection to spending money on her son's wedding—that led her to decide not to pay for the event. And because of concerns about the attitudes of elderly relatives, Merling and Wythe sent out two sets of invitations, one for a "wedding," the other for a "celebration."[30]

The Merling-Wythe ceremony clearly demonstrates that some same-sex couples crave the social legitimacy provided by the lavishness of this type of extravagant ceremony. Moreover, they also crave the magic and memories made possible by incorporating the romantic symbols and gestures such as engagement rings, champagne toasts, and kisses. And although commitment ceremonies range from the opulent to the simple, the ceremonies, receptions, and honeymoon travel that come closest to resembling straight marriage—like that of Douglas and Andrew—have attracted the most attention. Even if more opulent and conformist than most, their ceremony embodied the elements of spirituality, appeal to tradition, and statements about romantic love common in most commitment ceremonies.[31]

LAS VEGAS WEDDINGS

The divorce rate in the United States indicates marriage is a risky proposition, so what better place for a prospective bride and groom to gamble on their future together than Las Vegas? The Las Vegas wedding is both a category unto itself and a prime force behind the increasing popularity of the destination wedding and the wedding package. Both strange and familiar, the Las Vegas wedding offers insight into how much celebrity and spectacle are reshaping modern nuptials. Las Vegas has welcomed pregnant, eloping, and encore brides for decades, and now welcomes gay couples. Whether driven by pregnancy for straight couples or for many other reasons for gays and straights, many couples want their ceremonies to happen quickly. With no waiting periods or required blood tests in Nevada and a well-established wedding industry since the 1950s, the ceremonies available in the state's cities, especially in Las Vegas, have become one of the most popular alternatives to full-blown lavish weddings in the hometown of the bride or groom. But at the same time, many couples create events closer to the lavish wedding than they first appear; in fact, some Vegas ceremonies can cost several thousand dollars and seem almost mainstream.[32] In the same way the Japanese offer packages, hotels offer brides and grooms dresses, veils, cakes, limousines, and all of the accoutrements of the standard lavish wedding. At one new luxury hotel, the Bellagio, a couple can purchase the Deluxe Wedding Package. For $1,500, they receive

> one hour of "chapel time," a Custom Bellagio Wedding Certificate, a Personal Bride Dressing Room (nothing for groom), a wedding coordinator, and express mailing of the photo package. . . . [F]or $1,000 more [the couple] could have the Luxury Bellagio Package. Included: Officiant Fee, Personalized Video, Rehearsal Time for Bride and Groom, and One-Day Spa Passes for Two.[33]

The first wedding chapel in Las Vegas, the Little Church of the West, opened in 1944, and quickly became known throughout the 1940s and 1950s for its "quickie weddings." It was the first to be built on what would become known as the Strip, which not only contains the glitzier casinos and attractions, but now houses most of the city's fifty-five wedding chapels.[34] Many who tie the knot in the city have been married before, and because of the city's connection to gambling, prostitution, and the Mob, Las Vegas weddings of the 1940s and 1950s typically possessed an air of unacceptability and garishness. But by the late 1960s, the Las Vegas wedding had acquired a celebrity patina, thanks to the nuptials of Paul Newman and Joanne Woodward, Elvis and Priscilla Presley, and Mickey Rooney and several of his wives. Also, by presidential order, August 26, 1965, became the last day young men could improve their draft standings by getting married, increasing their chances of not having to fight in Vietnam. To accommodate the crowds in Las Vegas that evening, Justice of the Peace James Brennan Jr. cut his normal five-minute service down to three minutes and managed to squeeze in weddings for sixty-seven couples.[35]

Throughout the last few decades of the twentieth century, the Las Vegas wedding experienced explosive growth, so much so that the city is now known as the wedding capital of the world. It is especially popular with Germans who fly there to marry, both for the sun and the absence of a waiting period. More than 121,000 weddings were performed in Las Vegas in 2001, and just a little over half of those in the city Bugsy Siegel made famous included someone who had been married before.[36] The increasing acceptability of remarriage means the Las Vegas wedding has lost its seedier connotations: "Getting married in Las Vegas used to be a tawdry thing to do. . . . [N]ow people look on a wedding day as fun. Las Vegas takes all the angst and difficulty out of getting married," pronounced Barbara Tober, former editor of *Bride's* magazine.[37]

Nonetheless, Las Vegas weddings appeal to particular types of brides and grooms because they offer unique benefits traditional ceremonies cannot provide. What is it about the "Vegas wedding" that makes it so popular? First, it is inexpensive. Marriage licenses cost $50, and the recommended fee for the minister is the same amount.[38] Brides and grooms can marry in any type of clothes they choose, or they can rent or buy all of the trappings of the lavish wedding from a hotel or chapel. However, many of the second- or third-timers opt to keep it simple: "Having gone through such a ceremony the first time, their dream wedding no longer incorporates [the] fantasy [of the lavish wedding]."[39]

Also, in the words of one observer, Las Vegas weddings are "built for speed."[40] A couple can get a license at the Clark County Courthouse from 8 A.M. to midnight on weekdays, and around the clock on weekends and holidays. The ceremonies are typically scheduled thirty minutes apart, and on Saturday nights couples stand behind a rope line waiting to get into a chapel. Couples can also get married at the drive-through of the famous Little White Chapel, where "the window opens and a head slides out and marries you."[41] This instant gratification model appeals to couples who want to have a wedding without all of the fuss so they can then gamble at the casinos or soak up the desert sun. The Las Vegas wedding is also typically small, with two-thirds of couples having no more than two guests present. This may be because some couples marry on impulse, while others elope with or without their parents' knowledge.

Figure 24.   Las Vegas drive-through wedding. Courtesy Las Vegas
Convention and Visitors Authority.

Given the number of people who opt for similar types of ceremonies
in Las Vegas, weddings in that city can hardly be called unique, so their
appeal must lie elsewhere. Perhaps what attracts people to "Vegas weddings" is that they are laden with borderline-vulgar kitsch, nonstop
entertainment, and humor—elements often muted or absent from formal church services—which appeal to the more carefree. In Las Vegas,
ordinary citizens can marry in chapels where the walls are plastered with

pictures of stars who have gone down the aisle before them. Indeed, signs outside the chapels announce the celebrities who were married there. A bride and groom can rub shoulders with the spirits of Elizabeth Taylor and Eddie Fisher, Richard Gere and Cindy Crawford, and other celebrities on their wedding day—and by doing so, acquire a little star power themselves.[42] It seems irrelevant that most of the stars who have married in Las Vegas have since divorced.

Couples can also parody the celebrity aspect of the Vegas wedding by selecting a minister dressed as an Elvis impersonator at the Graceland Wedding Chapel or a regular minister combined with Elvis, who serenades the couples and performs his own "preceremony ceremony." By doing so, couples inject levels of play and camp into their weddings that would likely have been missing from events held in their hometowns. But whether taken seriously or with tongue in cheek, this "star component" of the wedding is one of the reasons Las Vegas weddings are huge draws. The attraction to celebrity is different from the feeling a couple might experience if a photographer and videographer followed them around on their wedding day. It also does not offer the same thrill as seeing Harrison Ford on the street and asking for his autograph. Instead, the magic comes from doing something the stars did, being in the same place they were, being able to tell the folks back home your chapel was the place the stars took their vows. And by doing all of these things, being married in a chapel of the stars makes the wedding memorable.

Of course, other magical elements of Las Vegas—the spectacle of showgirls, fireworks, and exploding volcanoes on the Strip—rub off on its weddings as well. In a consumer, media-driven society, the neon-lit, 24/7 environment often proves more attractive than the wilderness. Rather than making a room or a hall of their own choosing into a spectacle, couples opt for an entire city that offers miniature landmarks such as the Eiffel Tower, the Statue of Liberty, and the city of Venice. For many, the hassles and worries of travel make the fake versions of these sights preferable to the "real" locales around the world, a phenomenon French sociologist Jean Baudrillard refers to as the "simulacrum."[43] With a Strip that is essentially "the world's largest and most spectacular carnival midway," sociologist George Ritzer claims Las Vegas is one of those magical tourist destinations that enables sightseers to reenchant their mundane lives.[44] While gambling is now possible in many U.S. cities,

Las Vegas was the first successful metropolis to combine gaming with celebrity, entertainment, retailing, cheap buffets, and strip shows. Small wonder, then, that wedding-minded couples seek the thrill of entertainment at all hours of the night. Among large, friendly crowds, they naturally gravitate to one of the country's best-lit cathedrals of consumption, where they can fulfill the need to marry instantaneously and worship both the stars and each other at the same time.

WEDDINGS OF (VISIBLY) PREGNANT BRIDES

In 1996, when President Clinton served as best man at the marriage of his brother, Roger, to a bride who was eight months pregnant, a new page was turned in nuptial etiquette.[45] There is nothing new about a pregnant bride having a big wedding. Nice girls got pregnant even in the 1950s; in fact, the rate of teen pregnancy was higher during that decade than at any other time in U.S. history.[46] But at that time, pregnant brides tried to conceal their conditions; otherwise, guests would snicker or make snide remarks in a voice sometimes audible to the bride's family. Priests were known to order pregnant brides not to wear white. If the bride started to show, or if her father found out, the couple had one alternative: to elope.

The issue of the wedding belly was so shocking that editions of Emily Post's etiquette book never mentioned it. When Post's daughter-in-law, Elizabeth, took over the series, she thought the subject had to be aired in the open, as in this passage from the 1975 edition:

> Many people feel that if the sanctity of marriage and the family unit is to be preserved the established standards of behavior in that regard should be maintained. Because this is so, these marriages should be kept relatively simple so that the couple does not appear to flaunt their situation in society's face.[47]

The bride, she wrote, should not wear a white gown, which would look incongruous given its connection with virginity. (Of course, while other brides in white were probably not virgins, the pregnant bride definitely was not!) Peggy Post, the daughter-in-law of Elizabeth Post, who took over the series in 1992, had to respond to changing times, even though she lagged considerably behind them. As late as 1997, she did not think the veil acceptable for the pregnant bride because it was a symbol for virginity; however, she gave the go-ahead for pregnant brides to wear long, white gowns.

Pregnant brides were soon joined by another group of women who violated the rules of sexual purity—brides who had previously been single mothers, and who carried their babies or young children down the aisle as part of their wedding ceremonies. If the wedding occurred at city hall, there was nonetheless often a fancy reception after it on the same day or a month or two later. Acceptance of these weddings owed as much to conservatives as to liberals. Liberals encouraged the groups of previously shunned people to hold their heads high at the altar. Conservatives wanted to tout marriage as the much-preferred alternative to either unabashed single motherhood or cohabitation, both of which they regarded as immoral. Relatives of single mothers breathed a sigh of relief when the woman found a loving man who would be a father to the child and provide needed income.

These formerly stigmatized women are now finding allies among a not-so-surprising group, wedding consultants and bridal retailers who stand to profit if a new group of brides is admitted into the fold. Although no wedding magazines cater specifically to pregnant brides, bridal Web sites such as theknot.com address issues of etiquette and dress. Kleinfeld and Son in Brooklyn attaches a brief note to the gown: "Bride will be a little larger upon return."[48] Sophia Demas Couture in Philadelphia makes one-of-a-kind white gowns for the pregnant bride.[49]

On the whole, gay couples, pregnant brides, and single mothers have demanded to be included as a civil right or quietly tried to make clear that when it came to having a lavish wedding, their money is as good as everyone else's. Both same-sex and "pregnant" lavish weddings prove that, after all, while these types of unions may be frowned upon, these couples share the fundamental right to purchase in a consumer society. The giants in the enormous wedding industry, and the money they stand to make as the lavish wedding extends its influence, have lagged behind the public in making lavish weddings increasingly inclusive. But except for conservative bridal consultants and like-minded manufacturers, they seem willing to respond to new groups of consumers.

In truth, there is nothing that alternative about marrying outside of one's ethnic group; this type of activity has become positively mainstream. Since the mid-1960s, couples marrying in the United States—and in many other countries as well—are crossing every possible barrier. Boundaries dividing couples by religion and race have begun to fall. About one-third of American Catholics are married to non-Catholics; in the 1990s, at least one-third of all Jews were marrying Gentiles. Interfaith wedding guides, mainly written for Christian-Jewish couples, have not kept up with the number of Hindu-Catholic or other-combination couples seeking advice. Meanwhile, the number of mixed-race couples in the United States has risen as well, to more than three million in 1999, or 5 percent of all marriages.[50]

More often than not, couples who cross racial, ethnic, and religious boundaries seek to placate relatives when creating their wedding ceremonies. By inserting customs and costumes into the ceremony and reception that are not part of the traditional lavish wedding, they demonstrate fidelity to their religious and cultural heritages and at the same time earn their relatives' approval. As we have seen, the globalized lavish wedding has already cleared the path for how this can be done, even though these weddings tend to feature endogamous couples (those marrying within their own ethnic groups). Relaxed immigration policies in the United States and other countries since the mid-1960s have meant there has been an influx of people from two different economic poles: the very poor looking for a new start and the wealthy and educated. In turn, immigrants have married within their own group but have also chosen recent émigrés from other countries as well as longtime U.S. citizens as spouses.

The lack of guidelines for couples needing to reconcile customs from such diverse backgrounds, while still honoring the families involved, has led to the creation of communities of brides helping each other in the chat rooms of wedding Web sites such as theknot.com and Weddingchannel.com. Given that these brides are literate and have access to computers, they tend to represent the upper end of the economic spectrum. In a study of the community building and socialization that occurred in these chat rooms, brides indicated language issues were some of the most difficult to resolve when planning bicultural weddings. Often, they reported having their vows conducted in one, two, or even three languages. One member of the couple usually ended up making statements in a language he or she did not understand so as to signal to members of the audience that he or she was ready to adopt membership in the other partner's group.[51] Sometimes the couple hired a translator or decided to hold the entire ceremony in the language they shared (typically English, especially if they had met in the United States). One bride reported on the difficulty of this issue:

> Now, I hate to be a little bit of a downer, but I went through HELL to find a bilingual invite. I don't know why, but I just couldn't find any invitation company that makes them. You can get them in one language or the other, but not in both. I finally did end up getting bilingual invitations but they cost me a fortune—$736 for 75!!!![52]

Since the bride and groom speak the same language, the point of vows in multiple languages is to communicate to monolingual guests, especially to relatives. The program explaining the customs of the wedding is another device that recognizes many of the guests do not understand the cultural customs of the ceremony and would therefore benefit from a brief description of them. Sometimes the explanation of customs is provided orally instead. It is not the presence of those unfamiliar with the ceremony that dictates whether a couple offers a program but rather their desire to offer an explanatory guide to a cultural event for their uninitiated guests. Moreover, such a program also encourages the inclusiveness and bonding that seems to occur naturally at weddings where the culture is shared by most in attendance.

Even when there are no language barriers, food, music, and dancing seem to be especially important in bridging cultures. When feeding their guests, many couples choose some hybrid solutions, such as including both the white wedding cake and sweets indicative of the bride's or groom's country of origin.[53] By appealing to the emotions, music stirs ethnic feelings and brings them to the surface. Dance, an intimate form of interpersonal communication, involves guests joining hands or bodies touching. Since each side takes steps to get to know the other at the reception, dancing is often a good way to show cultural acceptance, especially after everyone has had a glass or two of champagne. A Jewish bride and her Mexican American groom, both American-born, had considerable difficulty reconciling the wishes of their families for the ceremony, since they were unable to find both a priest and a rabbi to marry them. They deliberately used the dancing at the reception to try and soothe the ruffled feathers in both families. The bride recalled, "In the middle of the hora, the bandleader threw a sombrero out there on the floor, and started the Mexican Hat Dance. Everybody was brought together."[54]

The Catholic/Protestant divide is usually crossed by one partner converting to the other's faith in a gesture of amity. A bride marrying a Catholic invited her Lutheran minister to offer a prayer at the rehearsal dinner, even though she was converting to Catholicism and being married by a priest. A ceremony presided over by multiple officiants is something many couples seek but not all are able to achieve because of the religious barriers erected by many faiths. The path of least resistance for many couples is to find sanctuary with the Unitarians or liberal Protestants, who often deliver this message to couples: "You can do what you want to do; just tell me what it is you want." But when the religious traditions are too dissimilar, a couple has to choose among favoring one religion, a neutral ceremony, or two separate ceremonies, each presided over by a single religious officiant.

Since the mid-1960s, when renewed foreign immigration and the impact of black nationalism began to emphasize the assertion of cultural difference, people whose parents, grandparents, and other ancestors were born outside the United States have become more interested in displaying their ethnic identity at their weddings and/or receptions. Instead of valuing conformity and the bleaching out of one's ethnic heritage, American society has come to value having a definable ancestry. However, even though many middle-class or professional couples have no direct knowledge of the ethnic traditions of their descendants' countries of origin, they nevertheless would like a lavish wedding with a few ethnic touches. Moreover, couples often incorporate ritual elements that have nothing to do with their own heritage but simply stand for something they find aesthetically or politically pleasing, and they co-opt artifacts or ritual scripts from other cultures for their own ceremonies. In this age of bricolage, the creative recombination of products and/or rituals to give them new meaning,[55] ethnicity is an exercise in selective consuming. It is no longer a way of life defined by residence or membership in group organizations but a signal that one is seeking to combine a largely symbolic ethnic identity with a membership in the middle class. In such cases, couples turn to bridal books, which advise them to "rediscover your roots and . . . revive some of the signs and symbols that have special meaning for you, your families, and your community." One wedding planning book lists thirty-nine groups, with an average of three or four salient customs identified for each.[56]

Especially among recent immigrants to the United States, where ethnic traditions and backgrounds are too dissimilar, splashing just a few customs onto the lavish wedding canvas may leave either the bride or groom (or their families) feeling dissatisfied. In such circumstances, couples often add an additional ceremony and a change of costumes, as is true in the South Korean or Japanese ceremonies we have examined. Indeed, in the United States, most of the couples who incorporate changes of dress are Asian immigrants, and often they do so to demonstrate that their identities now represent a blending of both Eastern and Western cultures. Obviously, the double or triple ceremony (or change of clothes within one ceremony) has also expanded the opportunities for bridal businesses in both host and home countries, as demand increases for the now-required markers of luxury and distinction at a lavish wedding, as well as hard-to-find silk red gowns, red lanterns, and painted umbrellas.[57] Moreover, the demand for cuisine connected to the homeland has created opportunities for caterers who can serve chicken curry or pad thai.

When blending customs from two disparate cultures into one ceremony becomes unwieldy or unappealing, some couples hold two ceremonies in different countries. If the bride or groom is from the United States, a typical lavish wedding with the various white accoutrements is held. The other ceremony occurs in the country where the spouse's relatives reside and conforms closely to the standards for that culture. This seems to be the only satisfactory way for some transnational couples to feel they have received the blessings of both families, albeit separately. In this case, honeymoons often revert to the nineteenth-century model of the "bridal tour" as the newlyweds travel through the spouse's country of origin to visit friends and relatives. A second ceremony seems not only festive but also absolutely vital when the two cultures being joined are North American standard with South Asian (particularly Indian). Because India and neighboring countries are resistant to so many symbols in the Western lavish wedding, to marry only in a white gown in a lavish ceremony in the United States may leave either the bride or the groom feeling as if the ceremony had not been sacrosanct in the way he or she had been brought up to understand it.

Other ethnic groups may not have to wrestle with synthesizing two cultures, but may seek ways to incorporate their folk history into the lavish wedding. Since the reemergence of black nationalism in the 1960s, many African Americans have been using rites such as the Christmastime festival of Kwanzaa created in 1966 and other African-inspired rituals as means of asserting ritual identity.[58] One of the "new" wedding traditions, jumping the broom, is actually an old one that has been revived.[59] Some slaves devised their own form of self-marrying by jumping together over an ordinary broomstick that was neither decorated nor saved as a special keepsake. These ceremonies were invariably short and could be held either in a cabin or outdoors. In some cases, masters, mistresses, and other whites attended. In most broomstick jumpings, those who witnessed the event were other slaves.

As is true of many folklore practices, the ritual was not standardized. A groom could jump over the broom while the bride stood still, or they could each jump over a separate broom. More commonly, an officiant instructed the couple to join hands and they jumped the broom together. Usually the couple jumped forward, but they could also jump backwards. Upon occasion, the ritual was an initiation into patriarchy; it was said the partner who jumped the broom first would be the "boss of the house." But to outsiders, the ritual appears to have sexual symbolism, with "stepping over" serving as a metaphor for sexual intercourse.[60]

Jumping the broom seems to have been borrowed from Welsh neighbors who lived among slaves in the South; the ritual was known in Wales, but not in West Africa.[61] After the Civil War, while some ex-slaves continued to have common-law marriages, others desperately wanted the kind of wedding they had been denied, a legal and luxury-laden one. Few still opted to self-marry. Jumping the broom had become relegated to a game, but was rarely, if ever, a custom in marrying until the airing of the 1977 televised drama of Alex Haley's family saga *Roots,* which showed

Figure 25.   Jumping the broom, around 1996. Courtesy Furla Studios, Chicago.

Kunta Kinte and his wife engaging in this ritual.[62] In contrast to the brooms used when slavery was allowed, these days ceremonial brooms are often decorated with ribbons and sold by black entrepreneurs. There are even souvenir miniature brooms to give out as keepsakes for guests.[63]

Black nationalism also encouraged African Americans to rediscover their lost heritage by adopting Western African names, dress, hairstyles, and rituals. Black bridal consultants and writers of etiquette manuals recommended West African ritual drumming, a head wrap for the bride, a dress with cowrie shells, or a kente cummerbund for a tuxedo as additions to white trappings. As is true with gay weddings, controversies often arise that center not around the marriage itself but around what part of the eth-

Figure 26. Rings against kente cloth, around 1996. Courtesy Furla Studios, Chicago.

nic heritage to include. For instance, the fact that jumping the broom originated as a slave tradition in the South is not in dispute. Rather, the issue is whether to commemorate any tradition originating in slavery. So while some black couples jump the broom to pay homage to their slave ancestors, others exclude this tradition because they believe the memory of slavery should not be part of a joyous celebration and instead emphasize their African heritage through drumming or a bit of kente cloth.[64]

In short, for ethnic weddings, adding rituals or practicing bricolage constitutes a statement of identity, especially among middle-class couples who do not lead socially segregated lives. In some cases, the signals of cultural bridging are intended for guests and relatives more than for the couple. But because both the bridal and advertising industries are now stressing the message that heritage should be valued, couples respond as much to messages in media and popular culture as to their own desire to incorporate distinctive customs into the ceremony or reception. In other words, their definition of ethnicity is based on the proper purchase and display of commodities, as well as selected cuisine, music, toasts, and other cultural gestures.

ENCORE WEDDINGS

In 1996, 46 percent of all marriages involved a bride or groom not marrying for the first time—and one in seven were not marrying for the second time, either.[65] Moreover, most of these second- or third-timers were divorced rather than widowed.[66] Until recently, there was no nonstigmatized word for this group, reflecting their virtual nonexistence within the ceremonial landscape. Typically, the bride was married in a nice suit, and these occasions often took place at the courthouse or a hotel and featured a small, intimate party. One family therapist observes that the message of these downplayed ceremonies was "this is a complicated and difficult decision. . . . [S]ometimes [couples] wondered if they were 'really married.' "[67]

By the 1980s, divorce in the United States had become mundane and ordinary, but weddings for the divorced were still excessively bound by rules of etiquette formulated in an age when divorce proceedings were regarded as shameful. In 1989, Judith Slawson published the first etiquette guide for the second wedding.[68] Couples wanted to know where to seat the children at the ceremony and wondered whether to invite their ex-spouses. By 1990, the term "encore" was being used, politely suggesting a repeat but final performance. In 1992, one-fifth of second-time brides had formal weddings, even though half of Americans believed formal nuptial celebrations were inappropriate for previously married couples.[69] However, throughout the 1990s, the lavish wedding shifted from a testament to the bride's purity, virginity, and fertility to a celebration of luxury, romance, and magic—and, for repeaters, to the hope that this time the magic would stick. As a result, encore couples can create a lavish wedding on a par with that of first-timers, with participants and guests never mentioning the previous marital history of the bride and groom.

Even the most conservative etiquette advisers such as Peggy Post have caught up with the times, lifting the embargo on what these ceremonies are allowed to include. In the past, the list of forbidden elements in repeat weddings was quite long: no bridal showers, no gifts, no white dress—especially not a long, white one with a train. No orange blossoms, attendants, or a procession; likewise, no paternal escort down the aisle. Also, lavish receptions were frowned upon. By the 1990s, the only restriction Post mandated was that the encore bride should not wear a veil, which conveyed virginity (even though the first-time bride herself was rarely a virgin).

In truth, most brides who have previously had lavish weddings scale back their encore festivities to some extent. They offer two reasons for this adjustment: either they feel they have already had their day as Cinderella, or they are helping to pay for the occasion this time and are more budget-conscious than they were the first (or second) time around.[70] Couples are more likely to spend freely if either the bride or the groom had a simple ceremony for the first marriage.[71] Spurred by both changes in attitudes and a booming economy, by the year 2000, the average cost of a second wedding had increased to $12,000—a substantial sum, but still less than the amount spent by first-time couples. Moreover, since these couples were older and more established economically and since there were no etiquette restrictions against exotic travel, by the end of the twentieth century they tended to spend about twice as much on their honeymoons as first-timers.[72]

The bridal industry has been slower to recognize a distinctive encore market. The first magazine for repeaters, *Bride Again,* began publication in the summer of 1999. It now boasts over half a million readers with a median age of thirty-nine. Editor Beth Reed Ramirez, herself an encore bride, not only noted but encouraged the trend toward such events "going more elegant and upscale."[73] The mother of the bride has rarely been involved in the planning when her daughter begins this new chapter in her life, and most encore couples pay the total cost themselves. Encore brides and grooms also often try to accommodate children from previous marriages and provide them with roles in their weddings. Reverend Roger Coleman, an enterprising minister in Kansas City, has devised a new ceremony for blended families and a new ritual artifact, the "Family Medallion." It is given to the bride and groom and their

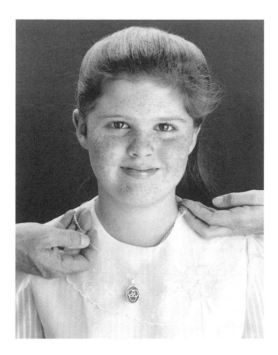

Figure 27.   Family Medallion. Courtesy Clergy
Services, Inc.

children during the ceremony as a sign of unity. This item, which costs $125, features three interlocking rings to symbolize the new family. Annual sales, made primarily over the Internet, now exceed $500,000.[74]

VOW RENEWALS

Thus far, we have described couples who because of social discrimination have typically been excluded from participating in the lavish wedding. If there is any single group who has already achieved social validation, it is long-married couples who, not content with a run-of-the-mill anniversary celebration, choose to restage their weddings. All of the alternatives to the lavish wedding discussed so far are designed to result in a marriage. For couples renewing their vows, the ritual is obviously detached from this act because participants have already been married to each other, typically for many years. Another difference is that compared to the other types of alternative ceremonies we have discussed, some vow renewals are group ceremonies that involve hundreds of couples participating at the same time, as was recently the case with 720 Catholic couples at a church in Chicago.[75]

In Italy, vow renewal ceremonies have been widespread for decades, and although present in the United States since the 1950s, such ceremonies increased in popularity during the 1970s. Almost all of these ceremonies take place in a church and involve a religious officiant. Nearly all also feature the exact wording of the couple's original marriage liturgy, which likewise typically mirrors the vows of the couple's chosen faith. Christian churches, long reluctant to encourage additional ceremonies in overscheduled facilities, gave the nod to such ceremonies as a ritual to reward marital stability at a time when divorce rates were soaring. Long-time married couples also wanted to demonstrate that their marriage vows had remained sacred to them. Still others regarded the vow renewal ceremony as an opportunity to have the wedding they always wanted. What is telling about these ceremonies is that regardless of the motive, these occasions often mirror the lavish wedding, even if the participants have been married fifty or sixty years.[76]

Some couples incorporate aspects of their earlier weddings and receptions, such as original cake toppers. Many shop as if for a first wedding: they buy guest books, photographs, videos, and new wedding rings. The authors of one study on vow renewal ceremonies indicated these newly purchased items and services perform precisely the same function as those in "real" weddings:

> Physical artifacts served for many of our informants as vivid memory repositories, linking the past to the present and the future in very material ways. . . . [They] serve as rhetorical devices through which a couple tells and retells their relationship story to themselves and to others.[77]

While their motives are obviously different, both encore and repeat couples often share the belief that the social norm of one lavish wedding per lifetime should be relaxed and are therefore in the vanguard of diffusing the idea of the luxury celebration, even when there is no life transition that needs to be recognized. Because vow renewal ceremonies often resemble lavish weddings, the "rule" that these occasions must result in a marriage also now seems to be passé.

RESISTING LAVISHNESS: OFFBEAT WEDDINGS

In some countries, laws have restricted couples' ability to marry in unconventional locations or to be married by officiants who might have acquired their licensing through more creative channels. Great Britain is still reconsidering laws that require couples to be married in the daytime by licensed local authorities; proposed changes to these statutes would permit couples to marry wherever and whenever they want, so long as they could find a "licensed celebrant" to conduct the ceremony.[78] But in countries such as the United States, where laws have not been as restrictive, some couples get married in a hot air balloon, in the aisle of the grocery store where they both work, on a mountaintop, on a roller coaster, or in a television studio. It is often the location as much as the event itself that is outrageous.

Offbeat or highly idiosyncratic weddings became more visible to the public in the 1920s, when flying solo across the Atlantic or sitting on a flagpole was testimony to one's ability to burn the candle at both ends. The Jazz Age seemed to encourage war-weary, educated youth to challenge formality—hence the weddings that took place at dance marathons or on water skis. Too many hard-drinking, fast-living couples like Zelda and Scott Fitzgerald were precisely why Emily Post felt her counsel was so urgently needed at that time.[79] These days, an offbeat wedding might make as much of a statement about a couple's embrace of consumerism as it does about the love of camp. The largest mall in the United States, the Mall of America in Minneapolis, Minnesota, hosts 475 weddings a year in its wedding chapel. One bride commented about her choice: "I just love shopping, so I thought it would be perfect."[80]

Offbeat weddings now seem to be more of a representation of the postmodern tendency toward bricolage.[81] Yet even these types of weddings incorporate a select few lavish items and convey the standard (but updated) meanings of these elements. Brides who marry in remote or unusual occasions often do so in a lavish wedding gown; even at one nude wedding in Las Vegas, the bride still wore a traditional wedding veil.[82] And many offbeat ceremonies still involve the clergy, even if the ceremony itself is conducted underwater, as is often the case for deep-sea divers in tropical locales.

These days, there seem to be two overriding motivations for a couple to engage in an offbeat wedding. First is the desire for exhibitionism and/or the need to be different, which seems akin to the reason offered by many Jazz Age couples. Some exhibitionists are daredevils who love skydiving and river rafting. Derring-do, once for men only, has become popular among couples, even significant in defining their shared identity. Because extreme sports and "extraordinary service encounters" can occur in the sky or on the rapids, couples often combine their enthusiasms with an adventure-destination wedding.[83] Moreover, couples who have often formed lasting bonds with members of sports clubs want these friends to share in the wedding in the way that reflects common interests. Such events are less unusual than they at first appear because these couples can glean both magic and memories from marrying in the air or in the depths of the sea. For these types of couples, perfection is not defined by the number of beads on a bridal gown but by the ability to demonstrate daring or athletic prowess in natural settings.

THE WEDDING AS PROTEST

There has always been a small group of people who have a political objection to lavish weddings. Even now, there are those who choose to emulate the model of the "hippie wedding," even though the term evokes the Summer of Love in 1967. At that time, the hippie wedding challenged the formality and etiquette of the traditional religious ceremony followed by a reception by occurring outdoors, espousing the back-to-nature attitude of the counterculture of the 1960s and early 1970s. But more significantly, the hippie wedding was always intended as a symbolic statement of anticonsumerism and generational conflict—a deliberate challenge to the parental generation's values, even when the parents attended and offered grudging if not genuine approval. Lisa Michaels, the daughter of two free spirits, presided over the "wedding" of her stepfather and mother in a public park at age seven and read quotations from Chairman Mao. She described the wedding as a "casual, God-free ceremony followed by a wild party."[84]

A "typical" hippie wedding (if one can be thought to exist) featured a

Figure 28.   Bridal daishiki, 1970. Courtesy Ann Cowan.

bride and groom who often wrote their own vows. During the ceremony, informally dressed guests sat on bales of hay or on the grass, rather than on chairs. The couple consciously rejected lavish trappings, creating hand-printed invitations and picking flowers from the garden. The dress code was Third World exotic, and featured inexpensive Mexican cotton or handmade wedding gowns and cotton pants and Guayabera shirts, daishikis, Nehru jackets, or plain white shirts for the groom. Receptions more often resembled picnics than fancy meals, and guests sometimes passed around joints of marijuana. Of course, there was the influence of the sexual revolution. At the early 1970s reception for Tim and Morning-Glory in Minneapolis, the bride and groom asked a female guest if she, along with six other women, wanted to "share their nuptial bliss." Never having engaged in a *ménage à neuf* and profoundly uncomfortable, the guest fell asleep on the couple's bed before the activities got under way. When she awoke several hours later, she recalls the happy newlyweds "were sleeping peacefully" beside her.[85]

John Lennon and Yoko Ono added a new element to the hippie wedding: a counterculture honeymoon. Being celebrities, however, their protest honeymoon was quite expensive. They married in the registry office in Gibraltar in March 1969, and then flew to Amsterdam and checked into the Presidential Suite of the Hilton Hotel. There they staged a "bed-in," a protest, intended as a pun on the sit-ins of the civil rights movement, the teach-ins of antiwar demonstrators, and the "be-ins" held in San Francisco. They invited photographers to take pictures of them nude and reporters to interview them in their white pajamas while they spent seven days in bed, advocating world peace and an end to the Vietnam War. Above their bed they had hung two signs, "Hair Peace" and "Bed Peace." When they were subsequently refused entry into the United States because of prior arrests for possession of cannabis, they took their bed-in to the Queen Elizabeth Hotel in Montreal.[86]

Because the hippie wedding is often rooted in the protest of symbols of matrimony that are viewed as oppressive, it has a common cousin in some variants of weddings created by male or female feminists, the staunchest of whom have always found much to dislike in the ritual. As far back as the 1840s, couples such as Amelia and Dexter Bloomer, Lucy Stone and Henry Blackwell, and Angelina Grimké and Theodore Weld protested the sexism of the wedding vows, and the women insisted on not taking their husbands' names at marriage. Such protests against the word "obey" in the wedding ceremony more than a century later led to removal of the word from the liturgies of a number of faiths.[87] In the late 1960s, many feminists were as interested in attacking the consumerism of the bridal fair as in critiquing the actual marriage ceremony itself. Feminists also took aim at the mandatory change in the woman's last name that marriage prompted, proposing the term "Ms." as a designation with no reference to a woman's marital status and leading many feminists to return to their maiden names, to combine their last names with their husbands', to hyphenate the names, or to create new names out of both.[88] Feminists also disagreed with the implication that being a veiled symbol of virginity was the proper way for a woman to enter into marriage.

But on a day when they want to look beautiful and their relatives will be attending, many feminists end up not rejecting the lavish wedding outright. Many maneuver within established ritual boundaries but modify or eliminate traditions that seem especially rooted in patriarchy. The word "obey" in the wedding vows has always been an easy target for feminists, but in truth, other sexist gestures abound in a traditional lavish ceremony and reception. Unwilling to decimate these events entirely, many women take a stand against one or two features they dislike. Only the truly daring have been willing to have a female "best man" or challenge the gender-segregated arrangement of attendants at the altar. Virtually no bride or groom, feminist or not, seems to give much thought to the stereotyped poses suggested by bridal photographers. Even at weddings of feminists, it is still common for only the men to deliver toasts. Most simply assume that the groom's attire will be rented while the bride's will be bought. But there are quite a few women who do eliminate the bouquet and garter tosses, and not many feminist brides permit their new husbands to remove the garter with their teeth. The feminist movement had also led to a major increase in women clergy, and these officiants often encourage a nonsexist liturgy.

Sometimes feminist grooms also object to wedding symbolism; one groom insisted on having an engagement ring as well, telling his fiancée, "If I just buy you a ring, it's like me making you mine."[89] His fiancée, a Jewish feminist writer, not only justified her decision to have a lavish wedding but employed the standard tactic of overlaying new meanings on old patriarchal symbols and rituals to make them more egalitarian:

> I still see the vestiges of male dominance in wedding traditions, but I also believe that traditions have beauty and power that I'm entitled to tap into: Two rings are better than none; the white dress signifies new life, not virginity; sexual commitment enriches our pleasure in each other, without possession or domination. . . . We broke two glasses under two heels at the ceremony's conclusion, claiming our cultural tradition but discarding the asymmetry. The veil framed my face but it didn't shield it. In a world

changed by feminism, we took what we wanted from tradition and left the rest.[90]

Nevertheless, protests to the symbolism of the wedding by feminist brides or grooms are most often voiced through the omission of certain standard elements at the wedding and reception, rather than the inclusion of artifacts not typically present. Sophisticated guests familiar with the "standard package" of these events are therefore expected to recognize these omissions as political statements.

The most recent celebrity/feminist/protest wedding featured Gloria Steinem and animal rights activist David Bale in September 2000. Steinem's wedding drew special attention because, like Simone de Beauvoir, sixty-six-year-old Steinem had insisted she would never marry, remarking in 1987, "Legally speaking [marriage] was designed for a person and a half. You became a semi-nonperson when you got married."[91] The fact that Steinem's wedding was the antithesis of lavish suggests there was no way for this prominent feminist to reconcile her ideological convictions with wearing a beaded wedding gown. A Cherokee ritual in Stilwell, Oklahoma, on September 3, 2000, not only provided the alternative but made an anticonsumerist statement as well. Steinem and Bales were married in a sunrise ceremony, and her feminist colleague and friend Wilma Mankiller and Mankiller's husband, a Cherokee medicine man, performed the ceremony, attended by four guests and a female Oklahoma judge. The bride and her new husband wore 95-cent beaded rings, which they took off after the ceremony. Neither Steinem nor the groom is Cherokee. But like many seekers of authenticity, they found in a Native American ceremony words, symbols, and gestures that did not evoke patriarchy, European cultural dominance, endless shopping and planning, or months of activity. While ritual theorist Ronald Grimes raises a red flag about people appropriating the rituals of the oppressed,[92] at the Steinem-Bale wedding, Cherokee friends freely offered these rituals as a gesture of welcome.

Last generation's hippie wedding has become this generation's environmental or "green" wedding. Both types value the outdoors and express a belief in the ideal of voluntary simplicity. But the green wedding came into its own long after former hippies had traded in their tie-dyed T-shirts for Armani. Moreover, green ceremonies typically accept a much higher level of consumption and make use of many more artifacts from the lavish wedding than the hippie one. Most green weddings feature invitations that are bought rather than made, flowers for the bridal party, gowns and tuxes, a catered reception, a wedding cake, and a honeymoon. Green weddings do not typically attack symbols perceived to be oppressive; rather, they permit consumption so long as it ascribes to the ideology of "voluntary simplicity." This movement, which owes its origins to the Puritans and Quakers, has always meant placing self-conscious limits on spending.[93] According to this line of thinking, money should not be the main way to demonstrate love, fidelity, and commitment.

Although environmental advocates typically bypass critiques of political or patriarchal symbolism, they do take the lavish wedding to task for espousing a "use once, wear once" consumer ethic. According to one wedding planner, basic principles of the "green wedding" include eliminating disposable and one-use-only items, using recycled paper and cloth for invitations and napkins, borrowing or renting items, wearing used or preworn clothing, serving organically grown vegetarian food at the reception, reducing fuel consumption by holding the wedding and reception at the same location, and setting up recycling bins for bottles, paper, and plastic.

Moreover, consistent with the voluntary simplicity movement is the idea that the green wedding not only endorses environmental consciousness but also advocates more modest levels of spending and turns this ethic into a statement about the couple's identity. Green guides to marrying advise buying a vintage gown at a consignment shop, both because doing so satisfies the environmental criterion of reuse and because it is cheaper to do so.[94] Carol, who married in accord with her green principles in 1999, described the importance of food and a few purchased objects, as well as her nostalgic longing for the simple life:

> Since there were only 32 guests, we got to visit with everyone. The reception was just the brunch, conversation, cutting the wedding cake and a brief toast with sparkling cider. We had EnviroMints as wedding favors, and our seven-

year-old niece had fun collecting the endangered animal cards from everyone who didn't want to keep them. . . . Weddings in the sixties used to be just a church ceremony with a cake and punch reception afterwards in the parish hall next door; we could save a lot of hassle with a return to that simplicity.[95]

Because the lavish wedding is the most powerful and best-known way to affirm love and commitment and gain social approval, more and more couples previously excluded from it now seek it, or at least seek to incorporate visible aspects that signal acceptance of the union of romance and consumption. In fact, except for a small group of weddings in the protest category, most of the weddings discussed in this chapter are planned with great pains taken to pay homage to the symbolism of the lavish wedding, even if it means defying etiquette rules that previously forbade their participants from incorporating elements of lavishness into their ceremonies and receptions. And because the wedding is an adaptable ritual, it can be molded into more appealing and more palatable forms for groups looking to bridge cultural, religious, and sexual divides. Once again, the right to purchase magic, as long as one has credit cards or cash, trumps the rules of the etiquette book.

Still, most people do not consider the diverse array of weddings described here to be "the real thing." These alternative ceremonies and receptions are always compared to full-blown lavish and distinctive ceremonies and are usually found lacking. Yet jewelers and stationers are continuously responding to previously untapped markets consisting of couples who want the magic, the memories, the perfection, and the romance—and, in addition, the social legitimacy—the lavish wedding provides. Certainly, there will always be some who consider the lavish wedding too loaded down with symbols, gestures, and stuff to be reformed. Their options come down to three: formulate ritual alternatives within the idiom of consumer culture excess; create rites that use more imaginative resources and fewer material ones; or skip the ritual altogether.

Given the many forms of alternative weddings discussed in this chapter, what are the implications for their coexistence with the lavish wedding in the future? It seems retailers and bridal consultants have been quicker than etiquette mavens and socially conscious family members to welcome some alternative forms. Yet this embrace by the wedding industry will only hold true if participants in alternative ceremonies are willing to incorporate the more costly aspects of the lavish wedding and to draw or expand upon the constellation of existing wedding artifacts. And of course, the bridal industry quivers at the thought that these challengers do not simply parody the lavish wedding but provide an attractive, low-cost option.

No doubt, the future of lavish weddings is secure, as alternative weddings themselves become more luxurious and elegant. For it has generally been true that couples participating in these alternative ceremonies are likely to first look to aspects of the socially sanctioned, full-blown occasion for guidance. Today, even offbeat weddings often include a white dress or veil, a nod to the dominant social form. As the rules of etiquette have been relaxed and reformulated, alternative weddings increasingly affect the evolution of the standard format. Likewise, since the lavish wedding is a consumer rite that thrives on novelty, it depends on new ideas. For example, the Las Vegas wedding has legitimized emulation of celebrity nuptials and aspects of the spectacle many couples now incorporate into their receptions. Other innovations—such as separating the time and place of the wedding and the reception, staging two ceremonies and receptions at different places and in different styles, eliminating sexist customs, redefining the old meanings of the wedding's symbols, and, of course, the hippie contribution of being allowed to marry barefoot— all originated in alternative forms of weddings. And even as couples choose to have more than one luxurious or semiluxurious wedding in their lifetimes (with the same or different partners), the potency of the wedding will remain intact. The seductiveness of the lavish wedding has never been rooted in its scarcity but rather in its promise to blend distinctiveness with luxury. As a result, whether couples choose an alternative wedding or a contemporary "traditional" variant, more and more they are able to satisfy their goal: "We want the wedding to be about us."

Chapter 10 | LUXURY, LAVISHNESS, AND LOVE

We began this book by describing a televised wedding that took place on a sunny July morning in Times Square in the summer of 2001, the grand finale to a contest sponsored by *Good Morning America.* The bride in that ceremony had chosen a long, white wedding gown and a traditional tiered white wedding cake. Just under ten months later, on May 17, 2002, ABC televised another winning wedding for *Good Morning America.* This time the successful couple—who, in their late twenties, were quite a few years younger than the 2001 winners—deviated a bit from the practices of the traditional lavish wedding. The bride, Sandy Bass, a schoolteacher by day and a kickboxing teacher several evenings a week, chose a multicolored wedding gown with a peach tulle skirt and chapel-length train. The cake, which had been featured in *In Style* magazine, was 16 inches high and was designed to resemble the pleats on a tuxedo shirt, with flowers on top. The couple chose their honeymoon location by tossing a heart-shaped beanbag through one of five precarved locations on a map of the world. All in all, the 2002 ceremony stressed distinctiveness as much as luxury—with the blessing of co-sponsor *Bride's* magazine, as well as the designers involved in the event.[1]

True, the lavish wedding in the nineteenth century permitted a certain limited deviation from the white gown—blue and brown silk were acceptable—but white frosted cakes in unusual shapes and honeymoons selected by playing what is essentially a carnival game would have been considered a travesty. None of this suggests that the lavish wedding is now endangered, but *Good Morning America* did permit a hint of post-modern irony in playing with some of the quasi-sacred elements of the lavish wedding. When first accepted as the standard among the elite in Europe and North America around the time of Queen Victoria, the opulent wedding was much more formal and proper. Etiquette advisers and later, in the 1930s, bridal consultants created the white rules of dress. After the end of the dual crises of the Great Depression and World War II, consumer abundance finally lay within reach of the middle class. Even so, the middle-class wedding eschewed the announcement that "we have arrived" and aimed to make a more common statement of modest family respectability. While celebrity and royal weddings influenced the "knockoff wedding dress," they had less of an impact on the style of the reception held in the family dining room. Only gradually were self-imposed barriers on spending lifted entirely as more and more couples and their families came to embrace two principles: it was good to be showy, and it was equally good to put on a show. The lavish event has now become a necessity, a right, and even an entitlement for middle- and working-class women in North America. Moreover, an increasing appetite for luxury throughout the culture, as well as the relaxation of the rules of etiquette, has contributed to the spread of the opulent wedding to the previously excluded: pregnant brides, gays, encore couples, those married fifty years ago by a justice of the peace, and even older first-time brides who feel they do not meet the ideal of the slender blushing virgin typically portrayed in ads in bridal magazines.

Despite this clear evidence for the democratization of luxury, it is too much to claim that the lavish wedding is a great social leveler, since much of the reason for the popularity of the occasion is its ability to help people purchase scarce, expensive, and prestigious goods and services and make statements about the superiority of their taste. At the bottom of the social ladder, couples are cohabiting more and marrying less frequently, and thus do not have the same opportunities for pomp. With this important exception, however, access to the lavish wedding has grown as restrictions of the rules about who can have one and who can shop for one have been lifted. If they have the money, couples across the board are now permitted to purchase a transcendent experience and are no longer considered morally corrupt for wanting it. Moreover, if they do not have the money, they are willing to exercise creativity and go to extreme measures to secure the necessary goods and services for their weddings—sometimes even setting up tables laden with free brochures for bridal retailers at their receptions and thanking sponsors in invitations in exchange for discounts or free goods and services.[2] In some cultures that value marriage highly, even those without the means to pay for their own weddings are joined in a group luxury ceremony sponsored by the government, a charity, or a religious institution.

Lavish wedding culture is also finding an ever-increasing number of adherents around the globe. Christian missionaries introduced the lavish wedding to many parts of the world in the nineteenth century. But the occasion only truly became popular worldwide with the development of post–World War II consumer-based economies. In Japan, wedding halls sprouted soon after the end of the war, and the lavish wedding flourished there as a means of cementing postwar Japanese identity. In most developing countries, the widespread adoption of the lavish wedding has arrived more recently, even though the desire to celebrate a wedding in luxury is centuries old.

This spread of the opulent wedding from continent to continent has been widely misunderstood as the Americanization of the globe. If anything, the globalization of the lavish wedding has tended to reproduce a division between the First World (where the occasion is seen as an enactment of tradition) and the Third World (where it constitutes an embrace of modernity). Scrutinized more closely, even a bipartite division of this kind does not hold. For if the lavish wedding does attract most of the world's couples to the offerings of luxury consumption, it also reinforces and transforms multiple meanings embedded in local culture, from the importance of prestige to ideas about beauty, fertility, kinship, social obligation, and national belonging. In sum, people around the world have adopted the lavish wedding to meet manifold needs and desires.

One of the major groups that remains excluded from partaking in the bounty of the lavish wedding are singles. No wonder some women like Jacyln Geller grieve over the fact that because they have chosen not to marry, they will not have a special day. Without a lavish wedding, they feel they cannot truly enjoy the abundance consumer culture offers. So while the lavish wedding has become more inclusive, it still excludes and creates envy. More and more, however, the recently divorced and the permanently single are honoring themselves at lavish parties, and the post-divorced are giving themselves permission to possess the branded, expensive goods typically acquired only at showers and weddings.[3]

Why have so many people found this way of celebrating the transition to marriage so appealing? The usual answers—prestige or a vain attempt to buy happiness—do not explain why a bride experiences a religious epiphany when she finds the right gown or why people will run into a burning house to save their wedding photos. The lavish wedding appeals to dreams, wishes, and fantasies stirred by romantic consumer culture. It appeals because couples and their families are trying to take goods, services, and experiences and turn them into symbols of *romantic love.* Like the elaborate proposal ritual that precedes it and the honeymoon that follows it, the luxury wedding is regarded as the perfect expression of such love. For almost a century, couples have expressed their attraction to each other through the purchase of goods and services, with florists, restaurants, Hollywood producers, and jewelers supporting their efforts. Through artifacts, photography, and videography, the lavish wedding is supposed to generate lasting *memories* that become not only the way the event is remembered, but also a way of keeping alive the belief in romantic love even when the flames of passion begin to flicker. With the growth of video and computer technology, ordinary couples not only can emulate celebrity lifestyles on their own wedding day but also can point to the videos and photographs that captured their star status for years to come.

As an event where luxury, distinctiveness, and beauty, rather than modest respectability, have become the dominant aesthetics, the lavish wedding is supposed to provide *perfection,* expressed through one-of-a-kind and use-once or wear-once items, attention to detail, makeup artists, and assistants. When the bridal industry first developed the concept of perfection, they preached conformity to the rules of etiquette and to a standardized script, along with attention to detail only professionals could help realize. But the industry and the public have been engaged in creating a new standard of perfection, especially in the last twenty years. This new standard not only embraces luxury in the form of items such as Vera Wang gowns, but also permits informality (for example, Krispy Kreme donuts and Rice Krispie treats at the reception) so long as this informality adds to, rather than substitutes for, the more expensive goods and services offered by the wedding industry. The new standard also allows for the mixing of highly selected elements from different cultures as a form of manufacturing an ethnic tradition (even if not one's own); greater theatricality and visual display; and high standards for cuisine, color coordination, and decoration à la Martha Stewart.

The new standard also emphasizes customization and recognition of a couple's creativity and personality—"this wedding is so Nancy and Michael." In a consumer culture valuing novelty, personalization is partly the response to the highly standardized script and assembly-line quality of the average wedding. It is also a response to increasing affluence, since people seek to distinguish themselves not only through spending on goods but also by their behavior through acting nutty or zany. Popular readings, music, wedding programs, wedding candies bearing the initials of the happy couple, blue versus ivory wedding gowns, the inclusion of carefully selected and long-forgotten ethnic traditions, and smashing the cake in the groom's face—all are ways the bride and groom can make the ceremony and reception unique.

Part of this emphasis on uniqueness can be traced to the hippie weddings of the 1960s and 1970s and to the backlash against so many Princess Diana–like extravagances of the 1980s. But at the same time, personalization in no way leads to a less elaborate event. At "theme" weddings, the wedding party and perhaps even the guests wear clothes, listen to music, and enjoy food and drink from a bygone era. Not surprisingly, Renaissance and Cinderella weddings—both of which evoke imagery of romance, royalty, and rescue—are extremely popular. This trend toward personalization may demonstrate the impact of professional party planners, but it may also be a way for the couple (and especially the bride) to add an extra layer of insurance that the event will be magical and unforgettable. In fact, the greatest fear of the bride and groom on their wedding day is not that their marriage will end in divorce (on that day especially, they obviously believe it will not), but that they will stage an event unworthy of prolonged (and positive) discussion among family members and friends.

We have devoted the most attention to explaining how couples want the wedding to be not only perfect but also *magical*. To be sure, the couple wants to feel they have been transformed from two single people into a family unit. More important, enlisting the aid of numerous expen-

Figure 29.   Wedding tennis shoes, 1997. Courtesy Museum of the City of New York.

sive ritual artifacts and experiences, they want to partake in a transcendent experience rarely, if ever, felt in the mundane world. Such a strong desire for magic obviously has its roots in multiple sources. Certainly it is a reaction to alienation from and profound disenchantment with a scheduled, bureaucratized world. It also emanates from De Beers, Disney, Kodak, Hollywood, Vera Wang, and myriad small retailers and cottage industries, including many female-owned businesses, each of whom has an economic stake in the public's belief in magic. Moreover, the beauty and entertainment industries that pervade consumer culture have long held out the promise that an ordinary person, through extraordinary means, can become a star and feel like one.

Couples who want bagpipers, horse-drawn carriage rides, Moet & Chandon champagne, and flowers to match their bridesmaids' gowns are not dupes succumbing to the appeals of bridal magazines and competition with their best friends. Instead, they are eager participants in a celebrity- and luxury-laden consumer culture who want not just the meanings such a culture offers, but its theatricality and pizzazz as well.

Yesterday's luxuries have become today's necessities; yesterday's excess is today's successful way to entertain. Few citizens of consumer culture would argue that telephones, televisions, cellular phones, microwaves, and home computers are really luxuries, although they once were regarded as such.[4] Similarly, many of the goods and experiences of the lavish wedding—a platinum or gold wedding band, a frosted white cake, and a honeymoon—are considered necessities. Today's luxuries—swan ice sculptures, monarch butterfly releases for receptions, and bouquets of rare flowers that cost hundreds or even thousands of dollars—have already begun to be defined as must-have items. Those who criticize the lavish wedding as an exercise in scripted extravagance miss the point that such events generate real meaning for the participants, despite the fact that the meanings are generated and reinforced by an industry that clearly stands to profit from extravagance.

With the increasing affluence of the last twenty years and the rejection by most of the ideals of voluntary simplicity, the dominant consumption ethic has encouraged personal qualities of self-indulgence and pampering—especially in the once-in-a-lifetime context of the lavish wedding, reception, and honeymoon. Hedonistic pleasure has become embedded in lavish theme parties, imported luxury goods, designer labels, cashmere socks, expensive cars, unique vacations, and days at the spa. Moreover, such pleasure is inevitably tied to the assumption that one can assume star status by acquiring and enjoying the right goods, services, and experiences. The idea of the bride and groom becoming celebrities during their special celebration and emulating the lifestyles of the rich and famous is made tangible through the purchase of products (a flawless diamond engagement ring), experiences loaded with stardust (being waited on, photographed, chauffeured, and served by white-gloved waiters), and travel to exotic or exciting places (Hawaii, Disneyland, Las Vegas).

The culture of celebrity is now replacing or revamping the meaning of the lavish wedding as a celebration of tradition. Marrying in the church of one's hometown is losing ground to the Las Vegas wedding chapels where celebrities like Billy Bob Thornton and Angelina Jolie exchanged vows or to receptions at Disney World where Mickey Mouse appears before the cake is cut. For many couples, especially those who are remarrying or who come from fragmented or unwelcoming families, the tie to celebrity culture through the wedding at Las Vegas or Disney World may be equally as important as or more important than discovering or enacting a link to family tradition. The Elvis impersonator serenading the couple appears not merely as a wedding soloist brought back from the grave but also as "a personal friend" or "intimate stranger" who provides a sense of community when a real one is lacking.[5] For those whose needs for spectacle go unfilled at the wedding, there is always the honeymoon at one of the "theaters of consumption" on land or on the high seas.

The cult of celebrity on the wedding day also exercises an increasingly powerful hold on both the calendar and on the other (minor) actors in the wedding itself. To be sure, several of the occasions that have a stepped-up luxury component—such as silver wedding anniversaries— are clearly related to the wedding. Yet this desire for luxury ritual has also spread throughout the life cycle—to the senior prom with its now obligatory white stretch limousines as well as to long-married women and men who reenact their earlier weddings, even if the original occasions were also lavish. Moreover, the irresistible pull of being admired and noticed means more and more people want to share the spotlight with the happy couple. These include mothers of the bride who have traded frumpy gowns for body-hugging designer dresses so they can show their adherence to the mantra often celebrated by advertising and the media: young, fit, trendy. In the same manner, bridesmaids want to demonstrate their personalities in gowns that reflect their style, and even the children of parents involved in encore marriages have made the transition from more passive roles such as flower girls and ring bearers and now actively participate by being honored with family medallions during the ceremony.

Certainly there are ritual celebrations other than proms and anniversaries—celebrations such as bar and bat mitzvahs and quinceañeras— that involve large outlays of time and money and are highly sanctioned as well.[6] But they do not have the same level of cultural visibility or religious and media support that the lavish wedding has acquired. A day for joy, a day to celebrate romantic love, kinship, acquisition, and beauty— such a day still requires some comparison shopping, but the choices are supposed to be made based on quality or aesthetic standards rather than on price. Shopping for the wedding may be tiring, but it is also pleasurable, because rules about penny-pinching applicable to other elaborate shopping scenarios do not have to be enforced; rather, indulgence and luxury are socially sanctioned. Brides, grooms, and their families are not only encouraged, but egged on by social and cultural forces to engage in unfettered spending. Even though brand-name items may not be as relevant to consumers purchasing items for their weddings (not many people think they must have a Sylvia Weinstock cake—or even know what one is), most wedding items cost more than their everyday variants because of their special and therefore extravagant status. Moreover, spending freely on a child's wedding has always been taken as a sign of a parent's love for a child, and an occasion that involves opening one's wallet to celebrate both romantic and familial love hardly requires rationalization in most cultures. Contrast the typical unabashed outlay of cash and credit for most weddings to situations where parents will not spend a dime on a gay child's wedding, which is viewed as the unkindest cut of all.

How much of the triumph of the lavish wedding can be attributed to the manipulations of the bridal industry, the bridal magazines, and seemingly innumerable Hollywood wedding films? As is true with other industries, these do not always speak with one voice. For example, bridal consultants emphasize to their clients the happy memories the wedding will bring while actively critiquing the ideal of perfection retailers and service providers go to such great lengths to promote. But an industry that makes contradictory statements can still be a manipulative one. The strongest case for the lure of advertising is the marketing of the diamond engagement ring. Tapping into women's needs for everlasting love, beauty, and status, the N. W. Ayer advertising agency in the 1930s and 1940s transformed a hard piece of crushed carbon in plentiful supply around the world into a publicly recognized symbol of enduring love and a key purchase for the engagement ritual. Men and women have been exchanging rings for centuries in marriage ceremonies. But De Beers, in concert with Ayer, provided consumers with an outlet to make a statement about their own standard of living and to demonstrate they understood the cultural rules of marrying and how to use material goods to express symbolic values. Ayer also recognized the ability of advertising to offer couples reassurances in the form of ritual scripts to help them avoid making visible and socially mortifying mistakes as they strove to get married "in the right way." Such insecurity explains the success of Ayer's rule that proposing successfully requires an engagement ring that cost the equivalent of two months' salary. Moreover, by varying its advertising rhetoric, Ayer has succeeded in reshaping demand in relationship to the changing supply of diamonds. True, the diamond engagement ring has little or no resale value, but as a symbolic object, it performs the multiple functions of therapy, talisman of love, and quasi-sacred item of prestige.

Granted, not all entreaties to spend instigated by advertisers proved successful. However, those that were transformed mass-produced objects such as plates and forks into bone china and silver place settings. Successful copywriters and art directors, many of them women, embedded their advertisements for the many products and services associated with the wedding with ideas of magic, memory, romance, and perfection. They harnessed and shaped desire to suit the needs of buyers. Advertising attached the fairy tale to products (from cans of tomato soup to bridal gowns) to make them symbols of romance and fidelity and concrete expressions of utopian fantasies. To put the products into action, however, required increasingly theatrical gestures, appropriate for items of luxury.

What, then, are the consequences of so many wishes fulfilled and so many fantasies being attached to the process of marrying? The claims for the impact of such a singular event are many, with some having more merit than others. Many people regard luxury consumption as a pyramid, similar to the one nutritionists use to describe food groups. In that image, the luxury wedding is the apex of all consumption. But with so much more affluence in recent decades, the metaphor of the pyramid no longer applies. Luxury consumption does not rise to a single peak, because there are many peaks and because opulence has become embedded in the standard of living. With the 1990s as the decade that featured the most sustained period of economic growth in U.S. history and with similar patterns of growth occurring in many other countries, many people have become accustomed to a life filled with high points. In fact, the wedding is no longer seen as the single time of luxury a couple can expect to enjoy. The economic boom of the 1990s meant special privileges once reserved for the wealthy—second homes, leather-appointed 3-ton SUVs, restaurant-quality refrigerators, Whirlpool Duet washers with twelve cycles—are now trickling down into the middle class with a vengeance.[7] In fact, in the last decade of the twentieth century, the consumption of luxury goods grew four times faster than spending in any other category.[8]

The lavish wedding has far more significant consequences when it comes to ideals of female beauty. Certainly, it reinforces the idea that women are creatures of fashion and beauty; one of the most entrenched cultural understandings of the wedding is that the bride is Queen for a Day. Just as consumer culture permits guilt-free spending for a wedding, so, too, it now permits—and practically requires—a woman to make her body and face a "project" in order to be beautiful on her wedding day. The ideal of perfection, once applied to the items and services used in the wedding, has increasingly included the bride's face, teeth, and body parts. But becoming Cinderella is not merely hard work; for some, it is also a deeply absorbing and rewarding activity. Historian Kathy Peiss points out that cosmetics, jewelry, and fashion offer aesthetic, sensory, and psychological satisfactions.[9] Many women perceive beautifying themselves as satisfying their intrinsic needs for sociability, creativity, play, and self-definition. The question remains whether today's woman is able to realize the ideal of being beautiful on her wedding day without subjecting herself to impossible demands for perfection.

What is the relationship between the lavish wedding and the marriage it inaugurates? Some argue the rituals of the engagement period, the lavish wedding, and the honeymoon encourage couples to adjust to traditional gender roles (which despite reinforcing the unequal status of women in public life presumably leads to greater stability in marriage). Others claim that couples, in spending so much time matching napkins to the color of rose petals, have no time left to contemplate the serious step they are about to take. According to this point of view, lavish weddings encourage Cinderella fantasies of happily ever after, which lead to disappointment and ultimately to divorce.[10] In fact, both propositions are difficult to demonstrate, because they simply attribute too much importance to the wedding as preparation for future marriage rather than as a highly unique consumer rite.

On the whole, the Cinderella fantasy today seems more detached from the future spousal relationship and more connected to the temporary, pure escape available through shopping for the "big day." Many women, like the title character in *Muriel's Wedding,* are more interested in the bridal fantasy than in a husband. Some have already chosen the designer for their gown without having any idea whom they will marry. There is also a fairly sizable group of single, unattached women—self-professed "wedding junkies"—who buy bridal magazines, visit wedding retailers, and become experts on the wedding simply because it makes them feel good.[11] As an Australian feminist collection of articles about weddings and marriage claims, "Many women want to have weddings: few of them want to be wives."[12] Bridal fantasy is usually seen as a reward for future sacrifice. But when divorced from marriage, it is more of an entitlement than a bribe—something women actively seek rather than something they passively wait for a man to bestow on them. A new trend, elaborate mock weddings, are fabricated purely for the purpose of enabling young college graduates whose marriages lie in the future to both plan a luxurious party and embellish it with zany postadolescent pastiche. For example, one of these recently featured groomsmen wearing jumpsuits with waffles glued to them, bridegrooms dressed in bear costumes, and a bride carried to an altar on a rocking horse.[13]

No doubt, the majority of contemporary weddings include nods to the gestures and beliefs of patriarchy. Some assume these dramas of gender subordination do lasting damage to women's status in the world. The active redefinition of the symbols—changing what it means when a father walks the bride down the aisle—takes some of the sting out of these gestures. More important, these days the lavish wedding functions less as a path to lifetime gender roles because larger social changes play a much bigger role in shaping women's lives and their marriages. Consider these trends for women in many Western (and non-Western) countries. The labor force participation of married women, even mothers with young children, has soared. The age for women's first marriage continues to rise, as does the age for first-time single motherhood and cohabitation. Women's wages are more closely approximating those of men, and more women occupy nontraditional jobs. With the growth in women's education and commitment to the labor force, fertility rates have continued to fall. Women have begun to claim a greater share of political power in governments around the world than ever before.[14] All of these trends have occurred even as the lavish wedding has become more opulent. One has very little to do with the other. Since that is so, it is best to conclude that having a lavish ceremony, hosting a pricey reception, and going on an exotic honeymoon do not act as a major brake on the social and economic progress women continue to achieve.

If the lavish wedding does not have a clear and direct impact on women's status, it does signify the sexual privilege of heterosexuals. Many religious ceremonies restate the norm that defines marriage as a heterosexual institution of husband and wife and celebrate the ideal of children as the necessary part of marriage. The mystique of the wedding masks the fact it is a legal ceremony as well as a consumer (and oftentimes a religious) rite and thus represents the state's legitimation of who can marry. European nations are ahead of the United States in challenging the views that homosexuals are second-class citizens. While the Defense of Marriage Act passed in the United States in 1996 permitted states to recognize only heterosexual unions, the Netherlands has passed a law permitting same-sex marriage. The more other nations follow the Dutch example, the more the heterosexual norm will no longer be taken for granted. Newspaper editors, bridal consultants, and television producers have proven less resistant than Hollywood, many religious leaders, and legislators. There are plenty of gay-friendly retailers and tourist industry promoters who offer equality of consumption, based on purchasing power. Ultimately the pressure for change emanates from gay couples who want not merely the lavish event but also the same religious blessings and legal rights heterosexuals enjoy.

There are economic and environmental consequences to the lavish wedding as well. It is part of the global wealth divide, a set of consumer purchases larger than a Gucci handbag or Hermes scarf, but far less costly than a Mercedes S 6000 or a vacation cottage. Diamond and gold miners in South Africa, Botswana, and Namibia; hotel employees in Cancún; and garment workers in Taiwan help to create the lavish wedding but rarely enjoy its special moments. Even if staged only once or a few times during a lifetime, opulent weddings also encourage the waste of natural resources. The standard honeymoon trip to a tropical island dotted with palm trees contributes to endangering a highly fragile tropical environment. Still, most of the world's people clamor for access to consumer choice and to both the great and small luxuries of life. Moreover, the desire for the lavish wedding seems so pervasive around the world that people will probably devise creative ways to participate and work within whatever environmental constraints have been placed on them. This situation already occurs in Japan and South Korea, where the lack of storage space in homes means wedding gowns are rented and complete wedding packages bought so families need not be responsible for the ritual artifacts after the event. Yet the fact that the dress is worn more than once and that exotic flowers in the bride's bouquet may be silk instead of fresh does not seem to dilute the magic of the event.

If we divide the world into people who do not want anything to do with the lavish wedding and those who have been excluded from enjoying it but who want to join in the excitement, the second group is clearly much larger than the first. Many people, if asked, might condemn individualism, materialism, celebrity worship, the desire to entertain and be entertaining, and status striving as shallow values. Nonetheless, the majority of couples in North America and a sizable minority of couples around the world have decided they want to emulate these values, even if only for a day, precisely because their wedding day is one where the usual rules do not apply. The fact that sumptuary laws have always proven unworkable suggests how ineffective and even pointless such prohibitions against opulence prove to be.

The group of couples that deliberately reject the luxurious wedding is a distinct minority. They share with other couples the desire to make a statement. But their statement is often intended as a protest against luxurious consumption, conformity, patriarchy, or the assumption that a couple is by definition a heterosexual pair. Yet we have had a difficult time defining what resistance to the luxurious wedding actually means, since so many of the alternative forms of marrying seem to incorporate nods to luxury. Even with minimalist ceremonies, there is no escaping opulence, since the alternative wedding is defined in part by the degree it departs from the standard lavish form. Such protest even seems to reinforce the dominant ideal. Today's barefoot bride on a sandy beach in Maui is yesterday's hippie. Because of the unrelenting demand of consumer culture for novelty, alternative weddings invariably serve as the incubator for innovations in the standard. The two are thus invariably linked as well as opposed.

If the lavish wedding has truly won over so many American consumers, why the recent rash of ambivalent wedding confessionals such as Kate Cohen's book *A Walk down the Aisle* and Jaclyn Geller's biting but sometimes wistful *Here Comes the Bride?* And why did a female therapist recently feel compelled to write *The Conscious Bride,* a book meant to console brides who found themselves on an emotional roller coaster while engaged in wedding planning?[15] Moreover, if the 1990s was the decade of the wedding movie, why did that decade end with a film that advocated a destination wedding (for a wedding planner, of all people)? The increasing scale, complexity, and length that now characterize planning the lavish wedding were bound to disenchant the experience; to impose demands for software, efficiency, and bureaucracy; and perhaps even to spiral out of control. The increasing reliance on bridal consultants is one solution to this hyperplanning, but Hollywood has picked up on the feeling of satiation among the public. Hence the destination wedding, the package deals, and David's Bridal, all of which reduce the work but retain much of the magic and romance of the wedding.

Real weddings may prove disenchanting, but the image of the wedding, divorced from reality, still contains the undiluted magic. As weddings have become established as fixtures on television programs, and as advertising has increasingly reinterpreted the visual and verbal components of weddings as symbols of joy and desire for myriad products and services, weddings have become increasingly detached from marriage, law, or religion and more closely aligned with the world of entertainment. The wedding has become a spectacle in its own right, an image of happiness, romance, and/or chaos that exists apart from any religious or marital context. In the early days of the entertainment industry, weddings were often inserted into musicals and even into silent films—and of course, the denouement of many theatrical events was a wedding. But what is new is that the wedding ritual itself has been transformed into the entertainment. Consider the popularity of the off-Broadway play *Tony n' Tina's Wedding,* which began in 1988 and has run continuously in New York since that time, as well as expanding to other cities. At most theaters, audience members typically pay more than $50 each to "attend" the same Italian working-class wedding staged week after week and enjoy ziti, wedding cake, and champagne at the reception. Along the way, members are drawn into the dramas of the wedding party, including the unmarried pregnant bridesmaid and the fights between the bride and groom.[16] That the wedding is ethnic and working class indicates the cultural distance traveled since the 1950 version of the movie *Father of the Bride,* the sense that Italian American families

Figure 30.   Cast photo, *Tony n' Tina's Wedding*. Courtesy Carol Rosegg Photography.

now best embody kinship, family, and belonging that the guests in the audience are seeking.[17]

We wrote this book neither to praise nor to condemn the lavish wedding but to emphasize how and why it has become so appealing in North America and now throughout the world. Far from being a one-size-fits-all ritual, the lavish wedding now embraces previously excluded groups and a number of different cultures. It generates standard meanings and local ones, too. It does the work expected of a commercial spectacle in a consumer culture: it provides status and entertainment; announces that a family has arrived and at the same time supports status differences; uses objects to make meaning, relieve anxiety, and provide emotional fulfillment; helps to create identity through processes associated with buying and using symbolic goods, services, and experiences; and makes it possible for people to feel elegant, sexy, teary-eyed, wacky, playful, and childlike within the space of a day, a weekend, and a pleasure trip.

In short, the lavish wedding allows participants to experience unabashed magic in their lives and to spend freely to achieve that magic, without a guilt hangover the next morning. It does so within the frame-work of a very famous fairy tale. Cinderella's dream was one of enchant-ment and escape, two goals often impossible to achieve in the real world. But under a lace veil, behind a 20-pound beribboned cake, in the reflec-tion of a flawless two-carat round diamond solitaire, or hand in hand on a beach in Aruba, the lavish wedding may be the one time when true transformation and transcendence of the ordinary seems not only pos-sible but also, to those who embrace the tenets of romantic consumer culture, well deserved.

1. ROMANCE, MAGIC, MEMORY, AND PERFECTION

1. *Good Morning America.* First broadcast 22 June 2001 by ABC.

2. *Who Wants to Marry a Millionaire?* First broadcast 15 February 2000 by Fox.

3. Rana Dogar, "Here Comes the Billion-Dollar Bride," *Working Woman,* May 1997, 32.

4. Condé Nast Bridal Infobank, American Wedding Study, 2002. Unpublished.

5. Seung-Kuk Kim, "Changing Lifestyles and Consumption Patterns of the South Korean Middle Class and New Generations," in *Consumption in Asia: Lifestyles and Identities,* ed. Chua Beng-Huat (London: Routledge, 2000), 68.

6. Chrys Ingraham, *White Weddings: Romancing Heterosexuality in Popular Culture* (London: Routledge, 1999), 177–83.

7. Shawna Malcolm, "The 100 Greatest Moments in Television: Rites of Passage," *Entertainment Weekly,* 19 February 1999, 36.

8. Ibid.

9. Lisa de Morales, "Fox's Farewell Gives 'City' Ratings a Nice Spin," *The Washington Post,* 26 May 2000, sec. C, p. 7; David Bauder, "NBC's Thursday Lineup Tops Nielsens," http://www.pagesix.com/upstories/V3126.html, 1 July 2001.

10. Angela Langowski, "Real People, Real Stories," *Cable World,* 6 December 1999, 44.

11. Rebecca Quick, "Federated and Wedding Channel Agree to Tie the Knot," *Wall Street Journal,* 25 May 1999, sec. B, p. 2.

12. Elizabeth H. Pleck, *Celebrating the Family: Ethnicity, Consumer Culture, and Family Rituals* (Cambridge, Mass.: Harvard University Press, 2000), 207–21.

13. Cele Otnes, Tina M. Lowrey, and Young Chan Kim, "Gift Giving for 'Difficult' and 'Easy' Recipients: A Social Roles Interpretation," *Journal of Consumer Research* 20 (1993): 229–44.

14. Richard Wilk, "The Binge Economy" (paper presented at the Eighth Interdisciplinary Conference on Research in Consumption, Paris, 26 July 2001).

15. Ronald L. Grimes, "Ritual," in *Guide to the Study of Religion,* ed. Willi Braun and Russell T. McCutcheon (London: Cassell, 2000), 261.

16. Diana Leonard, *Sex and Generation: A Study of Courtship and Weddings* (London: Tavistock Publications, 1980), 2.

17. Victor Turner, *The Ritual Process: Structure and Anti-structure* (Chicago: Aldine Pub. Co., 1969).

18. Tom Driver, *The Magic of Ritual* (New York: HarperCollins, 1991).

19. Leonard, *Sex and Generation,* 2.

20. Ronald L. Grimes, *Deeply into the Bone: Re-inventing Rites of Passage* (Berkeley: University of California Press, 2000), 153.

21. Frank F. Furstenberg Jr., "The Future of Marriage," *American Demographics,* June 1996, 34.

22. Ingraham, *White Weddings,* 169–70.

23. Eva Illouz, *Consuming the Romantic Utopia: Love and the Cultural Contradictions of Capitalism* (Berkeley: University of California Press, 1997), 73.

24. Christopher J. Berry, *The Idea of Luxury: A Conceptual and Historical Investigation* (Cambridge: Cambridge University Press, 1994), 18; Pierre Bourdieu, *Distinction: A Social Critique of the Judgment of Taste,* trans. Richard Nice (Cambridge, Mass.: Harvard University Press, 1984), 4–5.

25. Ellen K. Rothman, *Hands and Hearts: A History of Courtship in America* (New York: Basic Books, 1984).

26. Pamela Paul, *The Starter Marriage and the Future of Matrimony* (New York: Willard, 2002), 193–94.

27. A. Fuat Firat and Nikhilesh Dholakia, *Consuming People: From Political Economy to Theaters of Consumption* (London: Routledge, 1998).

28. Celia Lury, *Consumer Culture* (New Brunswick, N.J.: Rutgers University Press, 1996), 29–34.

29. Russell W. Belk, Güliz Ger, and Soren Askegaard, "Metaphors of Consumer Desire," in *Advances in Consumer Research,* vol. 23, ed. Kim Corfman and John Lynch (Provo, Utah: Association for Consumer Research, 1996), 368–73.

30. Jonathan Edward Schroeder, "The Consumer in Society: Utopian Visions Revisited," *Marketing Intelligence and Planning* 18, nos. 6–7 (2000): 385.

31. Berry, *Idea of Luxury,* 4.

32. Ibid., 27.

33. Illouz, *Romantic Utopia,* 13.

34. Benoit Heilbrunn, "In Search of the Lost Aura: The Object in the Age of Marketing Romanticism," in *Romancing the Market,* ed. Stephen Brown, Anne Marie Doherty, and Bill Clarke (London: Sage, 1998), 187–201.

35. Illouz, *Romantic Utopia,* 26.

36. This is one of the central arguments in Colin Campbell, *The Romantic Ethic and the Spirit of Modern Consumerism* (Oxford: B. Blackwell, 1987), as well as one made by Illouz.

37. Campbell, *Romantic Ethic,* 50. Campbell credits Thorsten Veblen with this idea.

38. Francesca Cancian, "The Feminization of Love," *Signs* 11, no. 4 (1986): 701; Janice Radway, *Reading the Romance* (Chapel Hill: University of North Carolina Press, 1984).

39. Cancian, "Feminization," 692.

40. Betsy [pseud.], interview by Cele Otnes, Urbana, Ill., 15 December 1997.

41. Laura [pseud.], interview by Cele Otnes, Champaign, Ill., 12 July 1991.

42. Russell W. Belk, "The Ineluctable Mysteries of Possessions," *Journal of Behavior and Social Personality* 6, no. 6 (1991): 17–55.

43. Ronald L. Grimes, personal communication, 19 December 2001.

44. Jelena Runser-Spanjol, Pamela Lowrey, and Cele C. Otnes, "Transformational Claims in Advertising: A Longitudinal Study" (paper presented at the Association for Consumer Research European Conference, Paris, 25 June 1999).

45. Russell W. Belk, Melanie Wallendorf, and John F. Sherry Jr., "The Sacred and Profane in Consumer Behavior: Theodicy on the Odyssey," *Journal of Consumer Research* 16 (1989): 1–38.

46. "Sharp Increase in Marriages of Teens Found in 90s," http.www. nytimes/com/2002/11/10/national/10TEEN/html, 10 November 2002.

47. Michelle R. Nelson and Cele C. Otnes, "How Do You Say 'I Do'? An Analysis of Community and Socialization in Intercultural Wedding Message Boards" (paper presented at the Eighth Cross-Cultural Research Conference, Kahuku, Hawaii, 14 December 2001).

48. M. Susan Burger and William B. White, *The Daguerreotype: Nineteenth-Century Technology and Modern Science* (Washington, D.C.: Smithsonian Institution Press, 1991); Merry A. Foresta and John Wood, *Secrets of the Dark Chamber: The Art of the American Daguerreotype* (Washington, D.C.: Smithsonian Institution Press, 1995).

49. John R. Gillis, *A World of Their Own Making: Myth, Ritual, and the Quest for Family Values* (New York: Basic Books, 1996), 3–19.

50. David Pillemer, *Momentous Events, Vivid Memories* (Cambridge, Mass.: Harvard University Press, 1998), 3.

51. Paula Mergenbagen DeWitt, "The Second Time Around," *American Demographics,* November 1992, 60.

52. Micaela di Leonardo, "The Female World of Cards and Holidays: Women, Families, and Work of Kinship," *Signs* 12 (1987): 440–53.

53. Russell W. Belk, "Art versus Science as Ways of Generating Knowledge about Materialism," in *Perspectives on Methodology in Consumer Research,* ed. David Brinberg and Richard J. Lutz (New York:

Springer-Verlag, 1986), 3–36; Russell W. Belk, "Multimedia Consumer Research," in *Representation in Consumer Research,* ed. Barbara Stern (London: Routledge, 1998), 308–38.

54. David Lowenthal, *The Past Is a Foreign Country* (New York: Cambridge University Press, 1985), 72.

55. Mihalyi Csikszentmihalyi and Eugene Rochberg-Halton, *The Meaning of Things: Domestic Symbols and the Self* (Cambridge: Cambridge University Press, 1981), 67.

56. Ingraham, *White Weddings,* 4.

57. *Modern Bride,* June–July 1999.

58. Focus group, interview by Cele Otnes, Urbana, Ill., 13 June 1991.

59. Marsha Seligson, *The Eternal Bliss Machine: America's Way of Wedding* (New York: William Morrow and Co., 1973), 26–29.

60. Pleck, *Celebrating the Family,* 209.

61. Russell W. Belk, *Collecting in a Consumer Society* (London: Routledge, 1995), 5.

62. See Berry, *Idea of Luxury,* chapters 2 and 3, for a discussion of the motivation for sumptuary laws.

63. Belk, *Collecting in a Consumer Society,* 5.

64. Ibid., 6.

65. Ibid., 7.

66. Ibid., 9.

67. Richard Lacayo, "About Face," *Time,* 3 December 2001, 46–47.

68. Ramona Faith Oswald, "A Member of the Wedding? Heterosexism and Family Ritual," *Journal of Social and Personal Relationships* 17 (2000): 349–68.

69. Jaclyn Geller, *Here Comes the Bride: Women, Weddings, and the Marriage Mystique* (New York: Four Walls Eight Windows, 2001), 72.

70. Elizabeth Freeman, *The Wedding Complex: Forms of Belonging in Modern American Culture* (Durham, N.C.: Duke University Press, 2002), 220.

71. A word is in order here about our research methodology. We utilized six basic sources: (1) published demographic data and marketing surveys; (2) interviews with brides from the United States

and many other countries conducted between 1991 and 2002; (3) observations of weddings and brides shopping for gowns in the United States; (4) historical research in magazines (bridal and otherwise), newspapers, bridal exhibits and photographs, etiquette guides, biographies and autobiographies, and archives of advertising agencies; (5) popular U.S. radio, television, films, and novels; and (6) scholarly literature on contemporary consumer culture and media history, culture, romance, ritual, and family history.

2. THE RISE OF THE LAVISH WEDDING

1. www.weddingsourcebook.com/page104.html, 1 February 2001.

2. Madonna Kolbenschlag, *Kiss Sleeping Beauty Good-Bye* (San Francisco: Harper and Row, 1988), 3.

3. Jack Zipes, ed., *The Oxford Companion to Fairy Tales* (New York: Oxford University Press, 2000), 165–67.

4. Arthur Waley, "The Chinese Cinderella Story," *Folklore* 58 (1947), 226–38.

5. Huang Mei, *Transforming the Cinderella Dream: From Frances Burney to Charlotte Brontë* (New Brunswick, N.J.: Rutgers University Press, 1990), 2.

6. Regina Lee Blaszczyk, *Imagining Consumers: Design and Innovation from Wedgwood to Corning* (Baltimore: Johns Hopkins University Press, 2000), 47–48.

7. Deborah Handy, ed., *Variety Film Reviews 1907–1980* (New York: Garland Publishing, 1985), 44.

8. Kay F. Stone, "The Misuses of Enchantment: Controversies on the Significance of Fairy Tales," in *Women's Folklore, Women's Culture,* ed. Rosan Jordan and Susan Kalcik (Philadelphia: University of Pennsylvania Press, 1985), 125–45.

9. Colette Dowling, *The Cinderella Complex: Women's Hidden Fear of Independence* (New York: Summit Books, 1981).

10. Lawrence Stone, *The Family, Sex, and Marriage in England, 1500–1800* (New York: Harper and Row, 1977), 180–81, 272–73,

282–87, 490–91; Marilyn Yalom, *A History of the Wife* (New York: Harper Collins, 2001).

11. Colin Campbell, *The Romantic Ethic and the Spirit of Modern Consumerism* (Oxford: B. Blackwell, 1987), 1–99.

12. Peter N. Stearns, *Consumerism in World History: The Global Transformation of Desire* (London: Routledge, 2001), 29.

13. Lisa Jardine, *Worldly Goods* (London: Macmillan, 1996); Simon Schama, *The Embarrassment of Riches: An Interpretation of Dutch Culture in the Golden Age* (New York: Knopf, 1987); Clare Haru Crowston, *Fabricating Women: The Seamstresses of Old Regime France, 1675–1791* (Durham, N.C.: Duke University Press, 2001).

14. Nancy Tomes, *The Gospel of Germs: Men, Women, and the Microbe in American Life* (Cambridge, Mass.: Harvard University Press, 1998), 62–63.

15. James O. Horton, "Freedom's Yoke: Gender Conventions among Antebellum Free Blacks," *Feminist Studies* 12 (1986): 50–76.

16. *Godey's Lady's Book* (1849), quoted in Maria McBride-Mellinger, *The Wedding Dress* (New York: Random House, 1993), 30.

17. Michael Deming, *Mechanic Accents: Dime Novels and Working-Class Culture in America* (London: Verso, 1987), 199.

18. Philip J. Reilly, *Old Masters of Retailing* (New York: Fairchild Publications, 1966), 66–71, 142–50, 151–56, 193–200.

19. William Leach, *Land of Desire: Merchants, Power, and the Rise of a New American Culture* (New York: Pantheon Books, 1993), 22, 36.

20. Ibid., 84.

21. Terence Witkowski, "The Early Development of Purchasing Roles in the American Household," *Journal of Macromarketing* 19 (December 1999): 104–14.

22. *Philadelphia Evening Bulletin*, 1 June 1911, 12; Vicki Howard, "American Weddings: Gender, Consumption, and the Business of Brides" (Ph.D. diss., University of Texas, 2000), 26.

23. See, for example, *The Jewelers' Circular* 97, no. 19 (4 December 1928): 28.

24. Blaszczyk, *Imagining Consumers,* 50.

25. E. A. Butterick, *Butterick's 1892 Metropolitan Fashion* (New York: Butterick Publishing, 1892), 41.

26. *The 1902 Edition of the Sears, Roebuck Catalogue* (New York: Gramercy Books, 2000).

27. Ted Ownby, *American Dreams in Mississippi: Consumers, Poverty, and Culture, 1830–1998* (Chapel Hill: University of North Carolina Press, 1999), 75–76.

28. Kathy Peiss, *Hope in a Jar: The Making of America's Beauty Culture* (New York: Henry Holt, 1998), 122.

29. Laura Mulvey, *Visual and Other Pleasures* (Basingstoke, England: Macmillan, 1989), 14–26.

30. Cele Otnes and Linda M. Scott, "Something Old, Something New: Exploring the Interaction between Advertising and Ritual," *Journal of Advertising* 25 (spring 1996): 33–50.

31. *The Jewelers' Circular* 98, no. 9 (4 April 1929): 3; *Philadelphia Evening Bulletin,* 3 May 1911.

32. Janet Brown and Pamela Loy, "Cinderella and Slipper Jack: Sex Roles and Social Mobility Themes in Early Musical Comedy," *International Journal of Women's Studies* 4 (1981): 507–16.

33. Beth Bailey, *From Front Porch to Back Seat: Courtship in Twentieth-Century America* (Baltimore: Johns Hopkins University Press, 1988).

34. Daniel Harris, "The Romantic," *Salmagundi* 123 (1999): 64–79.

35. Joanne J. Meyerowitz, *Women Adrift: Independent Wage Earners in Chicago, 1880–1930* (Chicago: University of Chicago Press, 1988), 129.

36. Barbara Tober, *The Bride: A Celebration* (New York: Harry N. Abrams, 1984), 116.

37. Juliet K. Arthur, "Here Comes the Bride's Business!" *Independent Woman* 18 (1939): 170–72, 183–84.

38. Marisa Keller and Mike Mashon, *TV Weddings: An Illustrated Guide* (New York: TV Books, 1999), 13–14.

39. Mark Caldwell, *A Short History of Rudeness: Manners, Morals, and Misbehavior in Modern America* (New York: Picador, 1999), 101–2.

40. Joan Jacobs Brumberg, *Fasting Girls: The Emergence of Anorexia Nervosa as a Modern Disease* (Cambridge, Mass.: Harvard University Press, 1988), 231–48.

41. Peiss, *Hope in a Jar,* 52–60.

42. Roland Marchand, *Advertising the American Dream: Making Way for Modernity, 1920–1940* (Berkeley: University of California Press, 1985), 19.

43. As quoted in Peiss, *Hope in a Jar,* 184.

44. Ibid., 215.

45. For a description of child labor and unsafe working conditions at Alfred Angelo factories outside the United States, see Chrys Ingraham, *White Weddings: Romancing Heterosexuality in Popular Culture* (London: Routledge, 1999), 47.

46. The first edition was Marie Coudert Brenning, *Wedding Embassy Year Book* (New York: The Wedding Embassy, 1934).

47. Diane Ackerman, *A Natural History of Love* (New York: Random House, 1994), 95–99.

48. *So You're Going to Be Married* (1934), quoted in McBride-Mellinger, *Wedding Dress,* 34.

49. Arthur Mayer, *Merely Colossal* (New York: Simon and Schuster, 1953), 178.

50. Norma Williams, *The Mexican American Family: Tradition and Change* (Dix Hills, N.Y.: General Hall, 1990), 30–31.

51. Kitty Hanson, *For Richer, for Poorer* (London: Abelard-Schuman, 1968), 114.

52. Elaine Tyler May, *Homeward Bound: American Families in the Cold War Era* (New York: Basic Books, 1988), 162–82.

53. Leach, *Land of Desire,* 295. See also James B. Twitchell, *Living It Up: Our Love Affair with Luxury* (New York: Columbia University Press, 2002), 153–73.

54. Arlene F. Saluter and Terry A. Lugaila, "Marital Status and Living Arrangements: March 1996," *Current Population Reports, P-20–496* (Washington, D.C.: U.S. Government Printing Office, 1996), 2.

55.   "Maryland in Focus," http://www.mdhs.org/library/MDF3.html, 15 January 2001; Ownby, *American Dreams in Mississippi,* 95.

56.   Adele Bahn, "Changes and Continuities in the Transitional Status of Bride into Wife: A Content Analysis of Bridal Magazines, 1967–1977, the Decade of the Women's Movement" (Ph.D. diss., City University of New York, 1979), 57, 59.

57.   Naomi Wood, "Domesticating Dreams in Walt Disney's *Cinderella,*" *The Lion and the Unicorn* 20 (1966): 25–49.

58.   Mary Jeffery Collier, "The Psychological Appeal in the Cinderella Theme," *American Imago* 18 (spring 1961): 408.

59.   Anna Quindlen, "*Ms.* Goes to a Wedding," *Ms.,* December 1978, 73–75.

60.   *Sears Christmas Wishbook,* 1965, 623, reprinted in Thomas W. Holland, ed., *Girls' Toys of the Fifties* (Sherman Oaks, Calif.: Windmill Press, 1997); Sears, Roebuck, *Sears Christmas Wishbooks* (Chicago: Sears, Roebuck, and Co., 1965), 623.

61.   Kitturah B. Westenhouser, *The Story of Barbie* (Paducah, Ky.: Collector Books, 1994), 32.

62.   *Sears Christmas Wishbook,* 1962, 410, reprinted in Holland, *Girls' Toys.*

63.   Ingraham, *White Weddings,* 93.

64.   Caitlin Flanagan, "The Wedding Merchants," *Atlantic Monthly,* February 2001, 112–19.

65.   Marybeth Nibley, "Editor to Divorce Herself from Long Career Helping Brides," *Los Angeles Times,* 7 December 1994, sec. D, p. 7; U.S. Census Bureau, *Statistical Abstract of the United States: 2000,* 120th ed. (Washington, D.C.: U.S. Government Printing Office, 2000), 65.

66.   "Once upon a Time . . . , the World Fell in Love with a Dashing Prince and His Enchanting Bride," *People,* 30 July 1991, 23, quoted in Ingraham, *White Weddings,* 36.

67.   Alvin Sanoff, "Marriage—It's Back in Style!" *U.S. News and World Report,* 20 June 1983, 44–53; Shari Miller, "The Big Wedding Is Back," *McCall's,* April 1981, 124–34.

68.   U.S. Census Bureau, *Statistical Abstract,* 65.

69. For discussion of the relentless marketing of luxury goods by French corporations beginning in the 1970s, see Twitchell, *Living It Up,* 123–39.

70. Jay Cocks, "Scenes from a Marriage: Checkbook Ready? Big Weddings Are Back," *Time,* 7 July 1986, 58–62.

71. Flanagan, "Wedding Merchants," 112–19.

72. Caldwell, *Short History,* 101–2.

73. Census figures do not include gay couples. "Sharp Increase in Marriage of Teens Found in 90s," http//www.nytimes/com/2002/11/10/national/10TEEN/html, 10 November 2002.

74. Nancy F. Cott, *Public Vows: A History of Marriage and the Nation* (Cambridge: Harvard University Press, 2000), 200–227.

75. Jay D. Teachman, Lucky M. Tedrow, and Kyle D. Crowder, "The Changing Demography of America's Families," in *Understanding Families into the New Millenium: A Decade in Review* (Minneapolis, Minn.: National Council on Family Relations, 2001), 453–65.

76. Robert H. Frank, *Luxury Fever: Why Money Fails to Satisfy in an Era of Excess* (New York: Free Press, 1999), 14–44, 159–72; Twitchell, *Living It Up,* 63–64.

77. "Wedding Bells," *Off Our Backs* 25, no. 4 (1995), 3.

3. THE ENGAGEMENT COMPLEX

1. Emily Post, *Etiquette in Society, in Business, in Politics, and at Home* (New York: Funk & Wagnalls, 1922), 308–9.

2. Victor Turner, *The Ritual Process: Structure and Anti-structure* (Chicago: Aldine Publishing Co., 1969), 94.

3. Anita Diamant, *The New Jewish Wedding* (New York: Summit Books, 1985), 143.

4. Cele Otnes, Tina M. Lowrey, and L. J. Shrum, "Toward an Understanding of Consumer Ambivalence," *Journal of Consumer Research* 24 (June 1997): 80–93.

5. George Frederick Kunz, *Rings for the Finger* (Philadelphia: J. P. Lippincott & Co., 1917), 201.

6. David Cressy, *Birth, Marriage, and Death: Ritual, Religion, and the Life-Cycle in Tudor and Stuart England* (Oxford: Oxford University Press, 1997), 268–69.

7. Ibid., 269.

8. Claudia de Lys, *How the World Weds* (New York: The Martin Press, 1929), 64.

9. Laurel Thatcher Ulrich, *A Midwife's Tale: The Life of Martha Ballard, Based on Her Diary* (New York: Vintage Books, 1990), 139.

10. Cressy, *Birth, Marriage, and Death,* 275.

11. Ruby Jo Reeves, "Marriages in New Haven since 1870: Statistically Analyzed and Culturally Interpreted" (Ph.D. diss., Yale University, 1938), vii–33.

12. We examined June wedding announcements in the *St. Louis* (Mo.) *Post-Dispatch* from 1890 to 1980.

13. Frances W. Kuchler, *Law of Engagement and Marriage* (Dobbs Ferry, N.Y.: Oceana Publications, 1966), 17–20.

14. Michael Grossberg, *Governing the Hearth: Law and the Family in Nineteenth-Century America* (Chapel Hill: University of North Carolina Press, 1985), 31–63; Rebecca Tushnet, "Rules of Engagement," *The Yale Law Journal* 107, no. 8 (June 1998): 2583–618.

15. Tushnet, "Rules of Engagement," 2586.

16. Ulrich, *Midwife's Tale,* 141.

17. Wilbur Cross and Ann Novotny, *White House Weddings* (New York: David McKay Company, 1967), 118.

18. Patricia Mainardi, "Quilts: The Great American Art," *Radical America* 7 (1973): 58.

19. Ellen K. Rothman, *Hands and Hearts: A History of Courtship in America* (New York: Basic Books, 1984), 166.

20. Stephen Fox, *The Mirror Makers* (New York: William Morrow and Company, 1984), 90.

21. Regina Lee Blaszczyk, "Cinderella Stories: The Glass of Fashion and the Gendered Marketplace," in *His and Hers: Gender, Consumption, and Technology,* ed. Roger Horowitz and Arwen Mohun (Charlottesville: University Press of Virginia, 1998), 142.

22. Emily Post, *Etiquette: The Blue Book of Social Usage* (New York: Funk & Wagnalls, 1927), 322–23.

23. Ibid., 323–24.

24. Ernest W. Burgess and Paul Wallin, with Gladys Denny Shultz, *Courtship, Engagement, and Marriage* (Philadelphia: Lippincott, 1954), 163–64.

25. Checklists in *Bride's* were examined from 1959 (the first year Condé Nast bought the publication) to 2000.

26. Diana Leonard, *Sex and Generation: A Study of Courtship and Weddings* (London: Tavistock Publications, 1980), 114.

27. Bride's Calendar, *Bride's,* summer 1959, 70.

28. Bride's Calendar, *Bride's,* February 1970, 16.

29. Bride's Calendar, *Bride's,* August–September 1995, 290.

30. Russell W. Belk, Melanie Wallendorf, and John F. Sherry Jr., "The Sacred and Profane in Consumer Behavior: Theodicy on the Odyssey," *Journal of Consumer Research* 16, no. 1 (June 1989): 1–38.

31. Jennifer Hunter, "Behind All That Glitters (De Beers)," *MacLean's,* 29 December 1997–5 January 1998, 89.

32. Edward Jay Epstein, "Have You Ever Tried to Sell a Diamond?" *Atlantic Monthly,* February 1982, 28–29.

33. Nicholas Thomas, *Entangled Objects* (Cambridge, Mass.: Harvard University Press, 1991), 19–20.

34. Barrymore L. Scherer, "Engaging Rings," *Town & Country Monthly,* December 1990, 190–93.

35. Kunz, *Rings for the Finger,* 199.

36. Antonio Bonnano and Antoinette L. Matlins, *Engagement and Wedding Rings* (Woodstock, Vt.: Gemstone Press, 1999), 14.

37. Advertisement for Jabel Ring Manufacturing Company, *The Jewelers' Circular,* March 1934, 24.

38. "Interview with Harry Oppenheimer," 28 October 1999, *Prime Club Magazine,* http://www.primeclub.co.za/birthstones.html, 1 March 2000.

39. Edward Jay Epstein, *The Rise and Fall of Diamonds* (New York: Simon and Schuster, 1982), 127.

40. Advertisement for De Beers, "For Him the Diamond Dawns Are Set in Rings of Beauty," *New Yorker,* 23 September 1939, 7.

41. Advertisement for De Beers, "On Wings of Hope," *New Yorker,* 14 July 1945, 5.

42. Richard W. Lewis, *Absolut Book* (Boston: Journey Editions, 1996).

43. Donald S. McNeil, "New Promotion behind Jewelry," *Advertising and Selling,* March 1941, 23.

44. Julie A. Ruth and Ronald Faber, "Guilt: An Overlooked Advertising Appeal," in *Proceedings of the 1988 Conference of the American Academy of Advertising,* ed. John D. Leckenby (Austin, Tex.: American Academy of Advertising, 1989), 83–89.

45. Advertisement for De Beers, "Thought for the Future," painting by Raoul Dufy, from the "Great Artists" series, 1940.

46. Advertisement tearsheet for De Beers, "My Most Precious Possession . . . but Grind It to Powder!" January 1943, from the Smithsonian Museum Advertising Archives.

47. Epstein, *The Rise and Fall of Diamonds,* 124. De Beers has used this strategy more recently by persuading the directors of the television series *Baywatch* to devote an entire episode to the purchase of a diamond engagement ring. See "Glass with Attitude," *The Economist,* 20 December 1997, 115.

48. Epstein, *The Rise and Fall of Diamonds,* 127.

49. McNeil, "New Promotion," 23.

50. N. W. Ayer & Son, Inc., press release for *Jewelers' Circular Keystone,* 3 July 1963.

51. N. W. Ayer & Son, Inc., "Princess Expected to Follow Family Traditions," feature story prepared for *You and Your City,* 12 August 1947, 1.

52. Epstein, *The Rise and Fall of Diamonds,* 124.

53. David Federman, "50 Years of Saying Forever," *Modern Jeweler,* April 1997, 31; Ayer Oral History Interview with Frances Gerety, n.d., N. W. Ayer, Inc., Papers, Smithsonian National Museum of American History.

54. Ibid., 38.

55. Bonny Schoonaker, "Sparkling Slogan Is Century's Gem," *Sunday Times* (Johannesburg, South Africa), http://www.suntimes.co.za, 25 April 1999.

56. Advertisement for "Little Queens and Big Diamonds," 1953. Archived at the John W. Hartman Center for Sales, Advertising, and Marketing History; Rare Book, Manuscript, and Special Collections Library; Duke University. N. W. Ayer & Son, "Tiniest Diamond Ever Made—2," press release exclusive to *You and Your City,* 6 March 1951. N. W. Ayer & Son, Inc., "Grace Kelly Doll Wears Real Diamond," press release, n.d.

57. N. W. Ayer & Son, Inc., internal research report, 1985.

58. N. W. Ayer & Son, Inc., "Feature Ring Going into Men's Lines," Trend Report no. 42 (internal document), 2 February 1956, 1; advertisement for Feature Ring Company, *National Jeweler,* April 1957.

59. Jim Hickman, "Oppenheimer Passes on at 92—Glittering Life All Thanks to Diamonds," http://www.rense.com/general3/glit/html, 30 June 2001.

60. Millie R. Creighton, "The Depato: Merchandising in the West while Selling Japaneseness," in *Re-made in Japan: Everyday Life and Consumer Taste in a Changing Society,* ed. Joseph J. Tobin (New Haven, Conn.: Yale University Press, 1992), 42–57.

61. Epstein, *The Rise and Fall of Diamonds,* 135.

62. Dennis Chase, "De Beers Changes Ad Tack," *Advertising Age,* 18 July 1983, 42.

63. Cheryl Lu-Lien Tan, "Attacks Lead to a Change of Heart," *Baltimore Sun,* 15 October 2001, sec. E, p. 1.

64. Lauren Webber, "In Search of Forever, Shoppers Return to 47th Street," *New York Times,* 9 December 2001, sec. 3, p. 9.

65. N. W. Ayer & Son, internal research report, 1985.

66. Harvey Green, *The Light of the Home: An Intimate View of the Lives of Women in Victorian America* (New York: Pantheon Books, 1983), 10–28.

67. Rothman, *Hands and Hearts,* 216–17.

68. Jaclyn Geller, *Here Comes the Bride: Women, Weddings, and the Mar-*

riage Mystique (New York: Four Walls Eight Windows, 2001), 108, 112–14.

69. Lucy Howard et al., "I Thought You'd Never Ask," *Newsweek*, 30 October 2000, 15.

70. Daniel Harris, "Zaniness," *Salmagundi* 104–5 (1994–95): 206–17.

71. Sheryl Nissinen, *The Conscious Bride: Women Unveil Their True Feelings about Getting Hitched* (Oakland, Calif.: New Harbinger Publications, 2000), 33.

72. Sheree Bykofsky and Laurie Viera, *Popping the Question* (New York: Walker and Company, 1996).

73. Heidi B. Perlman, "Proposal Planner Helps the Romantically Challenged," *Champaign-Urbana* (Ill.) *News Gazette*, 22 February 2001, sec. D, p. 2.

74. The introduction of this section on wedding gifts and showers is based on Elizabeth Pleck, *Celebrating the Family: Ethnicity, Consumer Culture, and Family Rituals* (Cambridge, Mass.: Harvard University Press, 2000), 212–13.

75. Ellen M. Litwicki, "Showering the Bride: A Ritual of Gender and Consumption" (paper presented at the conference "Holidays, Ritual, Festival, Celebration and Public Display," Bowling Green, Ohio, 30 May 1998), 9.

76. Pleck, *Celebrating the Family*, 213.

77. Ibid.

78. Edith Ordway, *The Etiquette of Today* (New York: George Sully, 1920), 187, quoted in Johan Casparis, "The Bridal Shower: An American Rite of Passage," *Indian Journal of Social Research* 20 (1979): 12; Gail Paton Grant, "Getting Started: Outfitting the Bride in Seaside," *Canadian Folklore* 15, no. 2 (1993): 69–81.

79. Jo-Ann Leeming and Margaret Gleeson, *Complete Book of Showers and Engagement Parties* (Garden City, N.Y.: Garden City Publishing Company, 1948).

80. Margaret Baker, *Wedding Customs and Folklore* (Totowa, N.J.: David and Charles, 1977), 44; S. P. Breckinridge, *New Homes for Old* (New York: Harper and Brothers, 1921), 49.

81. David J. Cheal, *The Gift Economy* (London: Routledge, 1988), 98–100.

82. Leeming and Gleeson, *Complete Book of Showers,* 60–61.

83. Beth Montemurro, " 'You Go 'Cause You Have To': The Bridal Shower as a Ritual of Obligation," *Symbolic Interaction* 25, no. 1 (2002): 67–92.

84. Casparis, "The Bridal Shower," 14.

85. Robbie Davis-Floyd to Reed Malcolm, personal communication, November 2001.

86. Dawn O. Braithwaite, "Ritualized Embarassment at 'Coed' Wedding and Baby Showers," *Communication Reports* 8, no. 2 (1995): 150–51.

87. Regina Blaszczyk, *Imagining Consumers: Design and Innovation from Wedgwood to Corning* (Baltimore: Johns Hopkins University Press, 2000), 258.

88. Barbara Tober, *The Bride: A Celebration* (New York: Harry N. Abrams, 1984), 78.

89. Graeme Lorimer, "Wedding Bills," *Ladies' Home Journal* 3 (1929): 27, 65, 67; Marion Edwards, "Wedding Presents Made Easy," *Saturday Evening Post,* 15 March 1930, 52; Robert F. Nattan and Harry R. Terhune, "Different Styles of Advertising," *The Jewelers' Circular* 25 (25 July 1929), 43, 45.

90. Blaszczyk, "Cinderella Stories," 145.

91. Kimberly Stevens, "I Do . . . Take MasterCard," *Wall Street Journal,* 23 June 2000, sec. W, pp. 1–4.

92. Amy Vanderbilt, *Amy Vanderbilt's Complete Book of Etiquette* (Garden City, N.Y.: Doubleday and Company, 1954), 99.

93. Advertisement for Franciscan China, *Bride and Home,* February 1962.

94. Roger Heeler et al., "Gift versus Personal Use Brand Selection," in *Advances in Consumer Research,* vol. 6, ed. William Wilkie (Provo, Utah: Association for Consumer Research, 1979), 325–28.

95. Russell W. Belk, "Gift-Giving Behavior," in *Research in Consumer Behavior,* vol. 2, ed. Jagdish Sheth (Greenwich, Conn.: JAI Press,

1979), 95–126; Russell W. Belk, "Effects of Gift-Giving Involvement on Gift Selection Strategies," in *Advances in Consumer Research,* vol. 9, ed. Andrew A. Mitchell (Provo, Utah: Association for Consumer Research, 1981), 410.

96. Stephen P. DeVere, Clifford D. Scott, and William L. Shulby, "Consumer Perceptions of Gift-Giving Occasions: Attribute Saliency and Structure," in *Advances in Consumer Research,* vol. 10, ed. Richard P. Bagozzi and Alice Tybout (Ann Arbor, Mich.: Association for Consumer Research, 1983), 185–90.

97. Judith Waldrop, "Here Come the Brides," *American Demographics* 12 (June 1990): 4.

98. Cyndee Miller, "Nix the Knick-Knacks: Send Cash," *Marketing News,* 26 May 1997, 1, 13.

99. John Naisbitt, *John Naisbitt's Trend Letter* 10, no. 6 (1 August 1991): 1.

100. "Bridal Registries: Older Couples Equal More Gifts," *Stores,* April 1988, 16.

101. Stevens, "I Do," sec. W, p. 4.

102. Marcy Magiera, "For Couple with Everything, Try Hardware Store," *Advertising Age,* 25 January 1993, 27.

103. Mike O'Connor, "Gift Honeymoons," *Courier Mail* (Queensland, Australia), 1 September 2001, sec. T, p. 2.

104. Nicole Swengley, "What a Wedding Present," *London Times,* 20 October 2001, Features sec.

105. Stevens, "I Do," sec. W, p. 4.

106. Emily Post decreed in 1952 that it was acceptable to display checks on the table, provided that the amount of the check was concealed. Emily Post, *Etiquette: The Blue Book of Social Usage* (New York: Funk and Wagnalls, 1952), 236.

107. Helen Kirwan-Taylor, "Bridezilla's Monster Appetite: Buying a Wedding Present for the New 'Aesthetic Compulsive' Can Be a Nightmare," *Financial Times,* 21 July 2001, 10.

108. Post, *Etiquette in Society,* 305.

109. Leeming and Gleeson, *Complete Book of Showers,* 10.

110. Charles Hanson Towne, *Gentlemen Behave* (New York: Julian Messner, 1939), 283.

111. Howard P. Chudacoff, *The Age of the Bachelor* (Princeton, N.J.: Princeton University Press, 1999), 262.

112. Clover Nolan Williams, "The Bachelor's Transgression: Identity and Difference in the Bachelor Party," *Journal of American Folklore* 108 (1994): 106–20.

113. Elizabeth Comte, "Good Food, Good Wine, and Good Storytelling," *Forbes,* 10 May 1993, 174–75.

114. Diane Tye and Annie Marie Powers, "Gender Resistance and Play: Bachelorette Parties in Atlantic Canada," *Women's Studies International Forum* 21, no. 5 (1998): 551–61.

115. Nicholas Kulish, "Turning the Tables: Bachelorette Parties Are Getting Risqué," *Wall Street Journal,* 3 September 2002, sec. A, p. 1, 8.

4. THE RITUALS OF WEDDING SHOPPING

1. Stephanie N. Mehta, "Bridal Superstores Woo Couples with Miles of Gowns and Tuxes," *Wall Street Journal,* 14 February 1996, sec. B, p. 1.

2. Emile Durkheim, "Definition of Religious Phenomena and of Religion," in *The Elementary Forms of Religious Life: A Study in Religious Sociology* (London: Allen & Unwin, 1915), 36–45.

3. Cele Otnes and Tina M. Lowrey, "Til Debt Do Us Part: The Selection and Meaning of Artifacts in the American Wedding," in *Advances in Consumer Research,* vol. 20, ed. Leigh McAlister and Michael Rothschild (Provo, Utah: Association for Consumer Research, 1993), 325.

4. See Russell Belk, Melanie Wallendorf, and John F. Sherry Jr., "The Sacred and Profane in Consumer Behavior: Theodicy on the Odyssey," *Journal of Consumer Research* 16, no. 1 (June 1989): 1–38.

5. Jaclyn Geller, *Here Comes the Bride: Women, Weddings, and the Marriage Mystique* (New York: Four Walls Eight Windows, 2001), 214.

6. Otnes and Lowrey, "Til Debt Do Us Part," 327.

7. For more on the development of the white gown, see Musée de la Mode de la Ville de Paris, *Mariage: Exhibition Catalog of the Musée Galleria,* trans. Richard Hertel (Paris: Editions Assouline, 1999); Linda Otto Lipsett, *To Love and to Cherish: Brides Remembered* (San Francisco: The Quilt Digest Press, 1989); "Millennial Bridal Fashions," http://www.weddingchannel.com, 30 March 2001.

8. Claudia de Lys, *How the World Weds* (New York: The Martin Press, 1929), 68.

9. John A. Ruth, *Decorum: A Practical Treatise on Etiquette and Dress of the Best American Society* (New York: Union Publishing House, 1877), 288.

10. Geller, *Here Comes the Bride,* 224–26.

11. Stanley Elkin, "In Praise of Tuxedos," *Harper's,* November 1985, 34.

12. Ilene Beckerman, *Mother of the Bride* (Chapel Hill, N.C.: Algonquin Books, 2000), 127–29.

13. Ruth La Ferla, "NOTICED: Here Comes the Mother of the Bride," *New York Times,* 7 May 2000, sec. 9, p. 1.

14. Luisa Kroll, "What Would Queen Victoria Have Said?" *Forbes,* 20 October 1997, 267.

15. Karen Robinovitz, "Bridesmaid vs. Gown: Can This Marriage Be Saved?" *New York Times,* 20 May 2001, sec. 9, p. 7.

16. "Camp America," *Times Magazine,* 30 March 2002, 69.

17. The average cost of a gown was reported to be $790 and the veil to be $150 in 2000. Costs of the men's (rented) formal wear was $500 for the groom and five ushers; bridesmaids' attire was $720; and the dress for the mother of the bride was $198; Charity Curley, "Hill Rollin' Romance," based on a *Bride's* magazine survey in 2000, http://www.ivillage.com/relationships/weddings/articles/00, 89536,00.html, 15 January 2001.

18. James Carrier, "The Rituals of Christmas Giving," in *Unwrapping Christmas,* ed. Daniel Miller (Oxford: Clarendon Press, 1993), 63.

19. Dennis Rook, "The Ritual Dimension of Consumer Behavior," *Journal of Consumer Research* 12 (1985): 252–64.

20. Danelle Morton, "Seventh Avenue: Here Come the Brides," *New York Times,* 26 October 1980, sec. 3, p. 19.

21. Angela L. Thompson, "Unveiled: The Emotion Work of Wedding Coordinators in the American Wedding Industry" (Ph.D. diss., Brandeis University, 1998), 71.

22. N. W. Ayer & Son, Inc., "New Aspects on the Bridal Consultant Business, from a Tour of Jewelry Stores with Barbara Wilson," internal document, February 1952, 1. Archived at the John W. Hartman Center for Sales, Advertising, and Marketing History; Rare Book, Manuscript, and Special Collections Library; Duke University.

23. Ibid., 2.

24. Belfield Carter, "Jerry Connor: Practical Dreamer," brochure of article reprinted from *The Southern Jeweler,* 1959, 2.

25. Ibid., 2.

26. Doris Nixon, National Bridal Service, personal correspondence, June 2001.

27. Carter, "Jerry Connor," 4.

28. Advertisement for National Bridal Service, "Meet the Other Woman in Your Romance!" *Modern Bride,* fall 1957.

29. This association is now named the Association of Bridal Consultants; http://www.trainingforum.com/ASN/ABC, 2 July 2001.

30. Donald H. Dunn et al., "Consultants Who Help You Tie the Knot," *Business Week,* 25 May 1987, 182.

31. Thompson, "Unveiled," 134–35.

32. Ibid., 73–76.

33. Ibid., 171–72.

34. Debi Kephart, interview with Cele Otnes, 3 July 2001.

35. George Myers Jr., "E-commerce Study Shows Women Did More Online Shopping in 2001," *Columbus Dispatch,* 7 January 2002, sec. E, p. 4.

36. Cele C. Otnes and Mary Ann McGrath, "Perceptions and Realities of the Male Shopper," *Journal of Retailing* 77 (spring 2001): 111–37.

37. Cele C. Otnes, Tina M. Lowrey, and L. J. Shrum, "Toward an Understanding of Consumer Ambivalence," *Journal of Consumer Research* 24 (June 1997): 83.

38. Robert K. Merton and Elinor Barber, "Sociological Ambivalence," in *Sociological Ambivalence,* ed. Robert K. Merton (New York: Free Press, 1976), 3–31.

39. Zygmunt Baumann, *Modernity and Ambivalence* (Cambridge: Polity Press, 1991), 199.

40. Otnes, Lowrey, and Shrum, "Toward an Understanding," 86.

41. Ibid.

42. Thompson, "Unveiled," 150.

43. Ibid., 179.

44. Otnes, Lowrey, and Shrum, "Toward an Understanding," 88.

45. Ibid., 89.

46. Ibid.

47. Thompson, "Unveiled," 106.

48. Letter from Jerry Connor to Dorothy Dignam, N. W. Ayer & Son, Inc., 10 January 1958, 2.

49. N. W. Ayer & Son, "New Aspects," 7.

50. Thompson, "Unveiled," 121.

51. Ibid., 44.

52. Charles Lewis, "Working the Ritual: Wedding Photography as Social Process" (Ph.D. diss., University of Minnesota, 1994), 97.

53. Focus group, interviews by Cele Otnes, 13 June 1991, 18 June 1991.

54. Debi Kephart, interview by Cele Otnes, 3 July 2001.

55. Diana Leonard, *Sex and Generation: A Study of Courtship and Weddings* (London: Tavistock, 1980), 33–34.

56. Focus group, interviews by Cele Otnes, 13 June 1991, 18 June 1991.

57. "Wedding Trends," with Kojo Nnamdi, http://www.wamu.org/pi/shows/piarc_010212.html, 15 February 2001.

58. "Getting the Groom Involved in the Planning," *The Cleveland Plain Dealer,* 27 January 2000, sec. F, p. 5.

59. Vicki Howard, "American Weddings: Gender, Consumption, and the Business of Brides" (Ph.D. diss., University of Texas at Austin, 2000), 209.

60. Focus group, interview by Cele Otnes, 18 June 1991.

61. Jennifer Tung, "Attack of Bridezilla: Demanding Perfection Before 'I Do,' " *New York Times,* 20 May 2001, sec. 9, p. 1.

62. "Groom's Involvement Leads Wedding Trends," *Women and Marketing,* 13 May 1998, 10.

63. Focus group, interview by Cele Otnes, 20 June 1991.

64. Thompson, "Unveiled," 132.

65. Ibid., 137.

66. Dina Bunn, "Something Blue: J. C. Penney Quits Bridal Business as It Closes Its Salon at Villa Italia," *Denver Rocky Mountain News,* 9 June 1999, sec. B, p. 1.

67. Greer Fay Cashman, "Something Old to Something New," *The Jerusalem Post,* 25 December 1997, 14.

68. Sheryl Nissinen, *The Conscious Bride: Women Unveil Their True Feelings about Getting Hitched* (Oakland, Calif.: New Harbinger Publications, 2000), 87.

69. Cele Otnes, "Friend of the Bride, and Then Some," in *ServiceScapes: The Concept of Place in Contemporary Markets,* ed. John F. Sherry Jr. (Lincolnwood, Ill.: NTC Business Press, 1998), 244–45.

70. Irving J. Rein, "The Rhetoric of the Bridal Salon," in *The Great American Communication Catalogue* (Englewood Cliffs, N.J.: Prentice Hall, 1978), 156.

71. Christopher Berry, *The Idea of Luxury: A Conceptual and Historical Investigation* (Cambridge: Cambridge University Press, 1994), 27.

72. "Real Brides Say . . . ," http://www.windsorpeak.com/bridalgown/mailbag/mailmay00.html, 21 July 2001.

73. Geller, *Here Comes the Bride,* 219.

74. Diane Clehane, "Style File/Gowns to Go/More Brides Are Looking for Wedding Dresses in a Hurry," *Newsday,* 24 June 1999, sec. B, p. 27.

75. Anne-Marie Schiro, "Fantasy and Taste in a New Bridal Salon," *New York Times,* 5 September 1990, sec. C, p. 8.

76. Marianne Wilson, "Wedding Stores Go Big," *Chain Store Age,* October 1995, 31–35.

77. Sheila Sullivan, press release included in publicity packet prepared for Kleinfeld (MediaVision, n.d.).

78. Kit R. Roane, "Kleinfeld, a Threatened Bridal Mecca, Gets New Owners," *New York Times,* 21 July 1999, sec. B, p. 3.

79. Pauline Greenhill, personal correspondence, October 2001.

80. Geller, *Here Comes the Bride,* 219.

81. Rein, "The Rhetoric of the Bridal Salon," 156.

82. N. W. Ayer & Son, Inc., "Status of Leading Bridal Services and Bridal Book Publishers, January, 1957," internal document, 25 January 1957, 2.

83. Susanne Friese, "A Consumer Good in the Ritual Process: The Case of the Wedding Dress," *Journal of Ritual Studies* 11 (winter 1997): 50.

84. Marisa Corrado, "Teaching Wedding Rules: How Bridal Workers Negotiate Control over Their Customers," *Journal of Contemporary Ethnography* 31, no. 1 (February 2002): 33–67.

85. Ibid.

86. Ibid., 61.

87. Cele Otnes, field notes, p. 404.

88. Stephanie Gutmann, "The Wedding Gown: Revealing the Nation's Mood," *New York Times,* 15 June 1997, sec. 1, p. 33.

89. Otnes, Lowrey, and Shrum, "Toward an Understanding," 83.

90. Gail [pseud.], interview by Stephenetta Hoff, 12 July 1995.

91. Kate Cohen, *A Walk down the Aisle: Notes on a Modern Wedding* (New York: W. W. Norton, 2001), 42.

92. Otnes, "Friend of the Bride," 236–37.

93. Geller, *Here Comes the Bride,* 222–23.

94. Chris Reidy, "Here Storm the Brides: Basement Bridal Sale Provides Unique Insights," *Boston Globe,* 21 May 1996, 64.

95. Susan Dobscha and Ellen Foxman, "Women and Wedding Gowns:

Exploring a Discount Shopping Experience," in *Gender, Marketing, and Consumer Behavior,* 4th ed., ed. Eileen Fischer and Dan Wardlow (San Francisco: San Francisco State University Publishing, 1998), 131–41; Susan Dobscha and Ellen Foxman, "Gendered Communication: Textual Analysis of Letters Written to Filene's Basement," in *Gender, Marketing, and Consumer Behavior,* 5th ed., ed. Jonathan Schroeder and Cele C. Otnes (Champaign: University of Illinois Printing Service, 2000), 176–77.

96.   Mehta, "Bridal Superstores," sec. B, p. 1.

97.   James B. Twitchell, *Living It Up: Our Love Affair with Luxury* (New York: Columbia University Press, 2002), 134.

5. THE WEDDING WEEKEND

1.   James S. Hirsch, "This Should Get Their Picture on the Studio Wall," *Wall Street Journal,* 16 June 1992, sec. A, p. 11.

2.   George Ritzer, *Enchanting a Disenchanted World: Revolutionizing the Means of Consumption* (Thousand Oaks, Calif.: Pine Forge Press, 1999), 104; Nita Rollins, "Something Borrowed, Something Taped: Video Nuptials," *Wide Angle* 13 (April 1991): 32–38.

3.   David Bouchier, "OUT OF ORDER: Romance Plus Finance Equals Extravagance," *New York Times,* 7 May 2000, sec. 14L, p. 8.

4.   Ronald L. Grimes, "Ritual and Performance," in *Religion and American Cultures: An Encyclopedia of Traditions, Diversity, and Popular Expression,* ed. Gary Laderman and Luis León (Santa Barbara, Calif.: ABC-CLIO, 2003).

5.   Jeffrey Jensen Arnett, "Learning to Stand Alone: The Contemporary American Transition to Adulthood in Cultural and Historical Context," *Human Development* 41 (1998): 295–97.

6.   Kate Cohen, *A Walk down the Aisle: Notes on a Modern Wedding* (New York: W. W. Norton and Company, 2001), 94. See also Sue Fleming, *Buff Brides* (New York: Villard Books, 2002); Tracy Effinger and Suzanne Rowen, *The Wedding Workout: Look and Feel Fabulous on Your Special Day* (Chicago: Contemporary Books, 2002).

7.   Sheryl Nissinen, *The Conscious Bride: Women Unveil Their True*

Feelings about Getting Hitched (Oakland, Calif.: New Harbinger Publications, 2000), 74.

8. Cohen, *A Walk down the Aisle,* 94.

9. Elizabeth Connelly Pearce, *Altar Bound: An Outline of the Duties of the Members of the Bridal Party* (Danville, Ill.: The Interstate, 1963), 19.

10. Paul H. Jacobson, *American Marriage and Divorce* (New York: Rinehart and Company, 1959), table 21, p. 58; U.S. Department of Health and Human Services, *Vital Statistics of the United States,* vol. 3, *Marriage and Divorce,* DHHS Pub. No. (PHS) 91–1103 (Washington, D.C.: U.S. Government Printing Office, 1991), table 1–18, p. 22.

11. Eric Morgenthaler, "People Are So Goofy about Disney World They Marry There—Fairy-Tale Weddings Become a Major New Attraction; Cinderella Weds the Prince," *Wall Street Journal,* 28 October 1992, sec. A, p. 1.

12. Milton Okun, *Popular Songs for the Wedding* (Port Chester, N.Y.: Cherry Lane Music Company, 1994).

13. We surveyed all June wedding announcements in *The St. Louis* (Mo.) *Dispatch* for 1950, 1960, 1970, 1980, and 1990. Information for 1991–92 comes from Cahners Research, *Modern Bride* Reader Service Survey, 1991–92.

14. Erving Goffman, *Gender Advertisements* (Cambridge, Mass.: Harvard University Press, 1976), 54.

15. Postings to "Wedding Forum," http://forums.thathomesite.com/forums/load/wedding/MSG0509190014578.html, 1 June 2001; Pamela R. Frese, "The Union of Nature and Culture: Gender Symbolism in the American Wedding Ritual," in *Transcending Boundaries: Multi-disciplinary Approaches to the Study of Gender,* ed. Pamela R. Frese and John M. Coggleshall (New York: Bergen and Garvey, 1991), 97–112.

16. The information comes from a survey of 1,088 respondents in "Facts about Our Brides!" http://www.ultimatewedding.com/polls, 1 February 2001.

17. In Protestant ceremonies in the 1920s, the couple would kneel in

prayer after the groom had put the ring on the bride's finger. E. B. Cabot, "Perfect Church Wedding," *Ladies' Home Journal* 36 (June 1923): 112.

18. Jenna Weissman Joselit, *The Wonders of America: Reinventing Jewish Culture, 1880–1950* (New York: Hill and Wang, 1994), 36; "Matched Ring Set," *The Jewelers' Circular-Keystone* 115 (December 1944): 278; Barbara Tober, *The Bride: A Celebration* (New York: Harry N. Abrams, 1984), 98.

19. Credit for the phrase "portable utopia" goes to Daniel Harris, *Cute, Quaint, Hungry, and Romantic* (New York: Basic Books, 2000), 15.

20. Charles Lewis, "Working the Ritual: Wedding Photography as Social Process" (Ph.D. diss., University of Minnesota, 1994), 139.

21. Ibid., 156.

22. This visual cliché appeared as early as the 1880s in bridal daguerreotypes. Elizabeth Freeman, *The Wedding Complex: Forms of Belonging in Modern American Culture* (Durham, N.C.: Duke University Press, 2002), 28, 30.

23. Cohen, *A Walk down the Aisle,* 126.

24. Lewis, "Working the Ritual," 324.

25. Musée de la Mode de la Ville de Paris, *Mariage: Exhibition Catalog of the Musée Galleria,* trans. Richard Hertel (Paris: Editions Assouline, 1999), 145.

26. Nancy Ann Jeffrey, "Wedding Photos Losing Focus," *Wall Street Journal,* 22 June 2000, sec. W, pp. 1, 4.

27. Steve Necaster, personal e-mail to Cele Otnes, 25 June 2001.

28. Chuck Delaney, *Wedding Photography and Video* (New York: Allworth Press, 1994), 42.

29. James M. Moran, "Wedding Video and Its Generation," in *Resolutions: Contemporary Video Practices,* ed. Michael Renov and Erika Suderburg (Minneapolis: University of Minnesota Press, 1996), 360–81.

30. "They Shoot Weddings, Don't They?" *Washington Post Magazine,* 13 January 1991, sec. W, p. 25.

31. Asra Q. Nomani, "The Wedding Night: Bliss These Days Is a Party with Pals," *Wall Street Journal,* 7 October 1999, sec. A, p. 1.

32. John H. Davis, *Jacqueline Bouvier: An Intimate Memoir* (New York: John Wiley and Sons, 1994), 177–98.

33. Katherine Jellison, "From the Farmhouse Parlor to the Pink Barn: The Commercialization of Weddings in the Rural Midwest," *Iowa Heritage Illustrated* 2 (summer 1996): 65.

34. Randy D. McBee, *Dance Hall Days: Intimacy and Leisure among Working-Class Immigrants in the United States* (New York: New York University Press, 2000), 221–26.

35. Katherine Jellison, "Getting Married in the Heartland: The Commercialization of Weddings in the Rural Midwest," *Forum* (1995): 48; Kitty Hanson, *For Richer, for Poorer* (London: Abelard-Schuman, 1968), 66.

36. Judith G. Goode, Karen Curtis, and Janet Theophano, "Meal Formats, Meal Cycles, and Menu Negotiation in the Maintenance of an Italian-American Community," in *Food in the Social Order: Studies of Food and Festivities in Three American Communities,* ed. Mary Douglas (New York: Russell Sage Foundation, 1984), 207; Fred L. Gardaphe, *Italian-American Ways* (New York: Harper and Row, 1982), 32.

37. Janet S. Theophano, " 'I Gave Him a Cake': An Interpretation of Two Italian-American Weddings," in *Creative Ethnicity: Symbols and Strategies of Contemporary Ethnic Life,* eds. Stephen Stern and John Allen Cicala (Logan: Utah State University Press, 1991), 44–54.

38. Beverly Reese Church, *Weddings Southern Style* (New York: Abbeville Press Publishers, 1993), 186.

39. Focus group, interviews by Cele Otnes, 13 June 1991, 18 June 1991.

40. Jodi Kantor, "A Bride's First Vow: My Feast Won't Be Dull," *New York Times,* 15 May 2002, sec. F, p. 1.

41. *Balloon Images* 8, no. 5 (November–December 1996): 6–12.

42. Delaney, *Wedding Photography and Video,* 122.

43. Simon R. Charsley, *Rites of Marrying: A Scottish Study* (Manchester: Manchester University Press, 1993), 74.

44. Jaclyn Geller, *Here Comes the Bride: Women, Weddings, and the Marriage Mystique* (New York: Four Walls Eight Windows, 2001), 321.

45.   Beverly Clark, *Wedding Cakes* (Philadelphia: Running Press Book Publishers, 1999).

46.   "Wedding Cake Talk with Sylvia Weinstock," 25 August 1998, http://www.modernbride.com/ChatEvents/Cakechat.cfm, 1 April 2001.

47.   Craig Wilson, "Gold-tiled Confection Takes the Cake," *USA Today*, 27 June 2002, 10B

48.   Lisa McLaughlin, " 'I Do' with Doughnuts," *Time*, 22 April 2002, 11.

49.   Denise Abbott, "Wedding Trends," *Flowers &* 12 (March 1991): 90.

50.   Harris, *Cute*, 103.

51.   Ibid.; Geller, *Here Comes the Bride*, 150.

52.   Delaney, *Wedding Photography and Video*, 122.

53.   Harris, *Cute*, 103.

54.   "The Way We Were: Fifty Years of Wedding Trends," *In Style*, 15 January 2000, 46.

55.   Chat with Jack Goodman, 11 November 1998, http://www.modernbride.com/ChatEvents/jackchat.cfm, 15 January 2001.

56.   Carolyn Lipson-Walker, "Weddings among Jews in the Post–World War II American South," in *Creative Ethnicity*, 171–83.

57.   *Picture Perfect*, 35mm, 100 min., 20th Century Fox, Los Angeles, CA, 1997.

58.   Elizabeth L. Post, *Emily Post's Complete Book of Wedding Etiquette* (New York: Harper and Row, 1982), 146.

59.   Carol Stocker, "Weddings," *Boston Globe Magazine*, 16 January 2000, 28.

60.   Cabot, "Perfect Church Wedding," 36, 112.

61.   Pearce, *Altar Bound*, 83.

62.   Maria McBride-Mellinger, *The Wedding Dress* (New York: Random House, 1993), 139; Lewis, "Working the Ritual," 353.

63.   "Featured Wedding: Allison and Mike Hash," http://www.weddingchannel.com, 15 March 2001.

64.   Tober, *The Bride*, 116.

65. Cohen, *A Walk down the Aisle,* 127.

66. Lewis, "Working the Ritual," 72–92.

6. FROM THE CABIN TO CANCÚN

1. The figure pertains to *Modern Bride* readers surveyed in 1990–91. These readers were more affluent than the general public. Judith Waldrop, "The Honeymoon Isn't Over," *American Demographics* 14, no. 8 (August 1992): 14.

2. Kris Bulcroft, Linda Smeins, and Richard Bulcroft, *Romancing the Honeymoon: Consummating Marriage in Modern Society* (Thousand Oaks, Calif.: Sage Publications, 1999), xviii.

3. Karen Dubinksy, *The Second Greatest Disappointment: Honey- mooning and Tourism at Niagara Falls* (New Brunswick, N.J.: Rut- gers University Press, 1998), 25.

4. Jesse F. Batten, "The 'Rights' of Husbands and the 'Duties' of Wives: Power and Desire in the American Bedroom, 1850–1910," *Journal of Family History* 22 (1999): 165–87.

5. Dubinsky, *Second Greatest Disappointment,* 155.

6. T. H. Van De Velde, *Ideal Marriage: Its Physiology and Technique* (New York: Random House, 1926), 262.

7. Paul H. Landis, *Your Marriage and Family Living* (St. Louis, Mo.: McGraw Hill Book Company, 1969), 238.

8. Kris Bulcroft, Richard Bulcroft, Linda Smeins, and Helen Cranage, "The Social Construction of the North American Honeymoon, 1880–1995," *Journal of Family History* 22 (1997): 475.

9. Ibid.

10. Carley Roney, *The Knot's Complete Guide to Weddings in the Real World* (New York: Broadway Books, 1998), 331.

11. Bulcroft et al., *Romancing the Honeymoon,* 95; Ellen K. Rothman, *Hands and Hearts: A History of Courtship in America* (New York: Basic Books, 1984), 175–76.

12. Daniel Scott Smith, "The Dating of the American Sexual Revolu- tion: Evidence and Interpretation," in *The American Family in*

Social-Historical Perspective, ed. Michael Gordon (New York: St. Martin's Press, 1973), 328–30.

13.   Asra Q. Nomani, "The Wedding Night: Bliss These Days Is a Party with Pals," *Wall Street Journal,* 7 October 1999, sec. A, pp. 1, 13. In 1976, on average, unmarried white girls were no longer virgins by age eighteen; the average age for African American girls to lose their virginity was sixteen. Sandra L. Hofferth, Joan R. Kahn, and Wendy Baldwin, "Premarital Sexual Activity among U.S. Teenage Women over the Past Three Decades," *Family Planning Perspectives* 2 (March–April 1987): 46–53.

14.   Russell W. Belk, "Been There, Done That, Bought the Souvenirs: Of Journeys and Boundary Crossing," in *Consumer Research: Postcards from the Edge,* ed. Stephen Brown and Durach Turley (London: Routledge, 1997), 22–24.

15.   Bulcroft et al., *Romancing the Honeymoon,* 42; J. Joseph Pine II and James H. Gilmore, *The Experience Economy* (Boston: Harvard Business School Press, 1999).

16.   Cindy S. Aron, *Working at Play: A History of Vacations in the United States* (New York: Oxford University Press, 1999), 49.

17.   Bulcroft et al., *Romancing the Honeymoon,* 50.

18.   DeSoto Brown, *Hawaii Recalls: Selling Romance to America: Nostalgic Images of the Hawaiian Islands, 1910–1950* (Honolulu: Editions Limited, 1982), 90.

19.   Orvar Löfgren, *On Holiday: A History of Vacationing* (Berkeley: University of California Press, 1999), 37.

20.   Ibid., 157.

21.   Randy D. McBee, *Dance Hall Days: Intimacy and Leisure among Working-Class Immigrants in the United States* (New York: New York University Press, 2000), 229.

22.   Interview with granite worker, n.d., American Life Histories: Manuscripts from the Federal Writer's Project, 1936–40, American Memory, Library of Congress; interview with Catherine Margaret Weber, 9 September 1938, American Life Histories: Manuscripts from the Federal Writer's Project, 1936–40, American Memory,

Library of Congress; interview with Harold J. Moss, 5 October 1938, American Life Histories: Manuscripts from the Federal Writer's Project, 1936–40, American Memory, Library of Congress. New Orleans white elite couples in the nineteenth century seem to have been waited on by servants for several days rather than go on a bridal tour. Beverly Reese Church, *Weddings Southern Style* (New York: Abbeville Press Publishers, 1993), 19.

23. August Hollingshead, "Marital Status and Wedding Behavior," *Marriage and Family Living* 14 (1952): 308–11; Martin K. Whyte, *Dating, Mating, and Marriage* (New York: Aldine de Gruyter, 1990), 57–59. The figure for Washington State is from Bulcroft et al., *Romancing the Honeymoon,* 49–50. The number of guests attending New Haven weddings and receptions was much greater than in Detroit, suggesting that New Haven couples were of higher social class than Detroit couples.

24. Dubinsky, *Second Greatest Disappointment,* 205–6.

25. Coretta Scott King, *My Life with Martin Luther King, Jr.* (New York: Holt, Rinehart and Winston, 1969), 74.

26. Aron, *Working at Play,* 216.

27. Beth Bailey and David Farber, "Hotel Street: Prostitution and the Politics of War," *Radical History Review* 52 (winter 1992): 54–77.

28. Aron, *Working at Play,* 217–18.

29. Dubinsky, *Second Greatest Disappointment,* 236.

30. Rhona Rapaport and Robert Rapaport, "New Light on the Honeymoon," in *The Psychosocial Interior of the Family,* ed. Gerald Handel (Chicago: Aldine Publishing Company, 1967), 336.

31. Kitty Hanson, *For Richer, for Poorer* (London: Abelard-Schuman, 1968), 66. On the decline of honeymoon hotels and the rise of honeymoon resorts, see Lawrence Squeri, *Better in the Poconos: The Story of Pennsylvania's Vacationland* (University Park: Pennsylvania State University Press, 2002), 186–87, 217–19.

32. Martha Saxton, "The Bliss Business: Institutionalizing the American Honeymoon," *American Heritage* 4 (1978): 80–87.

33. Dubinsky, *Second Greatest Disappointment,* 30.

34. There had also been separate hotels and boarding houses for African

Americans in the Poconos since the 1920s, and in 1948, black entrepreneurs opened a motel for "colored guests." Most Poconos hotels did not permit Jews. Squeri, *Better in the Poconos,* 165, 181.

35. Eugene J. Kanin and David H. Howard, "Postmarital Consequences of Premarital Sex Adjustments," *American Sociological Review* 23 (1958): 556–62.

36. Squeri, *Better in the Poconos,* 187.

37. Adele Bahn, "Changes and Continuities in the Transitional Status of Bride into Wife: A Content Analysis of Bridal Magazines, 1967–1977: The Decade of the Women's Movement" (Ph.D. diss., City University of New York, 1979), 264.

38. Marcia Seligson, *The Eternal Bliss Machine: America's Way of Wedding* (New York: William Morrow and Co., 1973), 247; Squeri, *Better in the Poconos,* 187.

39. Seligson, *Eternal Bliss Machine,* 247. In 1990s Hollywood films it became a commonplace for the large sunken tub to symbolize romance and intimacy. Even in the Pygmalion film *Pretty Woman* (1990), the prostitute and the corporate takeover king who met two nights before laugh, smile, and get to know each other in the large sunken tub in his penthouse bathroom. The first black wedding film, *The Best Man* (1998), copied the same scene, showing an erotic bathtub encounter between a Chicago novelist and his longtime girlfriend.

40. "Honeymoon Havens," *Time,* 23 June 1969, 90–91; Seligson, *Eternal Bliss Machine,* 250.

41. Seligson, *Eternal Bliss Machine,* 244.

42. Squeri, *Better in the Poconos,* 217.

43. Alvar W. Carlson, "The Spatial Behavior Involved in Honeymoons: The Case of Two Areas in Wisconsin and North Dakota, 1971–1976," *Journal of Popular Culture* 11 (1978): 977–88.

44. In a sample of fifty-four couples from Vancouver, Canada, Bulcroft et al. found that, on average, couples spent $3,287 on their honeymoon. The figure was probably for a honeymoon in 1999. Bulcroft et al., *Romancing the Honeymoon,* 183. Seven out of ten *Modern Bride* readers in 1997 said they wanted to honeymoon in an exotic

location. "They're Not Hitchhiking to Niagara Falls," *Adweek* 38 (1997): 25.

45. Polly Patullo, *Last Resorts: The Cost of Tourism in the Caribbean* (London: Cassell, 1996), 16; "Cruise Liners and Air," *Life,* 22 February 1957, 24–33.

46. Brown, *Hawaii Recalls,* 86.

47. Jane C. Desmond, *Staging Tourism: Bodies on Display from Waikiki to Sea World* (Chicago: University of Chicago Press, 1999), 134.

48. The figures were 37 percent for 1966, 47 percent for 1971, 58 percent for 1987, and 66 percent for 1992. *Modern Bride* surveys for 1966 and 1971 were reported in Lacey Forsburgh, "New Fashions in Honeymoons: Hips, Super Hip, and Super Square," *New York Times,* 13 June 1971, sec. 10, p. 22. The *Modern Bride* figures for 1987 and 1992 can be found in Waldrop, "The Honeymoon Isn't Over," 14. Because honeymooners were traveling greater distances, they added extra days to the length of the honeymoon. Detroit couples between 1925 and 1984 spent an average of seven days on their honeymoon. By the 1990s, the number of days had increased to nine. Whyte, *Dating, Mating, and Marriage,* 58.

49. The Scandinavians had their own fifth "s": spirits. Löfgren, *On Holiday,* 173.

50. Rosalie Schwartz, *Pleasure Island: Tourism and Temptation in Cuba* (Lincoln: University of Nebraska Press, 1997), 54–163; Mansel G. Blackford, *Fragile Paradise: The Impact of Tourism on Maui, 1959–2000* (Lawrence: University Press of Kansas, 2001), 20–21.

51. Löfgren, *On Holiday,* 235.

52. 1997 data for Hawaii can be found in *Repositioning Hawaii's Visitor Industry Products* (Honolulu: University of Hawaii, 1998), 18.

53. Ann Brown and Marjorie Whigham-Dear, "Honeymoon Hideaways," *Black Enterprise,* April 1992, 105–10; Cathy Lynn Grossman, "More Honeymooners Bet on Gambling Spots," *USA Today,* 10 October 1997, sec. D, p. 8.

54. Rafer Guzman, "Lions and Tigers and Brides—Oh, My," *Wall Street Journal,* 12 January 2002, sec. W, p. 5.

55. Dubinsky, *Second Greatest Disappointment,* 16.

56. Ibid., 234–35.

57. Tammerlin Drummond, "The Marrying Kind," *Time,* 14 May 2001, 52.

58. "Summertime, and the Facts Are Jumping," *New York Times,* 21 July 1999, sec. D, p. 2.

59. Forsburgh, "New Fashions in Honeymoons," *New York Times,* 13 June 1971, sec. 10, p. 22.

60. Roney, *The Knot's Complete Guide,* 309.

61. Jaclyn Geller, *Here Comes the Bride: Women, Weddings, and the Marriage Mystique* (New York: Four Walls Eight Windows, 2001), 340.

62. Löfgren, *On Holiday,* 317.

63. Ibid.

64. Ibid., 109.

65. T. J. Jackson Lears, *No Place of Grace: Antimodernism and the Transformation of American Culture, 1880–1920* (New York: Pantheon, 1981); Marianna Torgovnick, *Primitive Passions: Men, Women, and the Quest for Ecstasy* (Chicago: University of Chicago Press, 1998).

66. Desmond, *Staging Tourism,* 278.

67. Ibid., 136.

68. Brown, *Hawaii Recalls,* 109; Löfgren, *On Holiday,* 217.

69. Ellen Furlough, "Making Mass Vacations: Tourism and Consumer Culture in France, 1930s to 1970s," *Comparative Studies in Society and History* 40 (1998): 247–86; Ellen Furlough, "Packaging Pleasures: Club Méditerranée and French Consumer Culture, 1950–1968," *French Historical Studies* 18 (1993): 65–81.

70. On local resentment of the all-inclusives, see Patullo, *Last Resorts,* 75.

71. Geller, *Here Comes the Bride,* 349.

72. Bahn, "Change and Continuities," 168; Cindy Aron, e-mail to Elizabeth H. Pleck, 2 July 1999; Patullo, *Last Resorts,* 151–52. However, to the standard combination of white North American tourists and

darker-skinned employees who were nationals of a poor country were added black American honeymooners who often selected the Caribbean, both because of perceived kinship with formerly African people and a sense that in the Caribbean they would not experience racial discrimination.

73. Steven Watts, *The Magic Kingdom: Walt Disney and the American Way of Life* (Boston: Houghton Mifflin Company, 1997).

74. Pine and Gilmore, *The Experience Economy,* 38.

75. Löfgren, *On Holiday,* 284.

76. George Ritzer, *Enchanting a Disenchanted World: Revolutionizing the Means of Consumption* (Thousand Oaks, Calif.: Pine Forge Press, 1999), 168.

77. Ibid., 8.

78. Löfgren, *On Holiday,* 15–16.

79. Guy Debord, *The Society of the Spectacle* (New York: Zone Books, 1995), 11–12; Alladi Venkatesh and A. Fuat Firat, "Liberatory Postmodernism and the Reenchantment of Consumption," *Journal of Consumer Research* 22 (1995): 239–67.

80. Belk, "Been There, Done That," 37.

81. http://www.christianbride.com, 15 July 2001.

82. Diane Warner, *Picture-Perfect Worry-Free Weddings* (Cincinnati, Ohio: Betterway Books, 1998), 42; Dave Smith, *Disney A to Z: The Updated Official Encyclopedia* (New York: Hyperion, 1996), 601.

83. David Leonhard, "Do You Take this Resort for Your Wedding?" *Business Week,* 17 June 1995, 146.

84. Maria Puente, "Wedded to the Year 2000," *USA Today,* 12 June 2000, sec. A, p. 1.

85. Leonhard, "Do You Take," 146.

86. The Department of Business, Economic Development, and Tourism, *Annual Visitor Research Report* (Honolulu: DBEDT, 2000), table 2, 6; table 27, 42.

87. Bulcroft et al., *Romancing the Honeymoon,* 88.

1. Starshine Roshell, "Wedding Guide 2001," http://www. newspress.com/2001_wedding_guide/movies.html.

2. Betsy Bergeson, "My Reaction to *The Wedding Singer,*" unpublished paper, 4 May 2001; Jingj'ing Zhang, "*My Best Friend's Wedding,*" unpublished paper, 4 May 2001; Sheetal Shah, "*My Best Friend's Wedding* and Its Wedding Portrayal," unpublished paper, 7 April 2001.

3. Kerry Seagrave, *American Films Abroad* (London: McFarland and Co., 1997), 66.

4. James Harvey, *Romantic Comedy in Hollywood from Lubitsch to Sturges* (New York: Alfred A. Knopf, 1987), 12; Eric Harrison, "Laughing at Love: Depression-Era Screwball Comedies Are Evolving into Modern-Day Romances," *Houston Chronicle,* 8 March 2001, Houston sec., p. 2.

5. Jackie Stacey, *Star Gazing: Hollywood Cinema and Female Spectatorship* (London: Routledge, 1994), 85.

6. Ibid., 176–223.

7. Mary Ann Doane, "The Economy of Desire: The Commodity Form in/of the Cinema," *Quarterly Review of Film and Video* 11 (1989): 31.

8. Rebecca L. Epstein, "Sharon Stone in a Gap Turtleneck," in *Hollywood Goes Shopping,* ed. David Desser and Garth S. Jowett (Minneapolis: University of Minnesota Press, 2000), 179–204.

9. Richard Allen, *Projecting Illusion: Film Spectatorship and the Impression of Reality* (Cambridge: Cambridge University Press, 1995), 4.

10. Ted Sennett, *Lunatics and Lovers* (New Rochelle, N.Y.: Arlington House, 1973), 15.

11. Elizabeth Kendall, *The Runaway Bride: The Hollywood Romantic Comedy of the 1930s* (New York: Knopf, 1990), 19.

12. Ibid., 49.

13. Ibid.

14. Edward D. C. Campbell Jr., *The Celluloid South: Hollywood and the Southern Myth* (Knoxville: University of Tennessee Press, 1981), 124.

15. Margaret J. Bailey, *Those Glorious Glamour Years* (Secaucus, N.J.: Citadel Press, 1982).

16. Stanley Cavell, *Pursuits of Happiness: The Hollywood Comedy of Remarriage* (Cambridge, Mass.: Harvard University Press, 1981), 148.

17. Grace Kelly was able to terminate her seven-year contract with MGM by allowing the studio to film her marriage to Prince Rainier in Monaco. The film of the marriage was shown in theaters before the featured film began.

18. Helen Rose, *"Just Make Them Beautiful": The Many Worlds of a Designing Woman* (Santa Monica, Calif.: Dennis-Landman Publishers, 1976), 86; Ellis Auburn, *The Most Beautiful Woman in the World* (New York: Cliff Street Books, 2000), 39; C. David Heymann, *Liz: An Intimate Biography of Elizabeth Taylor* (New York: Brick Lane Press, 1995), 92; Kitty Kelley, *Elizabeth Taylor: The Last Star* (New York: Simon and Schuster, 1981), 64–67; "Something Old, Something New," *In Style,* February 2001, 258.

19. "Something Old, Something New," 256.

20. Diane Waldman argues that the characters played by Jane Russell and Marilyn Monroe in *Gentleman Prefer Blondes* were gold-diggers. They were legitimized, however, by the lace-trimmed identical sweetheart gowns they wore at their double wedding. Diane Waldman, "From Midnight Show to Marriage Vows: Women, Exploitation, and Exhibition," *Wide Angle* 6 (1984): 40–49.

21. Judith E. Smith, "The Marrying Kind: Working-Class Courtship and Marriage in 1950s Hollywood," in *Multiple Voices in Feminist Film Criticism,* ed. Diane Carson, Linda Dittmar, and Janice R. Welsch (Minneapolis: University of Minnesota Press, 1994), 226–39.

22. Julia Antopol Hirsch, *The Sound of Music: The Making of America's Favorite Movie* (Chicago: Contemporary Books, 1993), 91.

23. Parley Ann Boswell, "The Pleasure of Our Company: Hollywood Throws a Wedding Bash," in *Beyond the Stars II: Plot Conventions in American Popular Film,* ed. Paul Loukides and Linda K. Fuller (Bowling Green, Ohio: Bowling Green State University Popular Press, 1991), 6–20.

24. Gerard D. Plecki, "The Films of Robert Altman" (Ph.D. diss., University of Illinois, 1979).

25. The Hubbler-Eisner wedding in *Plaza Suite* (1950) is a Jewish *Father of the Bride*. The real hero is the beleaguered father, and the bride, instead of running away, locks herself in the bathroom of a suite at New York's Plaza Hotel.

26. Naomi Greene, "Family Ceremonies: Or, Opera in the Godfather Trilogy," in *Francis Ford Coppola's The Godfather Trilogy*, ed. Nick Browne (Cambridge: Cambridge University Press, 2000), 133–55.

27. The exceptions were romantic melodramas, or the old genre known as "weepies." Both *Terms of Endearment* (1983) and *Steel Magnolias* (1989) contain the ceremonies of their doomed main characters.

28. Marisa Keller and Mike Mashon, *TV Weddings: An Illustrated Guide* (New York: TV Books, 1999), 129.

29. See Chrys Ingraham, *White Weddings: Romancing Heterosexuality in Popular Culture* (London: Routledge, 1999), 130–31, for a more complete discussion of the prevalence of weddings on television programs.

30. Steve Neal, *Genre and Hollywood* (London: Routledge, 2000).

31. James Naremore, *The Films of Vincente Minnelli* (Cambridge: Cambridge University Press, 1993), 97.

32. Richard Curtis, *Four Weddings and a Funeral: Three Appendices and a Screenplay* (New York: St. Martin's Griffin, 1996), 106.

33. Table data from http://www.boxofficeguru.com, 21 July 2001, except for figures for *The Wedding Planner*, provided by http://www.boxofficemojo.com, 20 April 2002.

34. Jill A. Mackey, "Subtext and Countertext in *Muriel's Wedding*," *NWSA Journal* 13 (2001): 86–104.

35. Kathy Mayo, "Julia Roberts: America's Sweetheart as Sorry Bitch," *Sojourner: The Women's Forum*, 30 September 1999, 52.

36. Richard Corliss, "*In & Out* (Review)," *Time*, 22 September 1997, 90.

37. *Chicks in White Satin*, 16mm, 25 min., Holliman Productions, Santa Monica, Calif., 1993.

38. Amy M. Spindler, "The Wedding Dress That Ate Hollywood," *New York Times,* 30 August 1998, sec. 9, p. 1.

39. *Monsoon Wedding,* 16mm, 114 min., Arte France Cinéma/IFC Productions, New York, 2001; *My Big Fat Greek Wedding,* 35mm, 96 min., Playtone Co., Los Angeles, Calif., 2002.

8. THE LAVISH WEDDING GOES GLOBAL

1. Maris Gillette, "What's in a Dress? Brides in the Hui Quarter of Xi'an," in *The Consumer Revolution in Urban China,* ed. Deborah Davis (Berkeley: University of California Press, 2000), 96.

2. We use the term "West" here even though it is as much a rhetorical and imaginative term as an accurate descriptor. Western weddings consist of a great diversity of practices within and between nations. Moreover, most people in "the West" do not usually think of the area as a unified entity. In some countries, the white wedding is seen as the "Western wedding," but in most parts of the world, it is called the "modern" wedding. Vassos Argyrou, *Tradition and Modernity in the Mediterranean* (Cambridge: Cambridge University Press, 1996), 169.

3. For an example of criticism of spending on traditional Indian weddings, see S. Ambirajan, "Politics of Wedding and Wedding as Politics," *Economic and Political Weekly,* 2 December 1995, 3053–54.

4. "Toned-down Ceremonies: Japanese Weddings Enter Age of Tasteful Restraint," 1998, http://jin.jcic.or.jp/trends98/honbun/ntj971111.html, 22 July 2000.

5. Meki Cox, "Japanese Brides and Grooms Head to 'Paradise,' " *Chicago Tribune,* 9 November 1995, sec. C, p. 8.

6. Ann Docker Marcus, "In Cairo, True Love Calls for Chandeliers on Top of the Head," *Wall Street Journal,* 14 February 1996, sec. 1, p. 11.

7. Nancy Tasser, "Changing Marriage Ceremonial and Gender Roles in the Arab World: An Anthropological Perspective," *Arab Affairs* 1 (1988): 117–35; Cassandra Lorius, "Desire and the Gaze: Spectacular Bodies in Cairene Elite Weddings," *Women's Studies International Forum* 19 (1996): 513–23. For the revival of the "traditional village wedding" among Palestinian nationalists, see Yvonne J. Seng and Betty Wass, "Traditional Palestinian Wedding Dress as a Sym-

bol of Nationalism," in *Dress and Ethnicity,* ed. Joanne B. Eicher (Oxford: Berg, 1995), 227–54.

8. Élan Ezrachi, personal e-mail to Cele Otnes, 11 September 2000.

9. Anya E. Liftig, "A Union of East and West," *New York Times Magazine,* 15 April 2001, sec. 6, p. 66.

10. Fareed Zakaria, "How to Save the Arab World," *Newsweek,* 24 December 2001, 24; John F. Burns, "Relishing Beautiful New Freedoms in Kabul," *New York Times,* 15 September 2002, YNE 13.

11. Nicole Itano, "Goin' to the Chapel—and the Goat Dung Bath, Too," *Christian Science Monitor,* 11 June 2001, 1.

12. Patricia Romero Curtin, "Weddings in Lamu, Kenya: An Example of Social and Economic Change," *Cahiers d'Etudes Africaines* 25 (1984): 131–55.

13. *Novia,* August 2001, 138–44.

14. Eileen Ford, personal e-mail to Elizabeth H. Pleck, 2 February 2000.

15. Arjun Appadurai, *Modernity at Large: Cultural Dimensions of Globalization* (Minneapolis: University of Minnesota Press, 1996).

16. Hassan Mekki, "Two Dead as Gunman Opens Fire at Jordan Mass Wedding," *Agence-France-Presse,* 14 July 2000; "The Land and Its People," http://www.ecssr.ac.ae/Land/wedding.html, 28 March 2002.

17. Abdul [pseud.], personal communication to Cele Otnes, 15 November 2001.

18. José [pseud.], personal communication to Cele Otnes, 20 November 2001.

19. http://www.philippines1.com/abride/, 25 July 2000.

20. Russell W. Belk, "Leaping Luxuries and Transitional Consumers," in *Marketing Issues in Transitional Economies,* ed. Rajeev Batra (Boston: Kluwer Academic Publishers, 1999), 50.

21 Wesley Andrew Fisher, *The Soviet Marriage Market: Mate-Selection in Russia and the USSR* (New York: Praeger, 1980), 57–59.

22. Jane Perlez, "Here Come the Brides, Video Catching the Kisses," *New York Times,* 11 October 1995, sec. A, p. 4.

23. Joanne P. Cavanaugh, "Cuba's Marry-Go-Round," *Johns Hopkins*

Magazine, April 1998, http://www.jhu.edu/~humag/0498web/wedding.html, 3 March 2001.

24. Rona Tempest, "Weddings Have Marched a Long Way in China since Mao," *Los Angeles Times*, 28 April 1996, sec. A, pp. 1, 3; Helen Johnstone, "Bridal Firms Embrace New Boom," *Asian Business* 33 (June 1997): 54–55.

25. For descriptions of Hindu weddings in the 1990s, which indicate they have become shorter, see Yuko Nishimura, "South Indian Wedding Rituals: A Comparison of Gender Hierarchy," *Anthropos* 91 (1996): 411–23. See also Iao V. Juluri, "Global Weds Local: The Reception of Hum Aapke Hain Koun," *European Journal of Cultural Studies* 2 (1999): 231–48.

26. Lata Mani, *Contentious Traditions: The Debate on Sati in Colonial India* (Berkeley: University of California Press, 1998).

27. *Monsoon Wedding*, 16mm, 114 min., Arte France Cinéma/IFC Productions, New York, 2001.

28. Narinder, interview by Shimantika Kumar, 2000.

29. Anindita Ramaaswamy, "Bridal Trade Event Described as One Stop Wedding Shop," *India Abroad*, 1 September 2000, 38.

30. Steve Coll, "Asian Prosperity Spawns Conspicuous Consumption: Middle Classes Buying up Consumer Goods," *Washington Post*, 22 March 1994, sec. A, p. 1.

31. "The Young Find Diamonds More Trendy," *Economic Times*, 10 December 2001.

32. Meenal Atul Pandya, *Viva: Design a Perfect Hindu Wedding* (Wellesley, Mass.: Meera Publications, 2000).

33. Sunali, interview by Shimantika Kumar, 2000.

34. Denise Couture, "Japanese Brides Borrow Western Traditions," *Chicago Tribune*, 16 May 1993, sec. G, p. 1.

35. Giana M. Eckhardt, " 'India Will Survive': Understanding the Role of Consumer Agency in the Globalization Process in Emerging Markets," *Proceedings of the Eighth Cross-Cultural Research Conference*, Oahu, Hawaii, December 2002.

36. Michael Schuman, "There Goes the Bride: An Indonesian Isle Has

Odd Sense of Wedlock," *Wall Street Journal,* 29 May 2001, sec. A, pp. 1, 12.

37. Nicole Ranganath, e-mail communication to Elizabeth H. Pleck, 8 April 2001.

38. Sunali, interview, 2000.

39. Joseph Nevadomsky, "Wedding Rituals and Changing Women's Rights among the East Indians in Rural Trinidad," *International Journal of Women's Studies* 4 (1981): 484–96.

40. Per capita income in South Korea was about one quarter of that of the United States. Ethiopia's per capita income was $100 a year in 1999. World Development Indicators database, World Bank, 2 August 2000, http://www.worldbank.org/data, 2 February 2001.

41. Laurel Kendall, *Getting Married in Korea: Of Gender, Morality, and Modernity* (Berkeley: University of California Press, 1996), 63–64.

42. Ibid., 57, 64–65.

43. Bonnie Adrian, "Framing the Bride: Beauty, Romance, and Rites of Globalization in Taiwan's Bridal Industry" (Ph.D. diss., Yale University, 1999), 21–22.

44. Cheol Park, "Consumption in the Korean Wedding Ritual: Wedding Ritual Values, Consumer Needs, and Expenditures," *Journal of Family Economic Issues* 18 (1997): 191–209; Kendall, *Getting Married,* 33–34, 44–45; Kim Sung-jin, "Lavish Wedding Custom Pales True Love," *The Korea Times,* 13 September 2001, 18.

45. Gillette, "What's in a Dress?" 88, 90–91.

46. O-Young Lee, *The Compact Culture: The Japanese Tradition of "Smaller Is Better,"* trans. R. N. Huey (Tokyo: Kodansha International, 1982).

47. Masami Suja, "Japanese Wedding Packages as Aesthetic Expression among Elite Brides of Osaka" (Ph.D. diss., University of Minnesota, 1996).

48. One major difference between Japanese and South Korean wedding halls is the South Korean version does not have rooms for a wedding banquet. The bridal feast is usually held at a restaurant.

49. Haegyoung, interview by Shimantika Kumar, 2000.

50. Teresa Anne Heiner, "Shinto Wedding, Samurai Bride: Inventing Tradition and Fashioning Identity in the Rituals of Bridal Dress in Japan" (Ph.D. diss., University of Pittsburgh, 1997); Kiyoshi Shida, "The Shintoist Wedding Ceremony in Japan: An Invented Tradition," *Media, Culture, and Society* 21 (1999): 195–204.

51. Walter Edwards, *Modern Japan through Its Weddings: Gender, Person, and Society in Ritual Portrayal* (Stanford, Calif.: Stanford University Press, 1989), 108–13.

52. Kendall, *Getting Married,* 43–46.

53. Kyoungmi Lee, interview by Elizabeth H. Pleck, 14 February 2001.

54. Ibid.

55. Kyoungmi Lee, interview by Elizabeth H. Pleck, 18 November 2001; Kim Sung-jin, "Lavish Wedding"; Junyong Kim, interview by Cele Otnes, 10 May 2002.

56. "Trade and Investment Industry Canada," http://strategic.ic.gc.ca/SSC/dd80893.html, 6 June 2001; Ron Gluckman, "Honeymoon Island," http://www.gluckman.com/ChejuWed.html, 6 June 2001.

57. Nancy Hafkin, personal e-mail to Elizabeth H. Pleck, 11 September 2000.

58. Ibid.

59. Ibid.

60. Ibid.

61. The women make a high-pitched, rapid "la la la" sound.

62. Belk, "Leaping Luxuries," 296.

63. Itano, "Goin' to the Chapel," 1.

64. Arjun Appadurai, "Disjuncture and Difference in the Global Cultural Economy," *Theory, Culture and Society* 7 (1990) 295.

9. VARIATIONS ON A THEME

1. For other ways of conceptualizing those who decide on "alternative" weddings, see Jane Roos-MacDonald, *Alternative Weddings: An Essential Guide to Creating Your Own Ceremonies* (Dallas: Taylor Publishing Company, 1997).

2. For the history of clandestine marriages in early modern England, see David Cressy, *Birth, Marriage, and Death: Ritual, Religion, and the Life-Cycle in Tudor and Stuart England* (Oxford: Oxford University Press, 1997), 316–35. See also Lisa O'Connell, "Marriage Acts: Stages in the Transformation of Modern Nuptial Culture," *Differences: A Journal of Feminist Cultural Studies* 11 (1999): 68–111.

3. Quoted in Eugene D. Genovese, *Roll, Jordan, Roll: The World the Slaves Made* (New York: Pantheon, 1974), 481.

4. Nancy F. Cott, *Public Vows: A History of Marriage and the Nation* (Cambridge, Mass.: Harvard University Press, 2000), 151–55.

5. Russell W. Belk, e-mail communication, 8 October 2001.

6. Cott, *Public Vows,* 127–28.

7. "3,800 Couples Wed After Dutch Law," *Honolulu Advertiser,* 13 December 2001, sec. A, p. 3.

8. Jyotsna Singh, "Gay Couple Hold Hindu Wedding," BBC News, http://news.bbc.co.uk/english/world/south-asia/newsid_1357000/1357249.stm, 29 May 2001.

9. John Boswell, *The Marriage of Likeness: Same-Sex Unions in Premodern Europe* (London: HarperCollins, 1995), 65.

10. Lisa Duggan, *Sapphic Slashers: Sex, Violence, and American Modernity* (Durham, N.C.: Duke University Press, 2000), 147; Joan Nestle, "Excerpts from the Oral History of Mabel Hampton," *Signs* 18 (summer 1993): 932–35; Jonathan Katz, ed., *Gay American History: Lesbians and Gay Men in the U.S.A.* (New York: Thomas Y Crowell Company, 1976), 248, 250, 603.

11. Gustav Niebuhr, "Laws Aside, Some in Clergy Quietly Bless Gay 'Marriage,'" *New York Times,* 17 April 1998, sec. A, pp. 1, 20; Ellen Lewin, *Recognizing Ourselves: Ceremonies of Lesbian and Gay Commitment* (New York: Columbia University Press, 1998), 7.

12. Ramona Faith Oswald, e-mail communication, 29 November 2001.

13. Neil Schlager, ed., *St. James Press Gay and Lesbian Almanac* (Detroit: St. James Press, 1998), 113–15.

14. Susan Krieger, *The Family Silver: Essays on Relationships among Women* (Berkeley: University of California Press, 1996), 78.

15. Jane Eaton Hamilton, "Twenty-One Questions," in *Young Wives'*

Tales: New Adventures in Love and Partnership, ed. Jill Corral and Lisa Myers-Jarvis (Seattle: Seal Press, 2001), 26–27.

16. Lewin, *Recognizing Ourselves,* 235–51.

17. Krista B. McQueeney, "The New Religious Rite: A Symbolic Interactionist Case Study of Lesbian Commitment Rituals," *Journal of Lesbian Studies* (forthcoming).

18. Lewin, *Recognizing Ourselves,* 259.

19. Gretchen A. Stiers, *From This Day Forward: Commitment, Marriage, and Family in Lesbian and Gay Relationships* (New York: St. Martin's Press, 1999).

20. Kath Weston, *Families We Choose: Lesbians, Gays, Kinship* (New York: Columbia University Press, 1991), 161–62.

21. We are grateful to one of our anonymous reviewers for making this observation.

22. Tess Ayers and Paul Brown, *The Essential Guide to Lesbian and Gay Weddings* (San Francisco: HarperSanFrancisco, 1994). For a more liturgical and less consumerist view, see Kittredge Cherry and Zalmon Sherwood, eds., *Equal Rites: Lesbian and Gay Worship, Ceremonies, and Celebrations* (Louisville, Ky.: Westminster John Knox Press, 1995).

23. Robert Jensen, "The Politics and Ethics of Lesbian and Gay 'Wedding' Announcements in Newspapers," *The Howard Journal of Communications* 7 (1996): 17; "Times Will Begin Reporting Gay Couples' Ceremonies," *New York Times,* 18 August 2002, sec. A, p. 23.

24. Smashing the glass probably originated in Germany no earlier than the twelfth or thirteenth century. The Jewish groom would smash a full glass of wine on the north side of the wall of the synagogue. Suzanne Weiss, "Deciphering Nuptial Rites: The Devil's in the Details," *Metro West Jewish News,* 22 May 1997, sec. S, p. 21.

25. Karla Jay, ed., *Dyke Life: From Growing up to Growing Old, a Celebration of the Lesbian Experience* (New York: Basic Books, 1995), 30.

26. Chuck Delaney, *Wedding Photography and Video* (New York: Allworth Press, 1994), 94.

27. Lewin, *Recognizing Ourselves,* 56.

28. Douglas Wythe et al., *The Wedding: A Family's Coming Out Story* (New York: Avon Books, 2000).

29. Ibid., 9–10.

30. Ibid., 166–68.

31. Lewin, *Recognizing Ourselves*, 44–46, 235–51.

32. Russell W. Belk, e-mail communication, 8 August 2001.

33. James B. Twitchell, *Living It Up: Our Love Affair with Luxury* (New York: Columbia University Press, 2002), 234.

34. Evelyn Nieves, "Las Vegas Journal: Endless Laws on Valentine's Weekend," *New York Times,* 17 February 2002, sec. 1, p. 16.

35. Joan Didion, *Slouching Towards Bethlehem* (New York: Farrar, Straus and Giroux, 1961), 79–83.

36. Nieves, "Las Vegas Journal," 16.

37. Nina Mink, "Easy Nuptials," *Forbes,* 25 April 1995, 178.

38. "Las Vegas NAACP Investigates Lack of Black Ministers on Wedding Chapels' Staffs," *Jet,* July 1996, 32–33.

39. Nieves, "Las Vegas Journal," 16.

40. Young-Hoon Kim, "The Commodification of a Ritual Process: An Ethnography of the Wedding Industry in Las Vegas" (Ph.D. diss., University of Southern California, 1996), 82.

41. Vendela Vida, *Girls on the Verge: Debutante Dips, Gang Drive-Bys, and Other Initiations* (New York: St. Martin's Press, 1999), 135.

42. Russell W. Belk, Melanie Wallendorf, and John F. Sherry Jr., "The Sacred and Profane in Consumer Behavior: Theodicy on the Odyssey," *Journal of Consumer Research,* no. 16 (June 1989): 1–38.

43. Jean Baudrillard, *Simulacra and Simulation,* trans. Sheila Glaser (Ann Arbor: University of Michigan Press, 1994).

44. George Ritzer, *Enchanting a Disenchanted World: Revolutionizing the Means of Consumption* (Thousand Oaks, Calif.: Pine Forge Press, 1999), 108.

45. David Flick and Todd J. Gilman, "Veiled in Secrecy: Dallas Wedding of Roger Clinton to Be Strictly Private," *Dallas Morning News,* 25 March 1994, sec. A, p. 1.

46. Maris Vinovskis, *An "Epidemic" of Adolescent Pregnancy? Some His-*

tory and Policy Considerations (New York: Oxford University Press, 1988), 25.

47. Elizabeth L. Post, *The New Emily Post's Etiquette* (New York: Thomas Y. Crowell, 1975), 693.

48. Stuart Mieher, "Great Expectations: The Stork Is a Guest at More Weddings," *Wall Street Journal,* 6 April 1993, sec. A, pp. 1, 6.

49. Patricia McLaughlin, "Pregnant Brides: Trade Frills for Grace," *Cleveland Plain Dealer,* 12 September 1996, sec. E, p. 6.

50. Roberto Suro, "Mixed Doubles," *American Demographics,* November 1999, 58.

51. Wendy Leeds-Hurvitz, *Wedding as Text: Communicating Cultural Identities through Ritual* (Mahwah, N.J.: Lawrence Erlbaum, 2002), 98–99.

52. Michelle R. Nelson and Cele C. Otnes, "How Do You Say 'I Do'? An Analysis of Community and Socialization in Intercultural Wedding Message Boards" (paper presented at the Eighth Cross-Cultural Consumption Conference, Kahuku, Hawaii, 14 December 2001).

53. Bhargair C. Mandava, "A Suitable Union," in *Young Wives' Tales,* 91.

54. "Rachel and Eddie Flores' Wedding," http://www.weddingchannel.com/azIndex/search.asp [keywords: Rachel and Eddie Flores' wedding], 10 May 2001.

55. John Clarke et al., "Subcultures, Cultures, and Class," in *Resistance through Rituals: Youth Subcultures in Post-War Britain,* ed. Stuart Hall and Tony Jefferson (London: Routledge, 1976), 53.

56. Cele Goldsmith Lalli, *Modern Bride Wedding Celebrations: The Complete Wedding Planner for Today's Bride* (New York: John Wiley and Sons, 1992), 186; Jerry Adler, "A Matter of Faith," *Newsweek,* 15 December 1997, 50–51.

57. Fotter Indica Vigue, "Brides Reclaim Their Ethnic Roots," *Boston Globe,* 14 June 1998, sec. B. p. 1.

58. Elizabeth H. Pleck, "Kwanzaa: The Making of a Black Nationalist Tradition, 1966–1990," *Journal of American Ethnic History* 20 (2001): 3–28.

59. Elizabeth H. Pleck, *Celebrating the Family: Ethnicity, Consumer*

Culture, and Family Rituals (Cambridge, Mass.: Harvard University Press, 2000), 230.

60.   Alan Dundes, " 'Jumping the Broom': On the Origins and Meaning of an African American Wedding Custom," *Journal of American Folklore* 109 (summer 1996): 324–29; C. W. Sullivan III, " 'Jumping the Broom': A Further Consideration of the Origins of an African American Wedding Custom," *Journal of American Folklore* 110, no. 436 (spring 1997): 203–5.

61.   Eugene D. Genovese, *Roll, Jordan, Roll: The World the Slaves Made* (New York: Pantheon Books, 1974), 475–81; Herbert G. Gutman, *The Black Family in Slavery and Freedom, 1750–1925* (New York: Pantheon Books, 1976), 274–76.

62.   Harriette Cole, *Jumping the Broom: The African-American Wedding Planner* (New York: Henry Holt and Company, 1993), 20; Marybeth Phillips, "Proud Heritage," *Philadelphia Bride,* spring–summer 1993, 52–55; Charisse Jones, "Bringing Slavery's Long Shadow to the Light," *New York Times,* 2 April 1995, sec. A, pp. 1, 14; *Signature Bride* magazine editors, *Going to the Chapel: From Traditional to African-inspired and Everything in Between—The Ultimate Wedding Guide for Today's Black Couple* (New York: Putnam, 1998), 87, 89.

63.   Diane Booth, "Jumping the Broom: An African-American Tradition Is Back," http://www.howardcounty.com/broom/bride 2000.html, 15 February 2001.

64.   Cherise Trahan, "Soulmates," Netnoir.com, http://www.blacknetwork.com/feature/wedding/soulmates.htm, 2 April 2001.

65.   Barbara Rosewicz, "Here Comes the Bride . . . and for the Umpteenth Time," *Wall Street Journal,* 10 September 1996, sec. B, p. 1.

66.   Peter Frances, "Marriage—United States," *Marketing Tools,* June 1996, 76.

67.   Evan Imber-Black, Janine Roberts, and Richard A. Whiting, *Rituals in Families and Family Therapy* (New York: W. W. Norton & Company, 1988), 290.

68.   Judith Slawson, *The Second Wedding Handbook: A Complete Guide to the Options* (New York: Doubleday, 1989).

69. Paula Mergenhagen DeWitt, "The Second Time Around," *American Demographics* 14 (November 1992): 60.

70. Field notes, Cele Otnes, October 1991.

71. Walter Kirn and Wendy Cole, "Twice as Nice," *Time,* 19 June 2000, 53–54.

72. Ibid., 53.

73. Ibid.

74. Ibid., 54.

75. C. Schreuder, "For These Couples, It Was a Very Good Year," *Chicago Tribune,* 1 September 1992, sec. I, pp. 9–10.

76. Dawn O. Braithwaite and Leslie A. Baxter, " 'I Do' Again: The Relational Dialectics of Renewing Wedding Vows," *Journal of Social and Personal Relationships* 12 (1995): 177–98.

77. Ibid., 195.

78. "Where Would You Like to Get Married?" BBC News, 25 January 2002, http://newsvote.bbc.uk/hi/english/talking_point/newsid_1775000/1775078.stm, 14 May 2002.

79. For a cultural history of the Jazz Age, consult Lynn Dumenil, *The Modern Temper: American Culture and Society in the 1920s* (New York: Hill and Wang, 1995).

80. *Buyology,* first broadcast 24 November 24 2001 by The Learning Channel.

81. John Clarke et al., *Resistance through Rituals,* 53.

82. Alice Lea Mast Tasman, *Wedding Album* (New York: Walker and Company, 1982), 93.

83. Eric J. Arnould, Linda L. Price, and Cele C. Otnes, "Magical Romance: Commercial Rafting Adventures," in *Romancing the Market,* ed. Stephen Brown, Anne Marie Doherty, and Bill Clarke (London: Routledge, 1998), 233–54.

84. Lisa Michaels, "Diamonds Are an Ex-Hippie's Best Friend," http://underwire.msn.com/underwire/social/vp/60firstP.asp, 1 April 2000.

85. Margot Adler, *Heretic's Heart: A Journey through Spirit and Revolution* (Boston: Beacon Press, 1997), 163–64.

86. Philip Norman, *Days in the Life: John Lennon Remembered* (London: Century, 1990), 90–91.

87. In the Catholic medieval prayer service, the bride was called on to vow obedience. In the Anglican Prayer Book service of 1552, she had to do so in English, even though the idea of obedience seemed to contradict that of symmetry in the wording of the other parts of the vows. Marilyn Yalom, *A History of the Wife* (New York: HarperCollins, 2001), 110.

88. Ruth Rosen, *The World Split Open: How the Modern Women's Movement Changed America* (New York: Viking, 2000), 204–5; Rosalyn Fraad Baxandall, "Catching the Fire," in *The Feminist Memoir Project: Voices from Women's Liberation,* ed. Rachel Blau Du Plessis and Ann Snitow (New York: Three Rivers Press, 1998), 214–15.

89. Kate Epstein, "A Marriage of My Own," in *Young Wives' Tales,* 11.

90. Ibid.

91. "Feminist Icon Gloria Steinem First-Time Bride," 5 September 2000, http://www.cnn.com/2000/US/09/05/steinem.marriage.ap, 5 September 2000.

92. Ronald Grimes, *Deeply into the Bone: Re-inventing Rites of Passage* (Berkeley: University of California Press, 2000), 207.

93. Juliet Schor, *The Overspent American: Upscaling, Downshifting, and the New Consumer* (New York: Basic Books, 1998), 136–37.

94. Carol Reed-Jones, *Green Weddings That Don't Cost the Earth* (Bellingham, Wash.: Paper Crane Press, 1996).

95. Posting by Carol to Greenweddings Web site, http://www.ilovethisplace.com/wwwboard/greenweddings/messages/49.html, 1 March 2001.

10. LUXURY, LAVISHNESS, AND LOVE

1. http://abcnews.go.com/sections/GMA/GoodMorningAmerica/GMA020516Honeymoon_wedding_times_square_html, 18 May 2001.

2. Julia Chaplin, "NOTICED: Here Comes the Bride, and Her Sponsors," *New York Times,* 24 September 2001, sec. 9, p. 1.

3. Julie V. Iovine, "Just Divorced, Gone Shopping," *New York Times*, 12 July 2001, sec. B, pp. 1, 12.

4. James B. Twitchell, *Living It Up: Our Love Affair with Luxury* (New York: Columbia University Press, 2002), 46.

5. Richard Schickel, *Intimate Strangers: The Culture of Celebrity* (Garden City, N.Y.: Doubleday, 1985), 23–64.

6. Ronald L. Grimes, *Deeply into the Bone: Re-inventing Rites of Passage* (Berkeley: University of California Press, 2000), 128–29.

7. Gregory L. White and Shirley Leung, "Middle Market Shrinks as Americans Migrate toward the High End," *Wall Street Journal*, 29 March 2002, sec. A, pp. 1, 8.

8. Twitchell, *Living It Up*, xiv.

9. Kathy Peiss, *Hope in a Jar: The Making of America's Beauty Culture* (New York: Henry Holt, 1998), 6–8, 268–70.

10. Pamela Paul, *The Starter Marriage and the Future of Matrimony* (New York: Villard Books, 2002), 189–99.

11. Kristin Griffith, e-mail communication to Cele Otnes, 5 May 2001.

12. Dale Spender, ed., *Weddings and Wives* (Ringwood, Australia: Penguin Books, 1994), quotation from book cover.

13. Elizabeth Breyer, "For Better, for Worse and for Fun," *New York Times*, 25 August 2002, sec. 9, p. 2.

14. Estelle B. Freedman, *No Turning Back: The History of Feminism and the Future of Women* (New York: Ballantine Books, 2002), 162–63, 377–79.

15. Sheryl Nissinen, *The Conscious Bride: Women Unveil Their True Feelings about Getting Hitched* (Oakland, Calif.: New Harbinger Publications, 2000).

16. Barbara Isenberg, " 'Tony n' Tina': Married to Their Work: Improvisational Wedding Satire That's an Off-Broadway Hit Is Planning an L.A. Ceremony," *Los Angeles Times*, 8 October 1989, Calendar sec., p. 4; Louisa Benton, "A Marriage Made off Broadway Takes the Cake," *New York Times*, 15 July 1990, sec. 2, p. 5.

17. Elizabeth Freeman, *The Wedding Complex: Forms of Belonging in Modern American Culture* (Durham, N.C.: Duke University Press, 2002), 198–209.

The 1902 Edition of the Sears, Roebuck Catalogue. New York: Gramercy Books, 2000.

"3,800 Couples Wed after Dutch Law." *Honolulu* (Hawaii) *Advertiser,* 13 December 2001, sec. A, p. 3.

Abbott, Denise. "Wedding Trends." *Flowers &* 12 (March 1991): 90.

Ackerman, Diane. *A Natural History of Love.* New York: Random House, 1994.

Adler, Jerry. "A Matter of Faith." *Newsweek,* 15 December 1997, 50–51.

Adler, Margot. *Heretic's Heart: A Journey through Spirit and Revolution.* Boston: Beacon Press, 1997.

Adrian, Bonnie. "Framing the Bride: Beauty, Romance, and Rites of Globalization in Taiwan's Bridal Industry." Ph.D. diss., Yale University, 1999.

Advertisement for De Beers. "For Him the Diamond Dawns Are Set in Rings of Beauty." *New Yorker,* 23 September 1939, 7.

Advertisement for De Beers. "On Wings of Hope." *New Yorker,* 14 July 1945, 5.

Advertisement for De Beers. "Thought for the Future." Painting by Raoul Dufy. From the "Great Artists" series, 1940.

Advertisement for Feature Ring Company. *National Jeweler,* April 1957.

Advertisement for Franciscan China. *Bride and Home,* February 1962.

Advertisement for Jabel Ring Manufacturing Company. *The Jewelers' Circular,* March 1934, 24.

Advertisement for "Little Queens and Big Diamonds." 1953. Archived at the John W. Hartman Center for Sales, Advertising, and Marketing History, Rare Book, Manuscript, and Special Collections Library, Duke University.

Advertisement for National Bridal Service. "Meet the Other Woman in Your Romance!" *Modern Bride,* fall 1957.

Advertisement tearsheet for De Beers. "My Most Precious Possession . . . but Grind It to Powder!" January 1943. From the Smithsonian Museum Advertising Archives.

Advertisements for Lenox, Pier One Imports, J. C. Penney Bridal Registry, and Gingiss Formalwear. *Modern Bride,* June–July 1999.

Allen, Richard. *Projecting Illusion: Film Spectatorship and the Impression of Reality.* Cambridge: Cambridge University Press, 1995.

American Life Histories: Manuscripts from the Federal Writer's Project, 1936–1940, American Memory, Library of Congress.

Appadurai, Arjun. "Disjuncture and Difference in the Global Cultural Economy." *Theory, Culture, and Society* 7 (1990): 295–310.

———. *Modernity at Large: Cultural Dimensions of Globalization.* Minneapolis: University of Minnesota Press, 1996.

Argyrou, Vassos. *Tradition and Modernity in the Mediterranean.* Cambridge: Cambridge University Press, 1996.

Arnett, Jeffrey Jensen. "Learning to Stand Alone: The Contemporary American Transition to Adulthood in Cultural and Historical Context." *Human Development* 41 (1998): 295–97.

Arnould, Eric J., Linda L. Price, and Cele C. Otnes. "Magical Romance: Commercial Rafting Adventures." In *Romancing the Market,* edited by Stephen Brown, Anne Marie Doherty, and Bill Clarke. London: Routledge, 1998.

Aron, Cindy S. *Working at Play: A History of Vacations in the United States.* New York: Oxford University Press, 1999.

Arthur, Juliet K. "Here Comes the Bride's Business!" *Independent Woman* 18 (1939): 170–84.

Association of Bridal Consultants Web site. http://www.trainingforum.com/ASN/ABC, 2 July 2001.

Auburn, Ellis. *The Most Beautiful Woman in the World.* New York: Cliff Street Books, 2000.

Ayers, Tess, and Paul Brown. *The Essential Guide to Lesbian and Gay Weddings.* San Francisco: HarperSanFrancisco, 1994.

Bahn, Adele. "Changes and Continuities in the Transitional Status of Bride into Wife: A Content Analysis of Bridal Magazines, 1967–1977: The Decade of the Women's Movement." Ph.D. diss., City University of New York, 1979.

Bailey, Beth. *From Front Porch to Back Seat: Courtship in Twentieth-Century America.* Baltimore: Johns Hopkins University Press, 1988.

Bailey, Beth, and David Farber. "Hotel Street: Prostitution and the Politics of War." *Radical History Review* 52 (winter 1992): 54–77.

Bailey, Margaret J. *Those Glorious Glamour Years.* Secaucus, N.J.: Citadel Press, 1982.

Baker, Margaret. *Wedding Customs and Folklore.* Totowa, N.J.: David and Charles, 1977.

Balloon Images 8, no. 5 (November–December 1996): 6–12.

Bashinsky, Ruth. " 'I Do'-ing It My Way." *New York Daily News,* 22 June 2000, 51.

Batten, Jesse F. "The 'Rights' of Husbands and the 'Duties' of Wives: Power and Desire in the American Bedroom, 1850–1910." *Journal of Family History* 24 (1999): 165–87.

Baudrillard, Jean. *Simulacra and Simulation.* Translated by Sheila Glaser. Ann Arbor: University of Michigan Press, 1994.

Baumann, Zygmunt. *Modernity and Ambivalence.* Cambridge: Polity Press, 1991.

Baxandall, Rosalyn Fraad. "Catching the Fire." In *The Feminist Memoir Project: Voices from Women's Liberation,* edited by Rachel Blau Du Plessis and Ann Snitow. New York: Three Rivers Press, 1998.

Beckerman, Ilene. *Mother of the Bride.* Chapel Hill, N.C.: Algonquin Books, 2000.

Belk, Russell W. "Art versus Science as Ways of Generating Knowledge about Materialism." In *Perspectives on Methodology in Consumer Research,* edited by David Brinberg and Richard J. Lutz. New York: Springer-Verlag, 1986.

———. "Been There, Done That, Bought the Souvenirs: Of Journeys and Boundary Crossing." In *Consumer Research: Postcards from the Edge,* edited by Stephen Brown and Durach Turley. London: Routledge, 1997.

———. *Collecting in a Consumer Society.* London: Routledge, 1995.

———. "Effects of Gift-Giving Involvement on Gift Selection Strategies." In *Advances in Consumer Research,* vol. 9, edited by Andrew A. Mitchell. Provo, Utah: Association for Consumer Research, 1981.

———. "Gift-Giving Behavior." In *Research in Consumer Behavior,* vol. 2, edited by Jagdish Sheth. Greenwich, Conn.: JAI Press, 1979.

———. "The Ineluctable Mysteries of Possessions." *Journal of Behavior and Social Personality* 6, no. 6 (1991): 17–55.

———. "Leaping Luxuries and Transitional Consumers." In *Marketing Issues in*

Transitional Economies, edited by Rajeev Batra. Boston: Kluwer Academic Publishers, 1999.

———. "Multimedia Consumer Research." In *Representation in Consumer Research,* edited by Barbara Stern. London: Routledge, 1998.

Belk, Russell W., Güliz Ger, and Soren Askegaard. "Metaphors of Consumer Desire." In *Advances in Consumer Research,* vol. 23, edited by Kim Corfman and John Lynch. Provo, Utah: Association for Consumer Research, 1996.

Belk, Russell W., Melanie Wallendorf, and John F. Sherry Jr. "The Sacred and Profane in Consumer Behavior: Theodicy on the Odyssey." *Journal of Consumer Research* 16, no. 1 (June 1989): 1–38.

Bellafante, Ginia. "In Rush Hour of the Brides, the Word Is Sexy." *New York Times,* 15 May 2001, sec. A, p. 22.

Benton, Louisa. "A Marriage Made off Broadway Takes the Cake." *New York Times,* 15 July 1990, sec. 2, p. 5.

Berry, Christopher J. *The Idea of Luxury: A Conceptual and Historical Investigation.* Cambridge: Cambridge University Press, 1994.

Blackford, Mansel G. *Fragile Paradise: The Impact of Tourism on Maui, 1959–2000.* Lawrence: University Press of Kansas, 2001.

Blaszczyk, Regina Lee. "Cinderella Stories: The Glass of Fashion and the Gendered Marketplace." In *His and Hers: Gender, Consumption, and Technology,* edited by Roger Horowitz and Arwen Mohun. Charlottesville: University Press of Virginia, 1998.

———. *Imagining Consumers: Design and Innovation from Wedgwood to Corning.* Baltimore: Johns Hopkins University Press, 2000.

Bonnano, Antonio, and Antoinette L. Matlins. *Engagement and Wedding Rings.* Woodstock, Vt.: Gemstone Press, 1999.

Booth, Diane. "Jumping the Broom: An African-American Tradition Is Back." http://www.howardcounty.com/broom/bride2000.html, 15 February 2001.

Boskind-Lodahl, Marlene. "Cinderella's Stepsisters: A Feminist Perspective on Anorexia Nervosa and Bulimia." *Signs* 2 (1976): 342–56.

Boswell, John. *The Marriage of Likeness: Same-Sex Unions in Pre-modern Europe.* London: HarperCollins, 1995.

Boswell, Parley Ann. "The Pleasure of Our Company: Hollywood Throws a Wedding Bash." In *Beyond the Stars II: Plot Conventions in American Popular Film,* edited by Paul Loukides and Linda K. Fuller. Bowling Green, Ohio: Bowling Green State University Popular Press, 1991.

Bouchier, David. "OUT OF ORDER: Romance Plus Finance Equals Extravagance." *New York Times,* 7 May 2000, sec. 14L, p. 8.

Bourdieu, Pierre. *Distinction: A Social Critique of the Judgment of Taste.* Translated by Richard Nice. Cambridge, Mass.: Harvard University Press, 1984.

Braithwaite, Dawn O. "Ritualized Embarrassment at 'Coed' Wedding and Baby Showers." *Communication Reports* 8, no. 2 (1995): 150–51.

Braithwaite, Dawn O., and Leslie A. Baxter. " 'I Do' Again: The Relational Dialectics of Renewing Wedding Vows." *Journal of Social and Personal Relationships* 12 (1995): 177–98.

Breckinridge, S. P. *New Homes for Old.* New York: Harper and Brothers, 1921.

Brenning, Marie Coudert. *Wedding Embassy Yearbook.* New York: The Wedding Embassy, Inc., 1934.

Breyer, Elizabeth. "For Better, for Worse and for Fun." *New York Times,* 25 August 2002, sec. 9, p. 2.

"Bridal Registries: Older Couples Equal More Gifts." *Stores,* April 1988, 16.

Bride's Calendar. *Bride's,* August–September 1995, 290.

Bride's Calendar. *Bride's,* February 1970, 16.

Bride's Calendar. *Bride's,* Summer 1959, 70.

Brooks, David. *Bobos in Paradise: The New Upper Class and How They Got There.* New York: Simon and Schuster, 2000.

Brown, Ann, and Marjorie Whigham-Dear. "Honeymoon Hideaways." *Black Enterprise,* April 1992, 105–10.

Brown, DeSoto. *Hawaii Recalls: Selling Romance to America: Nostalgic Images of the Hawaiian Islands, 1910–1950.* Honolulu, Hawaii: Editions Limited, 1982.

Brown, Janet, and Pamela Loy. "Cinderella and Slipper Jack: Sex Roles and Social Mobility Themes in Early Musical Comedy." *International Journal of Women's Studies* 4 (1981): 507–16.

Brumberg, Joan Jacobs. *Fasting Girls: The Emergence of Anorexia Nervosa as a Modern Disease.* Cambridge, Mass.: Harvard University Press, 1988.

Bulcroft, Kris, Linda Smeins, and Richard Bulcroft. *Romancing the Honeymoon: Consummating Marriage in Modern Society.* Thousand Oaks, Calif.: Sage Publications, 1999.

Bulcroft, Kris, Richard Bulcroft, Linda Smeins, and Helen Cranage. "The Social Construction of the North American Honeymoon, 1880–1995." *Journal of Family History* 22 (1997): 462–90.

Bunn, Dina. "Something Blue: J. C. Penney Quits Bridal Business as It Closes Its Salon at Villa Italia." *Denver Rocky Mountain News,* 9 June 1999, sec. B, p. 1.

Burger, M. Susan, and William B. White. *The Daguerreotype: Nineteenth-Century Technology and Modern Science.* Washington, D.C.: Smithsonian Institution Press, 1991.

Burgess, Ernest W., and Paul Wallin. *Engagement and Marriage.* Chicago: J. B. Lippincott Co., 1953.

Burns, John F. "Relishing Beautiful New Freedoms in Kabul." *New York Times,* 15 September 2002, YNE, p. 13.

Butterick, E. A. *Butterick's 1892 Metropolitan Fashion.* New York: Butterick Publishing, 1892.

Buyology. First broadcast 24 November 2001 by The Learning Channel.

Bykofsky, Sheree, and Laurie Viera. *Popping the Question.* New York: Walker and Company, 1996.

Cabot, E. B. "Perfect Church Wedding." *Ladies' Home Journal* 36 (June 1923): 112.

Cahners Research. *Modern Bride* Reader Service Survey, 1991–92.

Caldwell, Mark. *A Short History of Rudeness: Manners, Morals, and Misbehavior in Modern America.* New York: Picador, 1999.

"Camp America." *Times Magazine,* 30 March 2002, p. 69.

Campbell, Colin. *The Romantic Ethic and the Spirit of Modern Consumerism.* Oxford: B. Blackwell, 1987.

Campbell, Edward D. C., Jr. *The Celluloid South: Hollywood and the Southern Myth.* Knoxville: University of Tennessee Press, 1981.

Cancian, Francesca. "The Feminization of Love." *Signs* 11, no. 4 (1986): 692–701.

Carlson, Alvar W. "The Spatial Behavior Involved in Honeymoons: The Case of Two Areas in Wisconsin and North Dakota, 1971–1976." *Journal of Popular Culture* 11 (1978): 977–88.

Carrier, James. "The Rituals of Christmas Giving." In *Unwrapping Christmas,* edited by Daniel Miller. Oxford: Clarendon Press, 1993.

Carter, Belfield. "Jerry Connor: Practical Dreamer." Brochure of article reprinted from *The Southern Jeweler* (1959): 2.

Cashman, Greer Fay. "Something Old to Something New." *The Jerusalem Post,* 25 December 1997, 14.

Casparis, Johan. "The Bridal Shower: An American Rite of Passage." *Indian Journal of Social Research* 20 (1979): 11–21.

Cavanaugh, Joanne P. "Cuba's Marry-Go-Round, *Johns Hopkins Magazine.*" April 1998. http://www.jhu.edu/~humag/0498web/wedding.html, 3 March 2001.

Cavell, Stanley. *Pursuits of Happiness: The Hollywood Comedy of Remarriage.* Cambridge, Mass.: Harvard University Press, 1981.

Chaplin, Julia. "NOTICED: Here Comes the Bride, and Her Sponsors." *New York Times,* 24 September 2001, sec. 9, p. 1.

Charsley, Simon R. *Rites of Marrying: A Scottish Study.* Manchester: Manchester University Press, 1993.

Chase, Dennis. "De Beers Changes Ad Tack." *Advertising Age,* 18 July 1983, 42, 48.

Cheal, David J. *The Gift Economy.* London: Routledge, 1988.

Cherry, Kittredge, and Zalmon Sherwood, eds. *Equal Rites: Lesbian and Gay Worship, Ceremonies, and Celebrations.* Louisville, Ky.: Westminster/John Knox Press, 1995.

Chicks in White Satin. 16mm, 25 min., Holliman Productions, Santa Monica, Calif., 1993.

Chudacoff, Howard P. *The Age of the Bachelor.* Princeton, N.J.: Princeton University Press, 1999.

Church, Beverly Reese. *Weddings Southern Style.* New York: Abbeville Press Publishers, 1993.

Clark, Beverly. *Wedding Cakes.* Philadelphia: Running Press Book Publishers, 1999.

Clarke, John, Stuart Hall, Tony Jefferson, and Brian Roberts. "Subcultures, Cultures, and Class." In *Resistance through Rituals: Youth Subculture in Post-War Britain,* edited by Stuart Hall and Tony Jefferson. London: Routledge, 1976.

Clehane, Diane. "Style File/Gowns to Go/More Brides Are Looking for Wedding Dresses in a Hurry." *Newsday,* 24 June 1999, sec. B, p. 27.

Cocks, Jay. "Scenes from a Marriage: Checkbook Ready? Big Weddings Are Back." *Time,* 7 July 1986, 58–62.

Cohen, Kate. *A Walk down the Aisle: Notes on a Modern Wedding.* New York: W. W. Norton, 2001.

Cole, Harriette. *Jumping the Broom: The African-American Wedding Planner.* New York: Henry Holt and Company, 1993.

Coll, Steve. "Asian Prosperity Spawns Conspicuous Consumption: Middle Classes Buying up Consumer Goods." *Washington Post,* 22 March 1994, sec. A, p. 1.

Collier, Mary Jeffery. "The Psychological Appeal in the Cinderella Theme." *American Imago* 18 (spring 1961): 399–406.

Comte, Elizabeth. "Good Food, Good Wine, and Good Storytelling." *Forbes,* 10 May 1993, 174–75.

Condé Nast Bridal Infobank. "American Wedding Study." Unpublished, 2002.

Corliss, Richard. "*In & Out* (Review)." *Time,* 22 September 1997, 90.

Corrado, Marisa. "Teaching Wedding Rules: How Bridal Workers Negotiate Control over Their Customers." *Journal of Contemporary Ethnography* 31, no. 1 (February 2002): 33–67.

Corston Oliver, Monica. "The 'White Wedding': Metaphors and Advertising in Bridal Magazines." http://socrates.berkeley.edu/%7emoliver/weddingpaper .htm, 12 May 2001.

Cott, Nancy F. *Public Vows: A History of Marriage and the Nation.* Cambridge, Mass.: Harvard University Press, 2000.

Couture, Denise. "Japanese Brides Borrow Western Traditions." *Chicago Tribune,* 16 May 1993, sec. G, p. 1.

Cox, Meki. "Japanese Brides and Grooms Head to 'Paradise.' " *Chicago Tribune,* 9 November 1995, sec. C, p. 8.

Creighton, Millie R. "The Depato: Merchandising in the West while Selling Japaneseness." In *Re-made in Japan: Everyday Life and Consumer Taste in a Changing Society,* edited by Joseph J. Tobin. New Haven, Conn.: Yale University Press, 1992.

Cressy, David. *Birth, Marriage, and Death: Ritual, Religion, and the Life-Cycle in Tudor and Stuart England.* Oxford: Oxford University Press, 1997.

Cross, Wilbur, and Ann Novotny. *White House Weddings.* New York: David McKay Company, 1967.

Crowston, Clare Haru. *Fabricating Women: The Seamstresses of Old Regime France, 1675–1791.* Durham, N.C.: Duke University Press, 2001.

"Cruise Liners and Air." *Life,* 22 February 1957, 24–33.

Csikszentmihalyi, Mihalyi, and Eugene Rochberg-Halton. *The Meaning of Things: Domestic Symbols and the Self.* Cambridge: Cambridge University Press, 1981.

Curley, Charity. "Hill Rollin' Romance." Based on a *Bride's* magazine survey in 2000. http://www.ivillage.com/relationships/weddings/articles/00,89536,00 .html, 15 January 2001.

Curtin, Patricia Romero. "Weddings in Lamu, Kenya: An Example of Social and Economic Change." *Cahiers d'Etudes Africaines* 25 (1984): 131–55.

Curtis, Richard. *Four Weddings and a Funeral: Three Appendices and a Screenplay.* New York: St. Martin's Griffin, 1996.

Davis, John H. *Jacqueline Bouvier: An Intimate Memoir.* New York: John Wiley and Sons, 1994.

Dayan, Daniel, and Elihu Katz. "Electronic Ceremonies: Television Performs a Royal Wedding." In *On Signs,* edited by Marshall Blonsky. Baltimore: Johns Hopkins University Press, 1985.

De Lys, Claudia. *How the World Weds.* New York: The Martin Press, 1929.

De Morales, Lisa. "Fox's Farewell Gives 'City' Ratings a Nice Spin." *The Washington Post,* 26 May 2000, sec. C, p. 7.

Debord, Guy. *The Society of the Spectacle.* New York: Zone Books, 1995.

Delaney, Chuck. *Wedding Photography and Video.* New York: Allworth Press, 1994.

Deming, Michael. *Mechanic Accents: Dime Novels and Working-Class Culture in America.* London: Verso, 1987.

Department of Business, Economic Development, and Tourism. *Annual Visitor Research Report.* Honolulu: DBEDT, 2000.

Desmond, Jane C. *Staging Tourism: Bodies on Display from Waikiki to Sea World.* Chicago: University of Chicago Press, 1999.

DeVere, Stephen P., Clifford D. Scott, and William L. Shulby. "Consumer Perceptions of Gift-Giving Occasions: Attribute Saliency and Structure." In *Advances in Consumer Research,* vol. 10, edited by Richard P. Bagozzi and Alice Tybout. Ann Arbor, Mich.: Association for Consumer Research, 1983.

DeWitt, Paula Mergenbagen. "The Second Time Around." *American Demographics,* 14, November 1992, 60.

Di Leonardo, Micaela. "The Female World of Cards and Holidays: Women, Families, and Work of Kinship." *Signs* 12 (1987): 440–53.

Diamant, Anita. *The New Jewish Wedding.* New York: Summit Books, 1985.

Didion, Joan. *Slouching Towards Bethlehem.* New York: Farrar, Straus and Giroux, 1961.

Doane, Mary Ann. "The Economy of Desire: The Commodity Form in/of the Cinema." *Quarterly Review of Film and Video* 11 (1989): 23–33.

Dobscha, Susan, and Ellen Foxman. "Gendered Communication: Textual Analysis of Letters Written to Filene's Basement." In *Gender, Marketing, and Consumer Behavior,* 5th ed., edited by Jonathan Schroeder and Cele Otnes. Champaign: University of Illinois Printing Service, 2000.

———. "Women and Wedding Gowns: Exploring a Discount Shopping Experience." In *Gender, Marketing, and Consumer Behavior,* 4th ed., edited by Eileen Fischer and Dan Wardlow. San Francisco: San Francisco State University Publishing, 1998.

Dogar, Rana. "Here Comes the Billion-Dollar Bride." *Working Woman,* May 1997, 32.

Dowling, Colette. *The Cinderella Complex: Women's Hidden Fear of Independence.* New York: Summit Books, 1981.

Driver, Tom. *The Magic of Ritual.* New York: HarperCollins, 1991.

Drummond, Tammerlin. "The Marrying Kind." *Time,* 14 May 2001, 52.

Dubinsky, Karen. *The Second Greatest Disappointment: Honeymooning and Tourism at Niagara Falls.* New Brunswick, N.J.: Rutgers University Press, 1998.

Duggan, Lisa. *Sapphic Slashers: Sex, Violence, and American Modernity.* Durham, N.C.: Duke University Press, 2000.

Dumenil, Lynn. *The Modern Temper: American Culture and Society in the 1920s.* New York: Hill and Wang, 1995.

Dundes, Alan. " 'Jumping the Broom': On the Origins and Meaning of an African American Wedding Custom." *Journal of American Folklore* 109 (summer 1996): 324–29.

Dunn, Donald H., Bradley Hitchings, Irene Pave, Troy Segal, and Julie Flynn. "Consultants Who Help You Tie the Knot." *Business Week,* 25 May 1987, 182.

Durkheim, Emile. "Definition of Religious Phenomena and of Religion." In *The Elementary Forms of Religious Life: A Study in Religious Sociology.* London: Allen & Unwin, 1915.

Eckhardt, Giana M. " 'India Will Survive': Understanding the Role of Consumer Agency in the Globalization Process in Emerging Markets." *Proceedings of the Eighth Cross-Cultural Research Conference.* Oahu, Hawaii, December 2002.

Edwards, Marion. "Wedding Presents Made Easy." *The Saturday Evening Post,* 15 March 1930, 52.

Edwards, Walter. *Modern Japan through Its Weddings: Gender, Person, and Society in Ritual Portrayal.* Stanford, Calif.: Stanford University Press, 1989.

Effinger, Tracy, and Suzanne Rowen. *The Wedding Workout: Look and Feel Fabulous on Your Special Day.* Chicago: Contemporary Books, 2002.

Elkin, Stanley. "In Praise of Tuxedos." *Harper's,* November 1985, 34.

Epstein, Edward Jay. "Have You Ever Tried to Sell a Diamond?" *Atlantic Monthly,* February 1982, 28–29.

———. *The Rise and Fall of Diamonds.* New York: Simon and Schuster, 1982.

Epstein, Kate. "A Marriage of My Own." In *Young Wives' Tales: New Adventures in Love and Partnership,* edited by Jill Corral and Lisa Myers-Jarvis. Seattle: Seal Press, 2001.

Epstein, Rebecca L. "Sharon Stone in a Gap Turtleneck." In *Hollywood Goes Shopping,* edited by David Desser and Garth S. Jowett. Minneapolis: University of Minnesota Press, 2000.

"Facts about Our Brides!" http://www.ultimatewedding.com/polls, 1 February 2001.

"Featured Wedding: Allison and Mike Hash." http://www.weddingchannel.com, 15 March 2001.

Federman, David. "50 Years of Saying Forever." *Modern Jeweler,* April 1997, 31.

"Feminist Icon Gloria Steinem First-Time Bride." 5 September 2000. http://www.cnn.com/2000/US/08/05/steinem.marriage.ap, 1 May 2001.

Firat, A. Fuat, and Nikhilesh Dholakia. *Consuming People: From Political Economy to Theaters of Consumption.* London: Routledge, 1998.

Fisher, Wesley Andrew. *The Soviet Marriage Market: Mate-Selection in Russia and the USSR.* New York: Praeger, 1980.

Flanagan, Caitlin. "The Wedding Merchants." *Atlantic Monthly,* February 2001, 112–19.

Fleming, Sue. *Buff Brides.* New York: Villard Books, 2002.

Flick, David, and Todd J. Gilman. "Veiled in Secrecy: Dallas Wedding of Roger Clinton to Be Strictly Private." *Dallas Morning News,* 25 March 1994, sec. A, p. 1.

Foresta, Merry A., and John Wood. *Secrets of the Dark Chamber: The Art of the American Daguerreotype.* Washington, D.C.: Smithsonian Institution Press, 1995.

Forsburgh, Lacey. "New Fashions in Honeymoons: Hips, Super Hip, and Super Square." *New York Times,* 13 June 1971, sec. 10, p. 22.

Fox, Stephen. *The Mirror Makers.* New York: William Morrow and Company, 1984.

Frances, Peter. "Marriage—United States." *Marketing Tools,* June 1996, 76.

Frank, Robert H. *Luxury Fever: Why Money Fails to Satisfy in an Era of Excess.* New York: Free Press, 1999.

Freedman, Estelle B. *No Turning Back: The History of Feminism and the Future of Women.* New York: Ballantine Books, 2002.

Freeman, Elizabeth. *The Wedding Complex: Forms of Belonging in Modern American Culture.* Durham, N.C.: Duke University Press, 2002.

Frese, Pamela R. "The Union of Nature and Culture: Gender Symbolism in the

American Wedding Ritual." In *Transcending Boundaries: Multi-disciplinary Approaches to the Study of Gender,* edited by Pamela R. Frese and John M. Coggleshall. New York: Bergen and Garvey, 1991.

Friese, Susanne. "A Consumer Good in the Ritual Process: The Case of the Wedding Dress." *Journal of Ritual Studies* 11 (winter 1997): 51–62.

Furlough, Ellen. "Making Mass Vacations: Tourism and Consumer Culture in France, 1930s to 1970s." *Comparative Studies in Society and History* 40 (1998): 247–86.

———. "Packaging Pleasures: Club Méditerranée and French Consumer Culture, 1950–1968." *French Historical Studies* 18 (1993): 65–81.

Furstenberg, Frank F., Jr.. "The Future of Marriage." *American Demographics,* June 1996, 34.

Gardaphe, Fred L. *Italian-American Ways.* New York: Harper and Row, 1982.

Geller, Jaclyn. *Here Comes the Bride: Women, Weddings, and the Marriage Mystique.* New York: Four Walls Eight Windows, 2001.

Genovese, Eugene D. *Roll, Jordan, Roll: The World the Slaves Made.* New York: Pantheon, 1974.

"Getting the Groom Involved in the Planning." *The Cleveland Plain Dealer,* 27 January 2000, sec. F, p. 5.

Gillette, Maris. "What's in a Dress? Brides in the Hui Quarter of Xi'an." In *The Consumer Revolution in Urban China,* edited by Deborah Davis. Berkeley: University of California Press, 2000.

Gillis, John R. *A World of Their Own Making: Myth, Ritual, and the Quest for Family Values.* New York: Basic Books, 1996.

"Glass with Attitude." *The Economist,* 20 December 1997, 115.

Gluckman, Ron. "Honeymoon Island." http:www.gluckman.com/ChejuWed .html, 6 June 2001.

Goffman, Erving. *Gender Advertisements.* Cambridge, Mass.: Harvard University Press, 1976.

Good Morning America. First broadcast 22 June 2001 by ABC.

Goode, Judith G., Karen Curtis, and Janet Theophano. "Meal Formats, Meal Cycles, and Menu Negotiation in the Maintenance of an Italian-American Community." In *Food in the Social Order: Studies of Food and Festivities in Three American Communities,* edited by Mary Douglas. New York: Russell Sage Foundation, 1984.

Gottdeiner, M., Claudia C. Collins, and David R. Dickens. *Las Vegas: The Social Production of an All-American City.* Malden, Mass.: Blackwell Publishers, 1999.

Grant, Gail Paton. "Getting Started: Outfitting the Bride in Seaside." *Canadian Folklore* 15, no. 2 (1993): 69–81.

Green, Harvey. *The Light of the Home: An Intimate View of the Lives of Women in Victorian America.* New York: Pantheon Books, 1983.

Greenblat, Cathy S., and Thomas J. Cottle. *Getting Married.* New York: McGraw-Hill, 1980.

Greene, Naomi. "Family Ceremonies: Or, Opera in the Godfather Trilogy." In *Francis Ford Coppola's The Godfather Trilogy,* edited by Nick Browne. Cambridge: Cambridge University Press, 2000.

Grimes, Ronald L. *Deeply into the Bone: Re-inventing Rites of Passage.* Berkeley: University of California Press, 2000.

———. "Ritual." In *Guide to the Study of Religion,* edited by Willi Braun and Russell T. McCutcheon. London: Cassell, 2000.

———. "Ritual and Performance." In *Religion and American Cultures: An Encyclopedia of Traditions, Diversity, and Popular Expressions,* edited by Gary Laderman and Luis León. Santa Barbara, Calif.: ABC-CLIO, 2003.

"Groom's Involvement Leads Wedding Trends." *Women and Marketing,* 13 May 1998, 10.

Grossberg, Michael. *Governing the Hearth: Law and the Family in Nineteenth-Century America.* Chapel Hill: University of North Carolina Press, 1985.

Grossman, Cathy Lynn. "More Honeymooners Bet on Gambling Spots." *USA Today,* 10 October 1987, sec. D, p. 8.

Gutman, Herbert G. *The Black Family in Slavery and Freedom, 1750–1925.* New York: Pantheon Books, 1976.

Gutmann, Stephanie. "The Wedding Gown: Revealing the Nation's Mood." *New York Times,* 15 June 1997, sec. 1, p. 33.

Guzman, Rafer. "Lions and Tigers and Brides—Oh, My." *Wall Street Journal,* 12 January 2002, sec. W, p. 5.

Hamilton, Jane Eaton. "Twenty-One Questions." In *Young Wives' Tales: New Adventures in Love and Partnership,* edited by Jill Corral and Lisa Myers-Jarvis. Seattle: Seal Press, 2001.

Handy, Deborah, ed. *Variety Film Reviews 1907–1980.* New York: Garland Publishing, 1985.

Hanson, Kitty. *For Richer, for Poorer.* London: Abelard-Schuman, 1968.

Harris, Daniel. *Cute, Quaint, Hungry, and Romantic.* New York: Basic Books, 2000.

———. "The Romantic." *Salmagundi* 123 (1999): 64–79.

———. "Zaniness." *Salmagundi* 104–5 (1994–95): 206–17.

Harrison, Eric. "Laughing at Love: Depression-Era Screwball Comedies Are Evolving into Modern-Day Romances." *Houston Chronicle,* 9 March 2001, Houston sec., p. 2.

Harvey, James. *Romantic Comedy in Hollywood from Lubitsch to Sturges.* New York: Alfred A. Knopf, 1987.

Hawley, Michael. "I Was a Mail Order Minister." http://www.wedding channel.com, 1 March 2001.

Heeler, Roger, June Francis, Chike Okechuku, and Stanley Reid. "Gift versus Personal Use Brand Selection." In *Advances in Consumer Research,* vol. 6, edited by William Wilkie. Provo, Utah: Association for Consumer Research, 1979.

Heilbrunn, Benoit. "In Search of the Lost Aura: The Object in the Age of Marketing Romanticism." In *Romancing the Market,* edited by Stephen Brown, Anne Marie Doherty, and Bill Clarke. London: Sage, 1998.

Heiner, Teresa Anne. "Shinto Wedding, Samurai Bride: Inventing Tradition and Fashioning Identity in the Rituals of Bridal Dress in Japan." Ph.D. diss., University of Pittsburgh, 1997.

Heymann, C. David. *Liz: An Intimate Biography of Elizabeth Taylor.* New York: Brick Lane Press, 1995.

Hickman, Jim. "Oppenheimer Passes on at 92—Glittering Life All Thanks to Diamonds." http://www.rense.com/general3/glit/html, 30 June 2001.

Hirsch, James S. "This Should Get Their Picture on the Studio Wall." *Wall Street Journal,* 16 June 1992, sec. A, p. 11.

Hirsch, Julia Antopol. *The Sound of Music: The Making of America's Favorite Movie.* Chicago: Contemporary Books, 1993.

Hofferth, Sandra L., Joan R. Kahn, and Wendy Baldwin. "Premarital Sexual Activity among U.S. Teenage Women over the Past Three Decades." *Family Planning Perspectives* 2 (March–April 1987): 46–53.

Holland, Thomas W., ed. *Girls' Toys of the Fifties.* Sherman Oaks, Calif.: Windmill Press, 1997.

Hollingshead, August. "Marital Status and Wedding Behavior." *Marriage and Family Living* 14 (1952): 308–11.

"Honeymoon Havens." *Time,* 23 June 1969, 90–91.

Horton, James O. "Freedom's Yoke: Gender Conventions among Antebellum Free Blacks." *Feminist Studies* 12 (1986): 50–76.

Howard, Lucy, Susannah Meadows, Bret Begun, and Katherine Stroup. "I Thought You'd Never Ask." *Newsweek,* 30 October 2000, 15.

Howard, Vicki. "American Weddings: Gender, Consumption, and the Business of Brides." Ph.D. diss., University of Texas, 2000.

Hunter, Jennifer. "Behind All That Glitters (De Beers)." *MacLean's,* 29 December 1997–5 January 1998, 89.

Illouz, Eva. *Consuming the Romantic Utopia: Love and the Cultural Contradictions of Capitalism.* Berkeley: University of California Press, 1997.

Imber-Black, Evan, Janine Roberts, and Richard A. Whiting. *Rituals in Families and Family Therapy.* New York: W. W. Norton, 1988.

Ingraham, Chrys. *White Weddings: Romancing Heterosexuality in Popular Culture.* London: Routledge, 1999.

"Interview with Harry Oppenheimer." *Prime Club Magazine,* 28 October 1999. http://www/primeclub.co.za/birthstones.html, 1 March 2000.

Iovine, Julie V. "Just Divorced, Gone Shopping." *New York Times,* 12 July 2001, sec. B, pp. 1, 12.

Isenberg, Barbara, " 'Tony n' Tina': Married to Their Work: Improvisational Wedding Satire That's an Off-Broadway Hit Is Planning an L.A. Ceremony." *Los Angeles Times,* 8 October 1989, Calendar sec., p. 4.

Itano, Nicole. "Goin' to the Chapel—and the Goat Dung Bath, Too." *Christian Science Monitor,* 11 June 2001, 1.

Jacobson, Paul H. *American Marriage and Divorce.* New York: Rinehart and Company, 1959.

Jardine, Lisa. *Worldly Goods.* London: Macmillan, 1996.

Jay, Karla, ed. *Dyke Life: From Growing up to Growing Old, a Celebration of the Lesbian Experience.* New York: Basic Books, 1995.

Jeffrey, Nancy Ann. "Wedding Photos Losing Focus." *Wall Street Journal,* 22 June 2000, sec. W, pp. 1, 4.

Jellison, Katherine. "From the Farmhouse Parlor to the Pink Barn: The Commercialization of Weddings in the Rural Midwest." *Iowa Heritage Illustrated* 2 (summer 1996): 50–65.

———. "Getting Married in the Heartland: The Commercialization of Weddings in the Rural Midwest." *Forum* (1995): 46–50.

Jensen, Robert. "The Politics and Ethics of Lesbian and Gay 'Wedding' Announcements in Newspapers." *The Howard Journal of Communications* 7 (1996): 17.

The Jewelers' Circular 98 (14 April 1929).

The Jewelers' Circular 97, no. 19 (4 December 1928).

Jewelers' Circular-Keystone 113 (November 1942): n.p.

Johnstone, Helen. "Bridal Firms Embrace New Boom." *Asian Business* 33 (June 1997): 54–55.

Jones, Charisse. "Bringing Slavery's Long Shadow to the Light." *New York Times,* 2 April 1995, sec. A, pp. 1, 14.

Joselit, Jenna Weissman. *The Wonders of America: Reinventing Jewish Culture, 1880–1950.* New York: Hill and Wang, 1994.

Juluri, Iao V. "Global Weds Local: The Reception of Hum Aapke Hain Koun." *European Journal of Cultural Studies* 2 (1999): 231–48.

Kanin, Eugene J., and David H. Howard. "Postmarital Consequences of Premarital Sex Adjustments." *American Sociological Review* 23 (1958): 556–62.

Kantor, Jodi. "A Bride's First Vow: My Feast Won't Be Dull." *New York Times,* 15 May 2002, sec. F, p. 1.

Katz, Jonathan, ed. *Gay American History: Lesbians and Gay Men in the U.S.A.* New York: Thomas Y. Crowell, 1976.

Keller, Marisa, and Mike Mashon. *TV Weddings: An Illustrated Guide.* New York: TV Books, 1999.

Kelley, Kitty. *Elizabeth Taylor: The Last Star.* New York: Simon and Schuster, 1981.

Kendall, Elizabeth. *The Runaway Bride: The Hollywood Romantic Comedy of the 1930s.* New York: Knopf, 1990.

Kendall, Laurel. *Getting Married in Korea: Of Gender, Morality, and Modernity.* Berkeley: University of California Press, 1996.

Kim, Seung-Kuk. "Changing Lifestyles and Consumption Patterns of the South Korean Middle Class and New Generations." In *Consumption in Asia: Lifestyles and Identities,* edited by Chua Beng-Huat. London: Routledge, 2000.

Kim, Young-Hoon. "The Commodification of a Ritual Process: An Ethnography of the Wedding Industry in Las Vegas." Ph.D. diss., University of Southern California, 1996.

King, Coretta Scott. *My Life with Martin Luther King, Jr.* New York: Holt, Rinehart and Winston, 1969.

Kirn, Walter, and Wendy Cole. "Twice as Nice." *Time,* 19 June 2000, 53–54.

Kirwan-Taylor, Helen. "Bridezilla's Monster Appetite: Buying a Wedding Present for the New 'Aesthetic Compulsive' Can Be a Nightmare." *Financial Times,* 21 July 2001, 10.

Kolbenschlag, Madonna. *Kiss Sleeping Beauty Good-Bye.* San Francisco: Harper and Row, 1988.

Krieger, Susan. *The Family Silver: Essays on Relationships among Women.* Berkeley: University of California Press, 1996.

Kroll, Luisa. "What Would Queen Victoria Have Said?" *Forbes,* 20 October 1997, 267.

Kuchler, Frances W. *Law of Engagement and Marriage.* Dobbs Ferry, N.Y.: Oceana Publications, 1966.

Kulish, Nicholas. "Turning the Tables: Bachelorette Parties Are Getting Risqué." *Wall Street Journal,* 3 September 2002, sec. A, pp. 1, 8.

Kunz, George Frederick. *Rings for the Finger.* Philadelphia: J. P. Lippincott & Co, 1917.

La Ferla, Ruth. "NOTICED: Here Comes the Mother of the Bride." *New York Times,* 7 May 2000, sec. 9, p. 1.

Lacayo, Richard. "About Face." *Time,* 3 December 2001, 46–47.

Lalli, Cele Goldsmith. *Modern Bride Wedding Celebrations: The Complete Wedding Planner for Today's Bride.* New York: John Wiley and Sons, 1992.

"The Land and Its People." http://www.ecssr.ac.ae/Land/wedding.html, 28 March 2002.

Landis, Paul H. *Your Marriage and Family Living.* St. Louis, Mo.: McGraw Hill Book Company, 1969.

Langowski, Angela. "Real People, Real Stories." *Cable World,* 6 December 1999, 44.

"Las Vegas NAACP Investigates Lack of Black Ministers on Wedding Chapels' Staffs." *Jet,* July 1996, 32–33.

Leach, William. *Land of Desire: Merchants, Power, and the Rise of a New American Culture.* New York: Pantheon, 1993.

Lears, T. J. Jackson. *No Place of Grace: Antimodernism and the Transformation of American Culture, 1880–1920.* New York: Pantheon, 1981.

Lee, O-Young. *The Compact Culture: The Japanese Tradition of "Smaller Is Better."* Translated by R. N. Huey. Tokyo: Kodansha International, 1982.

Leeds-Hurwitz, Wendy. *Wedding as Text: Communicating Cultural Identities through Ritual.* Mahwah, N.J.: Lawrence Erlbaum Associates, 2002.

Leeming, Jo-Ann, and Margaret Gleeson. *Complete Book of Showers and Engagement Parties.* Garden City, N.Y.: Garden City Publishing Company, 1948.

Leonard, Diana. *Sex and Generation: A Study of Courtship and Weddings.* London: Tavistock Publications, 1980.

Leonhard, David. "Do You Take This Resort for Your Wedding?" *Business Week,* 17 June 1995, 146.

Lewin, Ellen. *Recognizing Ourselves: Ceremonies of Lesbian and Gay Commitment.* New York: Columbia University Press, 1998.

Lewis, Charles. "Working the Ritual: Wedding Photography as Social Process." Ph.D. diss., University of Minnesota, 1994.

Lewis, Richard W. *Absolut Book.* Boston: Journey Editions, 1996.

Liftig, Anya E. "A Union of East and West." *New York Times Magazine,* 15 April 2001, sec. 6, p. 66.

Lipsett, Linda Otto. *To Love and to Cherish: Brides Remembered.* San Francisco: The Quilt Digest Press, 1989.

Lipson-Walker, Carolyn. "Weddings among Jews in the Post–World War II American South." In *Creative Ethnicity: Symbols and Strategies of Contemporary Ethnic Life.* Edited by Stephen Stern and John Allen Cicala. Logan: Utah State University Press, 1991.

Litwicki, Ellen M. "Showering the Bride: A Ritual of Gender and Consumption." Paper presented at the Conference Holidays, Ritual, Festival, Celebration and Public Display, Bowling Green, Ohio, 30 May 1998.

Löfgren, Orvar. *On Holiday: A History of Vacationing.* Berkeley: University of California Press, 1999.

Lorimer, Graeme. "Wedding Bills." *Ladies' Home Journal* 3 (1929): 27–67.

Lorius, Cassandra. "Desire and the Gaze: Spectacular Bodies in Cairene Elite Weddings." *Women's Studies International Forum* 19 (1996): 513–23.

Lowenthal, David. *The Past Is a Foreign Country.* New York: Cambridge University Press, 1985.

Lury, Celia. *Consumer Culture.* New Brunswick, N.J.: Rutgers University Press, 1996.

Mackey, Jill A. "Subtext and Countertext in *Muriel's Wedding.*" *NWSA Journal* 13 (2001): 86–104.

Magiera, Marcy. "For Couple with Everything, Try Hardware Store." *Advertising Age,* 25 January 1993, 27.

Mainardi, Patricia. "Quilts: The Great American Art." *Radical America* 7 (1973): 58.

Malcolm, Shawna. "The 100 Greatest Moments in Television: Rites of Passage." *Entertainment Weekly,* 19 February 1999, 36.

Mandava, Bhargair C. "A Suitable Union." In *Young Wives' Tales: New Adventures in Love and Partnership,* edited by Jill Corral and Lisa Myers-Jarvis. Seattle: Seal Press, 2001.

Mani, Lata. *Contentious Traditions: The Debate on Sati in Colonial India.* Berkeley: University of California Press, 1998.

Marchand, Roland. *Advertising the American Dream: Making Way for Modernity, 1920–1940.* Berkeley: University of California Press, 1985.

Marcus, Ann Docker. "In Cairo, True Love Calls for Chandeliers on Top of the Head." *Wall Street Journal,* 14 February 1996, sec. A, pp. 1, 11.

"Maryland in Focus." http://www.mdhs.org/library/MDF3.html, 15 January 2001.

"Matched Ring Set." *The Jewelers' Circular-Keystone* 115, December 1944, 278.

May, Elaine Tyler. *Homeward Bound: American Families in the Cold War Era.* New York: Basic Books, 1988.

Mayer, Arthur. *Merely Colossal.* New York: Simon and Schuster, 1953.

Mayo, Kathy. "Julia Roberts: America's Sweetheart as Sorry Bitch." *Sojourner: The Women's Forum,* 30 September 1999, 52.

McBee, Randy D. *Dance Hall Days: Intimacy and Leisure among Working-Class Immigrants in the United States.* New York: New York University Press, 2000.

McBride-Mellinger, Maria. *The Wedding Dress.* New York: Random House, 1993.

McLaughlin, Lisa. " 'I Do' with Doughnuts." *Time,* 22 April 2002, 11.

McLaughlin, Patricia. "Pregnant Brides: Trade Frills for Grace." *The Cleveland Plain Dealer,* 12 September 1996, sec. E, p. 6.

McNeil, Donald S. "New Promotion behind Jewelry." *Advertising and Selling,* March 1941, 23.

McQueeney, Krista B. "The New Religious Rite: A Symbolic Interactionist Case Study of Lesbian Commitment Rituals." *Journal of Lesbian Studies* (forthcoming).

Mehta, Stephanie N. "Bridal Superstores Woo Couples with Miles of Gowns and Tuxes." *Wall Street Journal,* 14 February 1996, sec. B, p. 1.

Mei, Huang. *Transforming the Cinderella Dream: From Frances Burney to Charlotte Brontë.* New Brunswick, N.J.: Rutgers University Press, 1990.

Mekki, Hassan. "Two Dead as Gunman Opens Fire at Jordan Mass Wedding." *Agence-France-Presse,* 14 July 2000.

Merton, Robert K., and Elinor Barber. "Sociological Ambivalence." In *Sociological Ambivalence.* Edited by Robert K. Merton. New York: Free Press, 1976.

Meyerowitz, Joanne J. *Women Adrift: Independent Wage Earners in Chicago, 1880–1930.* Chicago: University of Chicago Press, 1988.

Michaels, Lisa. "Diamonds Are an Ex-hippie's Best Friend." http://underwire.msn.com/underwire/social/vp/60firstP.asp, 1 April 2000.

Mieher, Stuart. "Great Expectations: The Stork Is a Guest at More Weddings." *Wall Street Journal,* 6 April 1993, sec. A, pp. 1, 6.

"Millennial Bridal Fashions." http://www.weddingchannel.com, 30 March 2001.

Miller, Cyndee. "Nix the Knick-Knacks: Send Cash." *Marketing News,* 26 May 1997, 1, 13.

Miller, Shari. "The Big Wedding Is Back." *McCall's,* April 1981, 124–34.

Mink, Nina. "Easy Nuptials." *Forbes,* 25 April 1995, 178.

Monsoon Wedding. 16mm, 114 min., Arte France Cinéma/IFC Productions, New York, 2001.

Montemurro, Beth. " 'You Go 'Cause You Have To': The Bridal Shower as a Ritual of Obligation." *Symbolic Interaction* 25, no. 1 (2002): 67–92.

Moran, James M. "Wedding Video and Its Generation." In *Resolutions: Contemporary Video Practices.* Edited by Michael Renov and Erika Suderburg. Minneapolis: University of Minnesota Press, 1996.

Morgenthaler, Eric. "People Are So Goofy about Disney World They Marry There—Fairy-Tale Weddings Become a Major New Attraction; Cinderella Weds the Prince." *Wall Street Journal,* 28 October 1992, sec. A, p. 1.

Morton, Danelle. "Seventh Avenue: Here Come the Brides." *New York Times,* 26 October 1980, sec. 3, p. 19.

Mulvey, Laura. *Visual and Other Pleasures.* Basingstoke: Macmillan, 1989.

Musée de la Mode de la Ville de Paris. *Mariage: Exhibition Catalog of the Musée Galleria.* Translated by Richard Hertel. Paris: Editions Assouline, 1999.

My Big Fat Greek Wedding. 35mm, 96 min., Playtone Co., Los Angeles, Calif., 2002.

Myers, George, Jr. "E-commerce Study Shows Women Did More Online Shopping in 2001." *Columbus Dispatch,* 7 January 2002, sec. E, p. 4.

N. W. Ayer & Son, Inc. Ayer Oral History Interviews with Frances Gerety. Smithsonian National Museum of American History, n.d.

———. "Feature Ring Going into Men's Lines." Trend Report no. 42 (internal document), 2 February 1956, 1.

———. "Grace Kelly Doll Wears Real Diamond." Press release, n.d.

———. Internal research report, 1985.

———. "New Aspects on the Bridal Consultant Business, from a Tour of Jewelry Stores with Barbara Wilson." Internal document, February 1952, 1. Archived at the John W. Hartman Center for Sales, Advertising, and Marketing History, Rare Book, Manuscript, and Special Collections Library, Duke University.

———. Press release prepared for *Jewelers' Circular-Keystone,* 3 July 1963.

———. "Princess Expected to Follow Family Traditions." Feature story prepared for *You and Your City,* 12 August 1947, 1.

———. "Status of Leading Bridal Services and Bridal Book Publishers, January, 1957." Internal document, 25 January 1957, 2.

———. "Tiniest Diamond Ever Made—2." Press release exclusive to *You and Your City,* 6 March 1951.

Naisbitt, John. *John Naisbitt's Trend Letter* 10, no. 6 (1 August 1991): 1.

Naremore, James. *The Films of Vincente Minnelli.* Cambridge: Cambridge University Press, 1993.

Nattan, Robert F., and Harry R. Terhune. "Different Styles of Advertising." *The Jewelers' Circular* 25 (25 July 1929), 43–45.

Neal, Steve. *Genre and Hollywood.* London: Routledge, 2000.

Nelson, Michelle R., and Cele C. Otnes. "How Do You Say 'I Do'? An Analysis of Community and Socialization in Intercultural Wedding Message Boards." Paper presented at the Eighth Cross-Cultural Research Conference, Kahuku, Oahu, Hawaii, 14 December 2001.

Nestle, Joan. "Excerpts from the Oral History of Mabel Hampton." *Signs* 18 (summer 1993): 932–35.

Nevadomsky, Joseph. "Wedding Rituals and Changing Women's Rights among the East Indians in Rural Trinidad." *International Journal of Women's Studies* 4 (1981): 484–96.

Nibley, Marybeth. "Editor to Divorce Herself from Long Career Helping Brides." *Los Angeles Times,* 7 December 1994, sec. D, p. 7.

Niebuhr, Gustav. "Laws Aside, Some in Clergy Quietly Bless Gay 'Marriage.'" *New York Times,* 17 April 1998, sec. A, pp. 1, 20.

Nieves, Evelyn. "Las Vegas Journal: Endless Vows on Valentine's Weekend." *New York Times,* 17 February 2002, sec. 1, p. 16.

Nishimura, Yuko. "South Indian Wedding Rituals: A Comparison of Gender Hierarchy." *Anthropos* 91 (1996): 411–23.

Nissinen, Sheryl. *The Conscious Bride: Women Unveil Their True Feelings about Getting Hitched.* Oakland, Calif.: New Harbinger Publications, 2000.

Nomani, Asra Q. "The Wedding Night: Bliss These Days Is a Party with Pals." *Wall Street Journal,* 7 October 1999, sec. A, pp. 1, 13.

Norfleet, Barbara. *Wedding.* New York: Simon and Schuster, 1979.

Norman, Philip. *Days in the Life: John Lennon Remembered.* London: Century, 1990.

Novia, August 2001, 138–44.

Nylander, Jane C. *Our Own Snug Fireside: Images of the New England Home, 1760–1860.* New York: Alfred A. Knopf, 1993.

O'Connell, Lisa. "Marriage Acts: Stages in the Transformation of Modern Nuptial Culture." *Differences: A Journal of Feminist Cultural Studies* 11 (1999): 68–110.

O'Connor, Mike. "Gift Honeymoons." *Courier Mail* (Queensland, Australia), 1 September 2001, sec. T, p. 2.

Okun, Milton. *Popular Songs for the Wedding.* Port Chester, N.Y.: Cherry Lane Music Company, 1994.

Ordway, Edith. *The Etiquette of Today.* New York: George Sully, 1920.

Oswald, Ramona Faith. "A Member of the Wedding? Heterosexism and Family Ritual." *Journal of Social and Personal Relationships* 17 (2000): 349–68.

Otnes, Cele. "Friend of the Bride, and Then Some." In *ServiceScapes: The Concept of Place in Contemporary Markets,* edited by John F. Sherry Jr. Lincolnwood, Ill.: NTC Business Press, 1998.

Otnes, Cele, and Linda M. Scott. "Something Old, Something New: Exploring the Interaction between Advertising and Ritual." *Journal of Advertising* 25 (spring 1996): 33–50.

Otnes, Cele, and Mary Ann McGrath. "Perceptions and Realities of the Male Shopper." *Journal of Retailing* 77 (spring 2001): 111–37.

Otnes, Cele, and Tina M. Lowrey. "Til Debt Do Us Part: The Selection and Meaning of Artifacts in the American Wedding." In *Advances in Consumer Research,* vol. 20, edited by Leigh McAlister and Michael Rothschild. Provo, Utah: Association for Consumer Research, 1993.

Otnes, Cele, Tina M. Lowrey, and Young Chan Kim. "Gift Giving for 'Difficult' and 'Easy' Recipients: A Social Roles Interpretation." *Journal of Consumer Research* 20 (1993): 229–44.

Otnes, Cele, Tina M. Lowrey, and L. J. Shrum. "Toward an Understanding of Consumer Ambivalence." *Journal of Consumer Research* 24 (June 1997): 80–93.

Ownby, Ted. *American Dreams in Mississippi: Consumers, Poverty, and Culture 1830–1998.* Chapel Hill: University of North Carolina Press, 1999.

Pandya, Meenal Atul. *Viva: Design a Perfect Hindu Wedding.* Wellesley, Mass.: Meera Publications, 2000.

Park, Cheol. "Consumption in the Korean Wedding Ritual: Wedding Ritual Values, Consumer Needs, and Expenditures." *Journal of Family Economic Issues* 18 (1997): 191–209.

Patullo, Polly. *Last Resorts: The Cost of Tourism in the Caribbean.* London: Cassell, 1996.

Paul, Pamela. *The Starter Marriage and the Future of Matrimony.* New York: Villard Books, 2002.

Pearce, Elizabeth Connelly. *Altar Bound: An Outline of the Duties of the Members of the Bridal Party.* Danville, Ill.: The Interstate, 1963.

Peiss, Kathy. *Hope in a Jar: The Making of America's Beauty Culture.* New York: Henry Holt, 1998.

Perlez, Jane. "Here Come the Brides, Video Catching the Kisses." *New York Times,* 11 October 1995, sec. A, p. 4.

Perlman, Heidi B. "Proposal Planner Helps the Romantically Challenged." *Champaign-Urbana* (Ill.) *News Gazette,* 22 February 2001, sec. D, p. 2.

Philadelphia Evening Bulletin, 1 June 1911, 12.

Philadelphia Evening Bulletin, 3 May 1911.

Phillips, Marybeth. "Proud Heritage." *Philadelphia Bride,* spring–summer 1993, 52–55.

Picture Perfect. 35mm, 20th Century Fox, Los Angeles, Calif., 1997.

Pillemer, David. *Momentous Events, Vivid Memories.* Cambridge, Mass.: Harvard University Press, 1998.

Pine, J. Joseph, II, and James H. Gilmore. *The Experience Economy.* Boston: Harvard Business School Press, 1999.

Pleck, Elizabeth H. *Celebrating the Family: Ethnicity, Consumer Culture, and Family Rituals.* Cambridge, Mass.: Harvard University Press, 2000.

———. "Kwanzaa: The Making of a Black Nationalist Tradition, 1966–1990." *Journal of American Ethnic History* 20 (2001): 3–28.

Plecki, Gerard D. "The Films of Robert Altman." Ph.D. diss., University of Illinois, 1979.

Porter, Louis. "A Rite Rewritten." *Boston Globe,* 28 August 2000, sec. B, p. 7.

Post, Elizabeth L. *Emily Post's Complete Book of Wedding Etiquette.* New York: Harper and Row, 1982.

———. *The New Emily Post's Etiquette.* New York: Thomas Y. Crowell, 1975.

Post, Emily. *Etiquette in Society, in Business, in Politics, and at Home.* New York: Funk & Wagnalls, 1922.

———. *Etiquette: The Blue Book of Social Usage.* New York: Funk & Wagnalls, 1927.

Puente, Maria. "Wedded to the Year 2000." *USA Today,* 12 June 2000, sec. A, p. 1.

Quick, Rebecca. "Federated and Wedding Channel Agree to Tie the Knot." *Wall Street Journal,* 25 May 1999, sec. B, p. 2.

Quindlen, Anna. "*Ms.* Goes to a Wedding." *Ms.,* December 1978, 73–75.

"Rachel and Eddie Flores' Wedding." http://www.weddingchannel.com, 10 May 2001.

Radway, Janice. *Reading the Romance.* Chapel Hill: University of North Carolina Press, 1984.

Ramaaswamy, Anindita. "Bridal Trade Event Described as One Stop Wedding Shop." *India Abroad,* 1 September 2000, 38.

Rapaport, Rhona, and Robert Rapaport. "New Light on the Honeymoon." In *The Psychosocial Interior of the Family,* edited by Gerald Handel. Chicago: Aldine Publishing Company, 1967.

"Real Brides Say . . ." http://www.windsorpeak.com/bridalgown/mailbag/mail may00.html, 21 July 2001.

Reed-Jones, Carol. *Green Weddings That Don't Cost the Earth.* Bellingham, Wash.: Paper Crane Press, 1996.

Reeves, Ruby Jo. "Marriages in New Haven since 1870: Statistically Analyzed and Culturally Interpreted." Ph.D. diss., Yale University, 1938.

Reidy, Chris. "Here Storm the Brides: Basement Bridal Sale Provides Unique Insights." *Boston Globe,* 21 May 1996, 64.

Reilly, Philip J. *Old Masters of Retailing.* New York: Fairchild Publications, 1966.

Rein, Irving J. "The Rhetoric of the Bridal Salon." In *The Great American Communication Catalogue.* Englewood Cliffs, N.J.: Prentice Hall, 1978.

Repositioning Hawaii's Visitor Industry Products. Honolulu: University of Hawaii, 1998.

Ritzer, George. *Enchanting a Disenchanted World: Revolutionizing the Means of Consumption.* Thousand Oaks, Calif.: Pine Forge Press, 1999.

Roane, Kit R. "Kleinfeld, a Threatened Bridal Mecca, Gets New Owners." *New York Times,* 21 July 1999, sec. B, p. 3.

Robinovitz, Karen. "Bridesmaid vs. Gown: Can This Marriage Be Saved?" *New York Times,* 20 May 2001, sec. 9, p. 7.

Rollins, Nita. "Something Borrowed, Something Taped: Video Nuptials." *Wide Angle* 13 (April 1991), 32–38.

Roney, Carley. *The Knot's Complete Guide to Weddings in the Real World.* New York: Broadway Books, 1998.

Rook, Dennis. "The Ritual Dimension of Consumer Behavior." *Journal of Consumer Research* 12 (1985): 252–64.

Roos-MacDonald, Jane. *Alternative Weddings: An Essential Guide to Creating Your Own Ceremonies.* Dallas: Taylor Publishing Company, 1997.

Rose, Helen. *"Just Make Them Beautiful": The Many Worlds of a Designing Woman.* Santa Monica, Calif.: Dennis-Landman Publishers, 1976.

Rosen, Ruth. *The World Split Open: How the Modern Women's Movement Changed America.* New York: Viking, 2000.

Rosewicz, Barbara. "Here Comes the Bride . . . and for the Umpteenth Time." *Wall Street Journal,* 10 September 1996, sec. B, p. 1.

Roshell, Starshine. "Wedding Guide 2001." http://www.newspress.com/2001_wedding_guide/movies.html.

Rothman, Ellen K. *Hands and Hearts: A History of Courtship in America.* New York: Basic Books, 1984.

Runser-Spanjol, Jelena, Pamela Lowrey, and Cele C. Otnes. "Transformational Claims in Advertising: A Longitudinal Study." Paper presented at the Association for Consumer Research European Conference, Paris, 29 June 1999.

Ruth, John A. *Decorum: A Practical Treatise on Etiquette and Dress of the Best American Society.* New York: Union Publishing House, 1877.

Ruth, Julie A., and Ronald Faber. "Guilt: An Overlooked Advertising Appeal." In *Proceedings of the 1988 Conference of the American Academy of Advertising,* edited by John D. Leckenby. Austin, Tex.: American Academy of Advertising, 1989.

Saluter, Arlene F., and Terry A. Lugaila. "Marital Status and Living Arrangements: March 1996." In *Current Population Reports, P-20–496.* Washington, D.C.: U.S. Government Printing Office, 1996.

Sanoff, Alvin. "Marriage—It's Back in Style!" *U.S. News and World Report,* 20 June 1983, 44–53.

Saxton, Martha. "The Bliss Business: Institutionalizing the American Honeymoon." *American Heritage* 4 (1978): 80–87.

Schama, Simon. *The Embarrassment of Riches: An Interpretation of Dutch Culture in the Golden Age.* New York: Knopf, 1987.

Schaub, George. *Professional Techniques for the Wedding Photographer.* New York: Watson-Guptill, 1985.

Scherer, Barrymore L. "Engaging Rings." *Town & Country Monthly,* December 1990, 190–93.

Schickel, Richard. *Intimate Strangers: The Culture of Celebrity.* Garden City, N.Y.: Doubleday, 1985.

Schiro, Anne-Marie. "Fantasy and Taste in a New Bridal Salon." *New York Times,* 5 September 1990, sec. C, p. 8.

Schlager, Neil, ed. *St. James Press Gay and Lesbian Almanac.* Detroit: St. James Press, 1998.

Schmitt, Erich. "For the First Time, Nuclear Families Drop below 25% of Households." *New York Times,* 15 May 2001, sec. A, pp. 1, 18.

Schoonaker, Bonny. "Sparkling Slogan Is Century's Gem." *Sunday Times* (Johannesburg, S.A.). http://www.suntimes.co.za, 25 April 1999.

Schor, Juliet. *The Overspent American: Upscaling, Downshifting and the New Consumer.* New York: Basic Books, 1998.

Schreuder, C. "For These Couples, It Was a Very Good Year." *Chicago Tribune,* 1 September 1992, sec. I, pp. 9–10.

Schroeder, Jonathan Edward. "The Consumer in Society: Utopian Visions Revisited." *Marketing Intelligence and Planning* 18, nos. 6–7 (2000): 381–87.

Schuman, Michael. "There Goes the Bride: An Indonesian Isle Has Odd Sense of Wedlock." *Wall Street Journal,* 29 May 2001, sec. A, pp. 1, 12.

Schwartz, Rosalie. *Pleasure Island: Tourism and Temptation in Cuba.* Lincoln: University of Nebraska Press, 1997.

Seagrave, Kerry. *American Films Abroad.* London: McFarland and Co., 1997.

Sears, Roebuck. *Sears Christmas Wishbook.* Chicago: Sears, Roebuck, and Co., 1965.

Seligson, Marcia. *The Eternal Bliss Machine: America's Way of Wedding.* New York: William Morrow and Co., 1973.

Seng, Yvonne J., and Betty Wass. "Traditional Palestinian Wedding Dress as a Symbol of Nationalism." In *Dress and Ethnicity,* edited by Joanne B. Eicher. Oxford: Berg, 1995.

Sennet, Ted. *Lunatics and Lovers.* New Rochelle, N.Y.: Arlington House, 1973.

"Seventh Avenue: Here Come the Brides." *New York Times,* 26 October 1980, sec. 3, p. 19.

Shida, Kiyoshi. "The Shintoist Wedding Ceremony in Japan: An Invented Tradition." *Media, Culture, and Society* 21 (1999): 195–204.

Sidebotham, Timothy James. "Music in the Marriage Rites of Mainline Protestantism, 1983–1993: A Theological, Liturgical and Cultural Analysis." Ph.D. diss., Drew University, 1997.

Signature Bride magazine editors. *Going to the Chapel: From Traditional to African-*

inspired and Everything in between—The Ultimate Wedding Guide for Today's Black Couple. New York: Putnam, 1998.

Singh, Jyotsna. "Gay Couple Hold Hindu Wedding." BBC News. http://news .bbc.co.uk/english/world/south-asia/newsid_1357000/1357249.stm, 29 May 2001.

Slawson, Judith. *The Second Wedding Handbook: A Complete Guide to the Options.* New York: Doubleday, 1989.

Smith, Daniel Scott. "The Dating of the American Sexual Revolution: Evidence and Interpretation." In *The American Family in Social-Historical Perspective,* edited by Michael Gordon. New York: St. Martin's Press, 1973.

Smith, Dave. *Disney A to Z: The Updated Official Encyclopedia.* New York: Hyperion, 1996.

Smith, Judith E. "The Marrying Kind: Working-Class Courtship and Marriage in 1950s Hollywood." In *Multiple Voices in Feminist Film Criticism,* edited by Diane Carson, Linda Dittmar, and Janice R. Welsch. Minneapolis: University of Minnesota Press, 1994.

"Something Old, Something New." *In Style,* February 2001, 258.

Spender, Dale, ed. *Weddings and Wives.* Ringwood, Australia: Penguin Books, 1994.

Spindler, Amy M. "The Wedding Dress That Ate Hollywood." *New York Times,* 30 August 1998, sec. 9, p. 1.

Squeri, Lawrence. *Better in the Poconos: The Story of Pennsylvania's Vacationland.* University Park: Pennsylvania State University Press, 2002.

Stacey, Jackie. *Star Gazing: Hollywood Cinema and Female Spectatorship.* London: Routledge, 1994.

Stearns, Peter N. *Consumerism in World History: The Global Transformation of Desire.* London: Routledge, 2001.

Stevens, Kimberly. "I Do . . . Take MasterCard." *Wall Street Journal,* 23 June 2000, sec. W, pp. 1–4.

Stiers, Gretchen A. *From This Day Forward: Commitment, Marriage, and Family in Lesbian and Gay Relationships.* New York: St. Martin's Press, 1999.

Stocker, Carol. "Weddings." *Boston Globe Magazine,* 16 January 2000, 28.

Stone, Kay F. "The Misuses of Enchantment: Controversies on the Significance of Fairy Tales." In *Women's Folklore, Women's Culture,* edited by Rosan Jordan and Susan Kalcik. Philadelphia: University of Pennsylvania Press, 1985.

Stone, Lawrence. *The Family, Sex, and Marriage in England, 1500–1800.* New York: Harper and Row, 1977.

Suja, Masami. "Japanese Wedding Packages as Aesthetic Expression among Elite Brides of Osaka." Ph.D. diss., University of Minnesota, 1996.

Sullivan, C. W., III. " 'Jumping the Broom': A Further Consideration of the Origins of an African American Wedding Custom." *Journal of American Folklore* 110, no. 436 (spring 1997): 330–39.

Sullivan, Sheila. Press release included in publicity packet prepared for Kleinfeld. MediaVision, n.d.

"Summertime, and the Facts Are Jumping." *New York Times,* 21 July 1999, sec. D, p. 2.

Sung-jin, Kim. "Lavish Wedding Custom Pales True Love." *The Korea Times,* 13 September 2001, 18.

Suro, Roberto. "Mixed Doubles." *American Demographics,* November 1999, 58.

Swengley, Nicole. "What a Wedding Present." *London Times,* 20 October 2001, Features sec.

Tan, Cheryl Lu-Lien. "Attacks Lead to a Change of Heart." *Baltimore Sun,* 15 October 2001, sec. E, p. 1.

Tasman, Alice Lea Mast. *Wedding Album.* New York: Walker and Company, 1982.

Tasser, Nancy. "Changing Marriage Ceremonial and Gender Roles in the Arab World: An Anthropological Perspective." *Arab Affairs* 1 (1988): 117–35.

Teachman, Jay D., Lucky M. Tedrow, and Kyle D. Crowder. "The Changing Demography of America's Families." In *Understanding Families into the New Millennium: A Decade in Review.* Minneapolis, Minn.: National Council on Family Relations, 2001.

Tempest, Rona. "Weddings Have Marched a Long Way in China since Mao." *Los Angeles Times,* 28 April 1996, sec. A, pp. 1, 3.

Theophano, Janet S. " 'I Gave Him a Cake': An Interpretation of Two Italian-American Weddings." In *Creative Ethnicity: Symbols and Strategies of Contemporary Ethnic Life,* edited by Stephen Stern and John Allen Cicala. Logan: Utah State University Press, 1991.

"They Shoot Weddings, Don't They?" *Washington Post Magazine,* 13 January 1991, sec. W, p. 25.

"They're Not Hitchhiking to Niagara Falls." *Adweek* 38 (1997): 25.

Thomas, Nicholas. *Entangled Objects.* Cambridge, Mass.: Harvard University Press, 1991.

Thompson, Angela L. "Unveiled: The Emotion Work of Wedding Coordinators in the American Wedding Industry." Ph.D. diss., Brandeis University, 1998.

"Times Will Begin Reporting Gay Couples' Ceremonies." *New York Times,* 18 August 2002, sec. A, p. 23.

Tober, Barbara. *The Bride: A Celebration.* New York: Harry N. Abrams, 1984.

Tobin, Joseph J., ed. *Re-made in Japan: Everyday Life and Consumer Taste in a Changing Japan.* New Haven, Conn.: Yale University Press, 1992.

Tomes, Nancy. *The Gospel of Germs: Men, Women, and the Microbe in American Life.* Cambridge, Mass.: Harvard University Press, 1988.

"Toned-down Ceremonies: Japanese Weddings Enter Age of Tasteful Restraint." 1998. http://jin.jcic.or.jp/trends98/honbun/ntj971111.html, 22 July 2000.

Torgovnick, Marianna. *Primitive Passions: Men, Women, and the Quest for Ecstasy.* Chicago: University of Chicago Press, 1998.

Towne, Charles Hanson. *Gentlemen Behave.* New York: Julian Messner, 1939.

Tung, Jennifer. "Attack of Bridezilla: Demanding Perfection Before 'I Do.'" *New York Times,* 20 May 2001, sec. 9, p. 1.

Turner, Victor. *The Ritual Process: Structure and Anti-structure.* Chicago: Aldine Pub. Co., 1969.

Tushnet, Rebecca. "Rules of Engagement." *The Yale Law Journal* 107, no. 8 (June 1998): 2583–618.

Twitchell, James B. *Living It Up: Our Love Affair with Luxury.* New York: Columbia University Press, 2002.

Tye, Diane, and Annie Marie Powers. "Gender, Resistance and Play: Bachelorette Parties in Atlantic Canada." *Women's Studies International Forum* 21, no. 5 (1998): 551–61.

Ulrich, Laurel Thatcher. *A Midwife's Tale: The Life of Martha Ballard, Based on Her Diary.* New York: Vintage Books, 1990.

U.S. Census Bureau. *Statistical Abstract of the United States: 2000.* 120th ed. Washington, D.C.: U.S. Government Printing Office, 2000.

U.S. Department of Health and Human Services. *Vital Statistics of the United States,* vol. III, *Marriage and Divorce.* DHH Pub. No. (PHS) 91–1103. Washington, D.C.: U.S. Government Printing Office, 1991.

Van De Velde, T. H. *Ideal Marriage: Its Physiology and Technique.* New York: Random House, 1926.

Vanderbilt, Amy. *Amy Vanderbilt's Complete Book of Etiquette.* Garden City, N.Y.: Doubleday and Company, 1954.

Venkatesh, Alladi, and A. Fuat Firat. "Liberatory Postmodernism and the Reenchantment of Consumption." *Journal of Consumer Research* 22 (1995): 239–67.

Vida, Vendela. *Girls on the Verge: Debutante Dips, Gang Drive-Bys, and Other Initiations.* New York: St. Martin's Press, 1999.

Vigue, Fotter Indica. "Brides Reclaim Their Ethnic Roots." *Boston Globe,* 14 June 1998, sec. B, p. 1.

Vinovskis, Maris. *An "Epidemic" of Adolescent Pregnancy? Some History and Policy Considerations.* New York: Oxford University Press, 1988.

Waldman, Diane. "From Midnight Show to Marriage Vows: Women, Exploitation, and Exhibition." *Wide Angle* 6 (1984): 40–49.

Waldrop, Judith. "Here Come the Brides." *American Demographics* 12, no. 6 (6 June 1990): 4.

———. "The Honeymoon Isn't Over." *American Demographics* 14, no. 8 (8 August 1992): 14.

Waley, Arthur. "The Chinese Cinderella Story." *Folklore* 58 (1947): 226–38.

Warner, Diane. *Picture-Perfect Worry-Free Weddings.* Cincinnati, Ohio: Betterway Books, 1998.

Watts, Steven. *The Magic Kingdom: Walt Disney and the American Way of Life.* Boston: Houghton Mifflin Company, 1997.

"The Way We Were: Fifty Years of Wedding Trends." *In Style,* 15 January 2000, 46.

Webber, Lauren. "In Search of Forever, Shoppers Return to 47th Street." *New York Times,* 9 December 2001, sec. 3, p. 9.

Wedding announcements. *The St. Louis* (Mo.) *Post-Dispatch,* 1890–1980.

"Wedding Bells." *Off Our Backs* 25, no. 4 (1995): 3.

"Wedding Cake Talk with Sylvia Weinstock." 25 August 1998. http://www.modernbride.com/ChatEvents/Cakechat.cfm, 1 April 2001.

"Wedding Trends." With Kojo Nnamdi. http://www.wamu.org/pi/shows/piarc.010212.html, 15 February 2001.

Weiss, Suzanne. "Deciphering Nuptial Rites: The Devil's in the Details." *Metro West Jewish News,* 22 May 1997, sec. S, p. 21.

Westenhouser, Kitturah B. *The Story of Barbie.* Paducah, Ky.: Collector Books, 1994.

Weston, Kath. *Families We Choose: Lesbians, Gays, Kinship.* New York: Columbia University Press, 1991.

Wheeler, Blanche. *Party Plans: Showers.* St. Paul, Minn.: Webb Publishing Co., 1939.

"Where Would You Like to Get Married?" BBC News, 25 January 2002.

http://newsvote.bbc.uk/hi/english/talking_point/newsid_1775000/1775078. stm, 14 May 2002.

White, Gregory L., and Shirley Leung, "Middle Market Shrinks as Americans Migrate toward the High End." *Wall Street Journal,* 29 March 2002, sec. A, pp. 1, 8.

Who Wants to Marry a Millionaire? First broadcast 15 February 2000 by Fox.

Whyte, Martin K. *Dating, Mating and Marriage.* New York: Aldine de Gruyter, 1990.

Wilk, Richard. "The Binge Economy." Paper presented at the Eighth Interdisciplinary Conference on Research in Consumption, Paris, 26 July 2001.

Williams, Clover Nolan. "The Bachelor's Transgression: Identity and Difference in the Bachelor Party." *Journal of American Folklore* 108 (1994): 106–20.

Williams, Norma. *The Mexican American Family: Tradition and Change.* Dix Hills, N.Y.: General Hall, 1990.

Wilson, Craig. "Gold-tiled Confection Takes the Cake." *USA Today,* 27 June 2002, sec. B, p. 10.

Wilson, Marianne. "Wedding Stores Go Big." *Chain Store Age,* October 1995, 31–35.

Winer, Linda. "Take a Chance on 'Mamma': A Tale Told by ABBA, Full of Sweet, Loopy Fun." *Newsday,* 19 October 2001, sec. B, p. 2.

Witkowski, Terence. "The Early Development of Purchasing Roles in the American Household." *Journal of Macromarketing* 19 (December 1999): 104–14.

Wood, Naomi. "Domesticating Dreams in Walt Disney's *Cinderella.*" *The Lion and the Unicorn* 20 (1966): 25–49.

Wythe, Douglas, Andrew Merling, Roslyn Merling, and Sheldon Merling. *The Wedding: A Family's Coming Out Story.* New York: Avon Books, 2000.

Yalom, Marilyn. *A History of the Wife.* New York: HarperCollins, 2001.

"The Young Find Diamonds More Trendy." *Economic Times,* 10 December 2001.

Zakaria, Fareed. "How to Save the Arab World." *Newsweek,* 24 December 2001, 24.

Zipes, Jack, ed. *The Oxford Companion to Fairy Tales.* New York: Oxford University Press, 2000.

Zipser, Andy. "Viva, Las Vegas: Stratosphere Tower Fills an Inside Straight." *Barron's,* 4 April 1994, 15.

celebrity culture: *(continued)*
musical genre of, 107;
standardized experience of, 132–33;
transformation ethic of, 108–9, 114,
115–16, 117–18, 119–20, 268–69;
trappings/values of, 105–7, 270;
wedding receptions of, 120–21,
123–24. *See also* films; film stars
Cendrillion (Perrault), 27
Central Palace (New York City),
38–39
Central Selling Organization, 63
Chaplin, Geraldine, 177
Charles, Prince, 2, 50, 148
charmers (bridal salon clerks), 98
Cherokee wedding rituals, 260
Chicken Dance (popular dance), 129
Chicks in White Satin (film), 190
children: at encore weddings, 251; les-
bian couples with, 234; marriages
of, 206; as wedding attendants, 111.
See also Family Medallions
China, 197, 200, 205, 206, 207
China Hall (Rochester, Minnesota),
75
Christian Bride (magazine), 158
Christians: as honeymooners, 158;
lavish wedding identity of, 208; in
South Korean weddings, 215;
white dress custom of, 31
Cinderella (film), 46
Cinderella tale: Disney version of,
28–29, 46; Disney World wedding
of, 53, 158; feminists on, 29; Hollywood films of, 186–89, 192; of
Princess Diana, 50; wedding gown
of, 83; of wish fulfillment, 27–28,
53–54; women's recollections of,
46–47; written versions of, 26–27

class: and consumerism, 51–52, 53;
honeymoon as marker of, 140, 148,
311–12n22; in 1950s films, 172,
174–75; in 1990s films, 185–86;
reception's indication of, 120–22;
in screwball comedies, 168–70, 171;
wedding as marker of, 5–6, 39
Clinton, Bill, 235, 242
Club Med, 152–53
cohabitation: as alternative to marriage, 49, 184–85; by lower class
couples, 265; before marriage, 52,
138
Cohen, Kate, 100, 109, 277
Colbert, Claudette, 65, 166, 168,
169–70
Coleman, Rev. Roger, 252
commitment ceremonies, 232–33. *See
also* same-sex marriage
communal receptions, 121–22
Communist regimes, 20, 204–5
conga line (dance), 129
Connor, Jerry (jeweler), 86, 92
The Conscious Bride (Nissinen), 95,
278
consumer culture: advertising mechanisms of, 9–10, 36–37, 204; Barbie doll of, 47–49, 48 fig.; beauty
focus of, 40, 109, 274; celebrity
context of, 105–7, 270–71; department store strategies of, 32–35; diamond industry of, 63–67, 68, 70;
Ethiopia's lack of, 204, 219–20;
ethnicity element of, 246–47,
250–51; etiquette guides of, 39,
51–52; female focus of, 32, 34,
93–94; feminist critics of, 22; honeymoon experience of, 138–39, 162;
of India, 207; indigenous expres-

sions of, 210–11, 224–27; individualism's ties to, 6, 30, 226, 268; inequities of, 21; magic's role in, 28, 46–47, 53–54, 268–69; origins of, 30–31; perfection's ties to, 18–19, 42–43, 109; postmodern legitimation of, 8; protest weddings against, 256–57, 260, 261–62; romance linked to, 11–12, 19, 30, 76, 267; royal wedding model of, 50–51. *See also* luxury; perfection

consumption: as class marker, 5–6; as meaningful activity, 24; right to, 23–24; sumptuary laws against, 20–21, 198, 215, 277. *See also* consumer culture

Coppola, Francis Ford, 178

Corrado, Marisa, 99

cosmetics industry, 40

costs: of American weddings, 2; of encore weddings, 252; of groom's tuxedo, 300n17; of honeymoons, 149, 313–14n44; of Japanese weddings, 199; of Las Vegas weddings, 238; as socially sanctioned, 3, 9, 271–72; of South Korean weddings, 2; of wedding gifts, 19, 77; of wedding gowns, 18, 84, 101, 104, 300n17

Council of Trent (1563), 229–30

courtly love notion, 29

Cowrie, Colin, 87

Crawford, Cindy, 196, 241

cruise ship honeymoons, 147, 149, 156–57

Cuba, 147, 205

Cukor, George, 170

Cusack, Joan, 189

dancing, 129, 245–46

dating rituals, 38

David's Bridal (retail chain), 102–4, 278

Davis, Bette, 174

De Beers Consolidated Mines: advertising campaigns of, 63–65, 67 figs., 68, 70, 272–73, 294n47; diamond slogan of, 66; global markets of, 68; miners at, 62–63

The Deer Hunter (film), 179

Defense of Marriage Act (1996), 235, 276

Demetrios bridal gowns, 53, 205

DeMille, Cecil B., 152

De Rougement, Denis, 42

department stores: bridal magazine distribution by, 41–42; bridal registries of, 75–77 (see also individual stores); bridal salons of, 46, 95; merchandising strategies of, 32–35; racial segregation in, 45; urban location of, 204. *See also* bridal salons

destination weddings, 158–60, 160 fig., 161 fig., 224

"A Diamond Is Forever" (ad slogan), 66, 68. *See also* Gerety, Frances

diamonds: in Acceptance Rings, 67–68; Ayer's marketing of, 63–65, 67 figs., 294n47; De Beer's slogan for, 66; discovery of, 62; downsizing trend in, 68, 70; Four Cs of, 68; symbolic value of, 61–62, 272–73; of tri-set wedding band, 68

"Diamonds Are a Girl's Best Friend" (song), 66

Diana, Princess (née Spencer), 2, 50, 53–54, 148, 202

interfaith marriages, 244, 246

Internet. *See* Web sites

interracial marriages, 230–31, 244

Iraq, 200–201, 206

The Irish Honeymoon (film), 165

iskista (Ethiopian dance), 224

Israel, 200

Italian weddings: Hollywood films of, 178–79, 180; off-Broadway production of, 278–79, 279 fig.

It Happened One Night (film), 139–40, 168–70, 169 fig., 171, 191

Jane Eyre (Brontë), 27, 53

Japan: commodified identity of, 226, 266; cost of weddings in, 199; De Beers ad campaign in, 68; destination weddings from, 159–60; exported customs from, 211–12, 224–25; flexible religious boundaries in, 208; "picture brides" from, 230; two-wedding ceremony in, 215, 216; wedding gowns in, 199–200, 213, 277; wedding hall services in, 212–13, 215, 323n48

J.C. Penney, 95

Jeakins, Dorothy (studio designer), 176

Jean-Louis (studio designer), 166

jewelry stores, 34, 86–87, 98

Jews: honeymoon destinations of, 141–42; in interfaith marriages, 244; in Israeli weddings, 200; Reconstructionist, 232; Reform, 232; same-sex marriages of, 232; wedding films of, 177–78, 319n25; wedding/reception settings of, 122; wedding rituals of, 111, 236, 326n24

Jolie, Angelina, 270

Jordan, 203

jumping the broom ritual, 230, 248–50, 249 fig.

June Bride (film), 171–72, 174

J. Walter Thompson advertising agency, 68

Kay, Scott, 1

Kelley, Leola Coombs, 43

Kelly, Grace, 50, 117, 167, 202, 318n17

Kendall, Elizabeth, 169, 170

Kennedy, Jacqueline, 121

Kennedy, John F., 120–21

Kennedy, John F., Jr., 117–18

kente cummerbund, 249, 250 fig.

Kephart, Debi, 87, 93

King, Coretta Scott, 141

King, Martin Luther, Jr., 141

kinship. *See* family

kiss, nuptial, 114, 164

Kleinfeld and Son (Brooklyn), 97–98, 243

Kline, Kevin, 189

Kodak: FunSaver cameras, 119; hula shows, 152

Korea, 20, 230

Krieger, Susan, 232

Kwanzaa festival, 248

Landsdowne, Helen, 36

Las Vegas honeymoons, 156–57, 159

Las Vegas weddings, 229; celebrity component of, 238, 240–41, 263, 270–71; cost of, 239; drive-through type of, 240 fig.; length/size of, 239; magical elements of, 241–42

Latin America, 201–2, 204

Lauder, Estée, 1

Laumann, Edward, 138

Lauren, Ralph, 1

lavish weddings: alternatives' coexistence with, 228–29, 262–63, 277; of arranged marriages, 206–7; of bicultural couples, 247–48; charitable sponsorship of, 203–4, 266; Christian identity of, 208; as class marker, 5–6, 39, 174–75; in Communist regimes, 204–5; consumption ethic of, 8–11, 23; democratization of, 44–46, 54, 265–66; destination type of, 158–60, 160 fig., 161 fig., 224; detached from marriage, 274–75, 278; detached from women's status, 275–76; of encore couples, 251–53; environmental consequences of, 276–77; Ethiopia's adoption of, 220–22; in film hits (1994–2001), 185–86, 187 table; films' reevaluation of, 176–78, 186, 188, 191–95, 319n25; global desire for, 197–202, 266, 277; with indigenous innovations, 225–27, 266; as luxury goods, 10; as magical transformation, 12–14, 108–9; marginalization effects of, 22–23, 276; 1950s wedding versus, 180–83; perfection of, 18–19, 42–43; photographic preservation of, 15, 16, 17 fig., 18; planning calendars for, 61; of Princess Diana, 50–51; reasons for popularity of, 5–8; research methodology for, 285–86n71; socially sanctioned costs of, 3, 9, 271–72; standardization of, 132–33; sumptuary laws against, 20–21, 198, 215; on television, 1, 2–3, 179, 190; theatricality of, 105–7; time schedule of, 109; in urban centers, 201, 203–4; videography of, 118–20; of vow renewal ceremony, 254–55; as weekend event, 107–8, 184, 189. *See also* marriage; religious ceremonies; same-sex marriage

Learning Channel, 2–3

Lennon, John, 258

Lenox China, 75

Leonard, Diana, 4, 93

lesbian couples: bridal showers for, 233; with children, 234; civil unions of, 235, 276; honeymoon destinations of, 148–49; marginalization of, 22–23; parents of, 236–37; in religious ceremonies, 232; South Asian wedding of, 231; wedding guides for, 235–36. *See also* gay couples

Lewin, Ellen, 233

Lewis, Charles, 92

Lewis, Mary E., 66

Libbey ads, 28

liquor, 90–91, 124, 153

Listerine ads, 40

Little Church of the West (Las Vegas), 238

Little Rosebud's Lovers (novel), 32

Little White Chapel (Las Vegas), 239

London Daily Mail, 50

Lopez, Jennifer, 193–94

love. *See* romantic love

The Love Boat (television program), 147

The Love Parade (film), 165

Lury, Celia, 9

luxury: alternative wedding's incorporation of, 228–29, 262–63, 277; bridal salon's image of, 96–97; cake's image of, 126; as class marker, 6; Communist regimes' lack of, 204–5; contemporary standards of, 267–68, 270, 273–74; democratization of, 10, 44–46, 54, 264–66; Depression/wartime scarcity of, 43–44; of dinner reception, 123–24; engagement ring as, 63–64, 272–73; global desire for, 198–99; honeymoon's expression of, 137–38, 149; indigenous forms of, 225–27, 266; in 1980s, 51; in 1990s, 53; proposal's elements of, 71–72; registries' emphasis on, 75–76; right to, 23–24; size of wedding party as, 111; standardized creation of, 132–33; sumptuary laws against, 20–21, 198, 215; theatricality's ties to, 106–7; of trousseau items, 59–60; wedding as symbol of, 10. See also consumer culture; lavish weddings

Macarena (dance), 129
Macy's (New York City), 39
Madame Alexander doll, 47
magazines, 32, 35, 36, 64. See also bridal magazines
magic: of bargain-hunting experience, 101–2, 104; of bouquet toss, 129; of bridal salon experience, 96–97, 98; in consumer culture, 28, 46–47, 53–54; couples' desire for, 268–69; of engagement ring, 64–65, 66–67; of honeymoon experience, 162; of Las Vegas weddings, 241–42; of offbeat weddings, 256; of perfect gown, 95, 99–101; photographic preservation of, 15, 16–17, 114–16z; of the ring ritual, 70; standardized creation of, 132–33; of transformation by ritual, 12–14; of wonder tales, 26–27. See also Cinderella tale
Mall of America (Minneapolis), 255
Mankiller, Wilma, 260
Marie de France, 29
marketing. See advertising
marriage: arranged type of, 206–7, 209; of bicultural couples, 244–48, 250–51; booms in, 45, 50–51; broom jumping ritual of, 248–49, 249 fig.; cohabitation before, 52; of encore couples, 251–53; of feminist couples, 259–60; green ceremonies of, 260–62; of hippies, 256–58; historical rationales for, 29–30; historical restrictions on, 229–31; of interfaith couples, 244, 246; of interracial couples, 230–31, 244; lavish wedding's detachment from, 274–75, 278; legal benefits of, 4–5; of offbeat couples, 255–56, 263; opposition to, 22, 49, 184–85; patriarchal rituals of, 19, 22, 111–13, 232–33, 258–59, 331n87; of pregnant brides, 242–43; as rite of passage, 108; of single mothers, 243; statistics on, 5, 110, 244; vow renewals of, 253–55. See also lavish weddings; religious ceremonies; same-sex marriage
marriage licenses, 57
Marshall, Garry, 196
Martin, Steve, 180
Mary of Burgundy, 62

Matson steamship company, 152
Maximilian, Archduke of Austria, 62
McConaughey, Matthew, 194
McDonald, Jeannette, 165
McGraw, Ali, 177–78
Meet the Parents (film), 193, 195
memories, 15–18, 267. *See also* photographs
men: Acceptance Ring for, 67–68, 69 fig.; as advertising targets, 40, 64; as bridal salon charmer, 98; dating rituals of, 38; garter toss to, 130–31, 259; provider role of, 34; as toast makers, 124–25, 259; as wedding coordinators, 94–95. *See also* grooms
Mercedes rental cars (Ethiopia), 222, 223 fig.
Merling, Andrew, 237
Merton, Robert K., 89
Metropolitan Community Church (Los Angeles), 232
MGM pictures, 172, 174–75, 318n17
Middle East, 200–201
Minnelli, Liza, 84
Minnelli, Vincente, 172
mock weddings, 275
Modern Bride (magazine), 18–19, 155, 158, 175
Monroe, Marilyn, 66, 318n20
Monsoon Wedding (film), 196, 207, 209
Moonstruck (film), 179–80, 188
mothers of the bride: attire of, 83–84, 300n17; celebrity status of, 271; in South Korea, 218
movies. *See* films
movie stars. *See* film stars
Muriel's Wedding (film), 186, 188, 195, 274–75

Muslims, 206, 208
My Best Friend's Wedding (film), 185, 189, 195
My Big Fat Greek Wedding (film), 196

Nair, Mira, 207, 209
Nairobi, 204
names: in bridal registry, 93; feminists on, 258–59
Nassau, 147
National Bridal Service (NBS), 86–87, 88 fig., 92
Netherlands, 231, 276
newspaper announcements, 57, 235
Newsweek (magazine), 2, 71
New York Times, 235
New Zealand, 199
Niagara Falls, 142, 144, 148–49
Nigeria, 200
Nissinen, Sheryl, 95
Nixon, Doris, 86
Nixon, Tricia, 49
North Africa, 200
novels, popular, 32
N.W. Ayer advertising agency: diamond campaigns of, 63–66, 67 figs., 68, 70, 294n47; Fostoria campaign of, 75–76; symbolism rhetoric of, 272

offbeat weddings, 255–56, 263
Ogilvy, David, 154
Oklahoma (film), 175
The Old Maid (film), 170
Ono, Yoko, 258
Oppenheimer, Ernest, 63, 65
Oppenheimer, Harry, 63
Oswald, Ramona, 22

standard rituals of, 110–11, 112, 306–7n17; Unity Candle ceremony of, 113–14

Puritans, 20

p'yeback ceremony (South Korea), 214 fig., 217

racial discrimination: Caribbean's lack of, 315–16n72; against honeymooners, 141–42, 143, 312–13n34; against slave marriages, 230; white as signifier of, 31–32

radio programs, 38–39

Raging Bull (film), 179

Rainier, Prince of Monaco, 50, 167, 318n17

Ramirez, Beth Reed, 252

receptions: balloons at, 123–24; of bicultural couples, 245–46; bouquet toss at, 22, 129–30, 215, 259; cakes at, 125–27, 216–17; charitable sponsorship of, 203–4, 266; comedic routines at, 127; in Communist China, 205; disposable cameras at, 119; duration of, 120; in Ethiopia, 220, 222, 224; garter toss at, 130–31, 259; of green weddings, 261–62; of hippie weddings, 257; liquor at, 90–91, 124; meals served at, 121–23; musical entertainment at, 127–29, 128 fig.; settings for, 120–21; on Southern plantations, 170; in South Korea, 216–17; as theatrical performance, 105–7

Reggie, Denis, 117

registries. *See* bridal registries

rehearsal dinners, 108

Rein, Irving, 98

religious ceremonies: of engagement period, 56–57; gender roles of, 111–13, 258, 331n87; in Hollywood films, 167, 175, 176–77; of interfaith couples, 244, 246; nuptial kiss of, 114; of offbeat weddings, 255–56; romantic context of, 109–10; for same-sex couples, 232–33; simulation of, 115–16; Soviet Union's alternative to, 204–5; standard rituals of, 110–11; statistics on, 110; Unity Candle ritual of, 113–14; videotaping of, 118–19; of vow renewal, 254. *See also* Catholics; Hindus; Japan; Jews; Korea; Muslims

research methodology, 285–86n71

resorts: destination weddings at, 158–60, 160 fig.; entertainment value of, 161–63; for gay couples, 148–49; as honeymoon destinations (1966–1992), 145–47, 314n48; in the Poconos, 142–45; racial/ethnic discrimination at, 141–42, 143, 312–13n34; on tropical islands, 150–54, 315–16n72

retail stores. *See* bridal salons; department stores

Rhodes, Cecil, 62

Richards, Dorothy, 32

ritual artifacts: of encore weddings, 252–53, 253 fig.; memories tied to, 16–18; photographs as, 16, 18; sacred type of, 81–82; source of power of, 104, 107; transformative quality of, 83–84, 95, 99–101; of vow renewal ceremonies, 254; wedding gown as, 82–83. *See also* engagement rings; photographs; wedding gowns

rituals: of African Americans, 248–50, 249 fig., 250 fig.; of bicultural weddings, 245–47; of bridal photography, 114–18, 307n22; of bridal salon experience, 83, 96–98; of bridal shower, 73–75; of capping ceremony, 202; of encore weddings, 252–53, 253 fig.; of engagement period, 55–56, 72; of Ethiopian weddings, 222–24, 225–26; of Filene's sales, 101–2; films' commentary on, 184–85; of the honeymoon, 134–38; import/export of, 197–98, 201, 210, 224–25, 320n2; magical transformation through, 12–14, 101, 104; of Middle Eastern weddings, 200–201; patriarchal types of, 19, 111–12, 232, 258–59, 331n87; of the proposal, 70–72; at the reception, 129–31; of religious ceremonies, 110–12, 113–14; of smashing the glass, 236, 326n24; societal functions of, 4; of South Asian weddings, 206–7, 209; of South Korean weddings, 214 figs., 215–18; of vow renewal, 253–55; weddings as, 4–5
Ritzer, George, 241
Roberts, Julia, 166, 175, 189, 191–92
Rogers, Wayne, 97
romantic love: advertising's promotion of, 36–37, 272–73; bubble bath imagery of, 144–45, 313n39; consumption linked to, 11–12, 19, 30, 76, 267; dating rituals of, 38; diamonds as symbol of, 63–65, 67–68; of fairy tales, 28–29; honeymoon's goal of, 137–38; musical expression of, 128–29; as perfect love, 42; radio broadcasts of, 38–39; religious settings for, 109–10; South Asian taboo against, 208–9; South Korean ideal of, 212; standardized formula of, 132–33; of Western popular culture, 198–99
Rook, Dennis, 85
Rooney, Mickey, 238
Roots (Haley), 248
Rose, Helen, 166, 173
Ross, Katharine, 176
Rothman, Ellen, 7
Royal Brittania (yacht), 148
Royal Caribbean cruises, 147
royal weddings, 30–31, 50–51, 203
runaway bride (image), 169–70, 176, 178, 188–89, 191–92
Runaway Bride (film), 2, 185, 191–93, 195, 210
Russell, Jane, 66, 318n20

sacred objects: bride's ensemble as, 82–83; Durkheim on, 81–82; source of power of, 104, 107. *See also* engagement rings; photographs; wedding gowns
same-sex marriage, 234 fig.; commitment ceremonies of, 232–33; legalization of, 231, 235; motivations for, 233–34; parental reaction to, 236–37; redefined rituals of, 236, 326n24; Web site for, 235
Sandals resorts (Caribbean), 153–54
sati (widow immolation), 206
Saudi Arabia, 201, 204, 206
Savio, Mario, 176
Schroeder, Jonathan, 10
screwball comedies, 168–70, 171, 180, 193

wedding consultants, 87. *See also* wedding planners

wedding coordinators: counseling role of, 89, 90; men as, 94–95; services of, 87. *See also* wedding planners

wedding couples: ages of, 14, 45, 52; cohabitation of, 52, 138; destination wedding statistics on, 158; engagement period of, 55–56; as entertainers, 127; honeymoon statistics on, 134, 140–41, 147, 155, 310n1, 312n23. *See also* brides; grooms

wedding day directors, 87. *See also* wedding planners

Wedding Embassy Year Book, 41

wedding films. *See* films

wedding gifts: from bridal registries, 75–77, 86; of cash/checks, 77–78, 298n106; cost of, 19, 77; Ethiopia's substitution for, 224, 225–26; retail merchandising of, 34; in South Korea, 218

wedding gowns: in arranged marriages, 206–7; of Barbie doll, 47, 48 fig.; from bridal salons, 95–98; in China, 197, 205; of *cinema verité* ceremony, 264; cost of, 18, 84, 101, 104, 300n17; from David's Bridal chain, 102–4; in Ethiopia, 219; from Filene's Basement, 101–2, 103 fig.; in *Godey's Lady's Book,* 33 fig.; of green wedding brides, 261; of hippie brides, 49, 257; of Hollywood films, 166, 170–71, 173–74, 175–76, 192; in Japan, 199–200, 277; in Middle Eastern countries, 200–201; from

parachute silk, 44; perfection of, 95, 99–101; of pregnant brides, 242–43; of Princess Diana, 50; sacred quality of, 82–83, 84, 104; sewing patterns of, 35; in South Asia, 206, 248; in South Korea, 211, 213, 277; sweetheart style of, 174, 318n20; tripartite notion of, 41; white color of, 31–32

wedding guests: cash/check gifts from, 77–78, 298n106; gifts for, 127; honeymoon financing by, 77

wedding halls (South Korea and Japan), 212–13, 215, 216, 323n48

wedding invitations, 77–78

The Wedding Planner (film), 164, 193–95

wedding planners: bride's conflict with, 89–90; Ethiopian version of, 223; fees of, 87; of green weddings, 261; grooms as clients of, 91–93; in Hollywood films, 194; in India, 207; men as, 94–95; origins/services of, 85–87; on perfection goal, 91, 272; of same-sex weddings, 235–36; South Korean version of, 213, 215; three categories of, 87; training of, 86

Wedding Portrait Photographers International, 119

wedding receptions. *See* receptions

wedding rings: exchange of, 113, 306–7n17; as sacred object, 82; in same-sex marriages, 232–33. *See also* engagement rings

Weddings (magazine), 51

The Wedding Singer (film), 2, 191, 195

A Wedding Story (television program), 2–3

Compositor:	Binghamton Valley Composition, LLC
Text:	11/14 Adobe Garamond
Display:	Adobe Garamond
Printer and binder:	Thomson-Shore, Inc.